P9-DFZ-898

NEWTON'S

A DIGITAL NOMAD'S GUIDE

Law

Andrew Gore *&* Mitch Ratcliffe

RANDOM HOUSE
ELECTRONIC PUBLISHING

New York

Copyright © 1993 by Andrew Gore and Mitch Ratcliffe

All rights reserved. No part of the contents of this book may be reproduced in any form or by any means without the written permission of the publisher.

Published in the United States by Random House, Inc., New York, and simultaneously in Canada by Random House of Canada, Limtied.

Manufactured in the United States of America.

First Edition

9 8 7 6 5 4 3 2 1

ISBN: 0-679-74647-1

Illustrations and Icons by Laughing Trout used by permission:
  George discovers ... cartoon page 11
  Figure 3 page 19
  Figure 1.1 page 31
  The Apple Newton MessagePad (Model No. H1000) page 61
  The Sharp Newton Expert Pad (Model No. PI-7000) page 64
  Figure 11.1 page 349
  Assist, Easter Egg, and *Get Info* icons used throughout

Illustrations on pages 1, 29, 129, 247, 341, and 385 by Jeffrey Pelo used by permission.

The authors and publisher have used their best efforts in preparing this book. However, the authors and publisher make no warranties of any kind, expressed or implied, with regard to this book, and specifically disclaim, without limitation, any implied warranties of merchantability and fitness for a particular purpose with respect to techniques described in the book. In no event shall the author or publisher be responsible or liable for any loss of profit or any other commercial damages, including but not limited to special, incidental, consequential or any other damages in connection with or arising out of furnishing, performance, or use of this book.

Trademarks

A number of words in which we have reason to believe trademark, service mark, or other proprietary rights may exist have been designated as such by use of initial capitalization. However, no attempt has been made to designate as trademarks or service marks all words or terms in which proprietary rights might exist. The inclusion or definition of a word or term is not intended to affect, or to express any judgement on, the validity or legal status of any proprietary right which may be claimed in that word or term.

New York   Toronto   London   Sydney   Auckland

Dedicated with love to Kiera Lord-Ratcliffe, Taylor Ratcliffe,
Joanne Gore and to Ian MacKenzie Gore—welcome to the clan, laddy!

Kudos

Here we are again.

Newton's Law is the culmination of almost two year's worth of research. Although it is the third book in the Digital Nomad's series, it was actually conceived first.

We've had the assistance of many, many people. In fact, so many folks have earned kudos for their help that it's best to list their names and contributions.

The Random House Team. Tracy Smith, our wonderful and patient editor, once again managed to supply the perfect mix of pain and understanding that helped us deliver another book. Thank you, Tracy.

Although he is a member of the Newton Team at Apple, as our technical editor, Martin Gannholm deserved book-editing kudos along with Tracy. Thanks so much for being our Fact Policeman, Martin; no one picks nits better than you.

We also owe a tip our hats to our publishers, current Random House doyen Kenzi Sugihara and Michael Mellin, the ex-Random House publisher who gave us our start in the wierd, tense life of book-making. May you the jet stream always rise to meet you on your own terms, Michael!

The Apple Team. To Christopher Escher, Apple public relations director and master strategist, thanks for paving the way to the hearts and minds of the Newton Team. And to Tricia Chan, Apple public relations specialist and our good friend, thank you for walking a fine, hard line with the grace of a gymnast.

Most of all, thanks to our angel, Gaston Bastiaens, vice president and general manager of Apple's Personal Interactive Electronics division. Without that well-placed kick-start you gave us last June we might still be trying to finish the introduction to this book.

The Newton Team. We'd like to thank the entire Newton Team for their help. Kudos to every one of you for weathering the storm and for making that all-important first step. Working with the team was the single greatest pleasure in the production of this book. The folks down at PIE have managed a rare thing: to recapture the spirit that gave birth to the Macintosh. Thanks, everyone, for letting us stand over your shoulders at Newton's birth.

First on the roster of individuals who, almost without exception, worked with us on their own time is Newton Team Leader, Apple Genius and Father of the Finder (these titles barely begin to scratch the surface of this man's achievements), Steve Capps. Thank you so much, Steve, for greasing the wheels of progress.

Kudos also go to Marie D'Amico, the Newton Team's den mother who practically cornered the market on wheel grease for this project. Thanks to Walter Smith for raising our IQs a couple of points, to Tony Espinoza for bringing us back down to Earth and to James Joaquin for introducing us to Newton chic. Go Gorilla, J.J.!

Thanks to Rasha Bozinovic for helping us adapt our writing and to Rick Kapur for getting us Connected. And speaking of communications, thanks also to Susan Schuman, and Chris Bryant.

To Michael Tchao: thanks for opening the door! To Philip Ivanier: thanks for all the class, the ARMistice, and the nifty tee shirts. To Nazila Alasti: thanks for giving us your Newton demo unit. Don't forget to save us a seat on your next cross-country flight. To Maurice Sharpe: anyone who likes Kate Bush can't be all bad!

Special thanks to Steve Rea for all the nifty goodies (feel free to send us a few more PCMCIA cards, if the mood strikes, Steve!) and to Joseph Ansenelli for helping us correct our errors. And to Ken Wirt—hope you were serious about publishing the interactive version of this book. It'll be arriving on your doorstep before you (and probably we) know it!

And, finally, to Donna "Fi" Auguste, thanks so much for signing all the forms.

The Rest of the World. To the third-party developers who helped us pull things together including A.J. Jennings, Zyg Furmaniuk, Carlton Baab, Joyce Santos, John Payne, Norm Francis, David Ries, Rob Spector, Pete Snell, Andrew Anker, Bob Dillworth, David Rose, Howard Oakley, Dave Nanian, Brian Smiga, Clint Brown, Steve Riggins, and the unnamed thousands, merci beaucoup.

A special thanks, also, to the good people of the virtual Newton classroom conducted in the Newton Forum on CompuServe, who helped us beta test this technology and shared their ideas and tips.

At *MacWEEK*, thanks to Dan Farber for signing off on this project, and to Henry Norr and Mark Hall for giving Andy the time he needed to finish his part of the book. Thanks also to Jeffrey Pelo for giving us our "New Look", and to Nevin Berger for illustrating our lives.

And, to Unknown Sources everywhere, thank you!

—A.G. and M.R., Sept. 28, 1993

CONTENTS

COMMENTARY

Sir Isaac Newton's first law of motion states that a body in motion stays in motion unless otherwise compelled by an external force. This perfectly describes two aspects of the Newton: the user and the technology.

If you are a Newton user or are considering becoming one, you probably already live by Newton's Law. For many of us, life has become an endless stack of Post-It™ notes stuck to faxes tucked between random pages in a notebook you always seem to leave in the car. Sitting down in one place and doing the same thing for more than one hour is a rare event. That vague sense that something is forgotten or a call is unreturned or an appointment is missed seems to be ever present.

That's where Newtons come in. They are designed to tag along during the day and help control loose ends.

In contrast, a personal computer is a good example of a compelling force holding you back. Desktop computers do help you create useful spreadsheets or presentations, but that's probably not what you'd like to be doing while away from your desk. Sitting in a cafe writing spreadsheet macros on the latest MEGALOMANICAL 486DX with a super-twist color display, a 200 gigabyte hard disk and 64 megabytes of static RAM is undoubtedly some people's idea of a good time. But sometimes, worrying about all that work, whenever and wherever you are, is downright depressing. Newton is low-impact technology, something that helps you keep moving rather than tying you down.

So, imagine being in that same cafe, jotting down a new friend's phone number, or receiving a wireless invitation to a movie or sketching out a floor plan as you renovate the kid's bedroom. This is the design center of Newton: capturing those random bits of information, faxing a sentence or two, exchanging phone numbers via infrared. These little tasks definitely don't require a spreadsheet and a desktop computer (and if they did, the manual would be 500 pages long and the program would cost more than the entire MessagePad).

This is why Newton technology is different. Back in 1983, we allocated a large portion of the computing power of the Macintosh to present a pleasant graphical interface. At the time this was considered a pretty radical step in the established character-based world of computing. With Newton, we're continuing that tradition. Handwriting recognition and intelligent assistance occupy most of Newton's time. By making the machine more intelligent, the user is free to concentrate on their ideas instead of the mechanics of expressing them. And again, this concept seems radical to the status quo.

Since Newton is a new technology, it too must keep moving forward. We want to see Newtons that are bigger, smaller, for your kids, for your parents, for music, for games, for sports, for telephones, for televisions. Imagine tacking a keyboard and a mouse onto these devices and you appreciate the wonderful simplicity of a pen or finger interface.

The Newton evolution is far from done—the MessagePad is just the beginning. Over time, we'll make Newtons smarter, simpler to use and easier to integrate into your life. And, as more and more Newtons get out there, the real power will emerge. This ability to create and share ideas quickly and spontaneously enhances how we work, play and communicate. The next few years will be very exciting. We are breaking out of the wired desktop world into this new, somewhat wild, untethered frontier.

So, keep moving; and with luck nothing will act to slow you down.

—Steve Capps, Distinguished Engineer, The Newton Group, Apple Personal Interactive Electronics division, October 9, 1993

Principia Nomadica

The First Law: Bodies in Motion tend to stay in motion, bodies at rest get left behind.

Your Guide

It gets deeper every day, and too late we find that we are swimmers in a sea of unconnected data. The rain of facts bombarding us from the newspaper, telephone, television, radio, computer networks, and coworkers who pass us in the hallway collect in puddles on the desk, pour into boxes on the floor, and end up in meaningless pools in the closet and garage.

"Someday," we tell ourselves, "I'll extract some meaning from all this junk." We might even dig around in it, come up with an article on bee-keeping and wonder aloud: "What was I thinking?" Let's face it, we all need help, an assistant who will look at all this stuff, remember it, and identify connections we recognized only in that moment we clipped an article or made a note.

We need something like Apple Computer Inc.'s Newton, a collection of technologies that brings a little intelligence to the task of collecting, organizing and communicating our ideas. A personal device, Newton gathers the trivia of our lives, disappearing like a diver into that information after receiving a handwritten command as simple as "find this" or "remember that," to emerge seconds later with a precious pearl. It fits in the hand, hides in a pocket. When used with a little skill and a lot of attitude, Newton can be an intelligent tool for controlling the chaos around us.

What do we mean by intelligent?

Newton is dog-stupid, dumber than Lassie and more cooperative than the neighbor's terrier. It needs to be told what to do, but it can also divine from inexact instructions what must be done to satisfy your needs. No computer has ever been able to take the simple command "fax Bob" written on a notepad and format a letter, create a cover sheet, look up Bob's fax number and send the whole package—after asking "Did I do right?"

It's a revolutionary step, because dog-stupid is off the scale that we use to measure current computer technology. The ordinary personal computer doesn't have any intelligence, you have to add an application that can accept a command. Even then, the PC doesn't even qualify as stupid, because it can carry out commands given to it in only the strictest order—you have to adapt your workstyle to the machine process. People don't need to be dumbed down, yet that's what we've been putting up with since computers started showing up on our desks, like the pods in "Invasion of the Body Snatchers" (Kill it before it opens its eyes!). After re-configuring a crashed computer operating system, we all feel a little like Donald Sutherland, his body snatched, screeching at the last human in downtown San Francisco. Pathetic. Sad.

The computer has provided an inhuman environment for work—there's truth to the saying "Whom God would destroy she first makes use an IBM PC." Everyone knows personal computers aren't natural, that's why less than three percent of the human race uses one.

When sending a fax on any other device, whether it's a PC running Windows, a Macintosh or a VAX minicomputer, you must open a word processor to create a message, then open a fax program and an electronic Rolodex to address and send a fax to Bob (occasionally the fax program and address book are one-in-the-same, but not often). You also have to know exactly what to do at each step of the process, where to click, when to merge the address with the message, and how to set the modem protocols. Ugh.

Newton collapses the distinction between operating system, the basic operating instructions that control a computer, and application, the structured environment in which you enter data and tell the machine what to do with it. Included in Newton's basic instructions are the ability to interpret handwriting and guess what it means, as well as a predilection to wonder about the whereabouts of Elvis, the King. (We didn't just throw this in for fun; This capability is one of several "Easter Eggs" or undocumented features buried by fun-loving engineers in your Newton's brain.)

Newton intelligence is a computational quantum leap that draws on the physicist's view of the universe. The engineers who designed Newton understood that all data is relative, that it must be handled differently in each context, that when data is manipulated its very nature can change, and, most critically, they knew that people don't want a tool that crashes when it fails to understand a command. Like the universe, Newton can deal with a little chaos without collapsing in on itself. Of course, Newton isn't perfect. The first generation provides only limited capabilities, but it is replete with potential. The Apple MessagePad and Sharp Expert Pad point toward a future in which machines are our allies, customizing themselves to our needs, not just tools with an anal-retentive streak.

Newton can be your guide between the messy, scratchy, low-fidelity world of human life and the crystalline clarity of the computer's digital domain.

And Newton's Law is your guidebook.

Information Ocean

Look what we're up against.

During the next 24 hours, more data will churn out of human minds and their silicon minions than can be consumed in a lifetime. The English language newspapers printed in the next 24 hours alone would take weeks to read, let alone comprehend the meaning of the stories, the local issues and international intrigue. Add to that television programming, bank statements, mail, memos, schedules, books, magazines, advertising, stock reports, meetings, Post-It notes, and every phone call and casual conversation. We live our lives awash in an ocean of information.

The Daily Grind. Most of the information produced in a day is not germane to our lives. What's more, there's redundancy galore in the waves of data. Many of the stories in those daily newspapers cover the same event. A national election, a flood in the Midwest, a new movie, each provides the impetus for dozens of stories which are the same on the surface, and rich in their differing details. Getting the whole story, rather than the perspective of an individual reporter, requires that we read many renderings of the same event, as well as an exact transcription of the words spoken there. When a story is examined in this way even the reporter's prejudices can tell us something we would not otherwise know.

What do you need to know? And is finding it worth the search at libraries, in musty filing cabinets, through stacks of print, on your hard drive or the Internet (a global network of computers, libraries and people)?

Imagine that you can assemble a complete perspective with a minimum amount of time spent reading, rather than researching and collecting information for days or weeks. What if you could apply more effort to the application of reason to a problem than you do trying to cajole the basic facts from a database? What couldn't you undertake to do?

Newton, which provides the ability to collect data and access information over a telephone line or the airwaves, begins to deliver this kind of power.

For example, it is possible, through study of world weather patterns and agricultural science, to predict lima bean crop yields and prices with reasonable accuracy. Likewise, a student can compile a thorough profile of urban renewal policy by accessing the libraries of the world's universities through a computer network. Perhaps that student may someday find the keys to a decision which will awaken America's cities from their narcoleptic decay. A doctor can consult the histories of a thousand patients to test her theories about a new treatment. All of this will be easier with Newton than it has been when people were saddled with the complexities of computers, or the card file, at the local library.

Only connect, and we can begin a revolution of great ideas.

Meanwhile, back here in the real world, we need to track a great deal more than is dreamt of in our fields of specialization. That's why people turn to different sources of news, some to the *New York Times* while others to *USA Today*. Or why we'll read a story in the morning paper and then watch a segment on that same story in the evening television news. The selection of our own sources of information about the many goings-on in the world is what makes these peripheral relationships personal, even when this information is of interest to many thousands of people.

New services aimed at devices for the pocket and the home will eventually give us the ability to pick and choose or mix-and-match the news sources we read.

Odyssey of ideas. In the last decade, many people have ventured out of their comfortable data tide pools into the maverick waves and to distant, craggy boundaries of the information ocean. International stock reports, news of foreign intrigue, messages from tomorrow afternoon, currency exchange, keeping track of what time it is in Paris, Texas, or Cambridge, England; as we broaden our horizons we expand the information with which we must cope.

In today's "just-in-time" business environment, being on top of the situation wherever or whenever we are working is critical to success. It could be as simple as accessing an article on the business rituals of Japan or as complex as collecting a schedule, associated contacts, notes, and having a "smart" map that can help us find our way to a meeting at a mysterious five-star French restaurant while visiting clients in Boston. To bastardize a line from *Buckaroo Bonzai*, "Wherever you go, there you better be!"

FYI. Information contained in memos, marketing reports, group calendars, company inventories, price lists, and sales figures represent another class of data. It attracts the interest of far fewer people than news and entertainment. However, it's the data that is almost always more critical to our immediate well-being—and it spoils quickly. You might not mind reading a movie review a week or two after the movie opens, but a memo about a budget meeting delivered the day after the meeting isn't likely to do your career much good.

Spit in the ocean. On top of all the information created by others for our consumption are our own contributions to the raging waters: ideas, notes, memos, reminders, to-do lists, people to see, miles to go before we sleep. This is the most important information we try to keep in touch with, yet it's the hardest to keep organized. How many times have you been left standing at a pay phone, trolling for a number that you forgot to add to your little black book? Where did you put all the notes you jotted down yesterday—remember, the one on the envelope?

We know this guy who made a note about a meeting on the back of a postage stamp. Later that day, he mailed a letter, and he didn't realize until that night when he was brushing his teeth that he'd mailed his note. There was a blue streak on his tongue. It was too late to call about when the meeting was scheduled, and if he'd not had a memory for times, he'd have missed it all together.

From student to executive, from store clerk to computer programmer, we swim in the information ocean every day of our lives. We give birth to it, we grow in it and ultimately we can be ruled by it. In our society, being in the right place at the right time with the right information often spells the difference between success and failure.

The waters are rising, the flood is here. If we do not find a way to stem the tide of useless information, we will all be drowned in nonsense and fluff. Your working life depends on precisely how long you can tread water as the future rushes over the past and wipes away our parents' economy.

So, wax up your information surfboard, step out on the flashing digital water and change your world.

Hanging Ten in the Information Age

William Gibson, who launched the Cyberpunk movement, has said his darkly prophetic *Neuromancer*, which portrays a technocratic society dominated by mega-corporations and data gangsters, is "hopelessly optimistic."

With apologies to Mr. Gibson, we think he's dead wrong. Newton is proof.

The hero of the novel, Case, is a "console cowboy" who wields a personal device to access a vast network of computers to further the best laid plans of his patron, a mad artificial intelligence with a split personality. Newton is a precursor of such a device. However, Newton is a tool that many people can afford. So, unlike Case, you don't have to rely on the greed of others to pay for your information habit.

As long as individuals use Newton to remake their relationship with data, it will serve as a liberating technology. Gibson's pessimism will be borne out only if Newton and other personal digital assistants, as Apple's John Sculley likes to call them, are used to tether people even more tightly to the corporation. Personal devices should give time back to the person using them, not slice off more of the evening or weekend for work.

Figure 1 Welcome to your Information Surfboard!

The advent of the Newton may lead to fundamental changes in the way work is managed. People who can collect and process information from any place, at any time, don't fall into the typical job description. Invariably, the folks who master this workstyle will also be the most valued people in their organizations. It will not be easy, but we predict corporations will eventually have to bend to the expectations of these Newton-enabled data surfers.

At the same time, let's remember that PDAs speed up communication but they don't speed up people. An immediate response is not always a thoughtful response, and that the best ideas usually come when we are fishing, reading or just spending time with our families. Watch your boss shiver spasmodically when you say this, his paranoia rising to critical mass and his suit melting into a pool of wool and a century's worth of conceit. Then, hit him with this: "I'm asking you to require that I work a lot smarter and, perhaps, a lot less than I do now."

Sanity begins here.

The Disposable Computer

Fortunately for the data surfer wannabe, the computer industry is caught in a serious dilemma that will drive the development of ever more sophisticated information surfboards.

Once wildly successful companies are in trouble. They are running out of customers who will tolerate the pains of personal computing. (Face it, most of us have been forced to use PCs by the people we work for. We didn't ask to wrestle with device drivers in Windows.) So to consumer electronics they've turned, hoping for new profits generated by "hit" products, like Newton.

Companies like Apple have generated huge profits from relatively small revenue streams, at least in comparison to other big industries. Selling an average of only 1.1 million Macintoshes a year, Apple grew 10-fold in 10 years. This, even though the Macintosh grabbed only 15 percent or so of the total PC market.

But Apple was bound to hit a wall. If it wants to continue to double in size each year, a computer company must find twice as many new customers every year. And there are a finite number of potential computer buyers in the world.

Compounding Apple's problems was the declining cost of manufacturing. Apple's competition, most of whom buy components for about the same price Apple does, dropped their prices to try and grab more new users. The result: Apple must sell many more than twice the number of Macs each year in order to earn the same revenue—and many, many times more to make the same profit.

As the number of computers in the world has caught up with the number of people who want to use computers, computer companies have had to increase performance and the pace of technical innovation in order to grow their businesses. They have to sell computers to the same buyers year in and year out. So computer companies spend a lot of time and money convincing people that their computers are hopelessly obsolete, and that they must, in order to stay one up on their competition, purchase a newer, better, and probably cheaper computer. Just look at the computer trade press if you want proof. Computers have become as disposable as last year's fashions.

The computer industry is, quite literally, a snake eating its own tail.

Obviously, something is missing from today's computer products. That void between the ability of a computer to work with people and the people's willingness to work with computers has prevented computers from being adopted by the majority of customers in the industrialized world.

Get Info...Technophobia

James Coates wrote recently in the Chicago Tribune that a technophobe is a person who "rejects technology or avoids it whenever possible." According to the article, 55 percent of all Americans can be categorized as technophobic about using devices like computers, cellular phones, and even digital alarms clocks.

Some 25 percent of U.S. adults have never used a computer, set up a VCR to record a show or programmed the preset stations on a car radio; 22 percent are even afraid to type on a computer because they "might make a mistake and damage the machine."

The solutions to technophobia cited in the article ranged from the practical to the imperative.

Dan Gookin, author of the best-selling "DOS for Dummies," an introductory guide to using a DOS-based computer, was quoted as saying "When 55 percent of Americans say they don't like your products, you have some big problems to overcome—and you don't do that by blaming the people who can't figure out your machines." *(continued)*

Get Info...Technophobia (continued)

James Ray Wright, a spokesman for computer book publisher Sy-
bex Inc., was quoted as saying "Whether a person likes technology
or not, his or her economic survival depends on a basic knowledge
of computers."

Where Consumers and Computers Collide

Thus enters Newton.

Someone once said that computer companies sell us what we need while
consumer electronics companies sell us what we want. Newton was conceived by Apple as a way to break out of this mold, a consumer electronics
device that people will both need, because it handles the informational
tasks that clutter the day, and want, because it is a sexy device that sets its
user apart from the crowd.

As we said earlier, Apple calls the Newton a Personal Digital Assistant,
or PDA. Recently the company has begun to call them PCAs, swapping
out the "Digital" for "Communications" to contend with the appearance
of communications-oriented devices, like the AT&T EO Personal Communicators.

But Apple was on target at first, before marketing panic set in: Newton
is Personal because it controls the flow of one person's information; it is
Digital because it is based on computer technology; and it is an Assistant,
since it can handle mundane tasks automatically.

The term information surfboard is an apt description, because what
Newtons do best is let you skim through data to find what you want the
way a channel surfer uses a TV remote control. It also sounds a lot more hip
(see The First Axiom, Section I—*Understanding Newton*)

Newtons are relatively cheap—granted, not as cheap as a Walkman but
certainly cheaper than a first generation cellular phone—a key distinction
between consumer electronics and computers. Newtons can also perform
their primary function right out of the box. Imagine how well a boom box
would sell if you had to buy the radio tuner, tape deck heads and speaker
magnets separately. That's one reason why computers aren't for everyone,
but Newton may well be.

George discovers too late that a personal communications assistant is no solution for a lousy social life.

Newtons are disposable, but not in the marketing-driven sense that today's personal computers are. Walkmen have come and gone from everyone's life, they are replaced when a new feature comes along that compels you to upgrade. You don't think about it that much, and the old Walkman gets handed to your kids or a friend, who will get a lot of use out of it before it wears out or they pass it on.

Companies go through computers like razor blades for fear of being left behind the computational curve, even though computers are upgradeable. You can add an accelerator board to a Mac to speed its performance. Likewise, audio capabilities can be plugged into a PC with a Sound Blaster card.

You really can't change the basic operating capabilities of a Newton the way you can with a PC (although you can do considerable customization of a Newton by adding software and cards). Instead, Apple will build cooler functions into new models. This lack of upgradeability is a feature of the consumer electronics world. Upgrading consumer electronics devices would be very expensive compared to the original price tag of the device. That's why you're not likely to see a toaster oven with a slot for adding a coffee grinder.

Sharp Electronics Corp., the company that manufactures both Apple's MessagePad and its own Newton Expert Pad, drove down the cost of manufacturing the first Newtons to the point where upgrading the MessagePad or Expert Pad logic boards would cost nearly as much as buying a new Newton. It's a very Japanese way of looking at technology: If something does what you want it to do at a price you feel is worth it, you buy it. The concepts of upgradeability and compatibility never enter the equation.

Finally, like any good consumer electronics product from German beard trimmers to Japanese VCRs, Newtons are designed to please the eye. Newton hardware is sleek and sexy, it feels good when you hold it in your hand. From the puff of smoke that bursts on a Newton screen when you "scrub out" a word to the animation of a piece of paper being crumpled up and tossed in a trash can when you delete an entire note, Newton software was designed to make you smile as you work with it.

Newton is a combination of the best of consumer and computer technologies. There is technological sophistication hidden beneath Newton's surface, like the proverbial iceberg with nine-tenths of its mass hidden below the waves (just when you though you where safe from the nautical metaphors!)

Newton technology guarantees that the card, modem or printer you bought for your Apple MessagePad will also work with your Sharp Expert Pad. It also allows beaming of information to any other Newton device—Apple, Sharp, or one of the others that will hit the streets in the next year—as well as the ability to send messages to Macintoshes and PCs, or access a network of "real" computers.

Newton's computer technology guarantees that, if you know how to use one Newton you will probably know how to use another manufacturer's design. This consistency of interface and compatibility of software and add-on products is unheard of in consumer electronics. It also delivers a portable environment in which software can change the way Newton handles information.

Newton applications don't just add new capabilities to your MessagePad or Expert Pad, they can impose customized views of the information stored in them. That means you can explore different ways of managing information without first having to export and reformat information every time you change applications. This is simplicity mechanized, the restraints that constrain us in the PC world have been dropped.

As Easy As a VCR

There is a widely held belief that consumer technology must be easy to use or consumers won't buy it. Tell that one to the video tape recorder manufacturers and we're sure you'll hear some hearty laughter as you're given a quick introduction to the many features and draconian interface of VCR Plus recording.

Newton retains much of the flexibility that characterized its PC progenitors, but exploiting those options in Newton can prove complicated. Faxing, hooking up to networks, dialing into on-line services, and organizing your information can prove daunting tasks if you cannot first visualize the infrastructure you are tapping into. You could use a Newton without ever exploring the outlying regions of its capabilities—but even that is likely to require organizational skills and extensive planning. We hope to lend a hand in these areas.

A hammer is easy to use, but you wouldn't want to write a concerto with one. Newton has not yet achieved a level of technological sophistication that makes it easy for everyone to use, but with a little training most people can wield one with facility, organizing an address book, notes and calendar items with the best of them. While Newton's aren't as easy to use as a hammer, they're certainly not as hard to use as the time record function of most VCRs. They're only as difficult to use as they need to be, at least for now.

I'm Not Bad, I'm Just Trained That Way

One way Newtons try to be easier to use is through intelligence. We're not talking about intelligence in the way the HAL 9000 computer in *2001: A Space Odyssey* was intelligent. HAL understood everything he heard, and was able to place all information in context within his experience. Rather, your Newton understands that certain words represent specific functions and is capable of interpreting those words to carry out those commands. The process of interpreting words is called *parsing*.

For example, you write "I need to call Bob right now" in the notepad of your Newton. Newton parses the sentence, throwing away the words for which it finds no meaning, which reduces the sentence to the command phrase "call Bob." Newton understands that "call" means it needs to look for a phone number and open a telephone dialer slip. Newton also knows that Bob is a name, since it finds several references to Bob in its Name File. So, based on your command, Newton would look for Bob and display his phone number in a slip, ready to be dialed (see Figure 2).

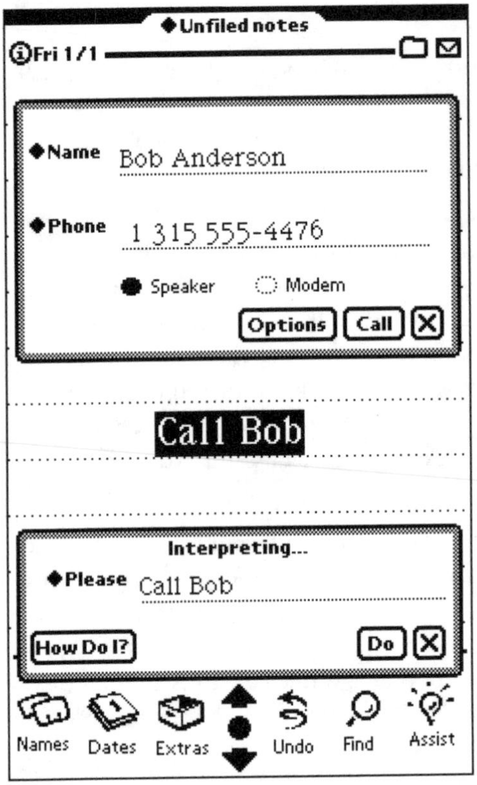

Figure 2 What about Bob? Newton's intelligent assistant helps you find your way.

Like your dog, Newton understands several variations on "fetch" and is capable of retrieving several kinds of electronic slippers for you. In most ways the assistant is dumber than your dog, because you can't teach it new tricks—hence our calling it dog-stupid.

The second aspect of Newton intelligence is its adaptive handwriting recognition that improves as you work with the device—to some extent, it learns to read your scrawl. Adaptive handwriting is one of the things that makes Newton a truly *personal* digital assistant.

Handwriting recognition is basically a game of percentages. When you write a word on the screen, Newton uses several tests to score candidate words on how closely they approximate the shapes of the letters you wrote. The word with the highest score wins. The adaptive handwriting recognizer collects information about how you write each letter, increasing the odds that what it thinks you wrote is what you really wrote.

At best, adaptive handwriting recognition is a "meet me halfway" game. While you're teaching your Newton how you write, your Newton will be teaching you how it recognizes. Both of you will adapt. But no other pen-based device available now can learn anything about your handwriting without requiring you open a special training application. (For more information on Newton handwriting recognition, please refer to Chapter Four —*The Written Word*.)

A word for those former technophobes out there: Once you've spent the time to train your MessagePad or Expert Pad to deal with the eccentricities of your scrawl, you won't want to let anyone else near it for fear they'll "screw it up." (My husband got hold of my Newton. After using it a few hours, it learned enough of his writing not to recognize either of our writing very well—it's not *personal* anymore!)

The barrier that prevents most people from using computers comfortably is a difference in the way wetware brains and silicon chips handle information. Humans think *dynamically*, in an unstructured and intuitive way that results in myriad connections between pieces of information, while computers compute *linearly*, with an emphasis on structure and rules. Newton intelligence tears down this conceptual Berlin Wall, because it lets a Newton process information dynamically. A Newton has multiple ways of going about everything it does. For instance, Newton can recognize "remember to pick up the laundry," whether you enter that command in the notepad or add it directly to your to-do list. So, no matter where you are, you can get where you want to be or do what you want to do.

The Right Connections

Apple likes to describe the Newton as a "communications assistant," but frankly, communications is only a means to an end.

Communications in this context means that Newton can use a variety of network and serial connections to collect and disseminate information. For example, you can take sales figures sent to you by a colleague via Newton-Mail, move the data into the notepad, add a few of your own ideas (as additional text or ink arrows pointing out key facts) and fax it to a client, complete with a cover sheet.

How communications-savvy is a Newton? The first generation is somewhere on the connectivity scale between the relatively deaf/mute Sharp Wizard and the cellular- and wireline modem-enabled AT&T EO Personal Communicator. With the addition of an external modem, a MessagePad or

Expert Pad can send faxes (it can't receive them, yet), as well as send and receive mail electronically. You'll need access to a telephone wall socket, since a cellular modem for the PCMCIA slot will not be available well into 1994.

On the wireless communications front, Newton is a catcher's mitt, since it can only receive data through the Messaging Card. This is very limited compared to first generation EOs, which include the ability to use a cellular connection to send and receive electronic mail, faxes and to even place voice telephone calls. However, the Messaging Card has a clever design which allows it to signal you when it receives a page. It can also store hundreds of messages while you carry it in your pocket. Newton can display those messages when the Messaging Card is plugged in to the Newton's PCMCIA slot.

We expect Apple, Sharp and third-party developers to expand the number of both wired and wireless communications options for Newton in short order. Newton is ready for wireless two-way communications, it will only be a matter of adding the software and hardware that supports it.

Newton exceeds all other communicators (including EO) and organizers in a critical area. Apple, through the Newton Connection software for Macs and Windows PCs, provides exceptional integration with the personal computer. Connection lets you take a snapshot of all the information in your Newton, including names, calendar items, text and notes preserved in ink, and move it to your computer. This capability alone makes Newton an important peripheral for mainstream computer users who want to make the transition to full-time computerization and the fabled "paperless office."

Connection also lets you use Newton data when you are working on a Mac or PC. So, while sitting at your desk, you can add an appointment to your Connection calendar which can be "synchronized" with your Newton calendar and carried along when you leave on a trip. A wide variety of third-party Mac and PC software will eventually include import/export capabilities that hook into Newton Connection, so look for Newton access to your company's shared calendar program, shared databases and other data sources.

The most obvious advantage of Connection is the ability to make backup copies of your Newton's data, all the handwriting recognition it has learned, and system updates added by Apple to fix problems with the software that is embedded in Newton's silicon heart. More important still, for those of us with no patience, you can use a keyboard instead of a pen to add names, notes and appointments to the data. Lastly, Newton Connection will save you money, since it lets you buy and load applications onto your Newton which ship on floppy diskettes, instead of expensive Flash RAM or ROM PCMCIA cards. (Look in Chapter Two—*Your Information Surfboard*, for information on RAM, ROM and PCMCIA cards).

Nothing remotely like Newton Connection currently exists for any other PDA or personal communicator, although we both have prayed to a pagan god and sacrificed a few casual acquaintances in a quest for a Connection-like product for the EO. The EO's relationship with the desktop computer, by comparison to Newton, is like a spouse after a contested divorce.

Newton also supports AppleTalk, the Apple networking protocol (which controls the way computers communicate over a network), allowing you to plug a Newton into a Macintosh computer network and share printers with the big kids on the wire. Newton can act as a direct, or native, "client" to databases and other services residing on a network server. (Don't worry, if you're unfamiliar with these terms, all will be explained in Chapter Three—*The Invisible World*.) Your tiny PDA can act as a network peer in some respects with bigger and much more expensive computers.

This Ain't No Stinkin' Wizard!

On a recent trip from Chicago to San Francisco, we had the opportunity to watch former Apple Chairman John Sculley, the man who unleashed Newton and the whole PDA concept upon the world, work in a seat three over.

Here, indeed was the person for whom Newton was invented, both literally and in terms of the demographics that describe the initial market for Newton. The man has no Off switch—he never once paused to watch the movie or for a quick cat nap. He started the flight by skimming through a copy of Silicon Dreams, a novel by Joe Hutsko, his technology advisor for three years. Sculley was making notes in the margins. He then proceeded to read through various newspaper articles gathered for him by a clipping service. A while later the chairman of Apple opened a tattered spiral notebook and wrote neat little lines of text, in pencil, the lines evenly spaced from each other, as though they were typeset. He referred back and forth between the articles and the notebook; the gears were meshing, this was Sculley the visionary, using his pencil.

We won't hold it against him, but at one point he even pulled out a small keyboard-based electronic organizer that looked suspiciously like a Casio B.O.S.S. Is John a traitor to the vision he articulated? Let's give him the benefit of the doubt. Newton had only been introduced days before and he probably hadn't had time to stand on line to get his yet.

Of course, John Sculley also said at the Newton announcement: "I really like taking notes using [Newton's] soft keyboard!." Yeah, right. And we like to pick up broken glass with our fingers while blindfolded.

It's the growing crush of information in our lives that drove Apple to build devices to help us ride the flow; they're betting that we need the help. And while we feel there are many advantages the first Newton have over their handheld competitors, many of which we've outlined above, Sculley provided us a look at the distance between these first devices and what we finally need to bring together: books, newspapers, Newton intelligence and assistance. It all comes down to this: If a device doesn't work the way you need it to work, you won't use it.

Most of our lives are text-based. The written word is still where we turn for knowledge, and we use it to make our livings. Sculley's flight home emphasizes the need for more work, different hardware designs and lots of cool applications, so Newton can be fitted to more lifestyles.

By investing in Newton now, you'll be better able to shape the Newtons of tomorrow to the way you work and the places you go.

No matter how much it might, on first blush, resemble products like the Sharp Wizard, Casio B.O.S.S., H-P 95LX or Tandy/Casio Zoomer, the Newton is more than an electronic organizer. All these devices have this in common—they're small, they run a long time on a battery charge and, in the case of Zoomer and the Sharp Wizard OZ-9600, let you use a pen to control their graphical (picture-based) interfaces.

But Newton's organizer capabilities are only one possible extension of Newton technology. The underlying architecture provides so much elbow room that it's not inconceivable in the next few years we'll have Newtons teaching our children penmanship, helping us share ideas with a room full of people, controlling the light and temperature in our homes, or perhaps even guiding us to our destinations while driving cross-country (see Figure 3).

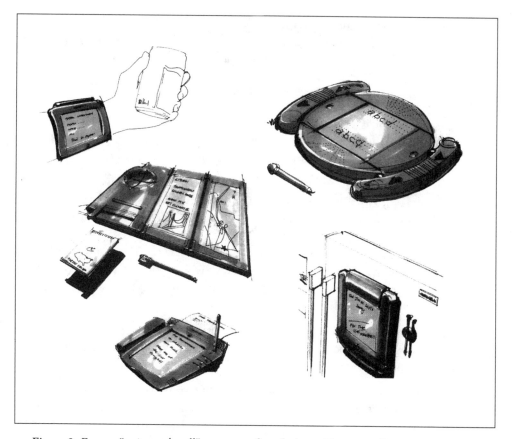

Figure 3 From a "write-and-spell" to a smart fax telephone, Newtons will come in every shape and size imaginable.

Sharp is only one of many manufacturing partners with which Apple has signed agreements to populate the world with Newtons of every size, description, and function set. Others include Siemens, Matsushita (you know them as Panasonic), and Motorola, so you can expect to see desktop telephones, cellular telephones, and more PDAs with a Newton flavor. Sharing Newton technology is an unprecedented business decision for Apple, and a very wise one. By licensing the Newton architecture, Apple is taking a real step toward becoming the Microsoft of PDAs. No more of the willful differentness of the Mac, where different spells problems for users.

With Newton, Apple is saying "Here it is and you can have it, too." The flexibility and power of Newton technology may well leave Microsoft, the mighty Windows leviathan, with a tiny slice of Apple's pie, at last. Then again, maybe not. Microsoft has a habit of taking 80 percent of a great idea, implementing the hell out of it, and making a market its own.

Equal Access

Newton is a subversive machine. By placing the power to manage information in the palms of people's hands, Apple threatens the balance of power in the emerging information marketplace.

Knowledge is power (it also makes one heck of a dinner date, but we digress). Three qualities characterize the value of information in our economy: timeliness; appropriateness; and exclusivity. Timeliness, because nothing is less interesting than yesterday's news. Appropriateness, because Mongolian yak hunters are unlikely to be interested in a fax on semiconductor futures. Exclusivity, because what you know is valuable, what your competitor doesn't know is 100 times more valuable. But even these criterion of value will change as we segue into an information economy.

Knowledge is unique, because if one person possesses it, all others can possess it to the same extent. You can't do that with an ox or an Oldsmobile, but with knowledge everything is equal, except what you make of it.

Restricted access to information is the weapon corporations and governments use to gain an advantage over one another, and over the population. More frightening than restricted access to the day's baseball scores or the stock market results is the limitation on access to information about ourselves. When this happens (believe us, it already has), then institutions can make decisions about you that drastically effect your life with no justification whatsoever. We could all be cast in the role of Kafka's Joseph K., searching in vain for a cause, a meaning in his persecution.

The sheer mass of information in the world makes the best possible haystack to drop a needle into. A Newton, equipped with an assistant capable of sifting through all that hay, will work like a magnet that attracts the needle you need. It's equal access for everyone, because a computer network doesn't care what income bracket, color, race, sex or sexual orientation you are. Just so long as you have a valid password, and that's the trick.

In a "free" society that places a price tag on everything, the strategy used to limit access to information is placing that information where it is difficult and/or expensive to access. It's been going on for years, as government records, newspaper articles and corporate reports to regulatory agencies have been placed in the databases of a few commercial data merchants. The data collecting about each of us in the credit reporting agencies is all-encompassing and terrifying in its arbitrary nature.

A nation of Newton users, who will go about accessing data at will, and who will naturally want to access more and more data as they improve their information surfing skills, will make it increasingly difficult to hide or restrict access to information. Credit agencies will be at the mercy of the consumer who uses his Newton to charge purchases (through infrared point-of-sale devices that will be offered by American Express, MasterCard and VISA) and to pay his bills (using Quicken and NewtonMail to send electronic checks). It used to be that the credit report was considered incontrovertible, since it was the product of a computer. Newton, since it shares the mystic authority of the computer, and carries with it the individual's history, will be a powerful weapon in the case of a credit dispute. Consumers will be able to use Newton to watchdog their credit accounts and deluge the bureau with corrections if any inconsistencies appear. It takes years to clear erroneous data from a credit report, in part because of bureaucratic foot-dragging and the tortures of snail-mail. The Newton can short circuit the process and actually make it easier for the agency to deal with your problem rather than continue to deal with your inquiries (ah, the wonders of max-faxing).

People won't stand for a ruling class—that's how we got ourselves into a revolution and a great idea like the United States. Newton is a musket to be used in the fight against information tyranny.

I Am Nomad

The MessagePad and Expert Pad are quite small and easy to carry. Only goes to reason you'll want to use such a small device pretty much wherever and whenever inspiration strikes.

Anywhere, anytime computing is usually referred to as mobile computing, although in Newton's case it's more like mobile musing. As the marketplaces goes global and as companies use more temporary workers to achieve short term goals without allocating long term resources, the need for small, ubiquitous devices that can keep people in touch will grow.

Taking your creativity off the desktop and onto the road will free you to be creative (and productive) on a 24-hour basis, giving you the freedom to set your own hours. Work a New York day, a Tokyo day or a Frankfurt afternoon and a San Francisco morning—it's up to you, as long as you produce the kind of value companies will pay for. Doing so puts you in the driver's seat of your career and life, because you no longer need to be tied to an office.

The company you work for can eliminate substantial overhead required to maintain an office for you. Your company saves money and you get to be both more effective in your job, because you have your computing resources with you when you need them, and happier because you can spend more time getting the job done and less dealing with office bureaucracy.

At least that's the theory; your results may vary.

We believe that those individuals who set themselves apart through their use of information will become invaluable to corporations. They will be the first to truly succeed in an information economy, setting the terms of their work and where it will be done. If you could live in Boise but earn a Los Angeles wage with a Newton, a cellular phone and your PowerBook, wouldn't you be better off?

We have been following this trend toward a technology-enabled, nomadic society for some years now. Our books have focused both on the technologies and the ramification of their use. Based on research from Sharp, Apple, a couple of technology research firms and our own observations (you get to guess which we relied on most), we've identified four ways people will use their PDAs:

The Portable Peripheral. At well under $1,000, a MessagePad or Expert Pad makes a moderately-priced information peripheral for both desktop and portable users. Corporations spend millions equipping field sales forces with portable and notebook computers. Salespeople certainly appreciate it and quietly thank their company's information systems manager every time they step out of the car door on the way to see a client (remembering to leave the portable in the trunk).

No salesperson is going to put a wall between themselves and their customers and, no matter how small a portable computer gets, its flip-up screen will always form a wall as obscuring as if it was made of brick. Also, the tapping of keys can be very distracting and can give a client the impression that they are not the center of attention, something any good salesperson will endeavor to avoid. The same is true of field service representatives, claims adjusters or anyone whose focus is people—it doesn't pay to tell the customer you are ignoring them through your use of a computer.

Even when they're not in conference, using a portable to quickly get that phone number, check an appointment or take some notes can involve interminable seconds as the thing wakes up or turns on. And balancing a five-pound plastic clamshell on your knee in a phone booth while you dial the phone is a feat that could put the Flying Walendas to shame.

Newton is a powerful alternative for the portable-hobbled worker in the field. With Newton you can collect and access information all day and, with the use of Newton Connection, download it to your portable that evening at the hotel for more intense manipulation.

This is where Newton will find its widest application in the next year or two. As business users discover other uses for their Newtons, it will begin to seep into everyday life.

The Executive's Assistant. All those executives the IS managers couldn't get to use a computer at all will be turned on to the Newton. They'll buy them to help get organized, or their spouses will give them this latest, hippest tech for Christmas or a birthday. Executives are already the technological spoilers of otherwise well-integrated company information systems, insisting assistants do the dirty work for them.

Newton isn't a computer, right? But after they've gotten comfortable with their "organizer", the Trojan Horse of Newton's built-in networking will bring them, willingly, into the company information systems fold.

The Mobile Mailbox. While we're sure everyone who buys one will use Newton as an organizer and electronic notepad to some extent, working with a handheld mailbox will likely evolve into one of the most attractive Newton uses.

For people on the move, keeping in touch is the most important and difficult task. Newton's ability to sign on to an on-line mailbox to which anyone can send mail will certainly help achieve the goal of making people more accessible. Combine that with a Messaging Card, which can receive a page anywhere in the U.S. and you sever the umbilical cord that lashes us to the office. From it size to the communications intelligence it lends, Newton is a nearly perfect electronic mailbox that follows wherever you go.

Window on the World. We doubt large numbers of users will buy a Newton to read the daily paper. However, once a new breed of intelligent assistants, called agents, can jump off your information surfboard to swim the seas of data in search of facts and headlines that interest you, Newton-based news services will be one of those things you'll wonder how you ever lived without.

While we're waiting for nomadic assistants to become reality (it'll be sooner than you might think), a MessagePad or Expert Pad, in combination with third-party terminal emulation software, will allow you to do the foot work yourself. And, having that AppleTalk-based network connection to the company database sure might come in handy the next time you need some sales figures quick!

Get Info...Who Are You?

Who is 39 years old, makes $59,000 a year, has been to college, is male, has children and has probably used a computer? A Newton user, that's who, according to Apple.

Apple conducted some 600 interviews with people who lived in households with incomes greater than $40,000 a year to try and determine who's most likely to buy a Newton. Here's what they found:

- The average Newton user will be 39 years old and earn $59,000 a year. The average American adult, by contrast, is 32 years old and earns $30,126, according to the U.S. Census Bureau. The price of the typical house, $79,100, is only a little more than what Apple's typical Newton user earns each year. Do you sense a bit of unreality here?

- About 70 percent of Newton users will be male, 54 percent will be college educated and 80 percent should live in households with kids. Surprise! The average American is a woman, and only 20 percent earn a college degree. Kids are the only common denominator between Apple's vision and our reality.

(continued)

Get Info...Who Are You? (continued)

- As to what computers or organizer products they've used before, Apple expects 17 percent will have used a FiloFax, 7 percent will come from a portable computing background, 6 percent will have used an electronic organizer, and 32 percent will come from a life free from computers or organizers. Of personal computer users, 55 percent will use DOS or Windows. While the U.S. Census doesn't measure these variables ("Could you tell us about your kids, your computer and what's that you're taking notes on?"), let's just point out that the largest sector of the American economy is populated by clerical workers (18 million).

The number one emotional response, which Apple got from 95 percent of the audience, was Newton would be fun to use.

Getting Hyper

It seemed silly to us to write a book about a device that lets you access information dynamically if we didn't do the same. In order to help you navigate through all the advice, facts and nifty tricks in *Newton's Law*, we've include three kinds of sidebars in the book.

Get Info

Called "Get Info" notes, look here for interesting facts and stories pertaining to the Newton, PDAs in general, or the mobile computing market as a whole. This is where you'll find articles, statistics and other interesting trivia of the Newton phenomenon.

Assist

Assist sidebars contain specific information about using your Newton and how to get the most from your PDA. Look here for extended discussions on what terms like MIPS really mean and how to use keywords to boost your power Find.

Easter Egg

Easter Eggs are the hidden and/or undocumented capabilities of your MessagePad or Expert Pad. Many are just "gee whiz" tricks, sort of like getting the family dog to leap through a burning hula hoop. Others, however, can be quite useful and even help an ailing Newton recover its wits when all else seems to fail.

Assist...The Hyperactive Book

We've written *Newton's Law* in modules. The modules, which we call sections, are designed to explore some area of Newton technology while avoiding overlap with other sections. The sections are written in ascending order of complexity, so, while Section I presumes little about your knowledge of Newton, Section V presumes quite a lot. So, judge your competency and feel free to dive in where you please. To the best of our ability, we've tried to write Newton's Law so each section can stand on its own.

Further, within each section are chapters which, in turn, are divided into subchapters. Again, as much as possible we've tried to make chapters and subchapters "stand-alone."   *(continued)*

Assist... The Hyperactive Book (continued)

This way, if you jump from place to place within the book you shouldn't feel lost.

This "multiple points of entry" writing style is sometimes referred to as *Hypertext*. It's a style we've cultivated in all our books, not just because we think it's easier for the reader, but because it makes moving the text to electronic book format much easier (Remember the Sixth Newton's Law: *Revenue is the mother of invention*).

Who Are These Fools, Anyway?

We have followed the development of Newton since it was first uncovered in the pages of *MacWEEK*, and in that time we've collected a lot of information about the devices and the people who made them. So, here it is, *Newton's Law*. While it does contain much of the information you'd expect to find in a computer book, it also provides information you probably won't find in "Newton for Numskulls" or "Zen and the Art of Bit-Diddling." We try to do more than tell you that you get result B from tapping icon A. We also tell you why you'd want to get result B or, in fact, that you may not want result B at all and that result C might be an altogether friendlier result to have tea with Sunday afternoon.

As much as possible, we try to make learning about Newton enjoyable. This technology has a context—your life—and we think it's important that you understand what you're getting yourself into.

Our other books, *PowerBook: The Digital Nomad's Guide and AT&T EO Personal Communicator: The Digital Nomad's Guide* (notice a trend here?), tried to give readers guidance, not just on how to use those devices, but how they might fit them into their business and personal lives. While we feel Newtons are something of a different animal from either an EO or PowerBook, the basic challenge still exists—to explain what the heck these ground-breaking mobile technologies mean to you.

Make No Assumptions, Accept No Imitations

The First Law of Newton's Law could be expressed this way—if you're not keeping up you're falling behind. And there's nothing we can imagine more depressing than spending your life trying to catch up.

So, in the interest of keeping our readers up-to-date on the latest and greatest of what is sure to be an ever-changing line of products, we are publishing our electronic mail addresses below. If you're in search of an update or have any questions, criticisms or just want to tell us how wonderful you think this book is (we especially like those messages), please feel free to contact us. We will try to respond to every message we get.

Andrew Gore
AppleLink (AOS): ANDYGORE
CompuServe (CIS): 72511,224
America Online (AOL): MW ANDY
NewtonMail: AGORE

Mitch Ratcliffe
CompuServe (CIS): 72511,274
AppleLink: MRATCLIFFE
Internet: coyote@well.sf.ca.us
NewtonMail: RATCLIFFE

The water's warm and sparkling. Let's dive in!

Post Script

Shortly before press time, but too late to make changes throughout this book, John Sculley left Apple Computer. Perhaps we can look upon references to him in the text and figures in this book as a homage to one of the fathers of the PDA.

A. G. and M. R.

Understanding Newton

The First Axiom: Before technology can be considered truly advanced, it should look cool and have a hip name.

Corollary I: Steven Spielberg should want actors using it in his movies.

Welcome To The First Level

Ever wonder what PCMCIA or "data object" mean? How Newtons deal with data or what the difference is between AppleTalk and LocalTalk? Then this is the section for you.

In *Understanding Newton*, we cover the basics of Newton technology including hardware, the Newton architecture, and communications (which we call *NeWtworking*). If you already know about PCMCIA cards and the Internet, and you feel comfortable using your Newton, you can probably get by just skimming through these chapters. However, be sure to watch for Easter Eggs and other nifty tips and tricks embedded in the text!

If you don't own a Newton but are thinking of buying one, read on. You'll get a good grounding in the technology, and will be better able to decide when and how you want to jump onto the Newton bandwagon.

A Quick Start

If you already have a Newton but haven't used it yet, it's a good idea to spend a couple of hours playing with the device before reading further; the experience will provide some added context for the information here. We know, playing with a Newton is a tough job, but someone's got to do it.

You don't have to read the MessagePad Handbook or Expert Pad user's guide before you get started. However, do go through the Setup Guide and try the Handwriting Instructor and Guided Tour on the Getting Started card included with your Newton MessagePad. The Expert Pad does not include the Getting Started card and, instead, has a "Quick Guide" paper manual. However, the following instructions on how to insert a PCMCIA card apply equally to both Newtons (Expert Pad users, see below).

Or just jump in and follow the tradition of pioneers before you (As Mike Doonesbury said "Somebody has to go first!").

To use the Getting Started card, just remove the plastic protector card from your MessagePad's PCMCIA slot and insert the card. First, raise the PCMCIA card latch on the upper left corner of your Newton's face. Your Newton will turn on automatically when you raise the latch. Press the card ejector switch—flush with the top left edge of the MessagePad (see Figure I.1)—which will eject the slot protector card. Be sure to put the protector in a safe place, you'll need it again.

If this is the very first time you've turned on your MessagePad or Expert Pad, the Newton will ask you to align the pen (for more on pen alignment, see Chapter Seven—*Life's Little Extras*).

Now, slide the Getting Started card into the PCMCIA slot with the label side up and insert the edge with two rows of pinholes into the slot. Press the card all the way in—be careful not to force it—the card should seat itself so that the top edge of the card will be flush with the Newton's case. Push the card latch back down. Your MessagePad won't look for a card in the slot until this latch is closed.

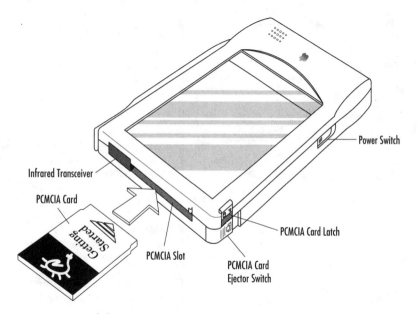

Figure I.1 *Sliding in a PCMCIA card*

After a moment, the Getting Started card will open your Newton's Extras drawer automatically, and a message slip saying "This is the Getting Started card" will appear on the screen. Just tap the close box—the box with the "X" in it in the lower right corner of the slip.

Try the Instructor, and then the Tour, by tapping the icons once with the pen; you'll see them at the bottom of the Extras drawer (see Figure I.2). Neither is an all-encompassing introduction to the Newton. They're valuable because they give you a place from which to start exploring. Avoid the game for the time being, we'll explain why in Chapter Four.

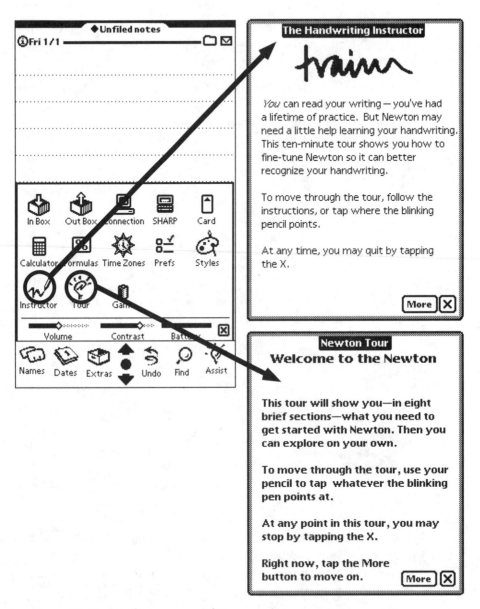

Figure I.2   Finding the Instructor and Tour.

Now, feel free to explore, change the settings, whatever you want. Don't worry about messing up; we'll show you how to get everything back to factory settings before the real work of training Newton starts.

You can remove the Getting Started card anytime you want. Just lift up the card latch and then press the card ejector switch. Don't forget to re-insert the plastic protector card and push the card latch back into place.

Expert Help

As we noted earlier, the Expert Pad does not include a Getting Started ROM card. Instead, Sharp has the "Quick Guide," a much more thorough introduction to Newton basics than Apple's Getting Started card. We highly recommend going through this guide and trying out some of the included examples.

It's unfortunate that Apple and Sharp couldn't combine forces and produce an electronic Getting Started guide as thorough as the Quick Guide and as accessible as the Tour. However, by playing around for a few hours, Expert Pad users should be able to get most of the "tactile" experience MessagePad users get from the Tour and Instructor.

By the way, both MessagePad and Expert Pad users can get a quick answer to a question by tapping the Assist icon in the permanent menu at the bottom of the Newton's screen and then tapping the "How Do I..." button in the Assistant slip (see Figure I.3). Choose a topic from the list by tapping it. The help here is pretty minimal, but it should be adequate for simple questions.

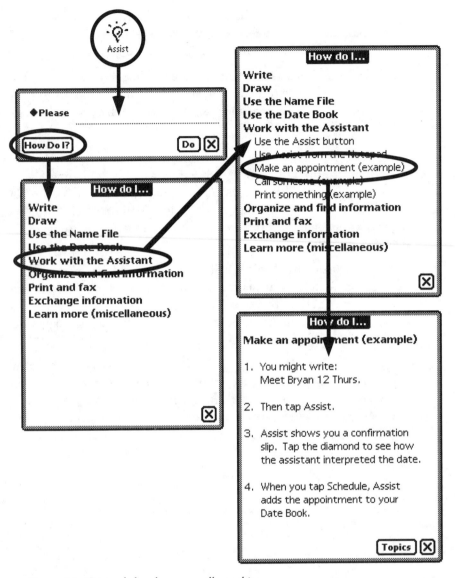

Figure I.3 Getting help when you really need it.

CHAPTER
1

SOFTWARE FOR THE
COMMON MAN

The observant reader may notice that we have deliberately avoided describing Newton as using an operating system (OS). There are several good reasons for this.

The Newton architecture, which is what Apple calls the gestalt of software (the instructions that run a computing device) and hardware technologies that make a Newton a Newton, is both more fluid and adaptable than traditional OSes. Because Newton is essentially a collection of software "modules" held together by the Newton framework (more on this later), it can be easily changed to fit the function of the device in which it is installed. For example, it's likely that sometime in the next year you'll see a Newton device that doesn't come with handwriting recognition, much, we're sure to the great relief of handwriting critics everywhere.

While handwriting recognition is one of the most visible features of the MessagePad and Expert Pad, it is simply a module which can be yanked out, added to, or replaced with a more sophisticated version in other Newtons. Newton software running a cable television controller might be more useful without handwriting recognition capabilities; the designers might feel that handwriting was a superfluous waste of processing power in such a device.

Other Newtons might feature a different calendar or Name file, or perhaps they would eliminate those applications altogether. A Newton Write & Spell probably won't come with a day planner or contact manager, although you can always add those applications via a PCMCIA card (for those of you with upwardly mobile toddlers).

Newton is just plain flexible, flowing into new shapes like the liquid-steel Terminator 2. Computer operating systems are much more structured and, therefore, more restrictive. The majority of today's OSes are fixed, like the supports in a very complex house of cards. Only the very highest levels of the house can be changed without bringing the whole structure down. Traditional OSes also bring along a lot of baggage, such as an inflexible interface or ingrained ways of doing things that make them less than ideal for certain tasks. While we're sure Microsoft Corp. is hard at work on an OS for running household appliances, we'd still steer clear of Windows for Whirlpools. The buttons and knobs we use today to control the washer need to be smarter, a graphical interface will do little to improve the performance of a washer, because icons are as structured as a steel timer and water-settings buttons.

In fact, it is tremendously difficult to use an OS to run different kinds of machines. This is because the part of the OS that controls hardware is so entangled with the rest of the OS instructions that it practically needs to be written again from scratch to move that OS to another platform. In Newton, because the part of the architecture that controls hardware (called the kernel) is just another technology module, it's a relatively simple matter to peel off the rest and drop it on top of a new kernel. Try that with the Macintosh OS! (In fact, Apple has been trying to do just that for a number of years, with limited success.)

Another key difference between the Newton Architecture and traditional computer OSes is applications. In most computers, the OS takes care of managing the hardware, defining the interface, and handling system management tasks. To actually do something, like word processing, requires separate application software.

There is a hard line between applications. So, every time a programmer writes an application they must reinvent the wheel. They must define the printing function, for example, whenever they write an application that they want to print from. In recent years, application frameworks have come into vogue which allow programmers to use software templates to define standard tasks. Even though this is a real time-saver, it's still like making a photocopy. Two practically identical pieces of software are required to do the same thing in two applications.

In the Newton Architecture, applications are an extension of the framework. That doesn't mean that you can only have better calendars or to-do list managers. Rather, it means that a new application can grab pre-existing instructions in other applications, modifying those instructions as needed. As a result, a Newton application is very small and very fast, being composed primarily of changes to instructions elsewhere in the Newton framework.

Applications and higher functions all exist on the same level of the Newton architecture. They are also all written in the same language, especially designed for this instruction-borrowing way of programming, called, logically enough, NewtonScript.

Even the information within Newton is community property. For example, the application that handles faxing, which you see as the fax slip where you enter the name and phone number of the recipient, looks into the Newton Names file for the fax number associated with the name you write in the To: field. When you enter Bob's name in the fax slip it calls Bob's number up from the Names file and dials it.

There is one other critical difference between Newton and a traditional computer OS. Today's GUI (Graphical User Interface) OSes, like Mac and Windows, are known by the way they manage data stored in files. This file management layer is the interface for the OS; applications define the interface for how you actually use the computer.

In Newton the applications are the only interface you'll ever see, there is no file management layer. In fact, there are no files! Information floats in a free-form soup unfettered by boundaries. Everything can be related to everything, a phone number to a name, and by extension, to all the names that work for the same company—it's only a matter of how the applications connect the data dots. Although this approach is preferable for a device, like Newton, designed to be used in quick bursts, the lack of data management facilities can be annoying at times.

Having taken the space to explain why Newton is both more and less than an OS, we must say that any comparison of the two is, by definition, flawed. A computer operating system works with fixed variables: Press a key and, depending upon the context in which you pressed it, one of several predetermined functions are transacted—the letter "a" appears in a word processing document or a database field, or the computer searches for the "a" in a document. With Newton, input is individualized. Handwriting is translated, the assist function adds the "a" you write to a string of letters in another application, and so on. The expectation that Newton would perform flawlessly out of the box is ludicrous, because there is no such thing as a standard human workstyle. Instead, Newton must be shaped by the application and the user to support a very individual way of thinking about your world.

Get Info...Foul Play and Frogs

"I always say if it walks like a duck and quacks like a duck it's a duck. So if it walks like a Macintosh and quacks like a Macintosh, it's a Macintosh. And if it runs Macintosh software and it has a Macintosh user interface, it's a Macintosh, no matter how big it is, no matter whether it's got a mouse, a track ball, a stylus, a finger, or talks.

(continued)

Get Info...Foul Play and Frogs (continued)

"Newton is different because its user interaction paradigm is totally different. The special applications that it runs will be different from the ones that define personal computers. In other words, desktop publishing isn't going to be what you do with a Newton.

"[Newton is] not an operating system in the same sense as UNIX or MS-DOS. When you buy a VCR, or microwave oven or an automobile, there are a lot of microprocessors and software built-in. But it's not what a commercial firm would call an operating system. The consumer is totally unaware of the electronics involved.

"[Newton] is halfway between a personal computer and a calculator... It's an amphibian."—Larry Tesler, former vice president of the Newton group. Taken from a September 1992 interview in *MacWEEK*.

Terms of Surrender, Part I

It's unfortunate that no one's invented a computing device that didn't require explanation. On the other hand, if a perfectly intuitive computer had come along, we'd be out of a job.

Like anything else, a good and thorough explanation usually comes couched in terms that are probably unfamiliar to the person the explanation was intended to enlighten. So, to help make sure that we and our readers are understanding the same meanings for the same terminology, we include this glossary of software-oriented lingo. For hardware-oriented verbiage, see *Terms of Surrender, Part II* in the next chapter.

Even experienced readers may want to skim through these two glossaries. It's amazing how much latitude there can be in such an exact science as computing.

Information. Unprocessed knowledge. The collected facts and figures that describe the world around us, but do not necessarily convey wisdom or insight. You can have a raft of information and still be stuck on a desert island of meaninglessness.

Data. Data is what information, like a phone number, name or lunch appointment, becomes once it's been converted into digital form. In the pre-computer world only scientists were said to handle "data," but that was because people believed that only the content of a scientist's mind was racing ahead of technology into the world of processing facts into new knowledge. In fact, life has been filled with data since the beginning of time, but putting all the pieces together has always taken a very long time. Data is the stuff a computing device processes, like the text in a faxed note, as opposed to the instructions for sending the data as a fax.

Code. These are the operating instructions that tell a computing device what to do and how to do it. The code that controls the calendar, for instance, tells your Newton that when you tap on a date in the calendar it should change the display to a view of that day. Software, like the Newton interface and applications, are made of code.

Applications. Applications are specialized collections of code that make your Newton perform a particular function. For example, the calendar is a built-in application and Fingertip for Golf is an add-on application. A Newton application is not like a traditional application running on your personal computer. Rather, it is a customized extension of your Newton's operating software.

Bits and Bytes. One of the most critical statistics you need to be aware of while using a Newton is available memory, which is measured in bytes.

Despite all it's feigned sophistication, at it's lowest level a computing device is nothing more than thousands of banks of microscopic switches. Depending on whether those switches are on or off, and the pattern they create, they make the computer behave differently.

A computer represents the state of each switch, or circuit, as a *bit*. There are two kinds of bits, either "0" or "1," with 0 representing a circuit without current flowing through it (switched off) and a 1 representing a circuit with power (switched on). This system of 0's and 1's is referred to as *binary*.

Bits in a Newton are measured in groups of eight binary numbers, which are collectively known as *bytes*. In your Newton, two bytes are used to represent every character of text.

If you already use a computer, you've probably heard that the standard character set used in a PC is known as ASCII, which stands for (get ready to duck) ANSI (American National Standards Institute—welcome to your first acronym within an acronym) Standard Code for Information Interchange. In ASCII, only one byte is needed to represent a specific character —a number, letter, symbol, punctuation mark or blank space (yes, even blank spaces take up space!) It's the pattern of bits in the byte that determine which character that byte represents. So, the byte "01100110" might represent the letter "G" (it doesn't, but it could).

The fancy fonts you see in a word processor or desktop publishing application take the ASCII character and draw it using more complex instructions. But for computers, it always comes down to ASCII.

The character system used in Newton, called Unicode, is much more versatile than ASCII. With twice as many bits per character, Unicode can represent many more characters than ASCII. You could run almost any language known on the planet on your Newton (after some modifications to the interface) because Unicode can handle the thousands of characters used in some languages. So, Newton is capable of handling writing in Japanese and Russian, for example, when Kanji or Cyrillic recognizers and dictionaries are built into ROM (Read Only Memory; see the next chapter for more). All Apple has to do is install the new ROMs and ship those international Newtons.

There are only two things you really need to know about bytes. One is that two bytes are a character and that each time you write a character into your Newton, you take away two bytes of available memory. (In reality, it can be more depending on what other code the Newton generates as a result of you writing in that character.) The other is that bytes are often measured in units of roughly one thousand, called kilobytes or KBytes (1,000 bytes), and one million, called megabytes or MBytes (1,000,000 bytes).

System update. A small bit of code loaded into a special place in your Newton's memory which fixes bugs and (less often) adds features. As we went to press, Apple had released three System updates: 1.02, the short-lived 1.03, and 1.04.

The Newton Framework

Thus far, we've tried to tell you what Newton isn't. Now we're going to try and tell you what it is.

Newton is a data framework. Inside that framework you can store many thousands of little bits of data and connect them and disconnect them at will. A minimal structure binds this framework together: the foundation, which consists of the hardware kernel, recognizers, communications and other technology modules, and the soup where data and code live in peaceful, if somewhat chaotic, cohabitation.

The components of the Newton data architecture are as follows:

Objects. In Newton parlance, object refers to the smallest unit of data or code in a Newton. So, for example, a street address is an object. So is a single line in a drawing.

Object oriented programming (OOP), which is the technique used to develop Newton applications and Newton itself, refers to a different kind of object than the sort we're primarily concerned with in this guide. An OOP object is a self-contained piece of code that performs some task, like drawing a form on the Newton's screen.

Frames. Frames are used by Newton to group objects together. So, for example, Rick Kapur's name, address and phone number could be grouped together within a frame, and this is the data that's accessed when you ask to see Rick's name card. Of course, the frame could just as easily be used to group the date, time and location objects that describe a meeting (in fact, the location could be the address object out of Rick's name frame). The places within a frame that holds objects are called "slots."

Frames can contain both code objects and data objects and often do. Frames are the primary building block of both Newton data sets and applications. A frame with code objects embedded in it can effect many different parts of an application. Most of the Newton architecture is built on these code frames.

Soups. Soups are pools of frames, usually associated with a particular application. So, for example, the Names file has a soup connected to it that contains all the personal information of the people in your contact lists.

All data in all soups in a Newton are readily accessible from other soups. In fact, multiple soups can be viewed collectively, poured into a bigger pot via a "Union Soup" instruction, enlarging the set of data available to an application. When you insert a RAM card into the PCMCIA slot, Newton creates a Union Soup of the names stored on the card and in its main memory to make all the data immediately available to the Names application. Newton simply combines its view of the internal names soup with the one of the card, with no more user input than plugging in the card.

The best part is, when you pull the card out (with no previous notification, by the way) Newton automatically sorts out the two soups.

Stores. The store is the physical location of a soup. So, in the example above, the store for the card soup was the PCMCIA card. Soups are always tied to their store. That way, soups can be combined and separated with minimal fuss.

Because the MessagePad and Expert Pad only have one PCMCIA slot, you'll never have to deal with more than two stores at a time—a card in the slot and Newton's internal memory. We do, however, expect that future Newton designs will include the ability to plug in multiple cards. And Newton is prepared: the software already exists in the device to deal with multiple stores.

Assist...Cold Soup

When Newton merges large soups from different stores, you may occasionally run into performance problems the first time you try to access the joined data.

This is because Newton is busy attempting to reconcile the new information with the data it already had. We call this "heating up the soup," and we have even seen it produce an error message. If you get an error after attaching a card with, or restoring through Newton Connection, a large amount of data, don't panic. Just close the error dialog box, close the application and then open it again (this will likely happen with the Names file, if it happens at all). The second time you open the application, the new data will be available after only a minimal delay. The caveat on that statement is that storage cards with more than 4 MBytes of data can take substantially longer to assimilate into the soup—like a really big pot of cold water takes forever to heat to a boil.

Another problem that can be caused by large amounts of data is something we call "frozen soup." This typically happens when, from inside an application, you change from one folder to another.

(continued)

Assist...Cold Soup (continued)

With about 250 names in the Names file, we've occasionally seen
Newton take up to two minutes to resolve a folder change! Having
the Overview window open only exacerbates the problem. So, be
careful to always close the overview window in the Names file
when you're done using it.

Forms. Forms are the face Newton turns to the world. This is where you
enter information, browse data and print it out. You can think of forms like
those "hidden message" pictures we used to get when we were kids. You'd
have this picture with a cacophony of colored images, purposefully hard to
distinguish from one another. The magic viewer—a piece of colored cello-
phane stretched over a cardboard frame—passed over the picture would
"decode" the hidden message. So, too, a form gives you a way to separate
out decipherable chunks of data in a soup (see Figure 1.1).

Forms serve a variety of functions, from giving you a place to take notes
to displaying a list. All Newton applications use forms to communicate
with the user. Some Newton applications are little more than forms laid on
top of a data soup.

House of mirrors. The sharing of objects between many applications is
a cornerstone concept in the arcana of Newton magic.

Imagine you have an object sitting in the middle of a house of mirrors.
There is only the one object, yet it can be examined from almost anywhere
within the mirrored labyrinth. Each mirror is a Newton application —able
to capture the substance of the object, from the application's particular perspective of needing a function contained in the object, without having to
recreate it. This way, if anyone causes the object to change in any manner,
that change is immediately reflected everywhere in the fun house. So too,
in Newton.

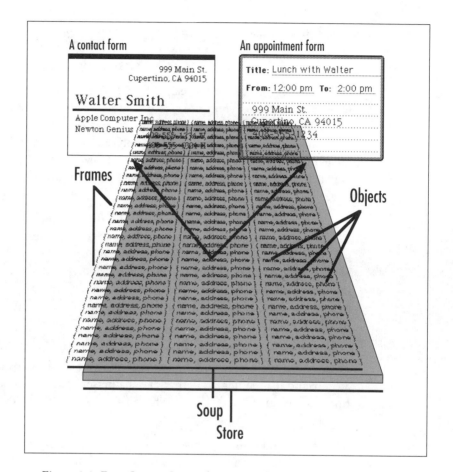

Figure 1.1 *From Soup to Stores, the Newton data framework.*

The Data Masquerade

With knowledge comes understanding, with understanding, structure. Although Newton doesn't really care very much about structure, humans do, so it's good to have some terms to describe how we organize information stored in Newton.

Newton deals with collections of data which on computers are called databases. However, computer databases have a great many more "rules" for handling data than Newton requires (for more on computer database structures, see Chapter Eight—*Ready, Set, Load!*) Newton databases are also called data sets. Although data sets often are comprised of an entire soup, it doesn't need to be that way.

A field is the space on a form where you enter, modify or view a specific piece of information. For example, when you enter someone's first name in the Names file, the space where you enter it is called a field.

A record is a collection of related fields. So, Steve Rea's name, address, phone numbers, etc. comprise a record. If you added Marie D'Amico to your name file, all her personal information would also form a record. In Newton a record can be a name card, a note, an event on the calendar, a to-do item, etc. Anything you can list in the overview window (by tapping the dot in the center of the row of icons on the bottom of your Newton's screen) is a Newton record.

A collection of related records is called a file. Although, unlike a personal computer, in Newton "file" is a term of convenience. Newton does not store data in a rigid format like a computer does and instead forms files on demand. So, when you put the names and addresses of family members into the Personal folder, you are putting them into a file. Unlike computers, Newton files can contain many different kinds of records—appointments, notes, names, etc.

In the Newton architecture, records can be created and dismantled as necessary by assembling and disassembling frames. So, it is possible to create a record for sending a fax that draws a person's name and fax number from their Name file record. After the fax is sent, the record is deleted from the file.

In fact, unlike most conventional databases, records in Newton are formed by connecting data objects. So, Steve's first name and last name might be connected to a lunch meeting in a day planner application. Instead of making you manually re-enter Steve's Name, Newton looks up Steve's Name record and copies the necessary information to the appointment record for you

For those familiar with computer databases this may sound like a relational link, where the contents of a field in one file can be called up from another file. However, nothing could be further from the truth. As we said above, Newton data is stored freeform, floating in the soups. So, relationships can be made and broken as the situation demands. There's no hard-wiring of relationships—this isn't a desktop computer, after all.

The most important thing to remember is this: beyond the object-to-frame-to-soup-to-store structure outlined here, all structures visible in Newton are created for your benefit.

Get Info...Tags, you're not it!

Newton's way of organizing records, in folders, is a simple two-dimensional means of looking at information. But it wasn't always going to be that way.

Early in Newton's development, the team had wanted to use "tags" instead of folders to group records. This would have had the advantage of letting you "slice" your data in many different ways.

For example, let's say you've got five people in your Names file. George, who is a friend and a coworker; Tanya, who is a coworker; Taylor, who sells you office supplies; April, who services your computer system and sometimes rounds out your golf foursome on Sundays; and Marc, who is the office janitor and also does landscaping work for you.

You create several tags including Friend, Company, Vendor, and Contractor and attach them to these people's names as appropriate. Now, you "cut" your data. Ask for a list of names with the Company tag and you get George, Tanya, and Marc. Ask for a Friend list and you get George and April. Ask for a Vendor list and get April and Taylor. And, ask for a combined Vendor and Contractor list and you get April, Taylor, and Marc.

Tags let you to organize data three-dimensionally and allow you much greater flexibility. Unfortunately, Apple's high, holy user tests showed that tags were too difficult a concept for many users to grasp. That's why the team went for the simpler folder system.

Tags, however, may make a reappearance in some future Newton.

Script, You Say?

As we said above, NewtonScript is the language used to create everything you see in your Newton. It's also the language used to create anything you're likely to add to Newton, except perhaps a new handwriting or communications module.

NewtonScript is an incredibly powerful, object-oriented, high-level programming language. Script, in fact, is something of a misnomer because the syntax of the language has nothing in common with other scripting languages, like Apple's HyperTalk or AppleScript, which are intended for use by especially adept users.

Let's be perfectly clear: NewtonScript is not for the faint-hearted! If you wouldn't want to program in C++, you wouldn't want to program in NewtonScript. However, if you're up to the challenge, NewtonScript is one of the best, most efficient and surprisingly flexible specialty programming languages we've ever seen. NewtonScript is what allows developers to borrow preexisting code to build their applications, which is one of the main reasons Newton applications are so much smaller than their computer counterparts. In fact, NewtonScript is so efficient, you're more likely to run out of screen real estate in the Extras drawer before you run out of space on a 2-Mbyte PCMCIA card for most Newton applications!

NewtonScript is the brain child of Newton Team member Walter Smith (NewtonScript was code-named WallyScript.) Walter is one of the brightest people we know. Engaging in a technical discussion with him is like being a kid sitting at the adults' Thanksgiving dinner table for the first time. We've heard a rumor that Walter is considering writing a book on NewtonScript. If he does, and you decide you want to learn the language, we'd highly recommend any book Walter writes, sight unseen.

NewtonScript is a very efficient language. We've seen some pretty robust applications go from concept to completion in as little as sixty days. (The average time it takes to develop a computer application from scratch is two years.) So, expect to see lots of Newton applications really quickly from a lot of different sources.

Newton Foundation

At the bottom of the Newton framework, below the applications, high-level communications, Assist and Find command, and data objects all swimming in a NewtonScript broth are the technology modules and hardware kernel. At this level, Newton borrows heavily from it's older sibling, the Macintosh, especially in low-level communications, communications protocols, and imaging.

Newton uses both QuickDraw, the imaging technology that Macs use to draw images on the computer screen, and the Mac's AppleTalk and Local-Talk networking technologies (for a complete discussion of AppleTalk and

LocalTalk, turn to Chapter Three—*The Invisible World*). This is also where the recognizers live as well as the data storage model.

The good thing about borrowing two of its key low-level technologies from the Macintosh is that Apple has had several years to work the kinks out of the software. Also, AppleTalk helps ensure Newton will fit into and be able to communicate within the existing Macintosh communications architecture.

As these technologies advance, such as when Apple ships QuickDraw GX (a more powerful version of QuickDraw), we expect to see those updates get integrated into future Newton models. The ease with which most Newton technologies can be swapped out, even at such a low level, will make it possible to keep Newton on the wave front on the latest and greatest.

The Critical Detail

We thought it appropriate to end this chapter with a brief discussion of the Te of Newton.

As part of their user testing, Apple brought the Taoist scribe Lao Tse to the Cupertino Headquarters and asked him to take a look at their plans for Newton. This was in the earliest days of the project, when Apple's Steve Sakoman and Jean-Louis Gassée were hawking a suitcase-sized computer with a pen. The ancient master shuffled into the conference room at the Bubb Road building during the fall of 1987. He wore a tattered flaxen Mao jacket that he'd picked off a dead guerrilla in the Yang-tse Valley during the 1940s. Cobwebs flowed from his mustache into the air with each word he spoke. Gassée thought Lao Tse smelled bad and said so under his breath.

But the master was too polite or too absorbed to make any show of noticing Gassée's comment. He was studying the pages of product plans and designs that were scrolling across the screen of a Macintosh. He asked for a print-out of the document and sat quietly reading it for more than three hours. Finally, he rose from his chair and walked to the door.

"Well, what do you think?" Sakoman asked as he rose to insinuate himself between Lao Tse and the door.

"There is something missing," Lao Tse said, a spider wafting from his lips to Gassée's shoulder.

"Of course," the Frenchman hissed. "It is an early design. We asked you here to tell us *what* is missing!"

"You've already found what's missing," the scribe whispered and turned back to the screen. He regarded the Macintosh mouse with curiosity, then seized it and scrolled through the document to the page that described the design of the first Newton. Lao Tse pointed at the screen.

Gassée and Sakoman leaned into the glowing plan, searched for what the old man seemed to be pointing at, then regarded one another suspiciously. What was this old coot trying to pull, after they flew him from China and put him up at the Cupertino Inn? Lao Tse had probably never seen the conveniences of modern living before and, now, here he was trying to bullshit the leading technical minds at Apple.

"What?" Gassée stood, pulling his leather jacket around himself to zip the zipper curtly.

"The critical detail," Lao Tse said as he pointed to an asterisk at the bottom of the page. Sakoman shrank perceptibly, he knew what the asterisk referred to, and he assumed Lao Tse had read the fine print to find out how tentative the Newton vision really was. "When I can actually write an asterisk on a computer, then I will be able to capture the critical detail, perhaps as deviously as you have," the old Chinese said with a smile.

Lao Tse turned and walked out the door, back into history. He'd never turned to the footnote.

Gassée said something derisive in French as Sakoman scrolled down the page to the footnote indicated by the asterisk. It said: "Handwriting recognition technology will not be capable of keeping up with the average person's untrained hand until the 21st Century."

The lesson of the story is not that handwriting recognition technology is poor. It is. But Lao Tse's lesson was that you don't have to write much to get the real message across to a perceptive reader. Just an asterisk will do.

Newton is optimized to handle little bits of data. In fact, if you try to either create large data objects, such as a note with hundreds of words, or handle a very large number of data objects, your Newton will come to a grinding halt.

This is Reason Number One why the MessagePad and Expert Pad don't make good notebooks. Even if handwriting recognition was perfect or you were willing to keep notes in ink format, you'd soon hit a wall. Newton is only willing to handle notes up to a certain size (see Figure 1.2).

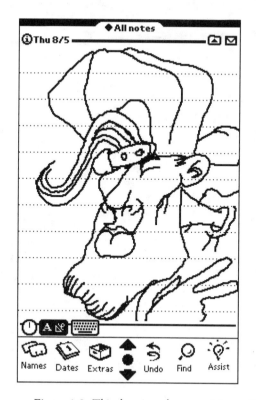

*Figure 1.2 This drawing, done on a MessagePad by urban graffiti artist "Crush,"
contains exactly the maximum number of ink strokes a single Newton note can contain.*

It's important that you start right now parsing the data you want to put
into your Newton into small, digestible bites. Lists, short messages, memory ticklers, these are all fair game for Newton. Think small; it'll save you a
lot of headaches down the road.

The ultimate goal of most writing is the search for the critical detail, the
one sentence, sometimes the one word, that brings an idea, a proposal, an
entire scene into focus. Sometimes it can be as little as the description of a
blood-stained handkerchief at a crime scene. Other times, it can be that
one figure which when placed correctly in a row of numbers, brings the financial condition of a whole company into sharp relief.

When working with Newton, search for the critical detail, the digital
piece of string that, when tied around Newton's electronic finger, will bring
back to your memory whatever you were trying not to forget.

CHAPTER
2

YOUR INFORMATION
SURFBOARD

The fog hugs the water just a hundred yards out from shore. A strong west wind blows a briny scent off the top of breakers that are high enough to get your heart racing. It's a great day to hit the waves. Like a good surfer knows every curve of that thin shield of wood and wax between her and the grinding surf, so too should you be familiar with the basic components of your information surfboard before you try shooting the digital curl.

Terms of Surrender, Part II

Before we delve into the mysteries beneath your Newton's plastic skin, take a moment to learn the terms you should be familiar with when reading this chapter. As with your Newton's software, hardware has a language all its own. Yes, we mean those dreaded computer acronyms and the code-wizened doublespeak that give the pocket-protector crowd the grim satisfaction of an evil snicker when they cluster in little flocks at Comp USA. Don't let these guys push their broken glasses up their nose at you!

No matter what Apple says about Newton being for the rest of us (really, they mean it this time), you still need to know what a byte of RAM is when it comes time to tune a PDA to your life. However, despite the need for familiarity with certain computer terms, we by no means propose you turn yourself into a computer scientist. If that's what it takes to use a Newton, you won't use it. Here is a brief glossary of hardware terms and a few conceptual markers to lend you bearings in the digital frontier. Software terms are defined in both the beginning of Chapter One and in the text of the book as we go along.

After reading this section be careful not to spook the gaggles of computer geeks with your new knowledge—the sound of all those corduroy-clad legs rubbing together as they flee makes fingernails on a chalkboard sound like a serenade. Because, you know what they say: An amateur armed with a few facts is dangerous to the complex world view established and maintained by experts.

None of this is terribly complex, if you let it be simple.

- **Crash.** It's an ugly word, but one with which you're likely to become quite intimate before long. A crash happens when code in the Newton encounters instructions or information that the programmer did not account for. The result: Your Newton either fails to do what you wanted it to do or shuts down altogether.

The Newton is extremely fault tolerant. That doesn't mean it'll excuse bad table manners or even that it won't crash very often; but it does go a long way toward ensuring that you don't lose data as the result of a crash.

- **CPU and ROM.** The central processor unit (CPU) is the gatekeeper of a computing device, controlling and evaluating the flow of bits and bytes using the instructions that are embedded in the ROM (Read-Only Memory, two chips in the MessagePad and Expert Pad that carry the basic instructions behind the Newton interface and intelligence). The CPU also executes code, so it is analogous to the heart in a human body, since it reacts to the state of the entire device and moves the bits and bytes that get things done.

  The ROM is like a brain, full of instructions learned during years of work by patient, impatient, and nerve-wracked programmers (sounds like some teachers we know). In the Macintosh environment, the ROM is static, interacting with the operating system which can be changed to alter the overall look and feel of the interface. Newton is a little different, since the ROM includes instructions about how to learn about the user. So, the Newton's brain actually expands over time, growing into the Random Access Memory (RAM) where applications live.

- **MIPS and Megahertz.** All those bits and bytes passing through the CPU are responsible for how fast your Newton performs, so the faster the CPU can pump that data, the more quickly handwriting will be recognized (depending on the settings you use in your Preferences), and the faster your Newton's intelligent assistant will be able to find significance in a few paltry words.

  As we said in *Principia Nomadica*, there's a lot of complexity in the code that makes your Newton run. Executing all the instructions in that code can be a tough task for something that is little more than a collection of metal traces crisscrossing a bed of silicon.

  How good a processor is at handling this difficult job is measured two ways, in MIPS (Million of Instructions Per Second) and clock rate, which is described in terms of megahertz or MHz (million cycles) per second. Many variables effect the performance of a computing device beside processor ratings, so take them lightly.

For example, while MIPS and megahertz are widely used in the computer industry to compare the performance of different computers, it should be remembered that what really determines final performance of a computer is the efficiency of the code the CPU is executing. If it takes half as many instructions on computer A to do the same job as computer B, even though computer B's CPU is 30 percent faster than computer A, computer A will still finish the job first.

A real-world example would be the MessagePad versus the AT&T EO Personal Communicator 880. The Newton CPU, called an ARM 610, is rated at 15 MIPS and runs a very efficient language that is known as NewtonScript (see Chapter One). The EO 880's Hobbit CPU is rated at 20 MIPS, but it processes a less efficient variety of code. Opening the calendar on the EO, which involves loading a set of instructions for drawing the calendar interface, determining the date, remembering appointments written in the calendar, and so on, takes a lot longer than opening the calendar on a Message Pad. That's because Newton executes far fewer instructions when opening its calendar.

The Newton's parsimonious coding requirements have a drawback, because it can limit the ease with which the device can perform certain tasks. Newton applications expand upon the code embedded in the ROM, rather than adding entirely new sets of code to the Newton. The EO, by contrast, allows programmers a very free reign in what functions they might try to render into computer code—looser code makes for broader latitude. You wouldn't want use your Newton to run a full-blown word processor with hundreds of fonts, while with an EO you could—if you didn't mind the small screen.

We should say that this doesn't mean you'll only be able to run bigger and better calendars and name files on Newton. Rather, it means Newton applications "borrow" freely from the code already stored in ROM, building on top of pre-existing pieces of code (called objects) to define new functionality (see Chapter One for a full discussion on the Newton framework). Programmers are not required to "reinvent the wheel" in NewtonScript to do something. Of course, not reinventing the wheel can also mean less flexibility. It might be possible to change the basic functionality of Newton, such as the way Newton handles electronic ink, but it could be a lot harder without changes first being made to the ROM.

- **Pixels.** When it comes time to show data, your Newton uses a touch-sensitive, low-power Liquid Crystal Display (LCD) screen. The images on this screen are made up of dots formed by little square blocks, called *pixels*. Everything you see on a screen is made up of pixels.

  The sharpness of an image depends largely on the density of pixels on the screen, or screen resolution. A screen with 72 dots per inch (dpi) is half as sharp as a screen with 144 dpi. Pixel density can be increased two ways, by reducing the distance between pixels or by reducing the size of the pixels themselves, called *dot pitch* (see Figure 2.1).

Figure 2.1 The pixel density (dpi) on the right is more pleasing to the eye and shows more detail than the pixel density on the left.

- **Font.** A font is a complete set of characters, or glyphs, that make up a single type style which is used to display characters stored as Unicode by your Newton. The entire alphanumeric range of characters in Times Roman constitute a font, as do all the characters in the Helvetica Bold type style. When you change a character from Plain to Fancy in Newton, you are changing its font (see Figure 2.2).

  There are two kinds of fonts: Bit-mapped, which are drawn pixel by pixel for each size and style; and outline fonts, which use a basic description of the font shape to draw the shape of each letter at different sizes. Outline fonts can be scaled to any size without the need for additional data. Newton uses bit-mapped fonts in several sizes to display characters on the screen, but can also substitute those bitmaps for outlines stored in Adobe Postscript-based printers. This results in sharper-looking printed text than you see on the Newton's screen.

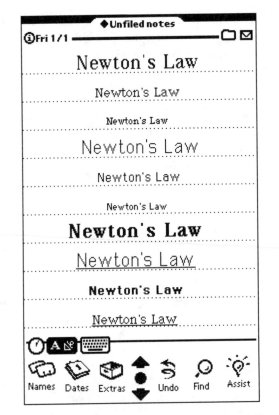

Figure 2.2 A selection of Newton fonts in different sizes and styles.

- **PCMCIA.** The acronym stands for Personal Computer Memory Card International Association, which is the name of the committee formed to figure out an add-on card standard. They've worked out two standards. Newton uses the second, known as PCMCIA 2.0. These cards are hardware, like memory chips, modems, or pagers.

  In theory, any PCMCIA 2.0 card should work in the Newton PCMCIA slot, which is located at the top of the MessagePad and Expert Pad. In practice, though, each kind of card requires special software drivers before Newton will be able to recognize them (see PCMCIA cards below).

- **Computer Terms.** There are several computer specific terms that we'll need to use in this book that don't pertain specifically to the Newton. The most important are *file*, a way of grouping related data in one place; *hard drive*, an enclosed, spinning platter of magnetic media capable of storing large amounts of data; and *floppy* or *diskette*, a small piece of removable magnetic media that can store less data than a hard drive, but that can be exchanged easily between similar computer systems. As other terms come up—and we promise to keep that to a minimum—we'll provide definitions.

The Vital Statistics

Okay, now for the nitty-gritty about the two breeds of first generation Newtons:

	Apple MessagePad	*Sharp Expert Pad*
Height	7.25 inches	7.25 inches
Width	4.5 inches	4.37 inches
Depth	0.75 inches	1.00 inches
Weight	0.9 pounds*	1.0 pounds*
Design Style	Notepad	Notepad w/cover
CPU	ARM 610	ARM 610
ROM	4 MBytes	4 MBytes
RAM	640 Kbytes	640 Kbytes
Screen	Low-power reflective LCD, 336×240 pixels	Low-power reflective LCD, 336×240 pixels
PCMCIA slot	Type II cards	Type II cards
Serial Port	LocalTalk, modem	LocalTalk, modem
Infrared	9,600 baud, half-duplex w/range of one meter (3 feet)	9,600 baud, half-duplex w/range of one meter (3 feet)
Pen	Passive stylus	Passive stylus

(continued)

(continued)

	Apple MessagePad	*Sharp Expert Pad*
AC Power Adapter	Universal, 100 - 240 Volts, 50 or 60 Hz	Universal, 100 - 240 Volts, 50 or 60 Hz
Battery	4 AAA Alkaline 6 Volt 1.1 WH output	4 AAA Alkaline 6 Volt 1.1 WH output
Rechargeable Pack	4 integrated AAA Nickel-Cadmium 4.8 Volt DC 200 mAh output	4 integrated AAA Nickel-Cadmium 4.8 Volt DC 200 mAh output
RAM Backup Cell	CR2032 or DL2032	CR2032 or DL2032

* With battery pack installed.

Newtons will operate reliably in temperatures from 0 to 40 degrees Celsius (that's 32 to 104 degrees Fahrenheit—use the Newton formulas calculator to figure it out!). You can store it in rooms as cold as -20 degrees and as hot as 60 degrees Celsius (-4 and 140 degrees Fahrenheit) as long as humidity in that room is between 20 and 95 percent.

In practical terms, you can put a Newton into luggage that will be stored in an unpressurized airline baggage cabin and use it afterwards. However, you'll want to let it warm up to 32 degrees Fahrenheit before turning it on, or you might cause condensation inside the device, and that can do serious damage.

A Newton that is too hot will show itself immediately: The screen will appear to have blackened, from the corners inward to the center. An overheated Newton, such as one that has been left in the sun, should be left to cool before powering it up. (Don't leave a Newton in the sun.) Electronics as delicate as those inside the MessagePad and Expert Pad can self-destruct at extreme temperatures.

The MessagePad

The Apple Newton MessagePad (Model No. H1000)

What It Comes With

- A slip cover (that barely accommodates the MessagePad)
- An Alkaline Power Pack with four AAA Alkaline batteries
- A coin cell battery
- A power supply
- Two plastic pens
- A really silly video tape
- The MessagePad Handbook
- The MessagePad Setup Guide
- Getting Started ROM card
- Warranty, registration, and various flyers that try to sell you more stuff for your Newton. Register to get a free metal pen to replace your plastic pens.

Apple MessagePad Bundles

Two MessagePad bundles were available as we went to press, in addition to the MessagePad sold all by itself.

The Newton Communications System includes the Newton and all the collateral materials listed above, as well as the fabulously clunky Apple external 9600/2400 send fax/data modem. The software you need to run the modem is already built into your Newton. Third-party applications, like Ex Machina's PocketCall, will also use the external modem.

The Newton Professional Communications System for Macintosh and the Newton Professional Communications System for Windows include Newton, the in-box stuff, the external modem and Connection Kit Pro software that runs on Windows-based or Macintosh computers. Except for the modem, this package includes everything you need to get data out of your desktop computer and into the Newton.

MessagePad in Review

The Apple design definitely avoids the tackiness of many other consumer electronics products. The flat black case gives it the feel of a Star Trek communicator that was carved from a solid brick of marble, or something dramatically important to the future of civilized space travel saved from

Romulan trade embargoes by Captain Picard, like "chromiomolybdoabo-minite compound."

The only blemish on the MessagePad's almost perfect veneer are the two rubber stoppers which cover the power and serial ports. Once you bend them up to plug in the cables, you'll be lucky to get them to lay flat in their sockets again. A chintzy detail on an otherwise seamless design.

The side-mounted pen caddie is especially handy. However, we believe the stylish Newtonian will probably opt for a larger stylus that fits in the pocket and, so, is not easily left behind (it's a matter of learning a new habit, and we all already know that we put a pen back into a pocket or purse).

The lack of an integrated screen cover is a major short-coming of the design, because in order to avoid scratching the screen you need to use the skin-tight slip cover, which prevents the MessagePad from fitting easily into a jacket pocket. The original design included a "flip-up" cover that folded over the top of the unit, like a reporter's notebook. It was dropped when users complained about it during marketing tests. For once, we wish Apple hadn't listened to users. In fairness, the complaints centered around not being able to lay the unit flat with the cover folded back and the general awkwardness of the "flip-up" cover design.

We liked the quick reference card and the production values on the in-box materials. There wasn't a lot to read, but what was there was very readable.

Apple can't be beat in a contest for best in-box kitsch. (The seven-color Apple decals in every Mac box were always a nice touch that felt like winning a merit badge. You get Apple and Newton stickers in the MessagePad box!) The Introduction video included with the MessagePad, about 10 minutes of "See Dick and Jane use Newton" propaganda, is a total waste of space. But save it anyway. It's bound to become a collector's item, just like Apple's "Helocar" video of 1989.

The Expert Pad

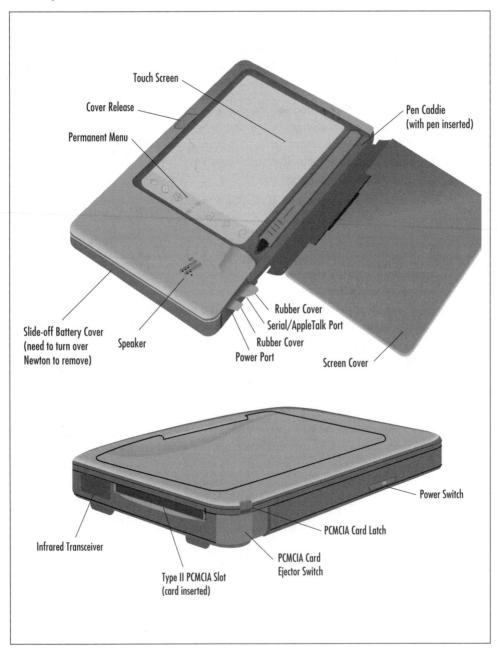

The Sharp Newton Expert Pad (Model No. PI-7000)

What It Comes With

- An Alkaline Power Pack with four AAA Alkaline batteries
- A coin cell battery
- Two plastic pens
- No really silly video tape
- The PI-7000 Personal Digital Assistant Operation Manual
- The PI-7000 Quick Guide
- Warranty, registration, and various flyers that try to sell you more stuff for your Newton, including a coupon for Newton's Law (The perfect opportunity, if you already have a copy, to buy one as a gift for your brother, sister or neighbors).

Sharp Expert Pad Bundles

At the time we went to press, Sharp was not offering any bundles for the Expert Pad. However, this may change over time. Meanwhile, Sharp offers both the same modem as Apple and the Newton Connection as separate items.

Expert Pad in Review

The Expert Pad's integrated cover puts it out ahead of the MessagePad; it's just easier to carry. The cover folds over the right side of the device to fit into a recessed panel on the back. The Expert Pad is comfortable in the hand when you use it. The inside of the cover also has a short, but potentially handy, quick reference list imprinted on it. Also, as if the cover wasn't protection enough, the screen has a thin sheet of plastic with a fake Newton interface on it. The sheet is easily removed and replaced and would probably be a good item to hold on to, although it didn't take long for us to misplace ours.

We did not have the equipment available to test the force the cover can withstand, but we whipped it around a lot without sustaining any damage. Don't flip it open like Captain Kirk in a Klingon-induced huff and you'll be fine.

While the cover definitely earns the unit some kudos, the pen caddie nestled in a cranny beneath the cover and to the right of the screen takes a lot of getting used to. You have to push the bottom of the pen to extract it from the plastic grip; it was a trick no one we handed the Expert Pad understood until we showed them a couple times. Of course, if you follow our advice and get a more hand-friendly stylus, you can leave the Expert Pad's pen where it seems to want to stay.

The Expert Pad's port covers are also better designed than Apple's and have a positive locking feature that snap them in place like rubber bottle stoppers. You won't be tempted to rip these plugs out after only a few weeks use.

There is a drawback to the cover. If the Expert Pad is not set to sleep after a fixed period of idle time, and you accidentally depress the power switch, with the cover closed there's nothing to indicate that the unit is drinking its power supply away on unproductive pocket time.

Sharp may be a great electronics manufacturer but when it comes to documentation, they live in the same Stone Age neighborhood that many computer makers do. Boring and virtually unreadable are the best ways to describe the aptly named PI-7000 Personal Digital Assistant Operation Manual. We've seen military manuals that are friendlier than this (i.e., *The Bradley Fighting Vehicle and Sexually-Transmitted Disease: An Operational Primer for A-14 Technicians*). The Expert Pad also comes sans some of the more refined goodies that are included with a MessagePad. We doubt too many people will miss the Getting Started ROM card, Newton video, or slip cover. But not including a power supply was a flash of unsurpassed stupidity. However, we do expect street prices to run about 50 bucks less than the MessagePad. With the addition of a power supply that should save you a grand total of $25.

As to extra materials, we just loved Sharp's listing of add-on products (like the power supply) called "Multiple Useful Options." Leave it to a consumer electronics company to come up with such a clever title. (Speaking of clever names, the original Japanese name for the Expert Pad roughly translated to "My Brain." What a marketing coup that would have been!) We also think that, if you want your customers to take a standardized test as part of the registration process, you should at least reward them with a free pen or something.

We preferred the Expert Pad mostly for the built-in cover. The items missing from the box are either easily purchased separately or unlikely to be missed much past the first week. Now, all we need is to find an airbrush to paint our Expert Pad black instead of battleship-gray.

For a full description of Apple and Sharp add-ons for your Newton, see *Parts & Parcel* and *Your Master Cards* below.

ARMed and Dangerous, a Technology Primer

In terms of their internal components and basic capabilities, the Message-Pad and Expert Pad are identical. You'll have to wait until sometime in 1994 before you'll start seeing more and different Newtons. There will be plenty, and in forms we traditionally associate with telephones, cellular telephones, portable computers and... well, the engineer's imagination is a perverse thing.

The following guide to Newton hardware applies to both the Message-Pad and Expert Pad, and the components described here will be used in future Newton-based products from Apple and other companies, as well.

ARMed for Battle

It may well be that a MessagePad or Expert Pad is not a computer. But whether it is a computer or not, at it's core is the latest in state-of-the-art CPUs, the ARM 610.

The ARM 610 is built for Apple by Advanced RISC Machines Limited, a British chip company which Apple owns a third of. The ARM chip employs two technologies to get the highest possible speed for the least power, making it the optimal heart for the battery-powered Newton.

The ARM chip is a RISC processor, meaning it uses a Reduced Instruction Set Computing machine language. It's probably easiest to explain RISC by contrast to CISC (Complex Instruction Set Computing) processors, like the Intel 80486, which powers many Microsoft Windows-based computers, or the Motorola 68040, used in Apple's Macintosh Quadra line of computers.

A CPU includes a number of basic capabilities, including the ability to load and unload bits and bytes from its circuitry, and a method for analyzing and acting on the instructions it finds encoded in those bits and bytes. A CISC chip must dedicate considerably more of its own resources to performing these tasks than a RISC chip does, meaning the RISC chip can focus more power on processing handwriting translation problems, telling the screen how to draw the Newton interface, and so on. As we said above, fewer instructions means fewer cycles to get the job done. It also means the chip itself doesn't need to be as complex. You could say that RISC has fewer but much more efficient instructions, and 90 percent of the time you don't need the extra complexity. When you do, the RISC chip just executes a few more simple instructions to achieve the same effect as a complex instruction on a CISC chip.

This way, a RISC chip can get by on fewer traces in silicon. RISC chips can be smaller than CISC chips (want proof, just compare the ARM 610 to the Intel Pentium).

RISC chips also produce less heat in a computer, which eliminates expensive design features needed to deal with that heat, and they cost less to manufacture. According to ARM, if you wanted to buy 100,000 ARM 610s, they'd charge you $25 a chip, a mere pittance compared to other high performance CPUs (such as the Hobbit). We know, you're just champing at the bit to run out and fill the family station wagon with ARM 610s.

The other key feature that makes the ARM 610 ideal for Newton is its especially efficient use of power. The ARM processor is a low wattage chip, consuming only 3 watts of power, and it also has the ability to "stop the clock" when it is not in use. Stopping the clock means it can turn off the cycling of the processor without shutting off the Newton or changing the performance of the interface.

Newton monitors activity from microsecond to microsecond and will stop the ARM chip's clock anytime it isn't being used to redraw the screen, do a calculation, process handwriting or send data to the modem. This reduces CPU power consumption dramatically, since it is not spinning its wheels and frittering away your battery power while it's waiting for your next move.

But let's get down to brass tacks for those of a more technical bent.

The MessagePad and Expert Pad use a 20-MHz ARM 610 that runs at a sustained speed of 15 MIPS. It is a 32-bit processor capable of true multitasking support, and combines a 4-Kbyte cache, write buffer and custom "object-oriented" memory management unit (MMU) into a single chip. For those with less tolerance for jargonese, what all this means is an ARM 610 can chew gum and jog backward down a flight of stairs while reciting the Iliad in ancient Greek and knitting a tea cozy.

Actually, the MMU is especially worth noting because it performs two critical functions. It helps protect ROM patches (Apple calls them system updates), which are installed in RAM, from being cleared from memory when you do a factory reset. It also contributes to your ability to plug in and remove PCMCIA cards without first putting your Newton to sleep, a feature unique to Newton.

The ROM's The Thing

There are two chips inside your PDA that form a Newton's brain. The 4-Mbyte ROM and the Newton System Services ASIC (Application Specific Integrated Circuit, known as the major and minor ROM). Together, these two chips define all your Newton's capabilities and contain all the operating and hardware control code, handwriting recognition, built-in applications and intelligence. Both chips use permanent memory, meaning that you can't add to or modify the code they contain. It also means that no power failure can clear the code.

The reason the Newton ROM is so large—the average Macintosh, by comparison, only has 1- or 2-Mbyte ROMs—is it contains almost everything that makes your Newton work. The Mac loads all these functions into the System Folder on the hard drive, and you get to spend your precious RAM loading it each time you boot the computer. The System Folder approach makes it easier to change and upgrade your computer's functionality. But, as we pointed out in the *Principia Nomadica*, upgrades aren't the point with a consumer electronics device. And a consumer electronics product is what Apple is convinced the Newton must be.

Because the MessagePad and Expert Pad store their basic instructions on chips soldered to the logic board (a plastic board in your Newton which contains all of its circuitry), you cannot make a major upgrade to the device. You can only add System Updates which can repair minor bugs or make small changes to your Newton's capabilities.

It's also possible to make significant changes in Newton behavior, but the operating instructions for doing so must be contained in a PCMCIA card or in an external device, like the Newton Print Pack, a printer cable with a built-in chip that lets the Newton communicate with certain third-party printers.

The other reason Newton's ROMs are so large is that they contain an extensive library of code that can be "loaned" to add-on applications. These functions, which range from special display features to a Unicode/ASCII character set translator needed to communicate with desktop computers, can become a part of a third-party application, eliminating the need for redundancy in code used by different programs. This keeps the programs that you load into the Newton RAM as small as possible, saving more memory for storing your personal information, name files, calendar, and more. (For more on Newton application structures, see *The Newton Framework* in Chapter One).

There's Static in my RAMpire

If the ARM 610 is the heart of your Newton, and the ROM is its brain, then RAM is a PDA's life blood.

The MessagePad and Expert Pad both come equipped with built-in 640 Kbytes of Static Random Access Memory (SRAM). Unlike most personal computers, a Newton uses RAM to store data when it isn't being used, as well as to store subsidiary operating instructions, like the system updates and your personalized handwriting information and additions to the dictionary used to translate the words you write on the screen. Newton RAM also serves as a "work table" for direct manipulation of data by the CPU. Most personal computers only use RAM as a place to hold data waiting to enter the CPU, or for data actually being executed in the CPU. A computer keeps much of the operating system, settings, applications, and stored data in some kind of permanent storage media, like a hard drive.

Basically, anything that isn't stored in ROM and anything you add to your Newton is kept in RAM, making RAM the most critical part of your PDA. And, considering the fact that RAM requires at least a trickle of electricity to "remember" the data stored there, it also makes RAM the biggest potential trouble spot in your Newton.

Luckily, Apple's engineers anticipated the problems inherent in a RAM-based computing device, and built several fail-safes into the Newton's design. The Newton has three power sources—a battery pack, backup battery, and AC power supply—all three of which must be disconnected or dead before the contents of RAM will be erased. Second, they made it nearly impossible to accidentally remove both batteries simultaneously.

Finally, and most critically, they used Static RAM instead of the Dynamic RAM used in most computers. In addition to requiring very little power to operate, SRAM also has the advantage of being able to retain a stored charge for short periods of time. So, if by some convergence of bad fortune and negligence both batteries were completely dead and your Newton was suddenly unplugged, the contents of RAM should be safe for a few minutes, at least according to Apple. Our results have varied so we don't recommend you try this at home!

Because your Newton uses its internal RAM for so many different jobs, it must partition the memory for use by different parts of the system. It sets aside more than half the total 640 Kbytes of RAM for system updates, handwriting data and the user dictionary. This means the space you have to work with is actually much smaller, only about 192 Kbytes (see Figure 2.3). For this reason, we recommend that you make a 1-Mbyte SRAM or 2-Mbyte Flash RAM PCMCIA card the first add-on investment you make for your MessagePad or Expert Pad (see *It's All In The Cards* below). A 2-Mbyte card, for example, will give you ten times the working RAM memory of a bare-bones Newton.

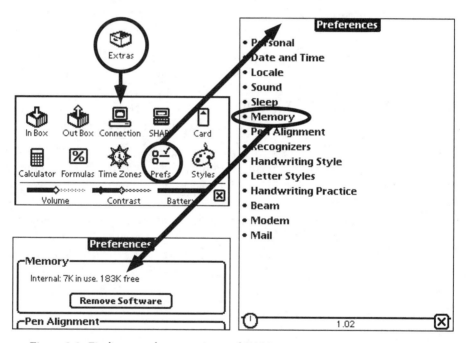

Figure 2.3 *Finding out about your internal RAM.*

When is a kilobyte not a kilobyte? When it's compressed using a special type of math that reduces the size of stored data. And that's just what Newton automatically does with all data that isn't actually in use by the CPU. Data is compressed until the very instant it is in use. For example, when you're looking at a name card, the data in the name card is uncompressed. In other words, where in a computer the CPU is the narrowest part of the digital road (all the data has to be funneled into it), in Newton it is the widest section, allowing data to take its full, useful form only for the time it is in use. Pretty cool.

Get Info...RAMpire Killer

As any computer user knows, PCs just love RAM. They suck it up like expensive champagne. In fact, these days most personal computers are absolute RAMpires (don't groan!)—they won't even run without at least 2 Mbytes of RAM, and then you can't run any applications.

Newton uses RAM for a lot more things than your average PC. So, how can a 640-Kbyte device like the Expert Pad or MessagePad possibly be useful for anything? Because a Newton doesn't put the byte on you like a PC (okay, you can groan now.)

Newton compresses text data and program code to as little as 1/6th of its actual size, drawings are reduced by a 4-to-1 ratio. That means every 6 Kbytes of text you enter into your Newton only takes up 1 Kbyte of RAM. Compression removes redundancy from the data (there's a lot of repeated information in most data).

Newton does a lot of other things to save on memory. However, we think that memory compression is one of the Newton team's cleverest and most unique hacks, even though Apple never talks about it. Just imagine the advertising: Kareem Abdul-Jabbar returns for a reprise of his airline seat ad for the PowerBook, only this time he shrinks to fit the tiny seats on a Boeing 757. "You gotta get your big man to the inside," he says smartly as he disappears into the seat.

Screen Test

Like Newton RAM, the Newton screen serves more than one purpose. It is display, keyboard and mouse (a mouse is the electronic rodent that hangs around many PCs and every Mac). The screen is the common ground where you and your Newton communicate with each other.

The Newton Expert Pad or MessagePad have very small screens, which are also used on the Sharp Wizard OZ-9600. With only 3.96 by 2.83 inches of active space, they squeeze a lot of pixels into this spare working area. The resolution is 240 by 336, or 85 dpi; Sharp also brought the dot pitch down to a mere 0.3 millimeters. This results in very sharp (no pun intended) and easy-to-read images.

The first Newtons display only black and white images, also called 1-bit images because they are represented by pixels that contain only one bit of data; they are either on or off—black when they're on or white (in Newton's case it's really gray) when they're off.

A disadvantage of the MessagePad and Expert Pad screens is that they rely on ambient light to illuminate the display. Anyone who uses a portable computer with a reflective screen can tell you that ambient light is a fickle thing indeed. Apple left backlit displays out of its first Newton designs to save power and to reduce cost; backlighting is a notorious power-hog and can be an expensive feature.

The MessagePad and Expert Pad try to make up for this lack of self-contained lighting with superior reflective screen technology, which is quite readable in even dimly lit rooms (we're talking 60 watts, not candle-dim). However, because the screens are supertwist LCDs (a type of liquid crystal display that directs light into a very narrow range above the screen, basically straight up and up to 30 degrees to each side), they have a lousy viewing angle. It's hard for someone standing next to you to read your Newton's screen while you're using it. But, hey, this isn't a bug—it's a feature! Another reason to think of a Newton as a *personal* digital assistant.

We feel confident that Apple will add both backlighting and grayscale screens to future Newton designs. Grayscale means instead of showing only one shade on a pixel, black for example, the unit can display many shades. In fact, we feel confident that these grayscale screens will appear on a certain larger Newton design early in 1994 (see Afterword—*The Next Newton*).

The MessagePad and Expert Pad screens' input capabilities are controlled by three transparent layers of film that cover the Newton's display. The first is a protective layer of mylar on which you actually write; the second two layers conduct a regulated flow of electricity. When your pen tip presses down on the protective layer, it pushes the second layer into the third layer, changing the current flow at that point. The point of contact is then sent to the LCD matrix, "capturing" your pen strokes, and Newton changes the pixel in the matrix to black to display your "digital ink" on the screen. The pen strokes are then interpreted by Newton's handwriting, drawing, or gesture recognizers. If you just tapped a button, Newton performs the task attached to it.

Assist...Conduction Unbecoming

Conductivity, the sensing technology used to identify the location of your pen on the Newton screen is a fickle aide to handwriting recognition.

The Newton screen, as we said, uses fluctuations in current running between two layers of electronically-sensitive material to trace your movements. It works well when your Newton is getting a steady flow of power from the batteries or an AC outlet. But add a fluctuating power supply to the picture and you can get false readings galore all around the actual location of the pen.

Just try it for yourself in the Notepad. With a new set of Alkalines installed and both the shape and letter recognizers turned off, draw a circle in a slow, deliberate hand. Now plug in the AC connector and draw another circle, which will probably appear more jaggy than the first circle you drew. This is because the power provided by the AC adapter fluctuates more than the fresh Alkalines, causing the screen to sense your pen contact point erratically.

Some pen-based machines, like the EO, use pens that include circuitry that reflects a particular frequency of energy back to the screen. The reflected power provides contact information that can be differentiated from power fluctuations.

Apple may have a fix for this by the time Newton's Law hits the bookstores, but don't be surprised if power fluctuations prove a permanent sore point with the first generation Newtons.

Permanent Press

If you ever want proof that Apple has no plans to make major changes to the first Newton, all you have to do is look at the row of icons permanently etched on the bottom of the screen. The silk-screened icons are the fingerprints of this generation, an indelible design feature that says "First Generation."

Called the permanent menu, the row of six buttons are divided into two parts. The first three open the application drawers: Name File, Dates, and Extras in that order. The second three are function buttons: Undo, Find, and Assist (We particularly like the coinage "Hard Icons" to describe the permanent menu). Separating the two halves of the permanent menu are the scroll arrows that make Newton shift its view of the notepad up and down (it can also move through overview lists). The overview, or "belly," button between the arrows will bring up a list of all the objects—names or notes, for instance—in the application you're working with (a good way to find the note you want when you don't know for sure what it says.)

PENishment

Unlike some other pen-based devices which use electrically conductive pens, your Newton's pen is about as smart as a twig. It's a simple piece of molded plastic with a rounded tip.

As such, any blunt-pointed stylus will work just as well. In fact, we found the Newton's flat pen difficult to hold and it gave one of the authors terrible hand cramps after only a few days of regular use. So, throw your Newton pen to the floor and find something to replace it. We'd wager that there is a significant market for Newton styli that fit in the pocket and which are larger, rounder and more ergonomically correct.

We tried the more normally-shaped pens that came with our EOs and found that they worked fine. The EO pens even seemed to improve hand-writing recognition slightly, probably the result of our being more comfortable with them. However, the EO pen is electrically sensitive and expensive. Those reticent to buy a $40 electronic stylus can check out your local art supply shop for a stencil pen with a rounded plastic tip used to rub dry transfer type onto paper. Actually, any stylus will work fine, as long as it has a solid, rounded tip and doesn't have real ink. A sharp point, including dried-up ball-point pens, will damage the protective mylar film layer. Ink just plain mucks up the screen.

Playing The Slot

Imagine that someone handed you a 2.1- by 3.3-inch plastic card and said the entire Encyclopedia Britannica could be embedded into the silicon inside the card.

You might look around real quick, making sure you weren't about to become this week's featured idiot on *Totally Hidden Video*. But, then, after you established that there were no suspicious-looking vans pointed in your direction, you might begin to wonder, what could I do with such a magical card?

The PCMCIA bus is quite possibly one of the most important developments for small, mobile devices to come along in the last three years. Through this magical interface, you can expand your Newton's mind, adding reference cards with intelligent mapping features, like the Fodor's Travel Manager '94; broaden its available storage space with a memory card; or you could bulk up its muscle with a wireless messaging card or a 14,400 bps fax/data modem. The single biggest criticism we've heard of the MessagePad and Expert Pad's slot is that they have only one (slot, that is).

For a complete list of available PCMCIA cards from third-party developers that will work with your Newton please see Chapter Fourteen—*Hot Hardware.* What follows is a brief PCMCIA primer and list of the card products Apple currently offers.

Know this about the Newton's PCMCIA slot: Never leave it empty. An empty slot is a magnet for dirt and long pointy things that can bend the tiny wires that plug into the business end of a PCMCIA card. Moreover, never, ever under any circumstances put anything into the Newton's add-in card slot but a PCMCIA 2.0 card or the plastic protector card. Anything else could damage the card interface hidden a few inches behind the slot.

The Newton PCMCIA slot is actually very smart compared with those installed on most other devices. It has a fully-interruptable bus, which means you can remove or install a card while the Newton is running without it crashing the device. On other devices with a regular bus attached to the PCMCIA slot, the power surge associated with inserting a card can knock the system out of commission. While testing the AT&T EO Personal Communicators, we learned that it's possible to erase a memory card just by inserting it into an EO that was turned on.

However, you should be careful to check before removing a Newton memory card that you are not running an application or using data that is stored on the card (for example, you shouldn't pull the card out if the intelligent assistant is searching for a name). If you do, you'll get a dialog box telling you the Newton still needs the card and that you should put it back. Should you ignore this warning, you'll most likely corrupt the data stored on the card.

We've found at least one piece of add-on Newton software that won't ever let you remove a card it's installed on. It's a piece of freeware (you don't have to pay for it) called Mr. Advisador, which was written by Newton team

member Bill Sharpe. To stop Newton from displaying the error message when you try to switch cards, you'll have to remove Mr. Advisador from the card. A new version of Mr. Advisador, which fixes this problem, is available now.

By the way, lifting the card latch will wake up a sleeping Newton, so don't think you'll be able to get around this problem by sneaking the card out while your Newton is snoozing.

Easter Egg...Coming Unlatched

Lifting the PCMCIA card latch is what actually interrupts Newton's interrupt bus. Until you push the latch back down, Newton won't acknowledge that a new card has been added to the slot. It won't even look for the card.

You can use this feature as another way to get the dialog box which displays the status of a PCMCIA card. From within this dialog you can remove software from the card, erase it, and backup your data to it. Just lift the latch and then press it down again without removing the card (for more on installing PCMCIA cards see *A Quick Start* at the beginning of this section). This will trick the Newton into thinking you've plugged a new card in and it'll display the card dialog (see Figure 2.4). It should be noted that this trick only saves you a few pen taps and can take a few seconds longer to display the dialog box while Newton re-installs the card soups, depending on how fast you tap.

```
Flash storage card
   703K in use, 1200K free
   ☐ Store new items on card
   [ Remove Software ] [ Erase ]


                 [ Backup ] [X]
```

Figure 2.4 You can trick Newton into displaying the PCMCIA card dialog box by lifting the card latch and pressing it down again.

PCMCIA Explained

PCMCIA cards are roughly credit-card sized and have a 68-pin interface along one edge. Three types of cards were defined by the PCMCIA 2.0 agreement. Type I, the skinniest at 3.3 mm, are most often the form used in storage card designs (both of Apple's storage cards are Type I). Type II at 5 mm are used primarily for devices like modems. Type III, the largest cards at 10.5 mm thickness, accommodate high-density devices like the H-P Kittyhawk hard drives or dual-purpose network/modem interfaces.

The MessagePad and Expert Pad ship with a Type II slot that can accommodate a Type I or II card. Type III cards, which tend to come in designs that would sap a battery pack of power in mere minutes, won't find a home in the first generation Newtons. Although PCMCIA storage is still quite expensive, costing up to 10 times the per-Mbyte cost of a computer hard drive, it has four advantages over any spinning storage medium. It's much smaller; it draws a lot less power; your Newton can access data stored on a card at least ten times faster than a computer can access a hard drive; it's very reliable—no moving parts, nothing to break.

Although the PCMCIA 2.0 specification (a fancy word that describes the limits a bunch of industry insiders decided to define for the rest of us) does support easy exchangeability of cards, you need to be careful that a card includes the *driver* software that explains to Newton what the card is and what to do with it. For example, SunDisk, one of the leading high capacity PCMCIA cards, will not work in a Newton because Apple did not put a SunDisk driver in the Newton ROM. The same goes for communication cards, like a modem, for which Newton has no driver; the slot will appear to be empty to Newton.

MessagePad and Expert Pad owners should know about three kinds of memory cards for their Newtons:

- **ROM cards.** Just like Newton's built-in ROMs, you can't change or add to the data in a ROM card, only read it. ROM cards are how the majority of third-party Newton applications will be delivered to users. They draw very little power, offer very fast access speeds and are the cheapest PCMCIA cards to produce (as little as $14 manufacturing cost for 2 Mbytes). Perfect as a publishing medium.

- **Flash EEPROM** (electrically erasable programmable ROM). You can add to and modify the data held on Flash EEPROM cards at any time. They come in capacities of up to 20-Mbytes, although Apple recommends you don't use storage cards of more than 4-Mbyte capacity, because it could cause your Newton to run very slow. Flash EEPROM cards also retain data without any battery power for an indefinite period of time, because each time you change them you are, in essence, reprogramming permanent memory that holds each bit.

  One drawback of Flash EEPROM is that they are the slowest of PCMCIA storage cards. They are also liable to "wear out" after you record, erase, and record data many millions of times. But you'll get plenty of life from the card before it fails—some manufacturers claim hundreds of years.

  In fact, one of the special smarts built into your Newton is the ability to track what parts of memory have been written to and how many times, allowing it to stay under the theoretical limit for the entire card as long as possible.

- **Static RAM.** These cards, which are based on the same kind of memory chips that make up your Newton's system RAM, need power to retain the data you add to them. Most SRAM cards come with built-in batteries that can be either replaced or recharged. The most ambitious manufacturers of SRAM cards claim they will preserve data for 100 years without a battery change.

  The main advantage of SRAM cards is speed. SRAM cards are roughly twice as fast as Flash cards when Newton goes to retrieve data stored there. Current SRAM cards for the Newton tend to the low end of the capacity chart for storage cards, and there is the nagging concern that a failed battery will cost you in lost data.

  A fourth kind of storage card, which uses traditional computer dynamic RAM (DRAM) is also available from some manufacturers. However, their high power draw make them undesirable choices for Newton users. In fact, Apple doesn't include any DRAM cards in their approved list of third-party memory cards.

Get Info...Taking the CardBus

It's a funny thing about standards... the moment you invent one, some know-it-all comes along who thinks they can do you one better.

For example, Apple, one of the most notorious know-it-alls in the computer industry, is currently pushing a new PCMCIA bus standard (a bus is the mechanism that transfers data between two parts of a computer—if data wants to move, it has to get on the bus). We'll call it PCMCIA 3.0 for simplicity's sake. By the way, this is not public knowledge, but you won't tell anyone, will you?

The new bus standard, which Apple calls CardBus (also code-named TRIMBus), stretches the capacity of PCMCIA to it's limits, expanding the upper end of the amount of memory on a PCMCIA card from 64 Mbytes to 256 Mbytes, far beyond what is actually possible with current memory wafer technology. Wafers are really thin, flat chips, but you can't stack them up like poker chips inside a PCMCIA card.

CardBus also blows the doors off the current PCMCIA bus' performance, doubling a card's capacity to move data from 16 bits to 32 bits per cycle. (The bit size of a bus describes how much data you can shove through it at one time.) Also, it allows a card to contain multiple software drivers so one device card could work on several different systems.

This all sounds very cool, but apparently the PCMCIA standards committee is reluctant to throw out the current standard. PCMCIA 2.0 is still pretty much a new standard, with low miles, plenty of rubber left on its first set of radials, and, well, they've still got to make a lot of payments on it.

The committee's reticence is probably due mostly to the domineering presence of chip maker Intel, which pretty much dictates every standard that is announced for PCMCIA. It's their baby and they don't like the father of this CardBus idea very much.

(continued)

Get Info...Taking the CardBus (continued)

Why? All of Apple's Macintoshes use Motorola processors rather than Intel chips. Apple has to wait for the standard to be approved before they can adopt it, because without a standard, no third-parties are likely to develop cards that use the CardBus. So it could be a long while before we see a CardBus in a Newton.

Your Master Cards

Although a number of other cards are reported to work in the MessagePad and Expert Pad, here is the list of cards that Apple and Sharp say will work in the first Newtons:

- **Sharp 512-Kbyte SRAM card.** Small and cheap just about says it all for this card.

- **Apple or Sharp 1-Mbyte SRAM card.** The least expensive sanctioned Newton storage card, Apple rates it's shelf life and number of read/writes as "indefinite."

- **Apple or Sharp 2-Mbyte Flash card.** The highest capacity storage card option currently offered by Apple or Sharp. Apple rates the card at 100,000 erasures per 128-Kbyte block. So, even if you completely erased the card everyday, it would have an active life of 100,000 days or 273 years!

- **Apple Messaging Card.** At press time, this was the only device card that Apple was offering. Its clever design (courtesy of Motorola Inc.), which incorporates an external radio receiver that sticks out of the Newton above the PCMCIA slot, can greatly expand your Newton's communications capabilities.

Infrared Vision

One of the simplest ways for a MessagePad or Expert Pad to communicate with another Newton or Sharp Wizard OZ-9600 is through the point-to-point infrared (IR) transceiver. Any piece of data in Newton can be sent through this port. Just select "beam" under the action button (beaming is

Apple's friendly name for the process of sending data via IR; we prefer "squirt"), stand or set your Newton within three feet or so of another Newton, top-to-top, and tap "Beam."

The transceiver can exchange data with another Newton at up to 9,600 baud in half duplex mode (that means each device has to take turns when sending and receiving data, they can't send data simultaneously). The transceiver is actually rated at up to 19,200 bps, but currently is limited to 9,600 bps to help reduce transmission errors. You can either set up the beamer to receive beams only when you tell it to or to always watch for an IR signal. The latter option burns extra power and is not recommended unless you do a lot of zapping.

There are only three things to remember about beaming. First, you can only send one piece of data at a time. So, you can send one business card but you can't send ten. Second, you should be sure to be within three feet of the other beamer, holding your Newton steady, and that the lights around you aren't too bright (Apple tried to demonstrate beaming under a fluorescent lamp during the Newton rollout at Macworld Boston '93 and the transfer failed, prompting a round of skeptical comments in the press). And, finally, never try to have multiple senders or receivers, it'll confuse the beaming process (no Newton a trois!).

Your Newton cannot beam an application, a limitation engineered into the PDA to prevent widespread pirating of commercial software. After all, two Newton users could exchange hundreds of dollars worth of software during only a few moments at lunch—"You haven't tried this new expense report application? Why, here you go!"

Actually, we understand from informed sources that there is a hack in NewtonScript that will get around this safeguard. Expect the company that discovered it to implement the feature so you can freely beam its software (the company probably won't enable it for other people's software).

For a full description of beaming, see Chapter Three—*The Invisible World*.

A Versatile Port

Newton comes with only one standard computer data outlet—a serial/LocalTalk port at the lower right corner of the device, next to the AC Power port. Through this lonely gateway you can access printers, networks, modems, and even personal computers.

The port uses an RS-422 mini DIN-8 connector, just like the modem or printer ports on most Macintosh computers. The port is interrupt-protected, which allows you to plug and unplug cables while the Newton is running almost at will without causing errors on the Newton or the networks you connect to.

You can use a Macintosh serial cable to connect directly to both non-network and networkable printers, such as the Apple LaserWriter series. With the appropriate connector, you can plug the serial port into your office LocalTalk network and browse it for many brands of Macintosh-compatible printers. (Your Newton won't necessarily work with all third-party Mac printers and may have trouble with the routers used in some multi-zoned AppleTalk networks.

With certain third-party applications installed on your Newton, you can use this same network connection to access databases on the network, and you can backup data to, or restore and download information from, a Macintosh or Windows PC running Newton Connection software. We call this *Newtworking*. (For more on Newtworking, AppleTalk and Local-Talk see Chapter Three—*The Invisible World*.)

The serial port is also the conduit for connecting external modems to the Newton.

The Foundations of Power

As we said earlier, Newton comes equipped with three power systems—an AC adapter, a battery pack, and a backup battery (coin cell). Your Newton can run on AC power or a battery pack alone, it won't run on a coin cell alone.

- **The AC adapter,** which comes with all Newtons, is a wonder on miniaturization. It's one of the smallest and lightest power supplies we've ever seen, and it was designed so as not to block the second socket on a wall outlet. The power supply is already internationalized and can, with the correct plug converter, be used in almost any industrialized country in the world. (It operates from 100 to 240 VAC, 50/60 Hertz.)

  If you're using a rechargeable NiCad power pack, the power supply will "trickle charge" the pack when plugged into the Newton and a working outlet. This takes about 10 hours to build a full charge that can power a MessagePad through a typical business day (if you don't do faxing with an internal PCMCIA modem).

- **The Alkaline Power Pack,** standard with every Newton, takes four AAA Alkaline cells. Barely discernible diagrams are etched into the power pack's black plastic are supposed to show you how to mount batteries. However, if you can't quite make them out just remember that the springs mate with the flat (negative) end of the battery.

  An Alkaline Power Pack is good for up to 16 hours of usage before the charge falls too low and the batteries must be replaced. You can't recharge Alkaline cells, because they can explode or leak acid into your Newton if subjected to a charge. But don't worry, your Newton can tell which power pack you've installed and won't attempt to trickle charge the cells. If you look inside the battery chamber of your MessagePad or Expert Pad, you'll see a blue switch that is depressed by the NiCad battery pack, but not by the Alkaline pack. This switch turns on the trickle charger.

  It should also be noted that you can force an Alkaline pack into the NiCad recharger. However, it doesn't fit correctly and doing so will damage both the pack and possibly the recharger, if you plug it in.

  Overall, we found the power from alkalines to be somewhat flaky. Alkalines provide good performance until they fall below the 50-percent charge mark, then the electrical quality seems to falter. In early MessagePads and Expert Pads older alkalines caused the screen to "jitter," momentarily distorting the images. Also common in our Newtons and those owned by folks on the major on-line services were unexplainable power failures, even though the batteries were still reported by Newton to have had half a charge. However, this particular bug was reportedly fixed in system update 1.04.

  By the way, the Newton's power manager is a lousy keeper of alkaline battery time, and readings on battery levels can be erroneous.

  For all these reasons, we recommend using alkalines only as your backup power source.

- **The Rechargeable Power Pack,** which uses integrated (you can't remove them) nickel-cadmium (NiCad) AAA cells, is our preference for day-to-day, away from an outlet Newton power. Although a fully charged pack only delivers about half the active usage time of an Al-kaline Power Pack, about 6-8 hours, we found the power was more reliable, of better quality generally, and caused fewer inexplicable errors.

The power manager was obviously tuned to work with NiCad cells, it gives a much more accurate measure of battery life with the rechargeable pack. Also, you should get 500 charges out of a NiCad pack before it'll need replacing, saving wear and tear on your wallet and on the environment.

You'll have to buy NiCad packs separately, and you should buy at least two. The NiCad recharger, which is a must-have, comes with one NiCad Power Pack. These tiny devices can recharge a NiCad pack in about three hours, plenty fast to put a full charge on two packs during an evening.

- **The lithium coin cell,** a CR2032 (Panasonic) or DL2032 (Duracell) 3-volt, flat battery, is your Newton's last line of defense against memory loss. If your power pack is dead and you aren't plugged in, the backup battery will protect the contents of SRAM for up to 12 weeks. Under normal usage conditions—when you haven't spent dozens of hours with just the coin cell installed—the backup battery will last about a year. In either case, Newton will open a dialog box that tells you when the time has come to replace the coin cell.

- **The power switch,** mounted on the left side of your Newton, is your primary power control. Just push it down quickly to turn your Newton on or off.

  In reality, your Newton is never really off, only in an electronic sleep in which it can get by on a trickle of current. When you hit the power button, Newton nods off; and when you wake it, it opens its metaphorical eyes in the same application or note that you were using when it went to sleep. Even the Undo button on the permanent menu will still work on the last item you entered, even if you entered it several days before.

- **The Reset Button.** Beneath the battery cover on the back of your MessagePad or Expert Pad is a Reset button that forces your Newton to restart itself, without causing the loss of any data. Learn this and remember it, because you'll need to press this button using the pen in order to wake your Newton when it lapses into a computerized coma. If Newton seems to lock up and refuse to translate handwriting (this bug is reportedly "worked-around" in system update 1.03 or 1.04), if you can't get it to turn on, or if the screen freezes and will not accept any input, press the Reset button.

The button is difficult to see, because it's in a hole on the upper left hand corner of the battery chamber. Look for the word RESET embossed in the plastic next to the battery slider that releases the power pack. Pressing reset forces your Newton to do a recovery restart (also called a warm boot), which will clear out the region of memory that holds untranslated handwriting and performs other housecleaning routines. This will usually free up a locked system. It does not, however, reload the system software, nor does it flush the contents of RAM used to store names, dates, and notes.

(For more on power states, battery life, power packs, replacing batteries, etc. see Chapter Eleven—*The Power of Newton*.)

Speaker

What can we say? Newton has a small speaker and can play sound. Sound takes up a lot of memory, so don't expect to use a lot of sound effects in Newton applications. Support for sound is, we speculate, ready and waiting for another generation of Newtons with built-in phones and remote voice mail client applications that let you dial in to your office and listen to your messages by tapping buttons on the Newton screen.

The most compelling activity you can engage in with the speaker is dialing the phone. Believe it or not, Apple seriously expects you to tap the dial button, hold your Newton up to the telephone microphone and wait as it sends the dial tones down the wire. Better than dialing by hand? We think not. The acronym for this technology is DTMF, which in the Newton lexicon stands for Dial Tone Macht Frei.

Parts and Parcel

While Apple may not have come out of the gate with an embarrassing wealth of card options, the company more than made up for it with a copious selection of Newton do-dads.

Goodies

- **Fax Modem.** The best thing we can say about Apple's first attempt at an external modem, manufactured by PSI Integration, is that it's cheap. About the size of a cigarette pack, the modem weighs only 7 ounces. It's also ugly, slow, and way too big.

  Apple's little mistake supports out-going faxing with 9,600 baud performance, the standard for fax machines. The MessagePad cannot currently receive faxes. The paltry 2,400 baud send and receive transmission for transferring data and electronic mail is pathetic performance in this day and age.

  Now for the good news: Unlike other Apple modem products, in our test the Newton modem proved very reliable and looked as if it might run forever on the two AA alkaline batteries that power it. You can also run it off the same AC power supply your MessagePad uses, but do you really want to make that choice? It's less expensive to put two batteries in the modem every once in a while.

  The Apple modem, however, seemed fragile. The batteries clattering around inside made it sound like a high tech rattle when we shook it. We didn't test this theory, but it seemed to us that one fall to the ground and the Apple modem would not be getting up.

  More than likely, you'll end up buying one of these modems because they are very cheap and, with care, should prove reliable. We only wish Apple had put a few more dollars into the design and come up with a smaller, more solidly constructed device.

  If you prefer your modem with the word "Sharp" on it rather than an Apple, Sharp will sell you the same exact modem out of its "Multiple Useful Options" flyer (we just love that name!)

- **Print Pack.** If you have a printer that requires a parallel port connector, which is common in the IBM-compatible computer world, you'll want this intelligent connector that converts the Newton's serial output. Embedded in the cable is a microprocessor that downloads instructions to Newton to tell it how to format data for output on these types of printers. A good example of Newton's modular communications architecture.

  Oh yes, you can get the Print Pack with a Sharp label on it, too (Sharp calls it the PC Printer Cable).

- **Power Adapter.** If you lose yours, isn't it good to know you can buy another?

  It should be noted that there is a minor difference between the Expert Pad and MessagePad power supply connectors. Differences in the plug receptacle make it so you can't quite fit the MessagePad power plug into the Expert Pad. However, the Expert Pad plug will fit a MessagePad, although it will be a little loose. Remember to buy the right supply for the right Newton.

- **Rechargeable Battery Pack.** Covered in *The Foundations of Power* earlier in this chapter. Definitely a "must have" for every Newton owner. Sharp also has one of these.

- **Battery Pack Recharger.** One of the cheapest NiCad rechargers we know of, this little device features such niceties as fold-up plug prongs to keep it from punching holes in the side of your favorite bag, a charge status light and an automatic four-hour shut off to keep it from overcharging batteries. It'll fully recharge a NiCad pack in less than four hours, three times faster than the Newton.

- **Battery Booster Pack.** Geek Chic is what this is. We have to admit to being somewhat baffled about this belt-hanging power dongle. We suppose if you were going on an expedition to the headwaters of the Amazon, a belt pack with eight AA alkalines capable of powering your Newton for weeks on end might be a neat survival tool. (Gad! We've had to roast and eat Hobson. At least his Newton has survived to tell us where to send what's left of the remains.) It also might be useful if you're going to deck out your Newton with some monster power-hungry PCMCIA card.

  Between you and us, we think the only reason Apple came out with this was to have something the company could stick under the noses of critics who think 16 hours from an alkaline pack is too short battery life for a consumer electronics product.

- **Level Converter Cable for Sharp Electronic Organizer.** The longest name deserves the shortest explanation. It's a special cable Sharp sells that can hook a Wizard to your Newton.

- **Carrying Case.** The cheapest Newton case and a must-buy for Newton users. It has space for three spare PCMCIA cards, a pen and place to stick your paper business cards, if your business cards are printed in abnormally small sizes. The case snaps closed leaving open gaps for access to power and serial ports, the PCMCIA slot and IR transceiver.

If you've got a MessagePad, lose the slip cover and invest in this relatively cheap case.

- **Leather Carrying Case.** The tops in Newton Chic. Lots of space for extra cards and Newton paraphernalia, the soft black leather zip-up carrier features an elegantly embossed rendering of the Newton light bulb logo. It's cool, expensive and way too big to fit in your pocket. However, if you're the kind of person who is impressed by Gucci bags, this might be for you. You'll need a Gucci bag to carry it.

- **Communications System Carrying Case.** Although it isn't listed as an option in the Newton's in-box materials, we got one of these cases just before going to press. The case has space for the modem, Messaging Card, and extra cards, which makes it the largest of the MessagePad cases. Oh yes, it's made of "fine leather."

It has one design flaw: it's nearly impossible to have the external modem plugged in to a Newton and an AC power source while stored in the case.

Alone in The Wilderness

One of the best stories to come out of the August 1993 Newton debut at Macworld Expo in Boston was told to us by Henry Norr, editor emeritus of *MacWEEK*.

While riding the bus between the two Expo show halls, Henry noticed that the man next to him was immersed in his newly acquired MessagePad. Henry interrupted him to ask what he thought of the PDA. The man looked up, a great, big smile spread across his face and he said, "It's totally changed my life!"

Surprised by the exuberance of his reaction, Henry pressed him for more information. "What do you do for a living," he asked.

"I'm a salesman for Lechmere's." (Lechmere's was one of three dealers selling Newtons at Macworld, where supply didn't even come close to filling demand.)

If you haven't already bought your Newton, hopefully the advice we've given you in this chapter has helped you make a choice. The odds are that after reading this chapter you already know more about Newton than most of the people trying to sell you one. There are, of course, exceptions, but even these people will be unlikely to want to spend a lot of time with you, unless you really want to spend some cash on add-ons, software and the ubiquitous Extended Service Plan (of the cost of the typical ESP, more than 50 percent is pure profit).

Apple has cleverly decided that, to give you the best possible price, they'd leave dealers with razor-thin margins. The profitability has been wrung out of the Newton itself. Considering the fact that the average dealer will make less than $75 on a Newton sale, they're not making enough to spend more than a few minutes on questions before pressing you to buy, buy, buy.

In fairness to Apple, the company isn't exactly raking in the cash. In fact, the MessagePad features the smallest profit margin Apple has ever made on a retail product. The company feels that, to compete in the consumer electronics market, it must drive the per unit cost of a Newton down to the lowest possible level. But with that trimming so goes some of the perks you may be used to when buying an Apple product.

As for Sharp, this is a company very familiar with cheap products and fast sales. You'll be able to find the Expert Pad in all the places you're used to seeing a Wizard; we expect the level of support to be familiar to Wizard users as well. The answers don't come from salespeople, they come from the customer support line. It's not that the consumer electronics outlets that Apple and Sharp have authorized to sell Newton don't want to give you good support. These stores generally aren't set up to support a complex device like a Newton. Cassette decks and toaster ovens are more their speed.

Seeing as you're unlikely to get a lot of post-sales support where ever you purchase your Newton, we recommend shopping based primarily on price. Keep in mind that there is no suggested retail on Newton products, only an expected street price. This makes it especially important to shop around. At Macworld, some dealers took the scarcity of MessagePads as an opportunity to gouge customers, charging as much as an extra $100 over expected street price.

However, price being equal, we'd buy from an authorized computer dealer long before we'd do business with the local Circuit City. The chances are that the computer dealer will at least know his MIPS from his megabytes, so to speak, and is less likely to give you erroneous information.

Okay, okay. Even at the local computer superstore, the chances are slim that you'll get really informed answers.

One last caveat: According to Apple policy, Newtons are not returnable unless they do not operate the very first time the buyer tries to turn it on. This will really hurt Newton in the long run. Not because dealers will tell Newton buyers they cannot return their products, but because dealers who do take Newtons on return will be discouraged to sell the devices in the first place. If a Circuit City has to eat the price of every Newton return, Newton won't be on the shelves for long.

The No-Return policy is only evidence that Apple has a very long way to go toward understanding the consumer electronics market. Long-time consumer electronics combatant Sharp, by comparison, will accept returns from dealers.

Get Info...FUD

We felt it was important to end this chapter with a brief discussion of a somewhat unhappy topic—Fear, Uncertainty, and Doubt (FUD).

You can't avoid it. In the ever-accelerating race to come out with newer, faster, cheaper products that capture more of your money, you can be absolutely guaranteed that within a few months there'll be another Newton with a better price tag and feature set. It will come from Apple or Sharp or Motorola or someone. With so many companies lining up to build Newton devices, if you wait and watch for the best deal your head will be spinning from the fast-paced changes.

So, you have two choices: wait for a better deal, in which case you may never buy anything, or buy now and risk feeling stupid in two months when they lower the price or add the incredible "predict the future of the stock market" option to Newton intelligence. (We didn't tell you Apple was working on clairvoyance? Silly us.)

(continued)

Get Info...FUD (continued)

Or you can do what we do. Look at the device, evaluate what it costs and balance that against what it does and how much you want those capabilities. Then, if you are willing to pay the price Apple or Sharp is asking for the MessagePad, Expert Pad, or God-Send Pad, buy it and don't look back. The choice is yours. If you wait you could miss out on all those months you could be using this tool to organize your life and manage information. Figure out what that's worth to you, and decide. That's the only answer anyone can give you in the face of FUD.

CHAPTER

3

THE INVISIBLE WORLD

Clothes make the man. Beauty is only skin deep. In Newton's case, it's what's inside and behind the friendly interface that counts. Newton without a network behind it is like a suit with no body to wear it. Easy-to-use, sure, but the connection-less Newton would be an ugly spud indeed. Because all your notes, appointments and name cards are of little use to you when they cannot be shared with others.

We've written a good bit about how great it is to take a note or make a calendar entry on the Newton, but in the workplace you will find the real power of digital technology is the ability to exchange information with others. All the information flying around the globe these days, the stuff changing our lives, is the product of people using digital tools to share ideas, attitude, and nonsense. Take a look at the computer magazines and you'll see that something called computer-assisted collaboration, or groupware, is hot. Calendars, electronic mail, and files are now exchanged as a matter of course on corporate data networks. Collaborative functions like this provide the benchmark from which Newton begins its life—where computers have only just arrived.

Computer users, however, suffer the inconveniences of communications technologies that are paradoxical by nature; connections don't always equal communications, and vice versa, because sometimes computer-mediated communication is more easily accomplished by printing a letter and shoving it into an envelope.

Computers, which are digital—they understand ones and zeros represented by electrical charges—have had to cope with a largely analog phone network, one that can transmit sound, but not electrical pulses. Modems, which translate silent bits into sonic screeching, don't conform to a single standard, and sometimes can't make a connection. Even when they find themselves on telephone or computer networks, computer users often have their messages blocked by miscommunication between different kinds of computers, or by the rules of the road, called protocols, which govern the way data travels over the network cable.

Newton does a great job of hiding the complexities of communications. It's a virtue that any computer user can appreciate immediately. For those folks picking up a computing device for the first time when they buy a Newton, rest assured many an hour has been wasted trying to set up modems or network connections to link computers. You are the lucky ones. (See Figure 3.1).

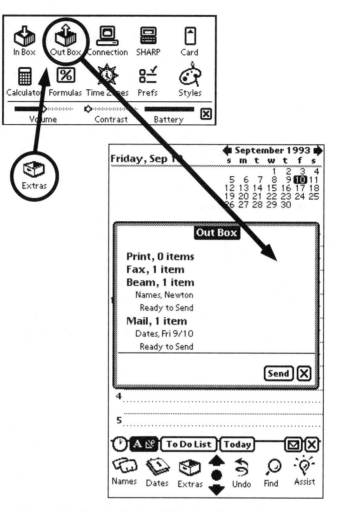

Figure 3.1 *The Out Box's unified view of network communications*

Apple's engineers automated the connections offered in Newton. Hardware and software are tightly integrated to minimize the decisions you have to make when faxing, sending electronic mail, or connecting to a network —most often all you need to do is tap the Send button. When beaming information through the infrared port, you don't even need to connect a cable. Just point and shoot.

Simplicity is the rule in Newton.

Let's say you are a company that wants to sell a fax/data modem on a PCMCIA card for the Newton. You are required to handle all the loose ends, like providing the connection between the fax card and the In Box. You also have to make the card work when it is inserted in the Newton's PCMCIA slot—without forcing the user to learn the ins and outs of modem settings before they can make it work. From the speed the modem will transmit a fax (standard fax machines operate at 9,600 baud), to the resolution of the image, all of it must be hidden behind the Send button.

Power users, those monks of the personal computer who can extract complexity from a stone, may chafe a bit when confronted with Newton simplicity (these are the guys who carefully examine a rock to determine the best angle for throwing it before doing so). But for the rest of us, the arbitrary decisions developers must make about communications features turn sending a fax, electronic mail or a beam into the easy part of communicating. Now, it's up to you to write clearly and concisely so that your message is understood!

Before you can forget the networks Newton uses, take some time to understand the problems that can derail a message. Knowledge will be critical when it comes time to troubleshoot. This chapter provides a firm foundation of network knowledge, offering primers on local area networks, telecommunications, paging, and printing. There is also a heavy helping of information about where Newton Connection software fits into the communications picture to let you blend Newton files with the files and features of the Macintosh and Windows PCs.

Use this chapter as a reference when confused about the basics of communications or if you are encountering trouble. It is designed for the networking novice, who thinks more about getting their job done than the cables connected to their computer (with a personal device like Newton, you'll find the network a more personal problem than ever before).

Networking experts and power users, should skip this section. It will just annoy you.

What is Newtworking?

You meet Bob, the quintessential example of a person in the Newton world (Try writing "Bob" on your MessagePad or Expert Pad; it'll get it right almost every time, because that is the name Apple told its marketing people to use during demonstrations. When recognizing Bob, Newton is rock-solid). Bob mentions that he has a meeting on the morrow and he'd like you to come. Out come your Newtons, and he beams the appointment to you. You can't see it, but a flashing infrared beam bathes the air in front of you with light. The port has a range of eight centimeters to one meter (Newtons out for a quick conversion: That's an infrared range of 3.14 inches to 1.09 yards). Infrared light can be received by another Newton held 13 degrees to the left or right of, and 10 degrees above or below, the infrared port on your Newton—about the height and width of the beam from a small flashlight at the same distance.

Just to be sure you can talk again before the meeting, he also beams his business card.

Later that day, you realize Bob doesn't know that the quarterly figures for the Borneo region are in. A couple taps with the pen bring up the Borneo numbers (boar futures are up!), and you write "fax Bob" on the screen and tap Assist—Newton looks up Bob's card while you wait and, for those of you with large address books, wait some more before your Newton brings up Bob's fax number in a fax slip. (Actually, a fax sent this way will include the "Fax Bob" text as part of the fax message.) Tap the Fax button. The Out Box opens, you tap the Send button, which brings up a list of options and, again, you tap Fax. Moments later, Bob has the Borneo numbers (see Figure 3.2).

That's networking Newton style: Newtworking.

An essential feature of Newton communications is the ability to work without wires. Every network or serial link you might use is available to your Newton at all times, even when there is no cable plugged in, through a deferred messaging architecture that stores beams, mail, and print jobs until you make the appropriate connection.

If you are walking down the street and think of something that you need to fax your boss, you can jot a note and tell Newton to fax it. Newton stores the message until the next time you connect the fax modem. The deferred communications feature is not unique to Newton, but when combined with the Newton interface in such a small device it provides an eminently practical tool for keeping in touch.

Personal computers, for the most part, are dependent on cabling to act as their data umbilical cord. Without a network or telephone connection, most PC and Mac communications applications whither and die. Some software does allow PowerBooks and Windows portables to support deferred messaging. However, try whipping open a notebook computer on a street corner to compose and address a fax and you'll see that deferred messaging does not a communications assistant make.

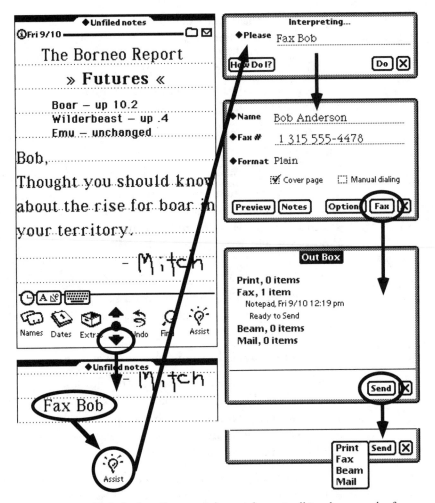

Figure 3.2 *To Bob about Borneo. A few quick taps is all it takes to send a fax.*

Newtworking also makes a big difference in the office or factory, where ideas can blast into the mind from left field during meetings, at the water fountain or in the elevator. When electronic mail software for local area network-based services are complete—look for in-office electronic mail for Newton by early 1994—you will be able to compose a note and put the message into the In Box while you're at lunch. Newton will save the message until you return to the office and plug a LocalTalk cable into the serial port.

"The bulk of a job cannot be done behind a desk," says Mark Vaschett, a member of Monsanto Corp.'s Innovation Team, the group responsible for integrating Newton into the chemical company's international network. "In a chemical plant, we can cable up to a certain point, but that is always several dozens of yards from the real job."

Newtworking will ease Monsanto's transition into the information age. The company will use Newton as a portable manual for service people, factory inspectors, and sales people in the field. New information will be mailed to employees' Newtons, which will blend the update with its existing data.

For example, chemical companies must maintain strict compliance with voluminous safety guidelines. When those guidelines are installed on a Newton that can be carried along by an inspector on the steel spine of a refinery, she can, for the first time, look up information as she works. That's going to improve safety standards compliance, Vaschett says.

"When a chemical plant goes haywire more people can die than in a 747 crash," Vaschett says. "So it's critical that we comply precisely to these standards."

Without access to a manual on the spot, even the best inspectors' memories can occasionally prove faulty. Newton doesn't replace a capable inspector, and it doesn't facilitate handing the job over to a lower-paid worker, it lets the best people do the job better. Certainly, some retrograde companies will try to fob off a very demanding job to lower-paid workers equipped with Newtons, but these companies will eventually find that the quality of work is lower. When looking at the Newton, think about it as helping your best people do better.

From the individual's perspective, Newton is a potential liberator. Personal computers have enhanced some people's ability to do their jobs, but at the cost of many more hours nailed to a chair behind a desk, a vantage point rationalized today by the "fact" that the PC is where information is available. Newton can let us be more flexible, if we are bold enough to demand flexibility, and if our employers are willing to brave the waters of decentralized access to information. The workplace can come to us, through electronic mail, infrared beams, over radio waves in pager messages, and, eventually, cellular telephone frequencies.

We should all be prepared to shut the doors of our personal lives against the workplace. Even a great stoic, like... Mr. Spock (duck, it's a *Star Trek* reference!), would get edgy if Captain Kirk was sending him mail and faxes, day in and day out. Sooner or later, the old Vulcan would hurl his Newton to the floor and lock Shatner in a death grip!

Stay unconnected to stay real. Use connections to free yourself from the structures of work that are counter-productive.

Communications of all sorts play an integral part in the Newton work-style, and some of the ports on your Newton can support several New-tworking connections. Let's take a look at your options.

What's that serial you're eating? Newton, honey!

Newton users can exchange data with Macs, PCs, and Sharp Wizard 7000, 8000, and 9000 series organizers through a cable attached to the serial port, which is located next to the AC power port at the lower right corner of the Newton. The Connection, Sharp, and In/Out Box applications in the Extras drawer are the tools you'll use with a serial connection.

Remember just one thing about a serial connection and you've got the concept: computers have to shake hands before they can talk.

Rather than talk Tech, let's anthropomorphize a meeting of two devices on a serial connection. A device on one end of a serial cable sends a signal that says "Hey, I'm here and I can send data at 9,600 bits per second." The other device says "I'm here too, and I can send data at 9,600 bits per second." If one of the devices is set to send data at a higher speed, it slows down to accommodate the slower setting of its new acquaintance. They synch-up, called "hand-shaking," and a clear pipe for data 9,600 bits wide is established between them, ready for use by an application.

But only one of the devices can talk at any moment. Each waits after the handshake, listening to their end of the data pipe. When one device wants to send data, it first sends a "Listen to me" signal, to which the other responds with an "I'll listen until you say 'stop.'"

Newton can be a particularly knowledgeable listener. Applications, as we said, must be designed to handle a particular kind of communication. Specialized listening is very important, because the data coming in over the serial cable won't always look like the data stored in your Newton. For example, if you connect to a Sharp Wizard 8200 and download its Business Card file into the Newton, the data will arrive in a Wizard format. Newton is trained by the built-in Sharp application to recognize how the Wizard data will look, what it means, and how to convert it into the card format used in its Names file.

Sometimes, though, all these neat pieces don't fall into place, and the serial connection fails. As a user, you can probably figure out what's gone wrong by paying a little bit of attention to the sequence of events.

If your Newton never gets a response from the Mac, PC or Wizard it is connected to, you may have a bad serial cable. Or, you may not have the right application running on the other machine. Make sure that the Newton Connection software is running and waiting for a reply from Newton (Look for a dialog box on the computer that says "Open a connection from your Newton.") Wizards must be running in PC-Link mode.

Should the connection fail repeatedly, despite the fact that all the software is set up correctly, change the serial cable. If it still doesn't work, there's a distinct possibility that the serial port on the computer or Newton is shot. Call 1-800-SOS-APPL, if you own a MessagePad; Expert Pad users should dial 1-800-732-8221, the Sharp Technical Support line.

The other problem to watch for is confused software. Serial communications happen in strict order. Imagine you are an application running on a computer. You've got a big bag of bits, ones and zeros, which you need to send to another computer. You open the serial connection and feed the first bit into the tube, and off it goes, dragging the rest of the bits out of the bag in the right order. When the last bit is gone, you add up all the bits and send the total to the other computer; this is called a checksum, a number that can be used to make sure what was sent is the same as the package that arrived. The other computer performs the same checksum computation on the file it received, compares the two and responds, saying "Got them all, thanks," and that's that.

If the checksum your Newton sent doesn't match the one generated by the recipient, something has gone wrong. This is what has happened when the Newton tells you a transfer failed.

As often as not, failed transfers happen because the software that is sending or receiving the information was sidetracked for a second by another process on the computer. Another possible culprit is the chip that controls the serial port, which holds the data in a memory cache for a split second before passing it to the CPU; if the cache overflows, because the CPU was too busy to process the incoming bits, some of the data will be lost.

An application can also become confused by data that it does not expect, as when the records sent as part of a business card file contain more fields than the Newton is prepared to translate. When working with pre-release versions of Newton Connection for Macintosh software that Apple distributed to MessagePad owners at Macworld Boston '93 (making beta testers of them all), we found that serial communications failed about 30 percent of the time. We expect the shipping software to be more stable, but it is very possible that for the first year or so, Newton serial communications may fall on rocky roads. It's a new technology, after all. (Often, the connection failed because things didn't happen in exactly the right order.)

The Newton serial port itself is an 8-pin connector, which is standard on the Macintosh; both the Modem and Printer ports on the Mac use this connector. Folks with a disdain for human language call it an RS-422 mini DIN-8. It can send or receive data at up to 1.5 megabits per second.

Serial cables are pretty ordinary, with a plug on each end. However, each kind of computer to which you'll connect your Newton requires a different kind of plug on its end of the cable.

On a Windows PC, the serial connection is the "COMM PORT," also called an RS-232 port. IBM PC/AT and some compatibles have a 9-pin RS-232 port, so you'll need to get a DIN-8 to DB-9 serial cable from your computer dealer. Several brands of IBM clones use a DB-25 connector, which has 25 pins.

If you have a Sharp Wizard 9000, 8000, or 7000 series OZ organizer, it uses a different serial connector. The Wizard must be connected to the Newton using a special serial cable that converts signals from the Wizard's port into the dialect used by the Newton. Ask your computer dealer for the RS-422 Level Converter cable Sharp sells for connecting Newton to Wizard.

Apple StyleWriter and Personal LaserWriter 300 printers can also be connected directly to the serial port. If you want to plug into a PC printer, you'll need to pick up Apple's Print Pack, a serial-to-parallel printer cable. Print Pack is unique, because embedded in the cable is a microprocessor that hands off the code, called drivers, needed to print to parallel printers with Newton. The five drivers in the Print Pack cable are for Hewlett-Packard LaserJet, Hewlett-Packard DeskJet, Canon BubbleJet, and Epson LQ and FX printers. These drivers will let you print to 947 different PC printer models, at last count.

Take a spin in the LocalTalk neighborhood

Apple set the standard for easy-to-use networks with its plug-and-play connectivity in the Macintosh. The lynchpin in that system is LocalTalk, a set of hardware and software specifications that control and transmit data on twisted-pair (standard telephone) wiring. Now, Newton arrives with the self same LocalTalk networking built in to its serial port. Two items in your Extras drawer use the LocalTalk port to do their work: Newton Connection and the Out Box.

A lot goes on in the cables that link computers together. Globs of data, called packets, rush over the wires. Computers check with one another to make sure they are still connected to the network. Often, packets crash into one another, obliterating the data inside. It's an electronic mob scene into which your Newton can fit quite comfortably, because it has a complete set of instructions embedded in the ROM that acts as its emissary on Local-Talk networks connected to the serial port.

The part of the ROM that contains the instructions on how to connect to a LocalTalk network connector also includes Apple's networking software, called AppleTalk.

When talking about a network, you must distinguish between the hardware—in this case LocalTalk hardware in the Newton (it is a part of the ROM and the serial controller chip that also handles serial, infrared, and modem communications) and external connectors that plug into the serial port to make a complete LocalTalk connection—and software. AppleTalk is a set of protocols written into software that manage network traffic, it controls everything from how computers exchange data and how messages are addressed, to how the packets sent by different computers are allowed onto the electrical highway without causing too many collisions. Apple-Talk works on LocalTalk hardware, as well as another kind of network cabling, Ethernet (see below). If your network runs on protocols other than AppleTalk, or on a different kind of cabling, you can't connect your Newton to it (though third-party developers will certainly remedy this at some point).

You'll need a special connector that plugs into the serial port when using LocalTalk. Apple offers a LocalTalk connector, but most people favor the PhoneNet Connector from Farallon Computing, which allows you to run LocalTalk over ordinary twisted-pair telephone wire. Apple's technology is expensive and requires that you use higher grade cabling. Just ask your

computer dealer for the connectors used with the Mac. Odds are he'll point
you to the Farallon products (If they point to the Apple LocalTalk products, that's a sign you're talking to the wrong guy).

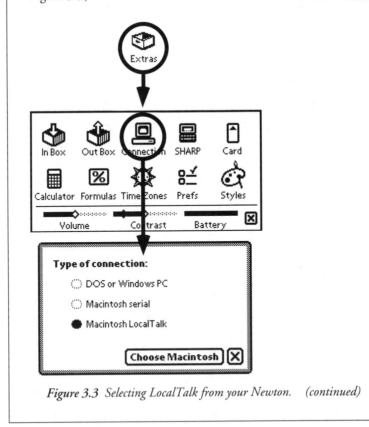

Assist...A Serial Shortcut

If you want to connect your Newton to a Mac via
LocalTalk, and that Mac isn't already connected to a
LocalTalk network, you can use the serial cable your
Newton Connection kit came with. Just plug the cable into the
Mac's printer port and make sure AppleTalk is enabled from the
Mac's Chooser. Then, tell Newton to connect via LocalTalk (see
Figure 3.3).

Figure 3.3 Selecting LocalTalk from your Newton.   (continued)

Assist...A Serial Shortcut (continued)

That's all there is to it! You'll get the performance of a LocalTalk connection (which is much faster than straight serial) without having to buy a LocalTalk connector.

For some reason, Apple doesn't like to tell users about this short-cut. But we've tested it extensively and found no problems using a serial cable as a single-connection LocalTalk solution. In fact, we can see no reason why you'd ever use the serial connection option when hooking up to a Mac. Either get to it over a "real" LocalTalk connection on the Network or just tell your Newton that the serial cable you've plugged in is really a LocalTalk connector.

In Mac network environments, computers grab and hold onto a network address the entire time they are turned on. An address is a number that represents the computer's "logical" location on a network. Computers imagine the network as a bunch of addresses in a conceptual structure, not as a lot of machines connected to a cable. So, your Newton may be searching for two computers which are next to one another on a desk, but they may appear in the Newton's perception as separated by dozens of addresses.

Newton behaves distinctively on LocalTalk networks, since it never claims an address. Rather it takes a look around the network for the Mac or PC that has the information it wants and, using a part of the AppleTalk network software, called the AppleTalk Data Stream Protocol (ADSP), sets up a communication session similar to the serial connection discussed above. Data is sent "point-to-point," the Newton ignores the rest of the traffic on the network. Newton also uses ADSP to communicate with printers on a LocalTalk network.

When you install the Newton Connection software on your Mac or PC (which must have a PhoneNet card to connect to an AppleTalk network), you also automatically install the ADSP driver in your Mac's System Folder —in the Extensions Folder. Windows users will find a new driver in the Windows Setup Network window. You'll have to select the PhoneNet driver and reboot your PC before running Newton Connection.

Your Newton can't see a Mac or PC on the network until you launch the Newton Connection software (or other Newton-savvy software) on the computer and click on one of the three main functions, Synchronize, Re-store, or Install Package. When you see the "Open a connection from your Newton" message, the computer begins to send an ADSP signal on the network that Newton will recognize.

When you open a Newton application that needs an AppleTalk connec-tion, Newton will present a network browser, called the Newton Chooser, that shows the names of the Macs or printers on a network. Tapping the name you want, and the Connect button, completes the ADSP connection (see Figure 3.4).

A connection failure, like when your Newton cannot seem to find any Macs or printers on a network, may be a simple matter of giving the Local-Talk connector on the Newton a shake. Check the other end of the connec-tion, too, at the Mac, PC, or printer. Sometimes, the pins inside the plug can be bent or broken, which severs the connection.

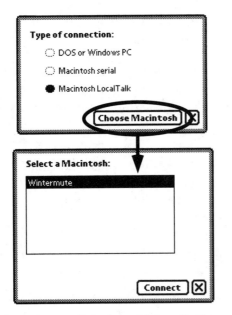

Figure 3.4 *Finding a Mac on the Newtwork.*

AppleTalk addressing cover up!

You'll never actually see the network addresses used by Macs and PCs on the network—that kind of addressing complexity is better left to other net-works. AppleTalk networks use the name entered in to the device by the user, binding the name to the number claimed by the machine for the duration of the network session. Macs use the name entered in the Sharing Setup control panel. Printers appear under names created by the network administrator, usually something strange, like "Dr. Faustus," or cute, like "Kathy's Kwick Printer."

When stopping in at a client's office to print a letter or business card that you'll hand to one of the analog troglodytes hanging around the place, you're going to run up against the name problem. You may be standing there looking at a LaserWriter Pro on their network, but when you try to find it in the Newton printing slip all you'll see is a list of funny, contra-intuitive names. When in doubt, ask.

Here's the second place you might encounter problems with your Local-Talk connection. Let's say you're looking for a networked printer in the printer Chooser. You tap the Printer list diamond and choose "Network printers" from the pop-up list. But nothing at all appears in the Chooser (the slip with the phrase Select a Printer at the top). You probably haven't connected the Newton to the network, or the cable is broken, or the pins in your LocalTalk connector are bent (time to replace the connector).

If all the printers but the one you want appear in the window, it is either switched off or disconnected because of a broken cable or bad connector (or someone took it home). Or you've stepped out of the right zone.

Did we say *zone*? Zones, which can contain up to 254 LocalTalk devices (computers and printers, for the most part), constitute the immediate neighborhood where your Newton lives on the network. Just like when you look out your window you can see only to the end of your street or over a few blocks worth of apartment buildings, AppleTalk devices can see only to the next corner on the network. When searching for a networked printer, or a Mac running Newton Connection software over a multi-zoned network, you can tap the Change Zone button in the printing slip to see a list of network zones. Newton will take a moment to compile a list of all the zones on the network, which you can tap to drop in for a look around. Again, in a large network, it's best to ask for instructions for finding the devices you want to access.

In some of our Newtworking tests, we found large multi-zone networks could prove problematic for Newton. Time-outs caused by routers, which are sometimes used to bridge large networks, and slow networks can reap havoc with your Newton. It's best to limit your explorations to devices in the same zone your Newton is connected to, unless you're sure of a solid, reliable connection.

Macs might not appear in the Connection dialog box on the Newton for a couple reasons. They may be off, but more likely you forgot to launch the Connection software on the desktop computer before asking your Newton to link up. Always do that first!

Actually, Newton will remember the name of the last Macs or printers you connected to and display their names in the Chooser, even though they are no longer available on the network. If you choose the device name and nothing happens, check to make sure the device is on the connection is solid.

Computer users are going to find their Newton's view of the network very different than the Mac's or PC's. Many different kinds of services, including filesharing through the AppleShare server, mail servers by CE Software and Microsoft, and collaborative applications will not be visible to the Newton in the first months or years of its life. Over time, as software and hardware companies build Newton connections into their products, your network view will become more complex.

Resist or Die!

Most Farallon PhoneNet connectors have two RJ-11 jacks. When using Newton, you'll probably use just one. The empty jack can bring on problems, if you happen to be connecting at the end of a string of devices on a network, because it can cause signals to bounce back down the wire. These echoes can cream real network packets—it's a digital reenactment of *When Worlds Collide*, and your data is going to be the loser.

In general, packet collisions are the source of most problems you'll encounter during a network session, after making the initial connection.

AppleTalk allows many computers to put data onto the LocalTalk cable at one time. Think of the network as a time-share condo where you're always bumping into the people who were supposed to be using it the week before you arrived. As the traffic increases, packets tend to crash into one another, just like tempers flare as folks barge into the bathroom when someone else's spouse is using it. Trouble occurs.

AppleTalk deals with collisions by having devices check that every packet made it to the destination. So, when your Newton sends a packet of data to a Mac, it waits for a signal that says "Got it." If you notice that the amount of time it takes to back up your Newton to a Mac increases dramatically—and you haven't recently added 200 people to your Names file

—your network is probably suffering from traffic overload. Newton isn't hearing the "Got it" from the computer running your Connection software. It's time to check with the guy who runs the network.

Sometimes installing a "terminating resistor," a plug that catches and eats stray signals, in the empty RJ-11 jack on your PhoneNet connector can help relieve the packet collision problem. The resistor prevents echoes from traveling back down the wire. Apple's LocalTalk connectors have built-in resistors, so you can leave the second jack open without unleashing a blizzard of ghostly echo packets (but LocalTalk connectors are still too expensive).

A terminating resistor isn't always going to solve your problems, neither is the network administrator. For early Newton adopters (putting a Newton on a network is kind of like taking a very disturbed child into your house), network problems are going to be a fact of life until Apple and software developers work out the bugs in a new communications architecture.

Copper into Ethernet, the alchemy of fast networks

LocalTalk, at 230.4 Kbps, is the slowest of networking standards. Many corporate networks have been upgraded to a faster cabling medium, called Ethernet. This 10-Mbps (approximately forty-three times faster than LocalTalk) networking technology stands as a barrier to Newton users. There is no way to connect your PDA directly to Ethernet, and there won't be for at least a year.

Some folks will argue, "Hey, you don't need Ethernet, because Newton uses such little bits of data that LocalTalk is more than sufficient." But they are missing the point about where data lives in a company. Important information, by nature, moves fast and frequently. That means it's going to be on an Ethernet network, for the most part. We won't even get into the faster networking schemes. Suffice it to say that the same principles we discuss here apply on those networks.

There are two ways to find a route to Ethernet for your little data junky named Newton. A third means to an ether-end will be on the way sometime in 1994.

Check to see if your network has a LocalTalk-to-Ethernet "bridge," a device that translates the signal used on LocalTalk to the type of signals proliferating on Ethernet. Your network administrator might talk about something called a "router," and that'll work, too.

If there is a bridge or router around, find out how to hook into the LocalTalk side of the network (just use a PhoneNet Connector, as we described above), and you'll be all set. Dayna Communications Inc. makes a good LocalTalk-to-Ethernet router, the PathFinder.

Don't go out and buy a bridge if you are the only Newton user clamoring for LocalTalk connectivity. That's the expensive route, the one to choose if a whole lot of Newton (and/or Mac) users show up for a data party.

The cheap route to Ethernet is a breed of software router that runs on a Macintosh with an Ethernet card installed. These applications, including PowerPath from Farallon, turn the Mac into a bridge that passes LocalTalk network traffic sent by your Newton to the Ethernet cable, and back again.

But variants on the cable theme are probably the least of your worries.

Did someone say *protocols*? (Gesundheit!)

Chances are your office network will be using a different set of protocols to control traffic. AppleTalk runs on Ethernet under the rubric EtherTalk, but it's considered by many to be a poor choice for larger organizations. If you want to really impress the boss and get a job in information technology —the cool way to say you take care of the computers around the office— tell her that EtherTalk is too chatty to be a high-performance networking protocol.

By chatty we mean that any AppleTalk network spends a lot of time and traffic on managing itself. So much so that it can bog itself down with messages intended to make it run more reliably.

Most companies instead rely on the network protocols in Novell Inc.'s NetWare network operating system or on a body of arcane Ethernet rules called TCP/IP (it was conceived by academics, so it shouldn't work in the real world, but somehow it does). You don't want to know what these protocol suites do. All the Newton user needs to know is that a router must be installed between the LocalTalk network they connect to and the NetWare or TCP/IP network where the company's data gets processed.

Once a router is in place, you'll need to find a Newton application that can handle the vagaries of these network protocols. A router can only shield you from so much complexity, and your Newton must still deal with a different way of handling network addresses if you want powerful connections to NetWare or TCP/IP-based services, like electronic mail, shared calendars, and databases.

You'll be waiting for a while before NetWare and TCP/IP protocols are supported in Newton applications. The instructions for these networks cannot be implemented in the NewtonScript environment inside the Newton. Instead, developers will have to use a traditional computer language, called C, when writing network protocols. These stacks, as the packages protocols come in are called, must be wrapped in the Newton's native language and must be plugged into Newton's modular software architecture. It'll take a while, and the first versions may not be very reliable. It took years for the Mac TCP/IP stack to work really well.

Modems: Let Newton do the screaming for you

If computers could talk, you wouldn't be able to listen. They speak a binary language of silence that doesn't carry well in a small room or over a noisy phone line. This is why computers, Newton included, have to use modems (which stands for MOdulator-DEModulators), which plug into the serial port or the PCMCIA slot, to convert their telephone calls into audible sound. On the other end of the phone line, another modem reverses the process, turning the tones back into the bits and bytes a computer can understand.

Newton will talk and listen through a modem when you fax, send or receive electronic mail, or log onto an on-line service through third-party software. As the Newton Mail service evolves, you'll probably be using your modem to shop for and buy application software, which will download directly into your Newton.

Modems perform a variation on the handshake made between computers on a serial connection, but the negotiations that happen beforehand are much more complex. In addition to the basic speed at which they will send data, called the modulation protocol, they agree on what kind of compression they will use to increase the amount of data sent within the signal. Error correction protocols—the language the modems will use to check that the data arrived intact—are also negotiated at the beginning of a call.

You've probably seen the modem protocols described in a thousand modem ads, as "V.32," "V.42bis," or "MNP-5." See the chart below for the low-down on what these protocols do for you, but know that the modem you use has to find a common ground for communication with any modem it connects with. If, for instance, they have no compression protocols in common, then they'll fall back to a slower, uncompressed signal. The

shifting tones you hear when two modems first connect are the questions
they ask one another as they attempt to find the protocols they will use.

Table 3.1 The Protocol Dance Card

Newton Fax Modem support	Protocol	Function
Yes	Bell 103	300-bps modulation protocol
Yes	Bell 212A	1,200-bps modulation protocol
Yes	V.22	1,200-bps modulation protocol
Yes	V.22bis	2,400-bps modulation protocol
	V.32	4,800/9,600-bps modulation protocol
	V.32bis	14,400-bps modulation protocol
	V.42	Error correction protocol
Yes	V.42bis	4:1 data compression protocol (requires V.42 error correction)
Yes	MNP-2	Error correction protocol
	MNP-3	Error correction protocol
Yes	MNP-4	Error correction protocol
Yes	MNP-5	2:1 data compression (requires MNP-4 error correction)
	MNP-10	Error correction protocol for cellular data connections
	V.32terbo	19,200-bps modulation protocol
	V.Fast	No standard has been set, but this modulation protocol should provide at least 28,400-bps throughput
Yes	V.29	9,600-bps fax modulation protocol
Yes	V.27ter	4,800-bps fax modulation protocol
Yes	V.21	300-bps fax modulation protocol

Apple's external modem for the Newton that lets you access the Newton Mail service at 2,400 baud, as well as send faxes at the requisite 9,600 baud speed used by most fax machines. Early in 1994, Apple will offer a much cooler, faster modem in a PCMCIA card. Get that one when it comes out, if you don't mind paying twice as much as you do for the external modem; pricing and the name of this PCMCIA modem were not set when this book went to press.

What does fast mean when one is talking modems?

Fast means several different things. Modems are generally described according to their base speed, which is measured in bits-per-second (bps) or baud. There is a slight difference between bps and baud as units of measure, but whichever way the modem maker describes their product, they deliver the same basic capacity, or "throughput." A 9,600 baud modem, for example, will transmit up to 960 characters per second of text and formatting information, like spaces or font sizes. If a typical page holds 3,000 characters, it takes three seconds to send at 9,600 baud.

These days, a 9,600 bps modem is *de rigueur*, and 14,400 bps modems are fast becoming commonplace; if a modem can't fax, it isn't a serious contender (why have both a fax machine and computer, anyway?).

The throughput requirements for a Newton user seem to diverge wildly from the data-starved telecommunications standards computer users endure. The typical Newton application is only a few thousand characters worth of data compared to the Megabytes of data required by a Windows application. Messages are even shorter. Newton's slim data budgets have convinced Apple that it can get away with a 2,400 baud (240 characters a second) data modem capability in its Newton modem. But the first time you get stuck sending a batch of mail messages between flights with a slow modem, you'll see that speed is speed, no matter how small the files you are sending.

Easter Egg...Newton-compatible modems

Apple has approved only one modem for use with
Newton, and that's its own external fax modem. Bah
humbug. There are plenty of modems out there that
will work with the Newton.

Newton is compatible with any modem that uses the Rockwell
224ATF chip set. That's what Apple uses in the Newton modem,
so both the MessagePad and Expert Pad are tuned to use these
chips if they find them connected to the serial port or the PCMCIA
bus (see Figure 3.6). When you tap the send button, your Newton
sends a command to the modem that returns a description of the
modem capabilities. If the modem doesn't match up with the
specifications embedded in the Newton ROM, you'll see a message
that the modem is not responding correctly. If it gets the right answer, Newton will automatically route faxes and electronic mail
connections to the modem, wherever it's connected.

A variety of third party modems also run on the Rockwell 224ATF
chip set. For the most part, they are compatible with Newton. Turn
to Chapter Fourteen—*Hot Hardware*, for a complete list of Newton compatible modems.

The coolest modem we used that relies on the Rockwell 224ATF
chips is the 14,400-bps Data/Fax Modem with XJack from Megahertz Corporation (Call 1-800-527-8677, it's part number
XJ1144). This PCMCIA card fits into the Newton card slot and
features a very smart pop-up RJ-11 telephone cable jack. There's
almost nothing as neat as pressing the top edge of your Newton
and having this XJack pop out.

The problem with the Megahertz modem, and any PCMCIA modem for that matter, is its thirst for power. We're not talking Nix-
onian delusions of grandeur here, it's simply a battery issue. This
modem uses 725 milliWatts (mW) of power when operating,
250mW when it's standing by while your Newton is running, and
29mW when the device is asleep.   *(continued)*

Easter Egg...Newton-compatible modems (continued)

Compare that to the 20mW to 40mW that a memory card uses when you are searching for data, and you'll see the problem. When faxing with the Megahertz card, a fully-charged Alkaline pack lasted only 28 minutes on average (we tested three sets of batteries); the first battery warning typically appeared at 19 minutes (these tests were conducted on a pre-production version of the Expert Pad; MessagePad users on CompuServe who tested the Megahertz modem reported even shorter battery life).

Apple is working with Rockwell and modem vendors to cut the power requirements of PCMCIA modems. But until they do, run your Megahertz modem only when connected to an AC power source.

By the time you read this, Apple and third-party modem makers will probably have solved many of the incompatibilities between non-Rockwell modems and Newton. Test your own modem before succumbing to an irrational urge to buy the Apple external modem.

Troubleshooting modem connections is complex work, since the modem on your end and the other end of the telephone line, the telephone network, and extraneous factors all impact on the success or failure of a connection.

Modems communicate asynchronously, meaning that they append a bit to the beginning and the end of every byte of data that they send. These bits, called parity and stop bits, tell the receiving modem where bytes begin and end, and they are stripped away from your data upon arrival.

If you have no success in making a connection or your modem seems to connect but nothing happens once the connection is made, your modem settings are probably incompatible with the settings used by the modem it's calling. Several third-party and shareware terminal emulation applications for Newton will let you change the parity and stop bits, and the length of the bytes your Newton sends, which should let you resolve modem-to-modem incompatibilities. Find out what settings are required by each service you call. PocketCall, by Ex Machina, will handle the settings for commercial services; all you'll need is the dial-up number.

The most common problem you'll encounter is interference of some sort that knocks your modem off the telephone line. Interference can be caused by older telephone switches (though most in the U.S. are digital these days) or electromagnetic fields from a computer, bad wiring, or the like. Someone picking up another extension in the house will almost always interrupt a modem call, too.

Finally, the phone cable may not be feeling too cooperative. Modems, as we said, are analog beasties, but many telephone systems, particularly those in corporate offices, are going digital. Now, that may sound like manna from heaven to a digital do-hickey like Newton, but it's not. Digital phone lines require a different kind of modem, called a terminal adapter, which converts the signal sent by a serial port into something comprehensible to the phone system. You can also go the cheap route with an adapter that fits between the handset and body of a digital telephone. We recommend that when confounded by a digital line you give a call to telephone adapter vendor TeleAdapt, of Campbell, Calif. They make a great little converter, called the TeleSwitch, that will let your Newton tap into digital connections.

Infrared Highways

The basic capabilities of the infrared port are covered in Chapter Two—*Your Information Surfboard,* so we'll focus on troubleshooting here.

The Newton infrared (IR) port can send and receive data at 9,600 baud at a range of up to one meter. Only one Newton can send data at a time, because the IR port is capable of half-duplex communications only, and therein lies the first hint to look for when trouble hits.

When you beam an object, Newton asks you to tell the receiver to send a signal saying its ready for the message. There are a lot of expectations to fulfill in a half-duplex communications session. A single missed acknowledgment can hang up both units as they search for the other device and try to re-synchronize their data (they try to pick up where they left off, rather than starting over).

We found that beaming fails at two different points in a data transfer: The beginning and the end.

If you can't get two Newtons, or Newton and a Sharp Wizard OZ-9600, to begin a beam, take a look at your surroundings and how the devices are positioned relative to one another. The IR ports won't work in bright sunlight or rooms bathed in fluorescent light—open a newspaper and drape it over the Newtons, if you can't find some natural shade.

Beaming failures also happen because you are too close to one another (give yourselves at least four inches between the Newtons) or because one of the Newtons is being held out of the horizontal field of approximately 30 degrees and vertical field of 15 degrees in which the IR signal is "visible." Basically, when beaming you have to aim the windows on the front edge of the Newtons at one another.

Newton takes two minutes for all communications connections before it declares a time-out and gives up. It allots two minutes to reestablishing contact with a receiver if it has lost the IR signal before confirming the beam; it's better to tap the Stop button in the Out Box or In Box, depending on whether you are receiving or transmitting, and start over.

If your Newton indicates that it has recognized another device, but it then cannot confirm the beam, you're seeing the results of interference that wiped out some of the data. Like other communications procedures, beaming involves the use of a checksum to confirm that the data arrived in one piece. In our experience, once Newton finds the checksum indicates an error, it seldom manages to reestablish the session to resend the data by itself. Maybe the other person has already walked away. It is better, once you see the "Confirming beam" message has been displayed for more than 15 seconds, to stop the transfer and resend the beam manually in the Out Box (see Figure 3.5).

Setting the Preferences for beaming takes a bit of IR savvy.

When you un-check the "Confirm before receiving" box in the Beam preferences, you are telling Newton that, when it receives a beam from another Newton or a Sharp Wizard, it should send a reply signal that indicates it is ready to receive the body of the message. If you do so, there is a remote possibility that you'll end up receiving beams you never asked for. This is doubly true if you have also checked the "Receive beams automatically" box *and* un-checked the "Open In Box while receiving" box (see Figure 3.6).

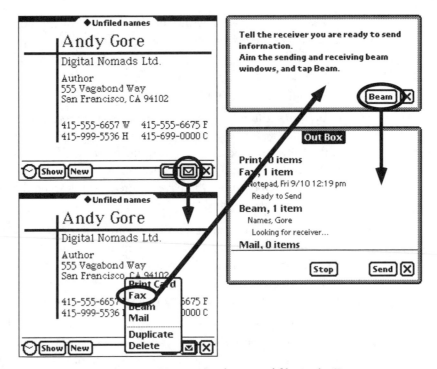

Figure 3.5 Beam me up, Newton! Sending a card file via the IR port.

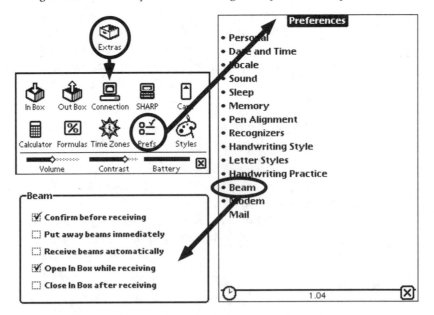

Figure 3.6 Options for beaming can be found in Preferences.

In general, though, you'll want to disable automatic receiving in your Newton. When this box is checked, the IR port will send a "Ready to receive" signal every two seconds, which consumes a lot of power. If left enabled, the IR port can reduce your battery life as much as 20 percent.

Assist...Connections Wrap-up: Built-in options

Now forget everything we've told you about networks. Shunt this knowledge off to the Mongolia of your mind and keep it there until you need it. What you need to pay attention to is getting along in your life. To help you remember when a particular bit of networking knowledge will come in handy, here's a chart that tells you when you'll be using each communications feature on the Newton:

Table 3.3 The Newtworking Master List:

Connect Newton to:	Newton Port	Hardware/Software add-ons required
Newton	Infrared	None
Newton via mail	Serial Port or PCMCIA slot	Modem and NewtonMail account
Macintosh	Serial Port	Serial cable with 8-pin mini-DIN plugs and Newton Connection or other Newton-savvy communications program for the Mac.
Macintosh via LocalTalk	Serial Port	LocalTalk or PhoneNet connector and cable and Newton Connection or other Newton-savvy communications program for the Mac.

(continued)

(continued)

Connect Newton to:	Newton Port	Hardware/Software add-ons required
Macintosh via mail	Serial Port or PCMCIA slot	Modem and NewtonMail account
Windows PC	Serial Port	Serial cable with 9-pin mini-DIN or DB-25 plug and Newton Connection or other Newton-savvy communications program for Windows.
Windows PC via mail	Serial Port or PCMCIA slot	Modem and Newton Mail account
Sharp Wizard OZ-9600	Infrared Port	Run the Wizard's IR transfer utility
Sharp Wizard 7000, 8000, 9000 series	Serial Port	Sharp CE135T Level Converter, run Wizard PC-Link mode
LaserWriter and StyleWriter printers	Serial Port	Serial cable or LocalTalk and PhoneNet connectors
Parallel printers	Serial Port	Print Pack cable (connects 974 models)
Fax machine	Serial Port	Fax modem

Newton's Private Mail Newtwork

Electronic mail, that stalwart of stodgy offices and the spice in the lives of fifteen million residents of Cyberspace gets a cool new ride in Newton. MessagePads, Expert Pads, and future Newtons will ship with built-in E-mail features that let you trade notes and drawings, calendar entries and Name files over a telephone line. Pricing for the service, called Newton-

Mail, hadn't been set when we went to press. Apple said they will charge a monthly fee that gives you "enough time to log on and check mail once a day."

If you are an active mail user, get ready to pay more. One of the lessons you learn after a few months of cruising the digital fringes is that E-mail expands to fill as much time as you give it. Mailing lists, collaboration with colleagues and general chit-chat are interesting, they consume time, and they consume money.

But that's what Apple is hoping. John Sculley, the chairman of the board of Apple has talked often and effusively about the huge market for on-line services. He talks in the billions of dollars, and they won't get there giving away unlimited mail services for a flat monthly fees. No, they want to sell you the Newton to use as a kind of communications razor—and network connections are the blades.

E-mail is a shock to the system that was weaned on paper mail sent by the U.S. Postal service. Where you are now used to a single exchange taking two weeks to travel back and forth, E-mail conversations happen at the speed of light. It is possible to converse in text throughout the day as you work on an idea, wrestle with a sticky negotiation, or get tangled in electronic dramas of love or intellectualized anger.

Once you get E-mail, you'll get hooked.

An E-mail system works like a quarterback. It takes the snap from the center, fades back, and looks for the receiver. If the receiver cuts back across the backfield, the quarterback hands the ball off. Or, he passes. Unlike the best quarterbacks, E-mail systems almost always hit their receiver—only modem problems or the wrong address can knock the message down in mid-pass.

Newton uses the modem to call the E-mail system, and a mainframe computer, called a server, uses a bank of modems to answer. After the modems negotiate, the Newton client tells the server the name of the caller and, when the server says, "Yeah, prove it," replies with a secret password. During the call, your Newton hands off all the messages you have composed, and scans the server for mail addressed to you, which it downloads to the In Box.

When you crack open your Newton package, look for the reply mail card in the Mail Registration Information pamphlet that you can send in to receive the Mail Starter Kit (if it's not already in the box). When this kit arrives, you'll find complete pricing information and a tip sheet, as well as a registration certificate.

Open the Preferences application and tap the Mail item to enter the NewtonMail configuration interface. If you have the account information already, write the account name in the E-mail Account field and tap the Set E-mail Password button. If the System ID field is blank, write "Newton" on that line. Write the password in the window that opens, and Newton will verify the word you entered (see Figure 3.7).

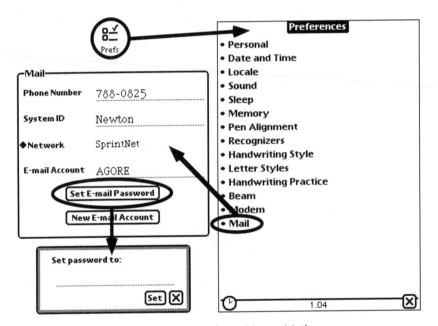

Figure 3.7 Setting up a new password on a NewtonMail account.

A word about passwords: NewtonMail supports passwords of up to eight characters in length. Use every character, and mix upper- and lower-case letters with numbers. Don't use a common word, since those are the first things that intruders use when testing the strength of E-mail security. Surely, you think, you won't be the target of a hacker, but don't be so sure. As more people go on-line, there is more incentive to invade the networks, whether one is an anti-social teen, crusading technologist with a point to prove, or the federal government looking for immoral activity on the network.

Bad people will try to crack your account two ways: They'll call you and, posing as a NewtonMail employee, ask for your password; or they will try logging on by running a dictionary of common words on an account's password. (Where do they get the account name or your phone number? They grab it off a business card, easy!). Nonsensical passwords, especially when they include numbers, force the intruder to try random combinations of characters, and there are a lot more combinations of the eight characters you are permitted by NewtonMail than there are common words in the dictionary. Besides, Newton remembers your password for you, so go with a confounding gob of text, not your son's first name, when choosing a password.

If you want to go on-line to register, you'll need to dig through all the paper in your Mail Starter Kit to find a NewtonMail certificate that contains a number and password that Newton will use to logon to the server in lieu of the account name and password. Tap the New E-mail Account button, fill in the fields, add the password you want to use to the Password Verification field, and tap the Continue button. Now, Newton asks you for your credit card number and expiration date. Big fun! It's like going shopping without ever leaving the house—that's the sensation Apple and home shopping doyen Barry Diller are counting on to boost their profit margins in the 21st Century! (see Figure 3.8)

Newton will connect to the NewtonMail server and upload your financial information, and in return it will receive an account name and verification of the password you chose. Now, your NewtonMail account is set up and you are ready to send messages. The virtual spending spree has just begun.

If you encounter difficulties when registering your account, or you cannot logon, call the NewtonMail customer support service at 800-775-4556.

NewtonMail lets you communicate with a wide variety of computers and networks, though making all these connections can be pretty complex. You can send Newton files to another Newton user's E-mail address without worrying about the recipient's ability to open them. But when you start fooling with Mac and PC users, or folks on UNIX networks, you'll be forced to fall back to the lowest common denominator in computing, the ASCII character set and plain text messages. So don't expect to sketch a map to dinner and send it from your Newton to a Windows user who will be able to print it out and carry it along on the road. During Newton's first year, however, look for Apple to extend its NewtonMail service to support the sending of electronic ink between Newtons and other computers (these come through as plain drawings).

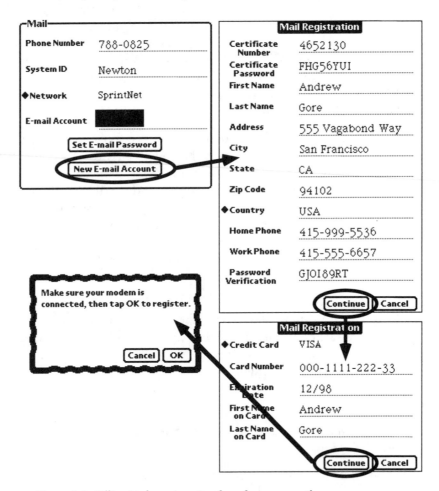

Figure 3.8 Filling in the registration form for a new mail account.

The Mail command is listed under the Action icon in notes, calendars, and Names cards. When you tap Mail, Newton will open an addressing slip. The name will be empty, unless you used the intelligent assistant to mail the letter. Just write "mail Mitch," for example, and it will open the Names file, check the E-mail address for Mitch Ratcliffe—it's "RATCLIFFE," by the way—and insert the name and address in the addressing slip.

Writing the name of the addressee in the Name field creates a link to the Names file, so Newton will fill in the address. Tap the Name field to see a list of other possible addressees, if Newton guesses wrong (see Figure 3.9).

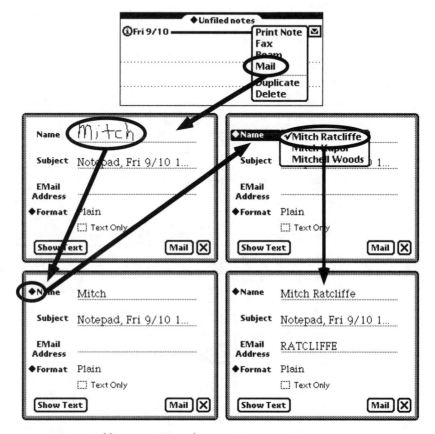

Figure 3.9 Addressing an E-mail message.

Once you finish addressing the message, tap the Mail button. Newton opens the Out Box, and you can send it immediately or close the Out Box to save the message for later delivery.

The Out Box is a bit complex. You can send the message, which you already told Newton you want to send, by tapping the Send button yet again and choosing from a pop-up list of actions (Print, Fax, Beam, Mail). Or you can open the message by tapping its name in the Out Box window and tapping the Try Again button at the bottom of the message screen (see Figure 3.10).

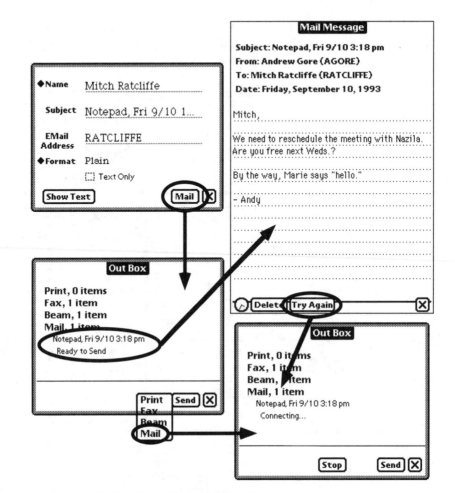

Figure 3.10 *Coaxing mail out of the Out Box.*

A clear problem with the NewtonMail interface as it stands in the first version of the MessagePad and Expert Pad is that you must tap too many buttons to get a message from the composition stage to the NewtonMail server.

There are some inconvenient glitches in the Newton-to-Newton mail environment, which we hope will have been resolved before you reach this page, but likely they will still be a problem. The In Box and Out Box does a poor job of integrating untranslated ink, like notes and drawings, into the mail message interface. When you open a message from the In or Out Box, only the text appears. Tap the Put Away button at the bottom of the window to file the note in the Notepad, where you can see the ink.

Calendar entries sent over NewtonMail, which should be integrated in-to the recipient's calendar like a beamed appointment, appear as text mes-sages that do not fit seamlessly into a calendar (they can be added by high-lighting the item and tapping the Assist icon).

If you haven't got any out-going mail, but you want to check your net-work mailbox, tap the Receive button in the In Box, choose Mail from the pop-up list that appears, and Newton will logon to the NewtonMail sys-tem. For more information on the In Box and Out Box, turn to Chapter Seven—*Life's Little Extras*.

The slow speed of the Apple modem is a hobble that will keep you on-line more than you need to be. It runs up your bill, and if you have any sense, you'll soon be searching for a third-party modem and E-mail appli-cation that lets you transfer messages more quickly, and over other systems than Apple's.

But be prepared for a few stumbles along the way. Even if you get, say, a Megahertz 14,400 bps PCMCIA modem, it is impossible to change the speed of NewtonMail access, unless Apple does it for you. The answer to this problem will come when modem manufacturers ship a Newton driver that lets you change the modem's speed in Preferences.

More importantly, though, third-parties will deliver client software for other networks, including the wonderfully anarchic Internet, where mil-lions of people are communicating for next to nothing. The first third-party E-mail application due out at the time we went to press is PocketCall, from Ex Machina of New York City.

PocketCall will blend pre-set functionality that lets Newton dial the phone with the ability to customize on-line sessions through the addition of PocketCom modules. So, for instance, you'll be able to add a graphical interface for browsing an electronic conferencing system, like Compu-Serve. Ex Machina promises E-mail client software for logging on to the CompuServe Information Service, MCI Mail, AT&T EasyLink, and GEnie in its first release.

PocketCall, and other applications that are in the works, will also pro-vide terminal emulation features. For those lucky enough to have avoided initiation into the cult of telecommunications applications for Macs, Win-dows workstations, or various desktop computers, a terminal emulator is an application that dumbs down the graphically-oriented machine to work with a mainframe or minicomputer. Unfortunately, most large communications services are still running on computers that expect to provide service to a text-based terminal, like the awful machines in many libraries and offices. Terminals, rather than operating as an independent device, are used to send commands to a remote computer.

The terminal is where the idea of the "computer user" was born—the concept lives on today in the hassles computer companies expect us to endure for a smidgen of added productivity. The terminal user has to memorize archaisms and anti-language, which computers eat up. PocketCall tries to smooth the way for Newton users by providing a library of these terminal commands which you will be able to tap, cutting down on the typing necessary to log on, collect mail, and send computer commands. Any terminal emulator for Newton that's worth its salt will offer similar command libraries.

Developers are also working to provide an Internet client application for Newton, which will give you access not only to mail but powerful search engines that can dip into libraries, databases and computer archives to find the answers to your questions. You'll also see a wide range of Newton client software for specialized information services, like the Dow Jones Dow-Vision network, which delivers news, analysis, and stock reports.

Third-party communications and information services will charge up your life. Check them out, try several and give up the ones that don't serve your needs. You may want to stick close to Apple's NewtonMail network as a home base, but we'll guarantee that the really vital "content" in Cyberspace won't be available from just one source, especially when it's a computer company that makes its decisions about what kind of information it offers after reading marketing reports. No, living your E-mail life in the Apple domain alone would be like a life lived in the bedroom at your parents' home. You got to, got to, got to roam if you want to taste the many flavors of experience in the Invisible World outside the electronic doorway.

Exploring Newton

The Second Law: Every action has an opposite and equal reaction, except handwriting rcognition.

The Second Axiom: The quality of data is inversely proportional to its mass.

You Are Here

Welcome to your guided tour of Newton. In this section we'll take you on an adventure through the Dark Continent of your PDA—the burning emptiness of the Notepad, the wide-open plains of the calendar and the lush and mysterious Names jungle. On your way you'll meet the many strange and indigenous Extras that populate this enigmatic landscape. And, of course, what adventure would be complete without at least one close encounter with a stampeding herd of folders, the lightening fast Find or the cunning Assistant. Just be sure to keep your hands inside our tour bus or more than your fingers could end up doing the walking!

Let's just hope we can avoid the vicious handwriting recognizer. We lost more than a few tourists to the less-than-kindly care of that evil beast!

This is *Newton's Law*'s quick and dirty guide to finding your way through your PDA, where you'll learn the basics of Newton applications, how they work, and get a healthy dose of tips and tricks, not to mention a few Easter Eggs sprinkled in for good measure!

This section is not intended to be a replacement for your MessagePad handbook or Expert Pad user's guide. If you haven't read through the manual, do so now. You'll be better prepared to take advantage of the information in Exploring Newton.

Anatomy of an Interface

One last bit of business before we begin our tour. We'll just be handing out the tour map. This way, if you get separated from the rest of the party you can find your way back to our main encampment. Just look for the red arrow that says "You Are Here."

You should also check out Chapter Five, which includes interface maps for the Names file, Calendar, To Do list manager, and Notepad applications. For more on the contents of the Extras Drawer, turn to Chapter Seven.

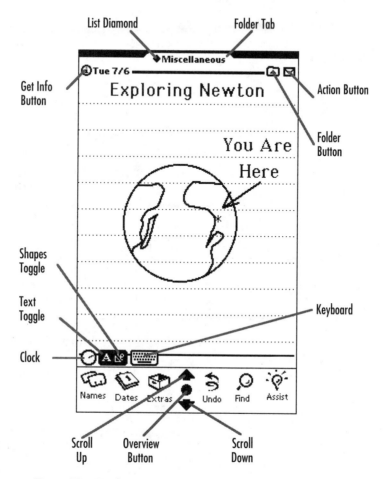

Figure II.1 Finding Your Way Around Newtonland

The Buttons

List Diamond

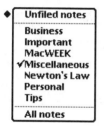

Anytime you see one of these little black diamonds next to a word or a field, it means there is more than one option that Newton knows of for that field or selection. For example, by tapping the diamond on any folder tab, Newton will show you a list of all available folders. Just tap on the name of the folder you want to change to.

Other examples of where you'll see the list diamond include the salutation field in the Names file, in the Find and Assist dialogs, and next to the name field in any dialer slip.

Folder Tab   ◆**Miscellaneous**

Folder tabs appear at the top of Newton applications which have records that can be stored in a folder. The name shows the current folder you're working in. Using the list diamond, you can also display the contents of all folders for that application (for example, All Notes), or just the records that haven't been filed (Unfiled Notes).

Get Info Button   ⓘ Tue 7/6/93 11:56 pm 977 bytes

Tapping a note's Get Info button displays the date and time stamp for when the note was created. It also displays its size. Get Info buttons appear on error dialogs as well; tapping them shows when the error occurred.

It's important to remember that the size displayed (in bytes) is compressed. The note probably takes up more space when in use and not stored away in Newton's memory.

Assist...Stamped and Delivered

You'll notice that the Get Info button in Figure II.1 is attached to the end of a note separator bar right before the date stamp. Note separators are how one note is divided from another in the Notepad. A quick, single stroke straight across the Notepad screen will usually cause one of these lines to appear.

There are a couple of things to keep in mind about date and time stamps. First, if the Newton's internal clock is set wrong, the date and time stamp could also be wrong. This is especially critical seeing as the date and time stamp records when the note was created, and doesn't change when it's modified.   *(continued)*

Assist...Stamped and Delivered

The other thing is that multiple notes in a folder are listed in chronological order. The stamp on the note, if the note is created out of order, will take the date of the previous note. For example, if you have three notes dated 9/20, 9/21 and 9/22 and on the 23rd you add another note, but you put it between 9/20 and 9/21, the date stamp on that note's separator bar will be 9/20. We don't know exactly why it does this. It seems to us it'd be better if Newton put the right stamp on the note and then, if it had to, move the note down to the correct position in the chronology.

One last item to be aware of about date and time stamps. If you fax, beam, print, or mail a note, unlike sending an appointment or Name card, the date that appears in the Out Box is taken from the note's stamp. (If the record is a Names card, no date appears in the Out Box; an appointment displays the date it is scheduled for.) If the wrong date is recorded on the stamp, this can make it difficult to distinguish exactly which note is which. (You'll have to tap on the item to display its contents). For more on time stamps and their effect on notes, see Chapter Five—*Newton 101*.

Action Button

Possibly the most useful button on your Newton's interface, the Action Button lets you do things to a record such as print, fax, beam or mail it. You can also use the Action button to delete a record (the Delete command causes Newton's otherwise invisible trash can to appear momentarily and swallow the crumpled remains of the record you deleted), duplicate it or move it on and off a PCMCIA card.

Not all Action Button options will be available at all times. For example, if you get a Find list with multiple records, you can use the Action button to move all the records or delete them, but you cannot gang fax, beam, print or mail Newton records.

The Action Button may appear on the bottom or the top of the screen, depending on the application or list you're in.

Folder Button

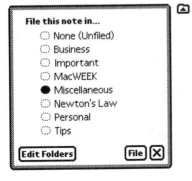

Tapping the folder button lets you move a record from one folder to another. You can also use this dialog to add, delete or modify the available folders. Select the folder where you want the record to reside and tap "File."

You may have noticed that the folder icon sometimes has a triangle in it. Folders with triangles indicate a record that is stored on an inserted PCMCIA card. If you remove the card, that record will no longer be available.

Shapes & Text Recognizer Toggles

When the letter "A" is highlighted (white text in a black field), the text recognizer is switched on. Anything you write, in the appropriate space, Newton will attempt to convert to text. When the little shapes to the right of the "A" are highlighted, Newton will try and "clean-up" anything you draw. For greater accuracy, toggle the recognizers on and off. For example, if you're trying to draw, tapping off the text recognizer will keep Newton from mistaking a short line for a letter.

Double-tapping on the text recognizer toggle will take you directly to the Recognizers section of the Preferences roller. Unfortunately, tapping the close box in Preferences doesn't take you directly back to where you were.

Clock Button

Tapping this icon displays the current date, local time and the amount of the charge left on the internal batteries. If the Newton is plugged in, the battery indicator will always display a full charge, even if the battery is completely discharged.

The icon itself is a working clockface and will show the current hours and minutes without the need to tap the button.

Keyboard Button

Tapping the keyboard button calls up the soft keyboard so you can type text into your Newton instead of relying on recognition. This is especially helpful when you're writing words that aren't in Newton's dictionary.

There are a total of four differently-configured keyboards which can be flipped through by repeatedly tapping the keyboard button. The first is the standard "QUERTY" keyboard used by most computers, the second is a number keypad, the third a telephone keypad and the fourth a keyboard designed to make entering dates and times easier (see Figure II.2). You can also get a keyboard by tapping twice on a field or anywhere in the Notepad.

Easter Egg...Have You Got The Temperature?

The next time you're checking the time for someone, give them the current temperature as well.

Instead of just tapping the clock button, hold your pen tip down on it. First the clock will display the time, date and battery status as always. But after a few seconds, up pops the current ambient temperature of the Newton!

We can't really vouch for the accuracy of Newton's thermal readouts. It's just a clever hack the Newton programmers slipped in that borrows data normally used by the screen to adjust contrast as the temperature fluctuates.

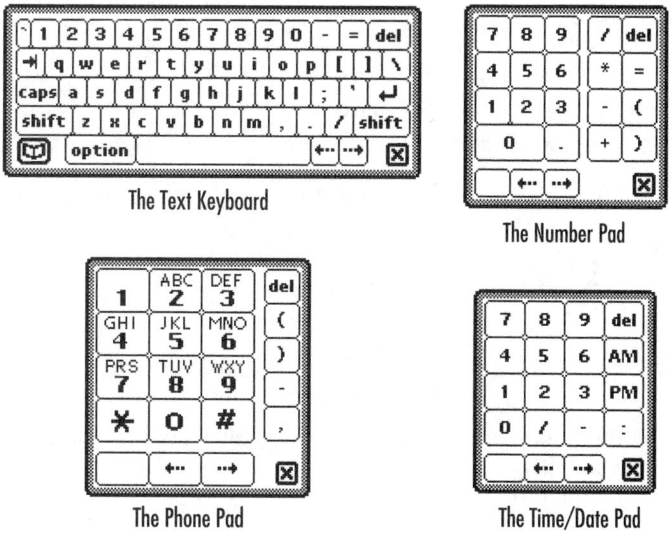

The Text Keyboard

The Number Pad

The Phone Pad

The Time/Date Pad

Figure II.2 The Four Keyboards.

Newton keyboards are at least a little context sensitive. For example, when you open a keyboard in the first and last name fields of the Names file data entry screen, the shift key will already be depressed on the keyboard. Also, when you tap on the screen, Newton will bring up the most appropriate keyboard for the application or field you tapped. If you tap in a phone field in the Names file, for instance, a phone keypad will pop up.

Newton keyboards also remember; if you hit the caps lock key on the standard keyboard and then close it, the next time you open that keyboard, the caps lock key will still be active (caps lock makes all the letters you type come out upper case).

With Newton soft keyboards, what you see is what you get. You won't see options that are not available, and you have to know standard key combinations that enable certain options. So, to get a question mark key, for example, tap the shift key first to make the question mark symbol appear on one of the keys. And you thought there was no need for typing skills in the Newton world! (For more on keyboards, see Chapter Four).

The Permanent Menu

Names File   Names

Tapping this icon calls up the Names file application. It should be noted that opening the Names file will close the calendar/To Do application, most third-party applications, but not the Extras drawer. The Notepad is always "open," even if you can't see it. (If you can see it, as will often be the case with the Names file, you can still write on the parts you can see.)

For more on the Names File see Chapter Five—*Newton 101*.

Calendar/To Do   Dates

Tapping this icon calls up the Calendar and To Do application. Like the Names file, opening this application will close most other applications except the Notepad and Extras drawer. For more on Dates see Chapter Five —*Newton 101*.

The Extras Drawer Extras

Tapping this icon opens the Extras drawer where add-on Newton applications are kept, as are built-in accessories such as Styles, Connections, and Preferences. For more on the Extras drawer see Chapter Seven—*Life's Little Extras*.

Scroll Up, Scroll Down, and Overview Button

The Scroll Up, Scroll Down, and Overview buttons are universal controls throughout Newton. Use the arrows to move up and down in the Preferences roller, the Notepad, and the To Do list or to move through cards in the Names file and the hours in the calendar. The arrows will also let you scroll through long lists in the Find and overview windows.

The overview button will display a complete list of everything in the current folder in the application you're using. So, for example, tapping overview from the Notepad in the Newton's Law folder will generate a list of all the notes stored in that folder, rather than all the notes in the Newton (see Figure II.3).

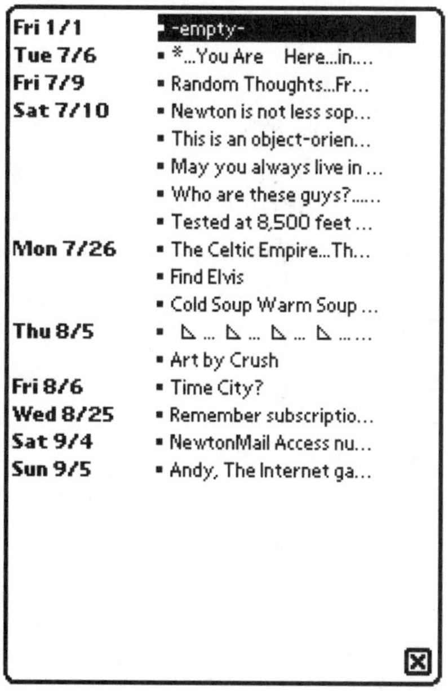

Fri 1/1	-empty-
Tue 7/6	• *...You Are Here...in....
Fri 7/9	• Random Thoughts...Fr...
Sat 7/10	• Newton is not less sop...
	• This is an object-orien...
	• May you always live in ...
	• Who are these guys?......
	• Tested at 8,500 feet ...
Mon 7/26	• The Celtic Empire...Th...
	• Find Elvis
	• Cold Soup Warm Soup ...
Thu 8/5	• ⌂ ... ⌂ ... ⌂ ... ⌂ ......
	• Art by Crush
Fri 8/6	• Time City?
Wed 8/25	• Remember subscriptio...
Sat 9/4	• NewtonMail Access nu...
Sun 9/5	• Andy, The Internet ga...

Figure II.3 The View From 40,000 Feet.

Unfortunately, unlike the rest of Newton, it's not always obvious when the scroll arrows and overview button will work. For example, if you load more than thirty items into the Extras drawer, you can't scroll to get access to the applications hidden below the bottom of the screen. You also can't use the Overview button to display a list of the applications and get at them that way. You've just got to limit yourself. Apple™ promises this shortcoming will be addressed in the near future.

When it doubt, try it out. The worst that can happen is Newton will beep you and display and error message saying you can't scroll there.

Undo   Undo

Tapping Undo erases the last data you entered or action you performed. This includes pen strokes, tapping buttons, scrub-outs and translated words. Undo remembers the last two actions you performed, so you can erase the second-to-last data entered by tapping the Undo button twice. In general, you go back one ink stroke, one translated word, or pen command per tap on the Undo icon.

Undo in Newton is universal: it works practically everywhere within the PDA.

Find   Find

Tapping this icon opens a slip which you can use to find a particular word or record or to create lists of records (see Figure II.4). For more information on the Find command, see Chapter Six—*Info Surfing*.

Figure II.4 Desperately Seeking...

Assistant   Assist

Tapping this icon calls up the assistant slip, which you can use to make Newton perform tasks, like scheduling a lunch or calling a person in your

Names file (see Figure II.5). If you select a text string which the Assistant can recognize as a command, you won't have to enter anything in the slip. For more information on the Assistant, see Chapter Six—*Info Surfing*.

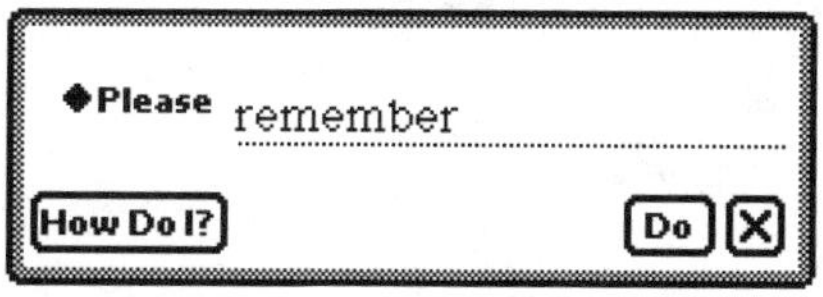

Figure II.5 Calling Your Assistant.

Slips, Boxes, Rollers, and Transporters

The Close Box

This is used to close an open form, application, dialog, or slip. The close box can be found practically everywhere in Newton, except on the Notepad which is always open.

Dialog Boxes

Dialog boxes are how Newton communicates with you. Dialogs will usually pop-up when Newton needs your input, such as when selecting a printer (the Chooser is essentially a nested dialog box that lets you drill down through a series of network views) or deciding what to do with a freshly inserted PCMCIA card. A dialog will also appear when Newton needs to tell you something important, like the fact that you're running low on battery power. Dialogs can also contain lists, such as the Overview or Find lists. Dialogs are sometimes referred to as Windows.

There are three kinds of dialogs. The first are static dialogs, which can't be moved and usually have a minimal number of options (see Figure II.6 for two examples of static dialogs). If a static dialog has an option that can remove data, it will usually have another dialog nested behind the button in question which will give you one of those "are you sure?" messages.

Movable dialogs usually contain more complex options which you might want to use over and over again, like the Styles dialog (see Figure II.7). To move a dialog box, hold the pen tip down of the gray border of the box and drag it without lifting the pen. Raise the pen when you get the box where you want it, and it will stay put. Dialog boxes remember their previous locations. So, the Styles dialog will usually reappear where you last moved it the next time you open it.

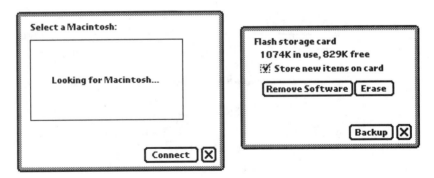

Figure II.6 Unmoving Dialogs.

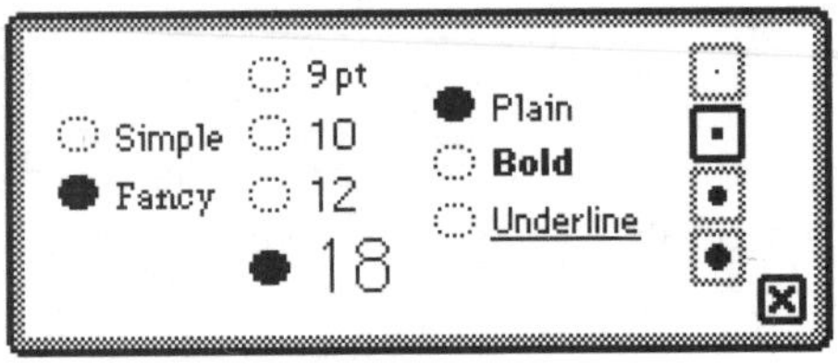

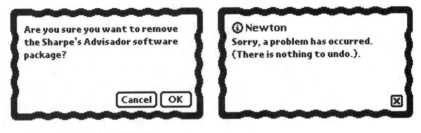

Figure II.7 A Moving Dialog.

The third, and most important, dialogs Newton displays are critical dialogs. They are displayed with solid, bold borders and usually warrant quick attention (see Figure II.8). These dialogs will contain messages that concern deleting applications, drained batteries and errors. They will almost always have one of two buttons on them, such as a close box or "cancel" and "OK" buttons.

If Newton displays an error dialog, tapping on the Overview Button while the error is displayed will cause Newton to list the most recent errors that have happened on the PDA.

Figure II.8 Critical Dialogs.

Slips

Slips are dialogs with input fields on them. They may also contain list diamonds and radio buttons (those empty circles that turn black when you
tap them). The mailing label and phone dialer are both examples of slips
(see Figure II.9).

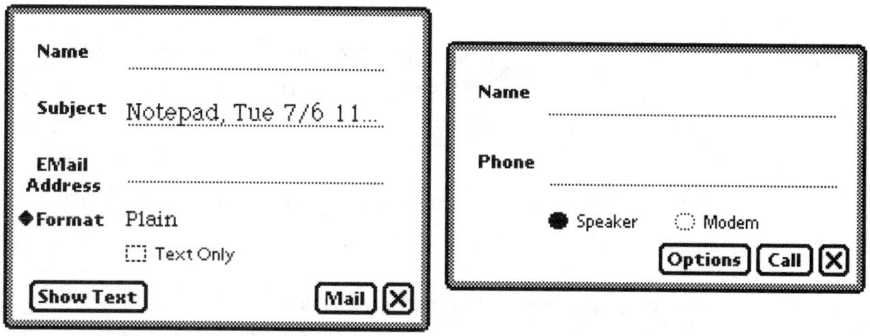

Figure II.9 Slipping Across Newton.

Rollers

Imagine a roll of toilet paper with forms drawn on each sheet. That's the
concept behind Newton's rollers.

Both the Notepad and the Preferences accessory use rollers to scroll
through notes in one case and settings in the other. The advantage of rollers
is that new software can add another sheet of viewable information on to
the Preferences, for example. And users can add on new notes without fear
of running off the bottom of the page (you only need worry about running
out of memory). The Notepad is a sort of infinite roller that you separate
into useful chunks by drawing a line across the screen.

Use the up and down arrows on the permanent menu to move through
rollers.

The Transporter

The Macintosh has the clipboard, Newton has the transporter.

Like the Mac clipboard, you can use the Transporter to move text or
drawings from one part of Newton to another. The only difference is that
you can't repeatedly paste in the same object over and over again in Newton
like you can in the Mac. For that, you need to use the copy gesture (see
Chapter Four—*The Written Word* for more on gestures).

Anything you can select can be moved in the Transporter. For example, let's say you want to move the title of Exploring Newton from the notebook to an appointment in the calendar (see Figure II.10).

First, select the text using the select gesture. Then, press the pen on the text and drag it all the way to the side of the screen. Your pen tip should actually meet the edge of the screen.

Newton will shrink the text and abbreviate it. Now, tap on the Dates icon in the permanent menu. When the calendar opens, find the appointment or add it; the Transporter will hold on to the text until you need it. Now, press the pen on the abbreviated text and drag it away from the side of the screen—the title will expand to its normal size. Position the text where you want it and let up on the pen.

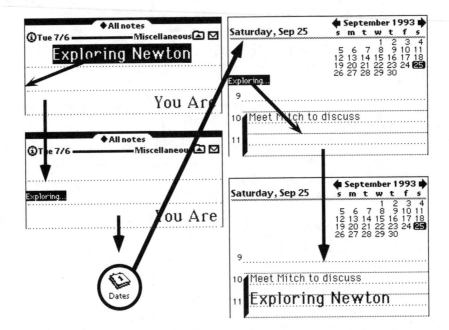

Figure II.10 *Energizing The Transporter.*

That's all there is to it! Newton will not let you have more than one selection in the transporter at one time. If you try to drag another object to the screen side while something else is in the transporter, Newton will kick the first selection out and suck in the new object.

Get Info...Apple Writes the Rules

One of the reasons the Mac is easier to use than other computers is Apple's reliance on a document called the *Macintosh Human Interface Guidelines* that sets out rules for software developers. Apple is now working on a set of Newton human interface guidelines.

The Mac guidelines dictate that the pull-down menus in applications must use the same names and commands for oft-used features, like Cut, Copy, and Paste. It also demands that windows and dialog boxes be used in specific ways, so that the user comes to expect the same "look and feel" in all applications. Developers' conformity with the Mac guidelines made people comfortable, and saved them from learning different keyboard commands for every application. Windows users continue to suffer.

In the Newton environment, things are a little different. There are fewer variables to control, since most of the command structure is hidden behind handwritten commands. There are no menu bars, no pull-down menus to Save, Print or Copy. Instead, there are standard interfaces for sending a fax and beaming, for instance.

What developers may do—what you are entitled to expect as a consumer—are products that expand on Newton intelligence to automate some of the tasks you handle with pen taps now. For example, when faxing in the standard Newton interface, you must tap several times between the time you decide to send a note as a fax and when the message finally leaves your Newton; developers may deliver true one-tap faxing.

Some companies just won't get the simplicity thing. They may screw up the interface by crowding it with buttons or new verbs (like "Fax" and "Print" that already exist—though it might be funny if someone brought "Energize" to the Newton verb-cabulary), adding so many functions that you'll have to carry a manual with you everywhere. *(continued)*

Get Info...Apple Writes the Rules

Eventually, the interface guidelines will probably say something like "Minimize user commands or get out." Apple's engineers will wrestle with these questions for some time before they rule on the final look and feel of Newton. And, because Newton is meant to flex more than the Mac ever did, adapting to devices with drastically different function sets, it could prove a big challenge to come up with Newton human interface guidelines to fit every circumstance.

CHAPTER
4

THE WRITTEN WORD

Under Siege

Set your expectations about the performance of Newton handwriting recognition like your grandfather chose the color of his Ford Model T: you can write in any style you want—as long as it's Newton's. The most misunderstood and controversial component of Newton technology, handwriting recognition is the launching pad for almost every tirade against Apple's first PDA.

True, Newton handwriting recognition is not as powerful, or as "adaptive," as Apple made it out to be. But it's not the *Chevy Chase Show* of input technologies, as some would have you believe. Newton gets more words right than Chevy does laughs.

Apple executives were determined to ship Newton by the self-imposed deadline of Summer 1993, but the result was a MessagePad that came out about a month before it was actually ready. Gaston Bastiaens, vice president and general manager of the Apple PIE division, had bet his wine cellar on making that summer deadline; Newton was already tardy, and his reputation was riding on delivery of a product. Apple took a beating in the press for the mistakes that slipped out the door in those first MessagePads. It might have been worth losing a few bottles of Dom Perignon to avoid the ensuing media backlash.

A couple of system updates later, Apple managed to stabilize things considerably. Unfortunately, Newton-bashing had become a self-sustaining firestorm. It's ironic, because the ongoing criticism is startlingly like the brickbats cast at Newton's big brother. When the Macintosh first came out, there was a lot of negative press concerning why a mouse was an awkward mechanism for navigating a file system. People were used to a command line interface. One journalist described using a mouse as being like "drawing with a pencil with a brick glued to the eraser." Now the majority of computer-using humanity can barely remember what a command line is (Windows users still know; they just like to pretend they don't).

We wouldn't describe Newton as pen-based computing anymore than we would describe the Macintosh as mouse-based computing. The pen is simply a method of input, better than some, worse than others. Even if handwriting recognition was perfect, anyone owning a passing familiarity with a keyboard could type faster, and for longer, than they can write with a pen. Compounding the frustration type-oriented folks feel, as we have already established, is the fact that Newton handwriting isn't perfect.

You learned to type to make the best use of a mechanical or electric machine that transferred ink onto paper, or to better use a computer. So, too, will you need to learn to write to make the best use of your Newton's pen. It is a mechanism with its peculiar eccentricities that you'll have to adapt to—machines are just that way. Driving a car is different from driving a buggy, too. If you follow the guidelines below, Newton will adapt somewhat; however, depending on how close your handwriting matches Newton's model, you will have to adapt, too. There are no free rides to the New Frontier!

Newton handwriting recognition is based on a strict model of the alphabet, numbers, and punctuation. The model is rigid, but sufficiently diverse to account for the handwriting styles of a large part of the population. However, every one of us will come to the Newton interface with a few peculiar letter styles that break the model. Learn where you and Newton can come to terms, and where you must change your style a bit, and the accuracy of recognition will skyrocket.

Most critics refused to admit that a Newton is a machine that recognizes handwriting. Even though these people would give nary a thought to learning the intricacies of the QWERTY keyboard, they bitch and moan about the infringements on their liberty when it comes to shaping a letter differently in order to help Newton recognize it. Part of the problem is the general laziness of the American hand. In Japan, where a standard method for writing each character of the alphabet is hammered into schoolchildren, people love pen computers, which understand them quite reliably from the very first time they pick up a PDA.

With English, Newton handwriting recognition starts out like a drunken sharpshooter. At times, it'll amaze you with it's accuracy; but when it misses, dive for cover against the surreal phrases it composes. "Guide" becomes "aide," and, as Garry Trudeau related in his Doonesbury comic strip, "Catching on?" is translated into "Egg Freckles." (Freckles is not in the Newton dictionary, Garry.) However, if you follow the suggestions outlined in this chapter, after a couple weeks of average usage, or a few days of intense training, you'll be surprised how well you and Newton will have adapted to each other.

Use Newton Connection when making major updates in your data to limit your exposure to handwriting hell. Like any tool, you need to evaluate when Newton works best for you and use it accordingly. If handwriting isn't a problem for you, or you don't have a computer or know how to type, then you'll probably want to use the pen most often. If your handwriting is a curse on paper that you can barely read two hours later, use a computer for heavy data entry and save the pen for surfing through your information. For those of you who have given up hope of ever reading a cursive or printed note in your own hand, hang tough, we understand a third-party hardware developer is working on a Newton keyboard. Apple also plans to support keyboards as an option on future Newton designs.

And the next time some know-it-all gives you a hard time about your Newton, ask them when was the last time they fit a DayRunner, notebook, fax machine, pager, and e-mail-savvy computer in their purse or jacket pocket!

Cold Boots and Warm Starts

Like any dog, it's best to start training a recognizer while it's young. Fortunately, you can send your Newton back to its infancy by performing a factory reset, which clears all the lessons your Newton has learned. (This is critical if your Newton has served time as a floor model at the dealer, where it will have learned many conflicting lessons as it was passed from hand to hand).

After reading Section I and experimenting with your Newton, now would be a good time to reset your system to factory settings. This will be helpful as we show you how to raise a well-behaved and helpful hand-writing recognizer.

Hopefully, you haven't put anything in your Newton you care about. If you have, please refer to Chapter Seven—*Life's Little Extras,* for instructions on how to copy data from Newton's internal RAM onto a PCMCIA card. Or turn to Chapter Eight—*Ready, Set, Load!,* and Chapter Nine—*The Information Sculptor,* to find out how to back up that data to a Mac or PC, and extract what you care about for reinstallation after shaping the recognizers.

Resets are a bit of dark science, allowing you to strip out parts of the RAM, or to clear the entire memory for a fresh start. The first step is turn your MessagePad or Expert Pad over and remove the battery panel. You'll see a small hole at the upper left corner of the battery chamber which is labeled "RESET." You can use your pen tip to press the recessed button.

Pressing just the RESET button will cause your Newton to perform a "Warm Boot," which clears operating memory. A Warm Boot collects the garbage lying around in your RAM, but doesn't touch your data. Several third-party applications already let you do a Warm Boot by tapping a button on the Newton screen. Check out Elegance from Tanis Development, a commercial application, or Howard Oakley's Memory Massager, a freeware application available on many on-line services. You'll need Newton Connection to install these applications. Just be sure to close all windows, slips, and dialogs before doing a software reset. These applications take advantage of an undocumented feature that doesn't always protect the most recently-entered data.

A factory reset, or "Cold Boot," wipes the slate clean—all settings and data contained in your Newton's internal RAM is erased. The only thing remaining after this electronic Neutron Bomb detonates are whatever system updates were stored in memory; the memory management unit in Newton protects that part of RAM from a cold boot. (If you take out the main and backup batteries for more than a couple minutes, you'll wipe out the system update, too). A cold boot is the digital equivalent of a plunge into a frozen lake after a sauna—Newton comes out clean, reduced to its elemental faculties, tingling with awareness and ready to start learning all over again.

This is the process for a cold boot. First, you hold down the power switch, but do not release it. Then, press the RESET button with your pen, without letting up on power switch. Let up on the RESET button first, then the power switch. If this has worked correctly, a small dialog box will pop up on the screen that says "Do you want to erase data completely?" There are two buttons in the box that say "Yes" and "No." Tap "Yes."

When you tap "Yes," a second dialog box appears on the screen that says "All your data will be lost. Do you want to continue?" This time the buttons say "OK" and "Cancel."

Tapping "OK" will nuke all the settings, your user dictionary and the notes, names and appointments stored in your Newton's RAM (Storage cards inserted in the Newton at the time will be left intact). If you choose to do so, you're Newton's mind will be as blank as the day it was first manufactured and ready for you to train it in earnest!

The Golden Rules

Before we launch into a detailed explanation of how handwriting works, here are the seven Golden Rules you should follow when writing on Newton. Some of these rules will help recognition improve over time, others will have an almost immediate impact.

You could probably get by just follow these guidelines; however, for more detailed instructions on setting Newton's recognizers and how recognition works (and doesn't work) read on. This will be especially valuable to those of you who are getting bad handwriting results from your PDA.

- **Golden Rule #1: Write Clearly and Carefully.** If a stranger can't read something you've written, neither will Newton. Also, avoid fancy flourishes or other eccentricities peculiar to your writing style. And don't write at an angle on the screen or slant your characters. Watch for the little things. Make sure your i's have dots directly over the top of the letter, for example, and make sure you close your letters properly.

- **Golden Rule #2: Don't Write Too Fast or Slow.** In all things, moderation. Writing too slow will cause Newton to think your done writing when you're not. Writing too fast will overload memory.

- **Golden Rule #3: Put Wide Spaces Between Words.** Newton cleans up empty space between words, so make plenty of room when you write; this way Newton won't think two words are actually one.

- **Golden Rule #4: Make Capitals Twice The Size of Lowercase Letters.** If you care about capitalization, follow this rule to make sure Newton doesn't mistake a capital for a lowercase letter.

- **Golden Rule #5: Don't Crunch Your Characters.** Make sure to leave distinct gaps between letters. But don't make the gaps too wide, Newton might think two letters are two words. Also, don't let letters run over each other—make sure your T's keep their horizontal strokes to themselves.

- **Golden Rule #6: Correct As You Go.** Never let a mistake in recognition lay. It'll screw up Newton's ability to learn your writing style. Write a few words, pause while Newton catches up, and if there are mistakes go back and fix them.

- **Golden Rule #7: If At First You Don't Succeed, Give Up.** While writing the same word over and over until Newton gets it will eventually improve your PDA's recognition, it'll learn faster if you just write a lot of different words, correcting the ones it gets wrong. Besides, it might be a word Newton doesn't know.

The Zen of Recognition

Be the Newton, let the Newton be you. The closer your handwriting style is to the model that Newton understands, the more Newton will be able to "adapt" its recognition capabilities to your hand. If the first time you picked up a Newton it accurately converted 75 percent of what you wrote, it should be able to improve its recognition to as high as 95 percent accuracy, over time. However, if your score was closer to 50 percent, then you're the one who'll be doing most of the adapting.

Newton can't recognize words absent from its 10,000 word dictionary. It might not understand your name, the name of your company or the street you live on—no matter how carefully you write these words. Don't be discouraged if Newton misses words that aren't in the dictionary, you shouldn't count those errors as part of your average score. You can turn off the dictionary to force the recognizers to translate each letter individually to improve Newton's handling of your name (in the Recognizers Preferences, check the "words not in dictionary" box and leave the "words in the word lists" box un-checked), but remember that you'll seriously degrade overall recognition performance.

Better to leave the dictionary on and add oft-used words, like your name and the names of your spouse and children, to your personal word list. For those words you rarely use, open the soft keyboard to type them.

Newton comes equipped with three core recognizers. You can turn two of them on and off by tapping the recognizer button at the lower left corner of the Newton interface (see *Anatomy of an Interface* for complete instructions). These are your allies in the battle for recognition:

Shapes. The shapes recognizer can straighten pen input it perceives as drawing rather than handwriting. We suggest you leave this recognizer switched off unless you are trying to create a very precise drawing. Turn the words recognizer off while you're drawing, so that it doesn't interfere with drawing by translating a short line into a letter.

Using the shapes recognizer to create a drawing is a bit like threading a needle with a rocket launcher. While it does a good job of straightening out larger objects, it doesn't work well with minute details and shapes.

Mixing text and drawings on the same line of the Notepad can be a true test of your patience. Newton dearly wants to line up newly added text with previous text, if possible. Confronted with failure to align text Newton will try to move your writing to the left side of the screen. It can be damn difficult to convince Newton that you really do want a word to be in the middle of a neatly rendered square.

If we do use the shapes recognizer, a mix of computer-aided and free-hand scribbling gives the best results. Just don't expect to produce any great works of art with or without shapes recognition, don't even expect to be able to do a reasonably accurate sketch of a ball joint on the Notepad. But, while Newton's own sketching application falls short of being a great canvas, third-party programs like Saltire Software's DrawPad provide additional drawing tools that make these kinds of drawings possible.

Words. It's the technological bad boy of the Newton architecture. The words recognizer is what we'll be concerning ourselves with in most of this chapter.

There are several factors that go into determining what you'll get back from Newton after you write "Dog" on the screen. Most important is the sub-recognizer, specific sets of letters and number styles against which the recognizer compares your handwriting (symbols and punctuation are standard across all sub-recognizers). Newton currently ships with three sub-recognizers; they are listed in the Recognizers Preferences:

- **Cursive.** This set includes 110 letter shapes and 34 numerals. The style they represent isn't purely script, you can get away with using letters that are not connected.

- **Printed.** If you're a block letter writer, this is the sub-recognizer for you. The character set includes 87 letter styles and 33 numerals, which do provide leeway for connected letters in a word, as when you link double T's. Select Printed if you're having trouble getting Newton to recognize words written in all capital letters.

- **Mixed Printed and Cursive.** As you might expect, this character set is vast by comparison to the others. It will compare your letters against 159 examples, but only 33 numeral styles (people tend to learn a standard set of numerals, it's the one thing schools do beat into us). Generally, the Mixed sub-recognizer takes slightly longer to translate a letter than the other sub-recognizers do when set to the same speed and accuracy in Preferences. It also provides the most give for people who've never made up their mind about how they write.

Each sub-recognizer has its own adaptive settings, the records of your handwriting used to adjust recognition to your style. So, if you start with cursive and decide, a few weeks later, that you really should be using the mixed sub-recognizer, you'll be starting over from scratch training your Newton. However, Newton does remember the settings for each sub-recognizer, even when you switch. So, you can go back to cursive and pick up where you left off if mixed doesn't work out as well as you expected.

Taking the test. As to which sub-recognizer will work best for you, it all depends on your writing style. Take the following handwriting test:

Grab a memo pad or whatever you usually use to jot down notes. Also, see if you can find a document on which you've recently written a few notes. Finally, if have a copy of something you've written to someone else, like a letter, fax cover sheet or memo, add it to your pile of test materials.

As carefully as you can (but not too slowly), write this sentence on the memo pad: "There may be a few questions you ask yourself about the future interdependency of man and machine, the emerging technological utopia, and our peculiar human desire for omnipotence."

Lay all three writing samples out on the table side by side. If two of the three are written in script, start with the cursive sub-recognizer. However, if you printed on either the memo pad or when you made notes on a document, you may want to opt for the printed sub-recognizer, instead. It may well be that you write in manuscript when you're more involved with the content, rather than the look, of what you're writing.

If you see a dramatic improvement in the quality of your writing between the quickly-written notes on the document you dug up and the test sentence you wrote on the memo pad, then, even if you'd describe your handwriting as bad, you and Newton should be getting along better after a few weeks of intensive training. Why? You were thinking about writing the test sentence—with the notes you were thinking only about the idea you were trying to convey—and the results show that you're able to improve your handwriting relatively easily. Now all you need do is think a little bit about the quality of your writing when using Newton. Don't worry, it'll train you.

Don't throw away that test note. You'll need it to compare with the Newton letter shapes gallery below.

Modes of Operation. The handwriting recognizer has two modes of operation, Normal and Guest. You change from one mode to the other from the Handwriting Style option under preferences. This is also where you select which of the three sub-recognizers you want to use (see Figure 4.1).

```
┌─Handwriting Style──────────────────────┐
│                                        │
│  My handwriting style is               │
│      ◌ Cursive Only                    │
│      ◌ Printed Only                    │
│      ● Mixed Cursive & Printed         │
│                                        │
│  My words are                          │
│      ████████◇···················      │
│      widely spaced   closely spaced    │
│                                        │
│  Recognize my handwriting              │
│      ████████████◇···············      │
│      slowly, more        fast, less    │
│      accurately          accurately    │
│                                        │
│  Transform my handwriting              │
│      ██████████████◇·············      │
│      immediately     after a delay     │
│                                        │
│  Configure for guest user  ▢           │
│                                        │
└────────────────────────────────────────┘
```

Figure 4.1 Selecting Your Handwriting Style.

What Guest mode does is switch from whatever sub-recognizer, style and adaptive settings your Newton currently has recorded for you to a temporary blank slate, as if you'd done a cold boot of your PDA. Don't worry, your settings remain in a nice safe place in RAM.

Once in Guest mode, the settings can be changed completely, including sub-recognizer, handwriting, and letter styles. If you use your Newton in Guest mode, it will start recording new adaptive settings for any and all sub-recognizers you're using. It will also begin improving its recognition once again—temporarily. When you switch out of guest mode, settings and everything your Newton has learned is purged from memory and your original personal settings are restored. The next time you go to Guest mode your Newton starts back at factory settings.

Sub-recognizers shouldn't be passed around carelessly. A half-hour with a stranger and the hard work you've put in training your Newton could be ruined. The next time someone at the office asks for a hands-on demo, be sure to switch to Guest mode before handing over your PDA. It'll save them the frustration of having to write with a recognizer adapted to your writing and you the trouble of breaking your Newton of any bad habits it might pick up in the process.

That's not to say that a Newton can't be shared. Let's say you share your Newton with your spouse. The only way to save adaptive changes for the two of you is for each of you to agree to use just one of the sub-recognizers.

He can use the Printed settings while you confine yourself to mixed cursive and printed writing. As long as both of you are careful to change between the two sub-recognizers when the PDA changes hands, Newton will record changes to your adaptive settings individually.

However, you'll both need to use the same spacing, timing and dictionary preferences, just as you have to share the den and the household chores. These settings apply to all sub-recognizers all of the time.

Ink, Strokes, Shapes

An understanding of what's happening behind the scenes—the mechanics of recognition—will help you get a head start on predicting what's likely to result when you put pen to mylar.

The basic component of all handwriting recognition is digital ink. Digital ink, or just ink, is the black trail you see following the pen as you move it across the screen.

Ink is a combination of a bit map, quite literally a map that determines what pixels are turned black on the screen, and some math behind it that records the shape and direction of the pen stroke that placed the ink. The data contained in ink makes recognition work.

Ink is the mud that makes the bricks of a recognition house, and strokes are the bricks. Every time you put a stylus on the Newton's screen, move it to another point and lift the stylus up, you create a stroke, a single line of ink. Sometimes it'll only take one stroke to form a shape, like the letter "o". It might also take a couple of strokes to form a shape, and, darn it, that's okay, too, like when you write an "H". But you can improve recognition by trying, as much as possible, to form every letter from a single stroke without lifting the pen off the screen. When you lift the pen you give Newton a cue that you've ended one letter and are about to begin another (the recognizer does know that sometimes you have to lift the pen and accounts for that by timing the interval between two strokes).

A shape is the ink equivalent of a letter, number, symbol or gesture, like the scrub-out that erases a mistake. Shapes are all wrapped up with the sub-recognizer you're using, and are the keystone of accurate handwriting recognition. You're more likely to get an accurate translation of a shape if it closely approximates one of the shapes Newton has recorded for that letter in the particular sub-recognizer's repertoire.

While perfectly reproducing shapes in ink that matches the letter styles Newton understands will certainly boost the accuracy of recognition, it's not the only factor in getting the right letter. Even though Newton's text recognizer is state-of-the-art (meaning it's the travois of recognition, we've a long way to go to the Space Shuttle), there are too many similar shapes in the alphanumeric range for Newton to make a judgment based solely on the shape of ink. Where shapes are very similar, such as with a lowercase "c" and "r," Newton factors in the direction of the stroke to help improve the odds (see Figure 4.2).

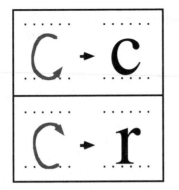

Figure 4.2 *R or C? Only the stroke direction knows for sure.*

Sure, we know that an "r" doesn't look much like a "c" to the human eye. But to a recognizer, which has a lot less ability to distinguish the nuances of a shape, especially since they are rendered in jagged bit maps of square pixels, strokes can look mighty similar.

Check out the shapes attribute for each letter, and the direction and the number of strokes Newton expects will form that letter, by tapping the Letter Styles item in Preferences. Tap the letter in the list of the alphabet at the bottom of the Letter Styles window to view your options. You can tap on a particular letter shape to make Newton play a movie of the stroke and direction for that shape.

Having said all this, we know some of you will get a "c" with a stroke in either direction. Chock it up to the fickle gods of recognition, and remember that shape counts more than stroke direction in determining recognition outcome.

Get Info...Ink as a standard

The 1990s may yet be the decade of the pen. A barrier to acceptance of digital ink as a useful medium for communications has been the many competitive ink standards.

Apple's ink is not merely a foreign language to an AT&T EO Personal Communicator or a Pen Windows computer, it's virtually invisible to these machines because it is encoded in a way they don't even recognize as ink. In the pen computing world we have a situation where everyone who uses blue ball-point pens can't read messages written by people who use black fountain pens. No wonder few in the press and corporations take this stuff seriously. While computers are linked together to unleash human communication, pen computing looks like cult activity conducted in mutually incomprehensible gibberish.

A band of computer companies have decided to make their ink compatible. Apple is one of the big chiefs in this movement. In the summer of 1993, Apple joined EO, General Magic, Lotus Development Corp., Microsoft, and application-developer Slate Corp. to announce the Jot 1.0 standard for digital ink. When implemented in their computers, Jot will allow users on a Newton to scrawl out a note and send it as untranslated ink to a Microsoft WinPad (the Microsoft pen portable coming in 1994), which will be able to display it and eventually translate it after the fact.

Whether Jot results in a new age of compatible assistants or just a level playing field for devices that will offer users other types of intelligence in a struggle to kill one another is for history to decide.

All The Shapes Fit To Print

Welcome to the Newton Letter Styles Gallery. The following diagrams (Figures 4.3, 4.4, 4.5, 4.6, and 4.7) contain all the shapes in the mixed sub-recognizer that Newton can convert into text. For the most part, the cursive and printed sub-recognizers use subsets of these letter shapes.

Newton does not have shape prototypes for entire words but builds them from the individual letters. In fact, one of the great myths of Newton recognition is that it is word-based. This isn't true. Newton recognition is two-tiered, and the tiers interact to improve overall performance. The actual shape recognition happens only at the letter level. Newton can check the words in the dictionary when deciding about the likelihood that an ink shape is a particular letter; if there is no word in which an "e" follows a "bz," it goes back to the letter-level recognition and tries a different translation on the shape. Translated letters, then, are assembled into words, which is why when you double-tap a word on the screen, you see a list of alternative translations. It's like a Scrabble contest played at light speed.

You'll notice that some of the hairline frames (which show the currently selected letter) in the gallery encompass more than one letter shape. That's because these letter shapes are all generated by the same shape prototype. Any changes you make to the adaptive settings will effect all the letters within the frame (see below).

Remember that writing test we asked you to save? Now would be a good time to take it out. As you go through the gallery, compare the letter shapes with your writing and highlight the letter shapes that most closely matches your scrawl. By the way, the text of the test was taken from an ad for the Sega Genesis CD system we clipped from an airline magazine. And here you thought it was some scientific approach that resulted in a perfect sample of handwriting!

If you run into a handwritten letter that doesn't have an equivalent shape in the gallery, put a star next to it. Later, you'll want to go into Letter Styles Preferences, call up that letter group and pick out a letter shape to teach yourself.

Also, remember that stroke direction is important. If you write a letter exactly as it appears in this gallery and you still can't get Newton to recognize it, check the stroke direction by tapping that shape in Letter Styles Preferences. Left-handers especially beware! Andy is left handed, and couldn't get Newton recognize his "4." Then, he checked Letter Styles to find that he was drawing the right-angle stroke of the number backwards.

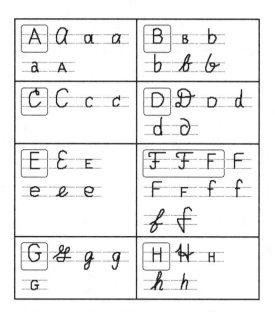

Figure 4.3 *Letter Shapes from A to H*

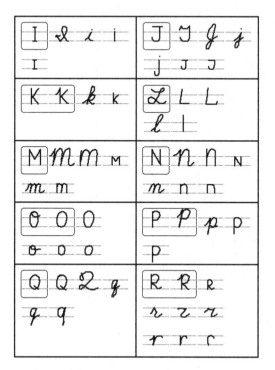

Figure 4.4 *Starting at I and going to R*

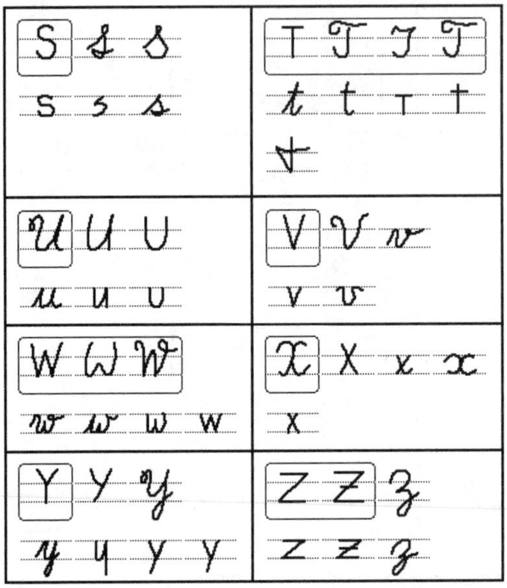

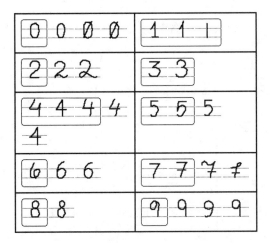

Figure 4.5 *S to Z, The Last Roundup*

Figure 4.6 *Your Number's Up*

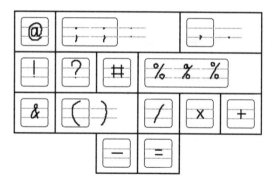

Figure 4.7 *Symbols of Recognition*

Adapt Yourself

Now we get to a touchy subject, that of the adaptive part of Newton's recognition.

It is true that Newton will adapt its handwriting settings over time to get better recognition results. It is also true that, while technically speaking, Newton does adapt, it is not adaptation in the sense that you and I would normally think of it.

Recognition is a numbers game. And one of the ways Newton loads the dice is to observe how you write and over time, increasing the likelihood that it'll match one letter shape to a written shape over another. It does this by changing the "statistical weight" of that letter shape, the one it thinks you write most of the time, and decreasing the weight of other shapes in that letter group that it thinks you write less often. This is the scores system, where the recognizer puts a value on each match it gets starting with shape, stroke direction, and then that shape's proximity to other shapes (this is where "word" recognition comes in). It tallies up numbers and whichever word gets the highest score wins.

Weight, by the way, is the score that Newton gives a particular letter shape. The higher the score, the heavier the weight of that shape and the more likely Newton will select it as the correct match. By lowering the score of one shape in a family compared to another, Newton decreases the possible outcomes and, in theory, increases the accuracy of recognition.

After a week's use, the Letter Styles Preferences displays scores that give a clear picture of how Newton thinks you write. For example, in Figure 4.8 the first shape for a lowercase "a" is displayed in black, because it is the one Newton has observed most often; it is weighted as a Sometimes in the Letter Styles window. The second shape, displayed in a dark half-tone, is one you've used occasionally, but not very often; it is weighted as a Rarely. Shapes displayed in light gray, which when highlighted in Letter Styles appear to be neither Sometimes nor Rarely, are scored as Almost Never. Newton won't consider this shape as an option unless it's stumped.

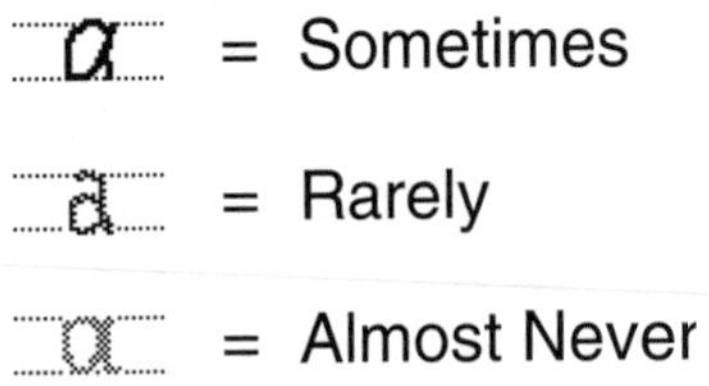

a = Sometimes

a = Rarely

a = Almost Never

Figure 4.8 Sometimes, Rarely, Almost Never; the scores in shapes recognition.

When Newton comes across a shape for which it finds two possible matches, if one is rated a Sometimes and the other a Rarely, the Sometimes wins. If both matches are scored Sometimes, Newton would have to look at other data, like possible word matches, for help in figuring out the correct letter translation.

Newton does not alter the shapes it knows. If your writing does not fit one of the shapes it understands, you should change your writing to improve recognition. It may be possible in some cases that the word score will help pull out the correct result for a single, erratic letter style, but word scores are used by the recognizer to rule out a letter, not confirm them. The hard truth is that you have to bend in order to avoid breaking your relationship with Newton, there is no substitute for writing the correct shapes.

After you've gone through the gallery and figured out which shapes match your handwriting, you can give Newton's learning a kick-start. Just go to Letter Styles preferences, select the letter group you want to work on and then select each letter shape and tap the Sometimes or Rarely buttons, depending on whether that shape is one you write often or not (see Figure 4.9). Only Newton can set a letter shape to Almost Never (fully grayed out).

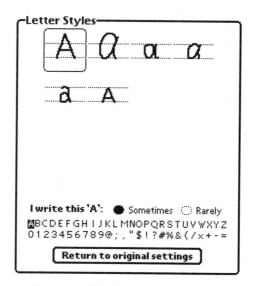

Figure 4.9 Teaching Your Newton To Read

When playing around with Letter Shapes remember that shapes contained in the same wireframe use the same prototype. So, even if only one of the three W's in Figure 4.5 matches your handwriting, you must leave all three set to Sometimes to get a correct result.

The Learning Process

So, just how does Newton figure out which shapes you write more or less often? The process is relatively simple. But, if you don't adjust your writing habits to fit this process, Newton adaptation can actually make handwriting recognition worse, not better.

Every fifth word you write that you don't correct, Newton assumes is accurate and adjusts the weights accordingly. So, if you wrote a sentence that Newton translated as "Isle got bats in my belfry," and didn't change "Isle" into "I've" (what you really wrote), by the time you get to "belfry," Newton would assume it guessed right and change the weights of shapes in the sub-recognizer accordingly. This would increase the likelihood that the next time you drew the shapes for "I", "v" or "e" Newton would translate those letters incorrectly.

By the way, Newton counts words for learning purposes across the entire interface. So, you could have written "I've got" in the Notepad, "bats" in the Names file and "in my belfry" in the Date Book and, as long as you haven't gone back and corrected the "Isle" result, Newton would still consider it correct and would change the recognizer weights.

Newton will only consider a word correct if it has been left totally unmolested. This includes choosing an alternative selection from the pop-up word menu you get when you double-tap on a word (see *Recognizable Gestures* below), writing over a letter in the word, scrubbing out any portion of a word and editing a word with the keyboard.

But not to worry if you leave a misspelling in a note. Just because Newton thinks it guessed the word right doesn't mean the weights of every letter shape in the word will change. Newton collects data over an extended period of time which it uses to change the weight of shapes. Newton is also capable of making a finer distinction between shape weights than you can set manually in the Letter Styles preferences. The recognizer is a glacier of electrons creeping toward chaos, not a volatile schizoid roaming your notes with a digital cattle prod.

Newton is always collecting data for its adaptive settings. There is no way to "train up" a Newton, get recognition almost perfect, and then take Newton out of learning mode to preserve the settings. People change, and so do their PDAs.

Just remember, Newton is always watching. If you start getting sloppy after you've gone to the trouble to train Newton, it may take a while but the quality of handwriting recognition will degrade.

Get Info... Take five, beautiful people

The "count five" learning system is the central cause of handwriting problems for most Newton users. Because Apple has been reluctant to try and explain this fairly complex concept to users it considers relative neophytes, and because handwriting recognition as a whole is something of a touchy subject down at Apple headquarters in Cupertino, Calif., most Newton users are dangerously ignorant of how handwriting works. A detailed explanation would tarnish the ease-of-use reputation Apple is fighting hard for on the televisions and magazine pages of America.   *(continued)*

Get Info... Take five, beautiful people (continued)

Most people probably sit down with the recognizer turned on, and start training their Newton by taking lots of notes. The problem is that when taking notes you probably don't take the time to stop every couple of words and correct bad recognition; recording your ideas is more important. So, if a wrong word makes it to number five in the queue without being corrected, Newton *thinks it's right* and adjusts recognition accordingly.

The result is handwriting recognition that gets steadily worse, not better. This is especially dangerous with virgin Newtons that don't have a lot of correct data to "drown out" the occasional incorrect assumption. This is Reason Number Two why Expert Pads and MessagePads make lousy notepads. Who can hope to take notes on a device that assumes you'll stop every couple of words to fix its mistakes? Not us, we still write mostly in paper notebooks.

The key to avoiding this pitfall is, for the first few weeks, to be careful to correct any mistake in recognition the moment it happens.

Try this simple training exercise to help bulk up your Newton with accurate data. Take a dictionary, and enter 10 common words from each letter of the alphabet into your Notepad. Be sure to sprinkle some punctuation into the mix, as well, so you and Newton can used to each other's periods, commas, and question marks. (Punctuation is the weakest link in Newton's recognition model— too few shapes in the sub-recognizers—so don't expect things to get much better.) The trick here is to get ten right guesses before you move on to the next letter.

Next, take the phone book and enter about fifty phone numbers at random. Remember, only right guesses count.

Sounds tedious. But you'll find recognition will work much better after you invest the time with this exercise. Also, all this work with the recognizer will help adapt your handwriting as well. Feel free when you hit a problem letter or word to go to Letter Styles to check the strokes and directions for that letter. This is probably the shortest route to a well-behaved Newton.

Word Scores

One last, but important, factor will effect the outcome of recognition. That's Newton's dictionary.

Newton uses a scoring system to measure the reliability of its recognition guesses. It is a dynamic process: as you write each letter of a word, Newton starts adding up the weights, figuring in the weight of each matched letter shape while it also produces a list of best guesses about the word you are writing.

The process works something like this. Let's say you're writing the word "bog." You write the "b" which Newton matches to "6," because you wrote your "b" with a single curving stroke and the weight for the "6" letter shape is heavier for that stroke than for the "b" letter shape. Next, you write an almost perfect "o" which Newton matches with 95 percent likelihood that it is, in fact, an "o."

A quick check of the dictionary and Newton finds no word candidates that start "6o". So, Newton knows that one of its two shape guesses is wrong. There was only a 72 percent likelihood that what it thought was a "6" was actually a "6," so Newton drops down to its next best guess for what you wrote, which is an "i." Don't laugh. Check the letter shapes group in Figure 4.4. A lowercase cursive "i" could look like a "6" to a recognizer.

Newton goes to the dictionary again with "io" and finds a match with "ion." So, even though the score for "i" is low, the likelihood that the overall word, based on the evidence at hand, is "ion" is high. Then you write a shape Newton gives an 80 percent likelihood is a "g". No word in the dictionary that starts with "iog," so it must have made a wrong turn someplace.

Worse yet, you haven't written anything else in a couple of seconds, or you placed the next letter pretty far away from the last one, both of which indicate to Newton that you've started a new word. So, Newton must do a final tally and give you what it thinks is the right word. It's stuck, painted into a recognition corner like a rat, a dirty, filthy, lice-ridden rat with nary a correct guess in its head (sorry, we got carried away). So, it shuffles through the dictionary, comes up with a final list of candidate words, and settles on "bog," because the "b" shape had a 60 percent likelihood for a match on your first letter and the word "bog" is in the dictionary and has, of all the other candidate words, the highest overall score.

This gives you a pretty good idea what Newton goes through every time you write a word on it. At any point in scoring a candidate word against what you've written, Newton can make a wrong turn and produce erroneous outcome. Unless you turn the dictionary off, when you enter a word Newton doesn't know you'll always get an incorrect result as it enforces its limited vocabulary upon your rich world of nouns, verbs, and adjectives. Not to mention adverbs and participles.

There are two tools available to help you work on recognition. One is Handwriting Practice in Preferences which asks you to write a word and shows you the recognizer's top five guesses for that word. You can see how close Newton came to guessing the right word by examining the scores, shown as percentages of its confidence in the match. All the words in Handwriting Practice come from Newton's built-in dictionary.

If you bought the MessagePad, you should have received a Getting Started card that contains another good handwriting trainer. Insert the card, open the Extras drawer and tap on the icon called "Game." Follow the instructions to play CalliGrapher, a Tetris-like game in which you must write a word correctly (it's really a game of cooperation between yourself and Newton's recognizers) before it reaches the bottom of the screen.

Both CalliGrapher and Handwriting Practice will do more to adapt your handwriting than they will Newton's. CalliGrapher especially will help you get the hang of writing fast and still get good results. (We've never made it past Level 2.)

One last thing about words. If you double-tap on a word, you'll get a word list which contains Newton's top five guesses, including an option to change the case of the first letter. Tapping on one of the alternate choices will replace what Newton guessed with the new candidate. You'll also get the ink form for the word on the pop-up list, which if you tap on it, will restore the ink. When you tap the keyboard icon, Newton selects the whole word and opens the keyboard.

When double-tapping on a word which precedes the last word you wrote by five words or more, you'll no longer have the option of restoring the ink. If it's twenty words or more behind, you'll no longer have the extended word list to chose from; just that word in lowercase or capitalized and the keyboard.

Newton will not accept words over twenty-five letters long. And the accuracy of recognition usually breaks down past twenty letters because Newton assumes you have finished the word and will translate, regardless of how many more letters you have to go. So, no Superkalifragilisticexpiealidocious on this PDA!

Newton does better translating longer words, which provide more strokes and shapes that it can use to divine the correct answer.

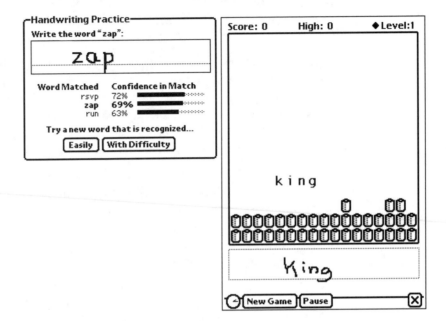

Figure 4.10 *Two ways to test your handwriting.*

Making Your Mark

Besides altering the weights of letter shapes in Letter Styles preferences, there are two other places you can go in Preferences to help customize Newton recognition to your style.

The first are the Recognizers settings, which you can get to without going through the Extras drawer by double-tapping on the text recognizer toggle (see Figure 4.11).

Your options here are:

Text Recognizer

Words in word lists. This is the default setting and means Newton will compare what you write to the dictionary and your personal word list. For best recognition results, leave this checked and leave the next item unchecked. (By the way, this is Reason Number Three why Newtons make lousy notepads. Who wants to take notes in a meeting where you have to worry if every word you write is in Newton's dictionary?)

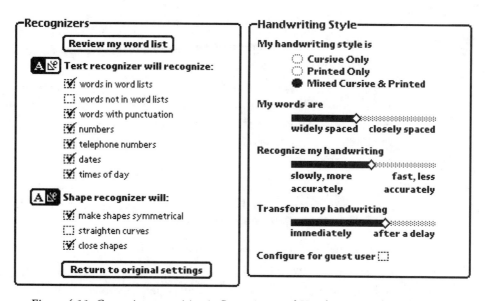

Figure 4.11 Customing recognition in Recognizers and Handwriting Style preferences.

Words not in word lists. This will let Newton recognize words based on letter shapes alone. While it avoids mistakes due to a word not being in the dictionary or personal word list, it also reduces accuracy considerably, since the recognizer has nothing to compare its translated shapes against when making words.

Words with punctuation. Newton will try to recognize symbols after words, like periods and commas. It also decreases accuracy slightly because the recognizer can occasionally mistake punctuation for a letter shape. (Really! I thought your "!" was an "i.")

Numbers. Enables number recognition. We can't imagine why you'd want your Newton recognizers to be ignorant of numbers. We guess Apple expects some users to enter numbers through the soft keypad exclusively.

Telephone numbers. Same as above, although we do find that Newton has a harder time with telephone numbers than it does with plain numbers. It can be hard to get it to recognize parenthesis or dashes between number clusters. You'll almost always have to add dashes separately and will probably have to delete a space or two as well.

Dates. This activates Newton's ability to recognize numbers in date formats. It does pick up dates expressed with slashes (e.g., 9/28/93) pretty well.

Times of day. Newton seems to grok time pretty well when it is expressed in an abbreviated format like 12:30 PM. Turning this off will help improve recognition slightly.

The "Off the deep end" configuration. If you uncheck everything but "words in word lists" you'll get the best possible results from the text recognizer. But, we don't feel the improvement in recognition is worth giving up numbers and punctuation.

Shapes Recognizer

Make shapes symmetrical. If you want the shapes recognizer to make your jaggy circles smooth, leave this checked.

Straighten curves. Makes curvy lines straight.

Close shapes. We'd leave this one checked. It means if you draw a square and your start and end points don't meet perfectly, Newton will fix it for you.

The other place to go to customize your handwriting settings is the Handwriting Styles preferences where you can modify Newton's recognition spacing and time-out parameters (see Figure 4.11).

Spaced out. Use the "My words are" slider to get Newton to properly separate one word from another. In general, you should write big, with capitals being twice the size of lowercase letters, and you should put wide spaces between your words. Newton doesn't use the size of the words you write to determine the size of text, so write as big as you want. Also, Newton will automatically bring words written one line below another word up next to that word when it recognizes it. So, feel free to spread out.

Slow hand. The "Recognize my handwriting" setting determines how long you're willing to wait before Newton gives you its final guess. The longer you give it, the better the results. But beware you don't slow Newton down so much that you write your fifth word before Newton finishes working on the first. Not only does this risk Newton learning the wrong shapes if that first word comes out wrong, you're likely to exceed the memory available for recognition with so many words being processed all at the same time.

Perfect timing. The "Transform my handwriting" setting controls how long before Newton "times-out" on a word. Setting it for longer delays gives you slightly more time between letters before Newton assumes you've finished writing that word. Just remember that writing too slowly can generate too much tablet noise and reduce the accuracy of recognition. And, like we said above, writing too fast is likely to give Newton a fit as it tries to deal with some much data. (Reason Number Four why Expert Pads and MessagePads make lousy notepads. You getting tired of these, yet? 'Cause we've got more!)

Keyboards and Dictionaries

So, what happens if you write a word Newton doesn't know? Well, just help your PDA expand its vocabulary.

There are three ways to add to your personal word list, which is an adjunct to the dictionary. First is by writing a word Newton doesn't know, double tapping the erroneous result to get the word list pop-up, and then tapping the keyboard.

Once you get the keyboard, type in the word you wanted. If the keyboard displays the message Add "XXXX" to word list? Then the word you typed is not in the dictionary. Tapping the "Yes" button adds the word to your list. Tapping "No" means that the word won't be added to the list (see Figure 4.12).

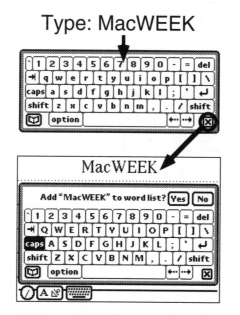

Figure 4.12 Adding a word to your personal word list from the keyboard.

The second method is to tap on the dictionary button on the lower left corner of the standard keyboard (see Figure 4.13). This calls up the Personal Word List manager. From here you can add as many words to your word list as you want and can examine and even remove words that you've already added.

Figure 4.13 One way to get to the Personal Word List manager.

You can also get the Personal Word List manager from the Recognizers preferences slip, which you can get to by double-tapping the Words recognizer toggle (see Figure 4.14).

There are two important things to keep in mind about adding to your personal word list. First, adding a lot of words will slow down your Newton's recognizer and will also decrease its accuracy. There are just too many words that will come up with the same score in the recognizer if you add the entire Random House unabridged dictionary to your Newton. Second, avoid adding short words (under five characters) that you don't use very often. Many short words look practically identical to the recognizer; there just isn't enough data there for it to distinguish one word from another.

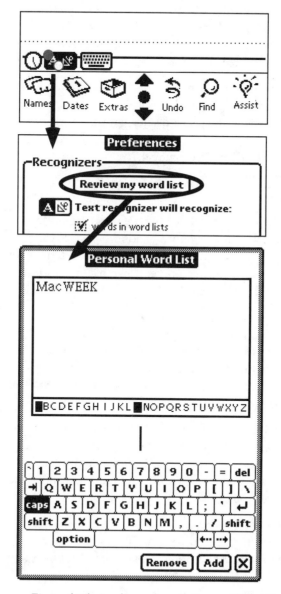

Figure 4.14 *Another path to the Personal Word List manager.*

Which brings us to the topic of rare and exotic words, like those foreign words with funny accent marks over the vowels. Newton does not recognize accented vowels and the like, unless you're using a foreign language recognizer. If you want to enter such words, you'll have to type them.

The good news is that, despite some reports in the press, you can type a veritable cornucopia of special symbols into your Newton that aren't supported by the recognizer. Please consult Figure 4.15 which contains a complete map of what keys to tap to get to what characters.

To get those special accented characters requires a couple of taps. First, tap the option key, and then select one of the four supported accent marks. Yet another keyboard map will display with the accents showing over the characters they'll appear with. Just tap the letter you want to get the exact right spelling of déjà vu (see Figure 4.16).

Recognizable Gestures

Unlike EO's PenPoint operating system, which supports some 50-plus gestures, in Newton there are only a handful of shapes you can draw to control everything from deleting to adding a new note to the Notepad. Unlike menu commands in most computer programs, most Newton gestures will work in any of the PDA's applications.

The first gesture you should get familiar with is for selecting objects. Just press the pen tip behind or in front of what you want to select and then, after you hear the "stepped-on mouse" sound (it's supposed to sound like a highlighter pen on a whiteboard), drag your pen across whatever you want to select. You should see a trail following the pen tip. What ever you selected will be highlighted.

You can select words, sentences, paragraphs, and objects. Drawing the selection trail around a group of objects, such as text and a drawing, will select all those objects. Drawing straight down through a couple of lines of text selects both lines. Drawing across and down at an angle ends the selection where ever you end the highlight (see Figure 4.17).

Once something is selected, you can do a number of things to it. For example, by placing the pen tip on one of the white dots, called handles, that appear when you select a graphic, you can break off lines or resize them by dragging.

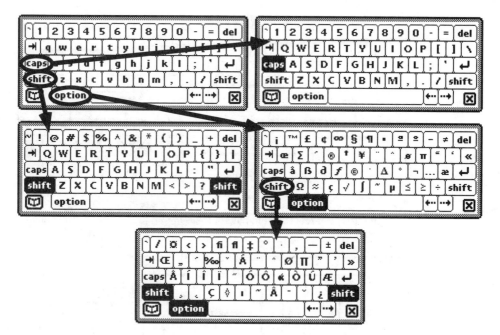

Figure 4.15 *How to get to all those funny-looking symbols.*

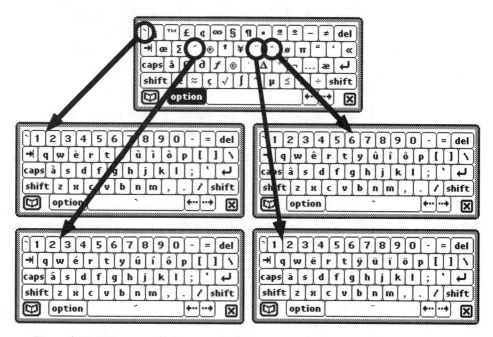

Figure 4.16 *How to get all those strange, foreign accents into your words.*

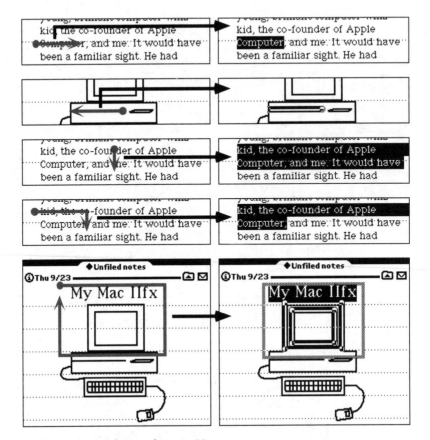

Figure 4.17 Selecting objects in Newton.

Practice makes perfect with the selection gesture. It can be especially difficult to get the selection to end on exactly the character you want.

The most often-used gesture in Newton is the "scrub-out" gesture. Just draw a sharply angled zig-zag (a "W" with too many jags) over what you want to remove and, if you've done it right, you should see the offending object disappear in a puff of smoke. You can scrub-out across or down. Just remember to have at least four lines in the scrub gesture.

For greater accuracy, select what you want to delete before trying to scrub it out (Figure 4.18). Also, you can scrub out individual letters in a word, although it takes some practice. Normally, you want the lines of your scrub-out gesture not to cross-over. However, to scrub out one character, start over the top of the character and draw straight down and up through it, careful not to run over other characters, at least five times.

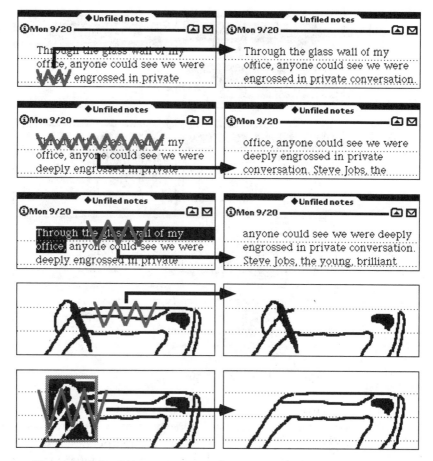

Figure 4.18 Scrubbing out your mistakes.

You can do more with the frame that surrounds multiple selected objects that just limit the effect of the scrub-out gesture. You can also grab (press the pen tip down on) the edges of the frame and resize or distort the shape of the image (see Figure 4.19). If it's a graphic object, you can grab one of the handles and change the shape of that part of the drawing.

If you put a selection frame around a block of text, taping the gray area will close up empty spaces between the letters. This will combine multiple paragraphs, for example. You can also grab and drag the frame to change the length and number of lines contained in the selection.

Having a hard time getting a block of text to behave? Try using a caret gesture to lead the text where you want it to go.

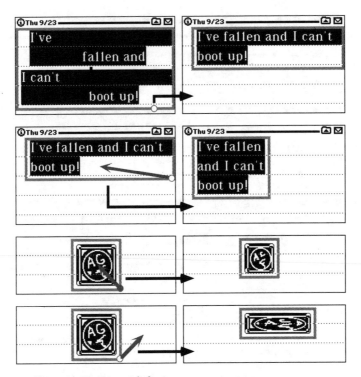

Figure 4.19 Fun with frames.

Five caret gestures can be used to break up text. In Figure 4.20 from top to bottom, they are the "add a single space" gesture, "add several spaces" gesture, "add a line" gesture, "add a couple of lines" gesture, and the "break up a paragraph" gesture. With the exception of the "add a single space" gesture, the amount of space or number of lines added will depend on where you end the stroke.

Always write caret gestures with a single, quick stroke, or they won't register with the recognizer.

Figure 4.21 contains a few odds and ends, gesture-wise. To correct a single letter just write the letter you want over it. This may require some practice. (Yeah, we know it's not really a gesture, but we though it fit here anyway.)

Draw a single straight line up through the first letter of a selected word to capitalize that letter. You must start below the letter and go through only that letter for this gesture to work. To capitalize all the letters in the entire selection, draw the same gesture up through any other part of the selection but the first letter.

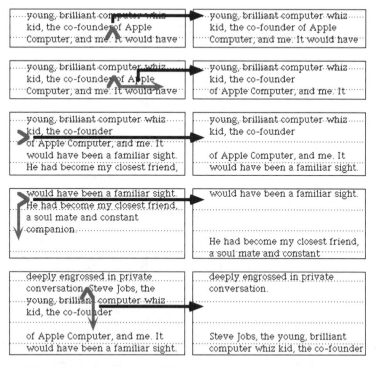

Figure 4.20 *A Caret is good for your sight.*

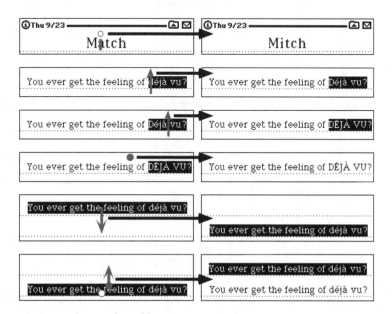

Figure 4.21 *A few odd gestures.*

To deselect something, tap anywhere on the screen but on the selection. To move a selection around the screen, put your pen tip on it and drag. To copy a selection, tap on it and then immediately press on the selection again and drag the copy away. It's like a double-tap, only you don't lift the pen up after the second tap.

We've already covered all the things you can do by double tapping elsewhere in this book; Figure 4.22 contains a quick review.

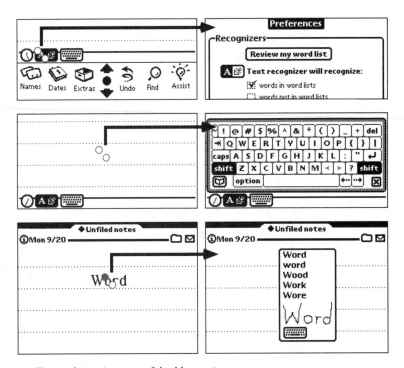

Figure 4.22 A review of double-tapping.

Figure 4.23 Behind bars.

To get a new note separator bar, place the pen tip on one side of the screen and draw a straight line across to the other. After a moment a new note should appear. To lengthen or shorten the note, put your pen tip down anywhere on the bar below the note (the next note's bar) and drag it up or down until the correct amount of space is displayed. This may require scrolling with the up or down arrows. You cannot drag one separator bar over another (see Figure 4.23).

You're Results May Still Vary

Despite your best efforts and even if you follow every guideline in this chapter and have the best handwriting for Newton there is, the fact is there are still going to be times when Newton will screw up and give you the wrong result.

All we can say is that Newton contains the best of 21st Century handwriting technology. Unfortunately, that makes it about a decade undercooked. It is the best on the market, and following the suggestions we've outlined above, it's not unreasonable for you to get from 75 to 90 percent accuracy on a regular basis.

It is the Zen of Recognition that we strive for perfection and are prepared for mistakes. Set your expectations accordingly, and we think you'll find Newton recognition quite serviceable.

After all, if things really go bad, you can follow John Sculley's advice and use the software keyboard to enter text during meetings (we think not!)

Get Info...Avoiding Recognition

Like we've said again and again, MessagePads make lousy notepads, regardless of what the Apple Newton ads have to say about it. Newton recognition just isn't up to the task. As we went to press, Newton users were faced with a choice between editing incorrectly translated words or leaving notes in untranslated ink format forever.   *(continued)*

Get Info...Avoiding Recognition (continued)

If you use the recognizer there's little hope of keeping up with a conversation while taking notes with any accuracy. It's a better idea to take notes in untranslated ink, synchronize your Newton using the Mac or PC Connection software, then open the notes and type keywords beside important passages. Now, synchronize again to reinstall the notes, which you can search with Find or Assist using the typed keywords. (You can enter keywords with the pen as well, it just takes longer.)

But, there is a drawback to ink. A word rendered in untranslated ink takes up more memory than translated text. Unless you have several spare PCMCIA RAM cards, ink is an uneconomical format for your notes.

A solution is on the horizon. Deferred recognition is a "write now, recognize later" scheme that lets you take all your notes in ink and translate the ink to text when you have more time for editing. This scheme requires more RAM than the bare-bones MessagePad has available, because it saves a record of the strokes and their patterns that you used to make each letter. In essence, the deferred recognizer can play back your input, watch the record of strokes and decide what you intended to put into text.

That capability will be available for inclusion in the second generation Newtons, due out in early 1994. It remains to be seen whether Apple will turn deferred recognition capabilities on in these models. The company may opt for another technology it is developing called "searchable ink." Searchable ink lets you do Finds on handwritten notes as if they were text. This way, there's no messy recognition you need to play with, just enter what you want in the Find dialog and Newton will ferret out the appropriate note, even if you recorded it in ink.

Who knows? Maybe Apple will combine both deferred recognition and searchable ink in a future Newton design. If this happens you could finally buy a Newton that would make a good notepad!

CHAPTER

5

NEWTON 101

Your Newton comes with three applications built into the ROM that will define how you collect, search, and disperse data (at least until you start loading up with third-party alternatives). Plenty of good information is served up in your MessagePad or Expert Pad manual about how to put the Notepad, Names, and Dates applications to good use; all it's missing are a little advice on how best to put these applications to work for you. And how to avoid a few pitfalls along the way.

Since the rest of this book talks about how to get information into and out of these applications effectively, we're going to focus on the practical issues and useful tips that will take your day-to-day Newton usage to a higher level. We'll look at the numbskull stuff, the booby-traps and aggravating details you won't get from a careful perusal of the manuals.

Before we jump in, here are the Chapters you need to turn to if you have specific questions about:

- The Newton architecture: Chapter One—*Software for the Common Man.*

- Networking and the technology behind the Action button: Chapter Three—*The Invisible World.*

- Handwriting, gestures, and editing: Chapter Four—*The Written Word.*

- Folders, Find, and Assist: Chapter Six—*Info Surfing.*

- Newton Connection: Chapter Eight—*Ready, Set, Load!* and Chapter Nine—*The Information Sculptor.*

- Printing, faxing, and electronic mail: Chapter Ten—*In the Out Door and Back In, Again.*

Everything in this chapter ties in somewhere else, and in some sense, it's an exercise in fulfilling obligations to traditional how-to book structure to cover these applications in isolation.

Taking Note

Your first real taste of using Newton probably happened in the Notepad. We've stood and watched a hundred times now: The buyer approaches the Newton with a certain hunger, a need really, to be understood. Pen clutched in hand, they wonder if what Mrs. Stephenson said in Second Grade was true. Is penmanship their great weakness? "You'll never make sense to anyone," Mrs. Stephenson lectured, "if you don't make an effort to produce a crisp 'C' and an equally well-defined 'd', not to mention the rest of the alphabet. Now, practice!"

Mrs. Stephenson is gone, pushing up daisies, but she convinced a lot of people that no one, not even a machine trained to recognize handwriting, will ever be able to read their writing. Hands shaking, the newcomer writes: "My name is...." The dialog begins, even if it get off to a rocky start.

But what can you do with a sentence once you get it on the electronic page of your Newton?

Well, you can organize it in relation to all the other sentences, notes and drawings you've scribbled into Newton. If the Newton lifestyle is a high-flying one, then the Notepad is life's holding pattern. Here is where you make sense of things, even if you have to use the keyboard an awful lot.

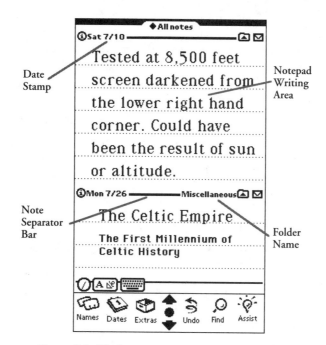

Figure 5.1 The keys to organization are in your hand.

Notes are arranged by when you added them. If Newton does nothing else, it preserves the order in which you have your ideas. After a few months, you should be able to tap the Overview button to see the genesis of several concepts, from a note to a memo to a full-blown plan.

Every note, in fact every object in Newton, is given a time stamp at the moment it is created. In the Notepad, you'll see only the day and date in the upper left hand corner (If you tap the Get Info button, you can see the time as well). You can also see the whole time stamp for a note after you send it to the Out Box, where it is listed by the date and time it was created —not the time when you sent it.

Time stamps work a strict regimen. If your Newton is shut down completely or you perform a cold boot, it will wake up at the beginning of 1993 (this could change from model to model, as more Newtons are introduced). Now, when you open the Notepad, you'll see that the first note is "Fri 1/1." Even items on your storage card that were created before your Newton was rebooted appear below this out-of-whack note, because Newton believes the 1/1 note was created first. All it looks at is the date.

If you have other notes, you can delete the 1/1 note, but if it's the only note in your Newton, it's not going to budge. Newton always keeps one note as a placeholder for the Notepad. You must open Time and Date Preferences and correct the time and date, then return to the Notepad, draw a line across the screen below the 1/1 note to create a new note with the correct date. The 1/1 note can be deleted now, because it's not the only note anymore.

So, what happens if your Newton does wake from a cold boot and finds itself full of notes that, according to the time stamps, were created sometime in the distant future? Newton thinks it is January 1, but all the notes on the installed PCMCIA card were created in September and October. Because Newton is always trying maintain order, if you try to add a note after the last note in the scroll—say it is dated 11/3, the real date—your messed up clock will make Newton move the new note right to the top of the queue. After all, you're trying to put a note created in January (the date Newton defaulted to) after October.

Some folks who'd had this experience described their notes "hopping up the page." If your notes make like frogs, check the Time and Date Preferences to see if your Newton's system clock has fallen behind.

The Glorious Form Nation

As we've said elsewhere, the best use of a Newton is as a trap for a lot of critical details. Applications like Names come with a structure that invites these important facts in. You have to do the same with the Notepad, if you want to make using Newton as efficient as possible.

Learn to use form letters. Come up with several forms that satisfy the majority of your typical correspondence with only a few changes, like the salutation and the address of the person to whom you are sending it. Now, create a folder that holds these form letters and categorize them so that you can open the folder and tap the Overview button to see the list of subjects. (We know this breaks the "don't create a one-application folder" rule discussed in the next chapter. But, if you want to use form letters, it's okay to create a folder just for these notes. We won't tell.)

This is a good example of what we're talking about when we discussed the critical detail: Your job probably consists of a lot of tasks you do routinely, and a small portion of time for a novelty, like thinking. Cut the time it takes to do your standard correspondence and you'll have more time for making the world a better place.

Begin by identifying those mundane communications and spend the time to write standard replies. Are you going to offend people if you happen to send them the same letter twice (this kind of guilt drives ordinary people to purple prose—there's very little originality in letters that are designed to be original). No, you're going to show them that you've got more important things to do. Stop paying tribute to bad habits and poor thinking, reward intelligent correspondence with a stimulating letter. Send forms to everyone else, so you've got the time to do the interesting writing.

When you send a form as a letter, Newton asks you to address the document. Write the addressee's name in the print or fax addressing slip, the information then flows into the address area of the letter. All you need to do to personalize—in that standardized corporate America way—is to place the person's name in the body of the letter (i.e., "Dear John....").

Assist... Is that ink on your fingers?

The Newton commercials running on The Late Show with David Letterman and other hip teevee give the impression that you can take notes on Newton while gunfire is breaking branches overhead, or even in a moment of passion. And you can, but only if you leave the recognizers off and work in ink mode.   *(continued)*

Assist... Is that ink on your fingers? (continued)

Ink doesn't lend itself to organization. When you tap the Overview button in the Notepad, ink documents are listed as a series of triangles (we suppose they're called "Isocellipses"). That's not the kind of heading that tells you what the note contains.

Adding keywords to an ink document after you are done taking a note is the best way to track the contents of these documents. Any text in an ink note, even if it is last thing on the scroll, will appear in the overview. Moreover, adding keywords to the ink lets you search for individual passages from anywhere in the Newton interface. Go through your notes and add a translated word that describes a paragraph, for example, it will grease the skids when you need to add that information to a plan for an upcoming project.

You can even go through notes in Newton Connection's Notepad application. When working on a PC or Mac, you can type the annotations very quickly.

For more on keywords, see Chapter Six—*Info Surfing*.

Moving notes within a single folder is impossible, since all the notes will be arranged by time stamp.

There are two ways to handle moving a note:

- **Place it in a folder.** This isn't rearranging the time-based organization (even in a folder, notes are ordered by time stamp), it's a thematic system of organizing information. See Chapter Six—*Info Surfing* for more.

- **Use the Transporter.** Highlight the text or ink you want to move, tap and drag the object to the side of the screen or double-tap and drag to copy the data, then go to the bottom of the scroll and create a new note. Drag the text from the Transporter into the new note. The information now appears under a different time stamp.

You can lengthen the writing space in an existing note by grabbing the separator bar below the note and dragging downward. Remember, however, that the absolute limit on note length is 4000 bytes.

From Order Comes Chaos

A final note on notes. Newton assumes when you input text that you are entering it as part of a single paragraph. Even if you write a new word a line below the last word you entered, the Notepad will usually bring the new word up next to the preceding text. If there isn't enough room at the end of the line for the new word, Newton will place it one line below that line. Any additional words you add will then go next to that word, until there isn't any room left on the new line. This is called word-wrapping.

The important thing to remember about word-wrapping is that Newton still treats the collection of words as if they were part of one line. Word-wrapping is only done so you don't lose sight of words off the end of the screen. That's why, if you take a note and print or fax it out using the letter format, what comprised several lines in the Notepad might only form one line in the printed letter.

To see how this works, just write a few sentences in a note. Select the block of text (it should be several lines long), open the Extras drawer and tap Styles. Once the Styles dialog box is open, close the Extras drawer.

Now, change the font size by selecting either a higher or lower number in Styles. The current size of the type you've selected will have a blackened radio button next to it. For example, if the selected text is 18 point, change the font size to 12 or 10 point. Once you've done that, close the Styles box.

If you reduced the font size, Newton will reformat the paragraph so that it takes up fewer lines on the screen. If you've enlarged the text, it'll take up more lines.

Let's say you're making a list and don't want Newton to reformat the lines. There are a couple of things you can do to stop it. First, you can select the text and drag it down more than one line below the bottom of the paragraph. This should force Newton to treat the text as a new paragraph. If that doesn't work the first time, try again. It can be hard to get the message across to Newton that you don't want it to clean up your "mistakes".

You can also open the keyboard and put the text insertion point in front of the text you want to separate (just tap in front of the text). Then, tap the return key (the key with the bent, left-pointing arrow on it) to be sure Newton knows you want the line separated. An add-a-line caret gesture will do the job as well, although it might add more than one line. For precision text editing, the keyboard is your most effective tool.

If getting Newton to break up lines is difficult, centering text on the screen or placing labels on drawings can drive you batty. The best advice is to try selecting the label or title you want to place and drag it far away from any preceding text. Newton should get the point that you want this to be a separate text object. Now, drag the text where you want it. Watch for the flashing, vertical insertion line. The line will indicate where Newton will place the text. For example, if the line appears in front of another word, Newton will place the selection in front of that word.

If all else fails, go to the keyboard, put the insertion point in front of the text you want to move, and add tabs or a bunch of blank spaces until Newton moves the text where you want it.

Your Little Black Book

You'll spend a lot of time in the Names application. It only makes sense. One of the most data intensive jobs anyone has is management of their contacts. Luckily, Newton makes it easy. It also makes getting the name you want when you want it simpler than it's ever been before.

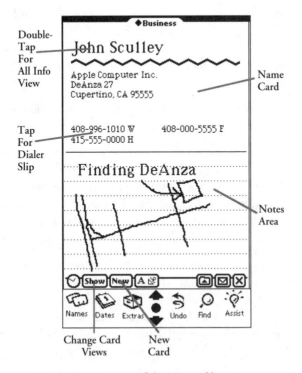

Figure 5.2 Anatomy of the Names file.

The basic component of the Names file is the name card which holds information about an individual or company. Newton offers only one form for people, places, and institutions. Whether it's a card identifying your best friend, your favorite restaurant, or your health plan, the options are the same.

A name card can contain first name, last name, a salutation like Mr. or Ms., title, company name, a two-line address, city, state, ZIP Code, country, e-mail address, birthday, and up to four different phone numbers (you get to pick from a list of eight types from home to mobile, just tap the list diamond above the field where you enter the number). You can also pick from four card styles which will change the look of the card—we're sure there's a booming market in custom card templates just over the horizon (see Figure 5.3). To enter information about a new contact, open the Names file and tap "New"; this will open the All Info view of a blank card. If you want to modify an existing card's data, first locate the card and then tap the "Show" button. Pick "All Info" from the list; this will display the same full screen form you used to create a new card, except the fields will already be filled in.

Figure 5.3 *Four looks for your name cards.*

If you double-tap the name on a name card in either the Card or Card & Notes view, Newton will immediately take you to the All Info view of that card.

By the way, when you fill in the phone fields, if you leave the first field blank, Newton will move the next phone number up to that position automatically after you leave the All Info view of the card.

If you want to add notes to a card, perhaps a map or list of personal information about a business associate, tap the Show button and select Card & Notes. This will call up a front-and-back view of a card. The top half is the front of the card and will look like what you see in the Card view. The bottom half, the "back of the card," however, will look more like a page torn out of the Notepad. Draw and write here to annotate a card. Whatever you add will stay with the card and can be searched with the Find command, as long as it is text.

The back of the card is an excellent place to attach keywords to people. For example, you can write the name of a project on the backs of the cards for each team member. Even if they are stored in many folders, when you do a system-wide search (tap All in the Find slip) the team members will appear in the overview with documents associated with the project.

The back of the card is fixed in size, it will hold only as much information as fits in a card-sized note (you can use smaller font sizes to squeeze in more notes). Items pasted onto the back of a card must not exceed the borders of the field.

Once you've added enough names to the Names file, you may want to try out the different methods available for surfing through the cards. Your primary tool for scanning the Names file is the overview button. When you tap it, a window will open up that lists all the name cards in the currently selected folder alphabetically (see Figure 5.4). Tap the scroll arrows to move through the list or use the letter index at the bottom of the screen. If you've got a lot of names and want the largest possible view, put Names in the Card & Notes or All Info views before tapping the overview button. The result will be a list of names that fills the entire Newton screen.

Once you've located the name you want in an overview, tap it to display the card. If all you want to do is dial the phone, tap the phone number to open a dialer slip with the number (think how useful this'll be when you can get a Newton built into a telephone).

Tapping the phone number on the Card or Card & Notes view will also display a dialer slip with the number you selected displayed in the phone field. If the number you tapped isn't what you were looking for, tap the list diamond to select another number for that card. Newton will not open a fax slip if you tap the fax number on a card. You must use the Action button to send a fax from the Names file.

Besides using the overview window, you can also flip through your cards by tapping the scroll arrows in any of the three primary card views.

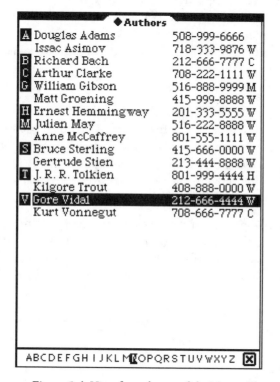

Figure 5.4 View from the top of the Names file.

Assist... Alphabet Soup

The overview window displays cards either by the last name field or by company. Depending on which you've selected in the "List By" pop-up, you'll either see the company name or the person's full name plus the first phone number of the four Newton can store.

Unless you've changed the "List By" field in the All Info view of your cards, Newton will list name cards alphabetically by last name (if there is no last name, it will default to the company name). This is a good thing. Because if you set your name cards to list by company name, you wouldn't be able to see any of your contacts names in the overview list.

And, if you have several people who work for the same company, you won't be able to tell one from another in the overview window, unless you recognize their number from memory. We recommend that you avoid the List By Company option, unless the card in question is for the company itself, not for an individual who works there.

You can change the List By setting for any card any time you want by selecting the All Info view and tapping List By. Just remember that the change only effects the card you're working on. All other cards will continue to be listed by whatever method you've set for them.

Too Much of a Good Thing?

In our tests we found that Newton worked fine with as many as 500 names in the Names file, more than enough for the average user. It may well have been able to support more, we just didn't have the patience to manually add more names (Newton Connection 2.0 hadn't shipped by the time we went to press).

However, there were problems with such a large data soup. When we went to change folders, the whole system would lock for up to a couple of minutes while Newton sorted out the soup (for more on folder lock, see Chapter Six—*Info Surfing*). The only way to avoid this problem was not to change folders, not a very practical solution.

We recommend limiting your Names file to about 200 cards if you think you're going to be swapping folders a lot. But, if you're like most people, you can spend most of your time in the All Cards view of the Names file without much trauma. Use folders only to help sort out large groups of contacts, like keeping the cards of colleagues in your office in a "Company" folder. This way, when you want to work with a particular group, you can select that folder, get a cup of coffee while Newton deals with switching folders, and come back to work with the data.

To assign a card to a particular folder, find the card and tap the Folder button at the bottom of the screen. Select the new folder and tap the File button. If you want to move a large number of cards to a new folder, we recommend you use the Find command to sort out the list and reassign the cards.

Here's Looking For You

Any application can query the Names file soup for information. Currently, the only ones that do are the various dialer slips. This means when you add a name to an appointment, it's a separate piece of data, even though that information may already exist somewhere else.

The disadvantage of this is you can't simply tap a name in the calendar to gain access to that person's name card. You must exit the calendar and enter the Names file to locate the card (you can do this from the calendar using the Find All command, but you still need to enter the name in the Find slip).

Other personal information managers (PIMs) allow users to do this simple trick. In fact, the AT&T EO Personal Communicators come bundled with an application called Perspective that let's you do this with relative ease. All you have to do is tap any name that appears on the EO in a bold font to display that person's profile.

We hope this shortcoming is addressed in future versions of the Names file. What's the use of having a dynamic data architecture like Newton's if it doesn't let you fly where you want as quickly as you can?

Dates. They were awkward in High School, too

Newton's calendar leaves something to be desired. There seem to be more holes in this application than in any other. In fairness, a calendar must be extremely flexible to satisfy everyone and is therefore destined to disappoint sometimes. Actually, considering Apple's track record in creating application software, we're surprised the calendar is as good as it is.

Dates, the application you use to control calendar functions, layers two functions that are time-based, one on top of the other. Appointments and To Do items are tied to particular dates and times, but they mean something very different to you. An appointment is an obligation to be in a location, to meet people, at a certain time—that can be a phone call or a flight to Denver. A To Do, on the other hand, is a commitment to yourself that you will complete a project or perform a task by a certain date; it is not tied so closely to the clock as an appointment.

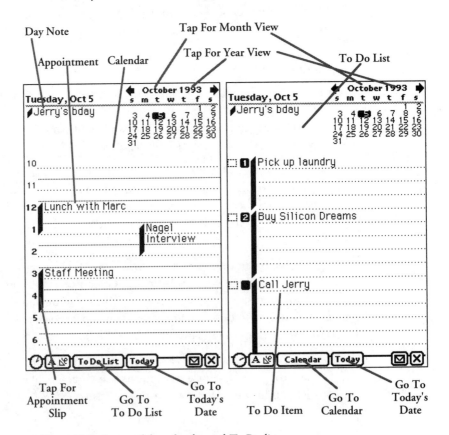

Figure 5.5 A tour of the calander and To Do list.

Yet they co-exist in the Dates interface. The conflict showed in several bugs in early versions of the application. We're hoping these are all fixed by the time you read this. But, just in case:

- If Newton went to sleep while the Dates application was open, it would not wake to display or sound an alarm.

- To Do items would disappear temporarily if the To Do page was left open when Newton went to sleep over night. The change in date caused the problem. In the morning the previous day's date would still be displayed, and no To Dos. Closing Dates and opening it again refreshes the To Dos, and items reappear when you turn back to the To Do page.

- Repeating calendar items reproduced like cats in an old warehouse. Setting a meeting to be repeated every Wednesday, for instance, caused Newton to replicate the item on every Wednesday before and after the date you entered the appointment the first time.

Assist... 'Lapping the leader

The calendar lets you set up conflicting appointments. Open Dates to the day that you want to schedule and draw a vertical line to the right of the first appointment, the line will turn into an item bar which you can tap to open an appointment slip. Fill in the slip, add alarms, or make it a repeating event, and close it. The second meeting will appear as an overlapping item in the calendar.

You can also drag an appointment into conflict with another meeting by tapping and dragging the item bar to the right of the first meeting in the time slot.

The Assistant will automatically place conflicting appointments to the right of the original appointment. However, it doesn't warn you that you have created a conflict. It's always a good idea to look carefully at the calendar when you've let the Assistant do the walking.

To Do items have confounded quite a few people, because they are difficult to delete after you complete them. Just as you can't delete the only note in the Notepad, you can't delete the last To Do on your list. The secret is to draw a horizontal line through the item bar, which forces Newton to create a second, empty To Do. Now you can use a vertical scrub-out (a "W" turned on its side) to wipe out the offending To Do; the empty To-Do will fill in the space that held your last item. Another way to remove an obstinate To Do is to first scrub out the text, and then try scrubbing the bar.

When a lot of To Dos have piled up in your calendar, you can turn to the To Do page and tap the Action button and select Delete. A dialog headlined "Delete To Do items older than 30 days" will appear. You can change the number of days, then tap Delete. A second dialog will open asking if you are sure you want to permanently delete items. Remember, unchecked To Dos follow you through the days like a lost puppy. And you can't delete them no matter what number of days back you set the delete command. You must check a to-do before Newton will remove it.

Could you repeat that?

Repeating meetings are set up in the appointment slip that you can acess by tapping the heavy black item bar next to the title of meeting. Tap the Frequency button; the slip that opens gives you several choices:

- **Don't repeat.** Then why did you tap Frequency?

- **Every week.** This option also enables days-of-the-week buttons on the right side of this slip, which you can tap to add specific days on which you want this appointment to repeat. Make sure you indicate a termination date for this repeating meeting in the "No Meetings After" field at the bottom of the slip.

- **Every other week.** Again, you can select the particular days of the week for repeating appointments.

- **Every month.** This button opens a month-long calendar in which you can select only one date. If you want to schedule the meeting more often than once a month, you must use the "every week" or "every other week" buttons.

- **Every year.** The month-calendar now appears with a month list diamond that lets you select on what date each year you want to repeat the appointment.

- **Week in month.** You can select a single day of the week and repeat the meeting during as many weeks of the month as you like. Just use check boxes on the right side of the slip for the first second, third, fourth, and last week.

If you are taking a trip to Minnesota on the third weekend in December and want to schedule the trip in a single appointment slip, follow these instructions (this process assumes that the repeating meetings bug mentioned above has been solved):

1. Write Minnesota in the calendar for the day of December 17.

2. Tap open the appointment slip and change the times from 12:01 AM to 11:59 PM.

3. Tap the Frequency button. Tap the "Every week" button.

4. Tap the Friday, Saturday, and Sunday buttons in the days-of-the-week palette.

5. Write "12/20/93" in the "No meetings after" field. This terminates the repeating meeting the following Monday. You've just blocked out the whole three days for your trip.

Repeating meetings come with a serious limitation. The notes slip attached to an appointment is static. If you repeat a meeting, the notes field is shared by all the appointments. You cannot make notes about a single meeting without those notes being attached to all the instances of that meeting. Apple should change this soon.

Deleting a repeating meeting is relatively easy. If you select the Delete option in the Action button list for any instance of the meeting, Newton opens a dialog asking whether you want to delete the single appointment or all the meetings.

Views of the day, week, and month

Getting a view on your schedule is as easy as tapping and dragging your pen over the days you want to see in the month calendar at the top of the screen. The only rule is that the days must be horizontally or vertically contiguous.

Selected days, as when you highlight Monday through Thursday, break out in the calendar or To-Do page of the Date application. If you want to view an entire month, tap the name of the month in the calendar above the scheduling pad; for a look at eight months, tap the year in the calendar.

You can also use the overview button to call up a list of appointments and their attached titles. Unfortunately, the overview button will only display that week's agenda.

Assist... Goals and special events

The blank field at the top left corner of the Dates application can serve as a designated location for special events, also called a day note.

To add a special event, write the name in the blank region of the calendar or double-tap to open a keyboard in which you can enter the name. Tap the item bar to add notes to the special event. As long as the item is in the blank region, you cannot attach a time to the slip; the times will be erased when you close the slip. You can, however, drag a special event appointment into the calendar and times will be appended automatically.

CHAPTER
6

INFO SURFING

It may seem strange that a chapter focused on Newton's tools for information surfing would be one of the shortest in this book. But, if you think about, it does make sense. The whole concept of information surfing is to make it easy for you to find what you're looking for. If the facilities for scanning and commanding your Newton needed lengthy explanation, they wouldn't be all that useful for quick access to critical facts.

The three facilities for info surfing in the first Newtons are admirably succinct and functional. Folders, Find, and Assist may seem somewhat limited in their scope, not the much-ballyhooed harbingers of hands-off computing able to leap tall data sets in a single bound, but they are more than adequate. Once data is in Newton, you'll spend a lot of time on Folders, Find, and Assist.

Now A Word From Our Concept

Here are a few guidelines for the budding information surfers out there. Remember, it's okay to try these stunts at home.

Start Making Sense. Newton is not a ready-made fulfillment of all your information needs, but neither is a personal computer nor a subscription to the *New York Times*. Newton's memory is too confined to hold a lifetime's worth of information, the 2 MB Flash RAM card will only hold as much data as a few day's worth of daily newspaper text. And even the meanest information surfer won't find data not loaded into their Newton.

There's an old saying in the computer industry: Garbage In, Garbage Out. (Hard to believe the computer industry's been around long enough to have any old sayings.) If data was disorganized to begin with, Newton isn't going to fix it. Get your house in order before laying the burden of a disorganized life at Newton's doorstep.

Keep in mind that information will gain significance only if it lends itself to Newton's ability to quickly access small bits of data. Phone numbers, lists, appointments, short messages, and to-dos are all things Newton can grind like a surfer in the curl of a good wave. If it's not something you need at your fingertips, don't waste Newton RAM on it. Pack rats need not apply.

I'm Fixing A Hole. They said it on *This Old House* and we'll say it here: Always choose the right tool for the job. Don't frustrate yourself trying to use Newton to write down voice mail messages while listening to them play. Write the messages on a scrap of paper, then transcribe the important stuff to Newton, where you'll be able to use it later. Every information act is also an editorial act. Slash and burn to get to the kernel of valuable information you need.

Mexican Radio. Context is everything! Information is worthless without the background necessary to comprehend it. You wouldn't record a news broadcast in a language you don't understand, and you don't want to fill Newton with cryptic notes which turn out to be little better than intercepted enemy codes. If you don't package important items with enough information for you to recall what it means days, or weeks, later, it's just more static. Even a critical detail becomes meaningless without the proper context.

Dancin' With Yourself. This is your *Personal* Digital Assistant. When organizing Newton data, the only rules you have to follow are your own. Some of the best reporters we know use special shorthand when taking notes, so, should their notebook ever get stolen, the information in it would be worthless to the thief.

The Long and Winding Road. Sometimes it pays to play it safe, and because five RAM cards would barely fill a pocket, take along the data you'll need on a trip. Don't cut out important data from your view of the world. If you're not sure you'll need it, take it. There's nothing worse than being on a long trip and getting caught without the information you need to get the job done. As long as you've exercised editorial discretion when entering data, the bulk you carry on the road will pay off.

The most important rule of information surfing is Keep It Simple! There's nothing that says you have to use the Assistant to make a phone call. If you'd like to, just dial the number yourself. You won't be betraying the revolution, no matter what Apple's advertising says (when we give in to using a machine for the machine's sake, all will be lost). If it's easier to just go to the To Do List and write in "buy flowers for the wife" than it is to write "Remember to buy flowers for the wife" in the Notepad and tap Assist, then do it that way. Guard your sanity first, employ cool technology second.

Folders—Newton's Little Helpers

It makes sense in an architecture like Newton's which thrives on chaos that the ability to impose order would be somewhat limited.

The first Newtons provide only one method for collecting data into groups for easier browsing: Folders. Newton folders can contain only two kinds of records, notes and name cards. Unfortunately, you can't file calendar items (although you can use keywords to help organize them).

In contrast to the folders you see in the Macintosh Finder or Windows Program Manager, which collect files in a hierarchical location on a single disk drive, Newton folders merely point to records in the data soup, records that can reside in internal RAM or on a PCMCIA card. Records stored on a PCMCIA card are visible only when the card is in your Newton; a triangle appears on the folder icon of records stored on a card. Records are quickly re-integrated into a folder after a card is reinserted. There's none of this Mac-like dragging and dropping a file into a folder, thus making it a resident of that folder, the contents of which are all contained on a certain disk. With Newton you simply assign a record to a folder, where ever it is.

Unfiled notes and names live in a catch-all folder which holds the pointers to records that have not been defined by the Newton user (see Figure 6.1). There's no analogous categorization on the Mac or PC, where an undefined file would float away into memory, never to be found again.

The advantage of having pointers to records instead of physically tying records to a folder is that, if the folder goes away, you're data remains intact. If you delete a folder in your Macintosh, all the files in that folder are deleted as well. Newton guards your data as tenaciously as a bear defends a fresh kill.

It's probably easier to understand how folders work if you think of the folder as a particular view of your data, the folder tab just tells you what view you're looking at. When you move a record from one folder to another, it will seem to vanish. It hasn't, rather it has just been moved to another view, one your not looking at.

For example, suppose you where to name your folders after U.S. states. You could put all your notes and cards related to California in the California folder, all your records for New York in that state's folder, and so on down to the Arkansas folder.

Now, just think of the states. Imagine that your Newton's screen is a window in a space shuttle through which you can see an entire state, one state at a time. When you select the California folder in the Notepad, it's as if the shuttle has changed its orbit to an aspect that allows only a view of the Golden State. Tapping the overview button or scrolling up and down will yield only records in the California folder. New York's not gone, the trajectory of the shuttle has just put it beyond the horizon.

Selecting the All Notes or All Names view, the bottom-most choice on the pop-up list that appears when you tap the folder tab, is like powering your shuttle into a much higher orbit that allows you to take in a view of the entire U. S.. The "All" option lets you see all your data in a particular application, regardless of what folder it is filed in.

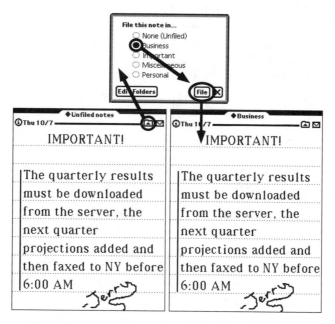

Figure 6.1 Putting a note away in the Business folder.

Records lay where they're dropped. So, if you're working in the Business folder, any notes or names you create will automatically become part of that folder's collection of records. Items end up in the Unfiled folder if that's where you happen to be operating at the time you created the item or if you were in the "All" view of your data (this shows all the records in that application). Unfortunately, this can't be said of Newton Connection—when you create new records, the application assumes they are Unfiled unless you tell it otherwise.

You can set up a total of 12 folders, not including the "Unfiled" folder. Newton comes with four predefined folders—Business, Important, Miscellaneous, and Personal (Newton lists folder names alphabetically, by the way). You can change the folders' names by tapping the "Edit Folders" dialog (see Figure 6.2) and writing in new titles. If you want to check which folder you're working in, look at the folder tab at the top of the screen.

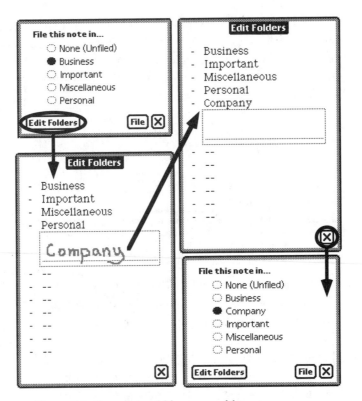

Figure 6.2 Customizing folders to your liking.

Assist...Internal Folders

Inside its paltry 192 Kbytes of internal RAM set aside for storing data, you Newton can store approximately:

- 475 calendar appointments of up to 20 characters each; or

- 235 name cards; or

- 190 notes of up to 50 characters each; or

- 76 screens worth of notes and drawings in untranslated ink.

(continued)

Assist...Internal Folders (continued)

This may not sound like a lot of data, but considering how little RAM Newton's got, it's a wonder it can squeeze in that much.

Most folks will grow tired of deleting records to open up space in Newton's main memory. They'll opt for one or more external PCMCIA RAM cards to hold the majority of their records. A 2-Mbyte Flash RAM card, for example, can hold over 10 times more data than Newton can store in internal RAM. That's 5,000 calendar items, 2,500 name cards and 2,000 notes containing 50 characters; more than enough for even the most compulsive scribbler.

The problem is, once you start loading data onto storage cards and into internal RAM, it can become difficult to sort out just what is stored where—until you eject the RAM card. Working with multiple cards can be an incredible headache, just think for a moment about how difficult it is to catalog data on floppy disks (it hasn't been very long since the floppy was the only digital backup storage medium available, unless you call standard cassette tapes storage).

Keep track of Important Stuff in the trackless depths Newton storage by separating the most important information both physically and logically from the rest of your data. Create a special folder where you'll store items that reside in internal RAM. Anytime you create a note or name card that you always want to have at your fingertips, place it in the Internal folder. Just remember to uncheck the "Store new items on card" box on the PCMCIA card dialog slip before creating the item. Tap the Card utility in the Extras drawer to switch off automatic saving of items to the card.

If you're ever unsure whether everything you need is stored in the internal RAM, just switch to the Internal folder and tap the overview button. Then scroll through the files to make sure you haven't accidentally put a storage card-based record in the Internal folder—just look for the telltale black triangle in the Folder icon. When you find one of these PCMCIA defectors, tap the Action button and select "Move from card" to place the record into Newton's internal RAM.

Organizing Your Info

So, you got a card, you got a Newton, and you've got reams of stuff you want to put in it. The only question left is, how are you going to organize this stuff so that you can find it later?

Because Newton lets you define your own folders, you should take some time to think about how you browse information now, in the pre-New-tonian world. Do you collect facts by topic, such as your interest in Western fungi, or do you organize by date and times that you encountered information, like that folder in the office called "January News Clippings"? Your analog habits will map nicely to the folder-oriented world of Newton.

Define your folders so that you can group records you want to be able to look at together, without other records getting in the way. For example, if you want to be able to peruse a list of your fellow employee's name cards, you should probably create a folder called Company and put their cards in it. It's a good idea, though, to create folder names that apply equally well to Names and Notepad files.

You'll always have a technological lifeguard at your fingertips, even if you muck up the folder approach to organizing data. The Find command traverses all folders when it looks for a keyword, so you won't lose anything for good. In fact, if you're in one folder and you do a find that locates a record in another folder, Newton will bring up the All Notes or All Cards view to display the found item, instead switching you to the other folder, which would put the document you were working in temporarily out of reach.

We divide folders into two groups of six each. In the first group are our permanent folders, with categories like Company and Personal for which we'll always have a use. The others are temporary folders, where we stick data that's specific to a project we're working on. Not only does this make organizing and managing information for that project easier, it makes deleting those records when the project is done simpler as well. We just open the folder and scroll through the list, deleting as we go.

Once you have your data organized, surfing through it can be as simple as tapping the overview button in a folder to locate what you want (see Figure 6.3).

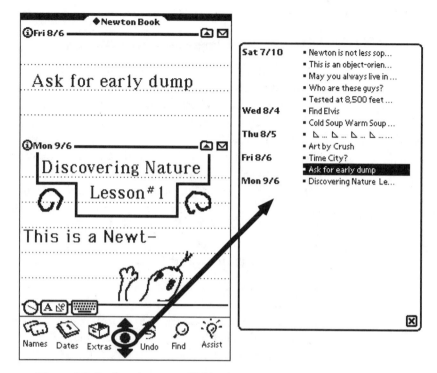

Figure 6.3 Surfing the waves of folder data.

Assist...Now, A Few Words About Keywords.

As we said in *Anatomy of an Interface*, folders are a two dimensional way of organizing data (see *Tags, You're Not It!* in that section). However, that doesn't mean you can't fool Newton into giving you multiple ways to slice your data.

Select some keywords you can append to all records that fit a category. If you don't have room for a folder called "Friend," for example, just add that word to the notes area of the Name Card of all your friends. Then, if you need to find some moral support and are wondering who to call, just go to the Names file, tap Find and write "Friend." Find will ferret out all your compadres for you.

(continued)

Assist...Now, A Few Words About Keywords. (continued)

Keywords can also identify drawings. You may have noticed that if you tap overview in the Notepad, a drawing will appear as some dots and triangles. When you want to make sure that a drawing will be in easy reach, add a line of keywords, like "Technical" and "Company" and "Car" to the top of a drawing for a new automobile concept you've been playing with. Use a combination of these keywords to locate the sketch, as well as to differentiate it from the technical drawings for the Puget Sound Casket Company that share the keywords "technical" and "company." Don't worry about printing or faxing keywords with your drawing. Just keep them together so you can select and drag them to the Transporter for storage while you print or fax the note.

You can also use keywords to get around Newton's inability to put calendar items in a folder. Just put the folder name you want the appointment related to in the Details area of an appointment slip. Then, say, if you need a list of business meetings and business notes, just tap Find and write "Business" in the search field.

Keep a list of keywords in the Notepad. This way, if you forget what keywords you've used in the past, you can look them up.

Vanishing Folders

So, you decided to get rid of the folder called "Business" and replace it with a folder called "Company." You go to the Edit Folder dialog and change the name to "Company." After a few minutes of digital shuffling, all the records in the Business folder are magically transferred to the Company folder. Why? Because the records retained their connection to the folder, even though it had been renamed.

If instead you had decided to remove the Business folder altogether, when you returned to the Notepad you'd find that without the folder to hold them together all the notes that had been in the Business folder would be scattered among the notes in the Unfiled folder.

Too, vanishing folders can confound when you share a PCMCIA card between two Newtons. Suppose you create a folder called "Trip to NYC." You put all the records for the trip, which are stored on a PCMCIA card, into that folder. Later, an associate who is making the pilgrimage to the Big Apple asks for a copy of those records—you knew about a great hotel and a killer bat guano cult nightspot. You just hand over your PCMCIA card and tell him to copy the folder contents to his Newton's internal RAM. No problem? No way!

When he looks for the folder on his own Newton, it's not to be found. He figures, because he doesn't have a folder called "Trip to NYC," that his Newton would put those records into the Unfiled folder. A logical assumption considering what Newton does with records that were linked to a deleted folder. But, what's this? He still can't find the records in his Unfiled folder.

Your colleague uses the Find command, and presto, the "Trip to NYC" notes magically appear. The All Notes or All Names views also unearth the notes from the card.

Here's what's going on. Newton keeps the definition of a folder, it's name, in the internal RAM. The definitions don't follow RAM cards, they stay at home in the Newton while the card goes visiting. Record designations, however, do follow the RAM card. All those records are still tagged "Trip to NYC," and they won't show themselves in the interface unless that folder exists or a system-wide search is conducted.

After he's found the files, all your coworker need do to restore the organizing influence of your folder is add a folder, called "Trip to NYC" to his Newton. All the data designated for that folder will be collected there.

Vanishing Folders can also prove an affliction for a Newton that has undergone a factory reset. Records stored in a custom folder on a PCMCIA card may appear to have been nuked with the rest of Newton's data after a Cold Boot. Not so. Recreate the folder names and the items on the card will return to their organizational homes in orderly fashion.

Assist...Folder Lock

Several CompuServe users have reported that their Newtons suffer from folder lock. When they change from one folder to another, Newton takes an interminable amount of time to complete the change of view. Most people cut Newton some slack, expecting folders that contain hundreds of names or notes to take a while to open. But when folder lock struck folders that contained only two or three records out of the hundreds on a Newton, it was hard for these on-line Newtonians to accept the slow performance. After all, they were sorting only a few records.

The reason switching views can take such a long time is that Newton scans the entire application soup to locate the records that belong to a particular folder every time you change views. This is true for folders containing hundreds of items and for folders that contain but a few records. You can link items stored all over Hell and back, but you have to look for them every time you hit the data surf.

The three prescriptions for folder lock are:

- Don't create folders that contain only a few records. Changes of views won't be processed any faster, but at least you'll feel like you got something for waiting. This might be called the "Folders as a Last Resort Solution."

- Limit the number of folders you use, you won't need to change so often. This is the "Modified Folders as a Last Resort Solution" or the "Data Half-Pike In and Out."

- Operate in the "All" view most of the time, assigning notes to folders for purposes of collecting data for reports, but working primarily in the larger world. This is the most sensible approach to living, because it shutters most of the organizational hassles behind the scenes until you need it. The fact is, Newton's filing system is screwed up in the right way. But that's not to say it can't get better.

In the end, we all have to learn a little patience. If we wrestle with the filing system, it will come.

Find—The Info Surfer's Best Friend

In Newton, nothing could be simpler than finding yourself, or anyone else. Just tap the Find icon on the Permanent menu, enter the name you're looking for and tap the find button (see Figure 6.4).

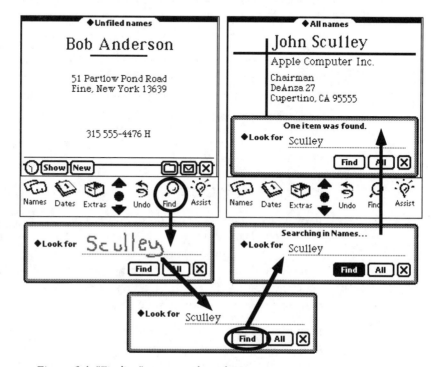

Figure 6.4 "Finding" your way through Newton.

Newton's Find command is an equal-opportunity search utility. It ignores folder boundaries, searching the entire soup of the active application (the active application is the one on top) whenever you hit the Find button. If you tap the All button in the Find slip, the search is expanded to every corner of the Newton architecture, and will track down the word or words you entered anywhere they occur, including the Date Book, Names file, Notepad, and third-party application records (assuming they support the Find command).

Find can search based on both multiple and partial words. It is also "case-insensitive" meaning it doesn't need to match capital letters to capital letters and lowercase to lowercase to return a match.

For example, let's say you want to find that guy you met about a year ago who works at the National Security Agency. His vital statistics are stored somewhere in your Newton, but you can't remember his name, exactly. It was Gary, something. You could search by entering "Gary," but that would probably produce a list of about twenty names. You could enter "NSA," but there are more spooks in your Newton than in a haunted house.

So, you opt to do a compound search. First, you tap the Names icon, opening up the Names file. Next, you tap the Find icon. When the Find slip appears at the bottom of the screen you enter "gary nsa" and tap "Find." A message appears that says "searching in names..." (watch this message, it'll tell you where Find is looking). A moment later, Gary Armbuckle's name appears.

Easter egg...Elvis Lives!

If you're nothing but a hound dog who's crying for your hunka hunka burnin' love, you don't have to step on your blue suede shoes to dig up the last location of The King. In fact he's turning up all over the world these days, and you don't have to head down to the store for a copy of the *Weekly World News* to find out where.

Just write "Find Elvis" on the Notepad, select it and tap the Assist icon. Watch the status message above the search field carefully, because a message will flash by informing you that "The King was last seen in..." and the name of a city in the Time Zones cities list. Then an overview will open that contains the name of the city where Elvis was spotted, tap it to see the world map and follow the King of Rock n' Roll on his continuing journey. Every time you search, he moves on to another city.

We've heard from a reliable source that this feature was added at the insistence of the *National Inquirer*, which has committed to buy several hundred MessagePads for Purposes Unknown. Just don't quote us, okay?

The Listmaster

The previous example demonstrates using Find to select one Name card. But, suppose you want to scan multiple records?

Let's say you're one of those passive aggressive character types who never deletes her e-mail, knowing that you can always send a complaining homily to each of the people who unluckily had a message land in your In Box. You've invested in a 4-Mbyte Flash RAM card, because you keep everything, office memos, e-mail, even pages that came over the Messaging Card in hopes of finding something to leverage to your own twisted ends.

One morning you come into the office to find your partner sitting behind his desk staring into space. He looks up at you and says that Natasha, one of your employees, just went to work for your biggest, most cut-throat competitor. Your partner fears the worst. After all, trade secrets in your business get passed around like a joint at a rock concert.

This could be bad. Natasha worked on so many confidential projects that neither of you are sure which ones could be at risk. But you are prepared. You whip out your Newton, and tap the Find icon. You enter "Natasha" in the slip and, instead of tapping the Find button, you tap All. For a few tense moments, your Newton is locked in thought. Then, the message "Creating a list of found items..." flashes on screen and you are rewarded with a list of the correspondence and appointments you have involving Natasha. God, you're going to make this woman feel guilty, feel really bad.

It's a long list. But you scan through it quickly using the up and down arrows in the permanent menu. Something catches your attention, so you tap it. Nope, not terribly likely your competitor hired Natasha to get at details about this product. They already have one of these they sell for a lower price than you do.

But, rather than tapping the overview button to display the Find list again, you use the arrow buttons to scroll through the items in the list one at a time. The Find dialog is still open, allowing you to scroll through the retrieved items while keeping track of where in the list you are.

After an intense half hour of surfing through the list, it looks like your exposure with Natasha was minimal after all. She hadn't been involved in any really crucial projects for months. You close the Find dialog and breath a sign of relief. Now you can really let her have it, because she's probably not even guilty of any double-dealing. It's so good to make others suffer, the mere sound of tension in other people's voice puts a delightfully dreary edge on your day. You think, "Gee, I'll just call her and whine about how I was about to give her a raise."

Find will remember what you entered the last time you used it. Should you need to run the Natasha search again while tormenting her, you can do so without having to reenter it.

While most of the time you'll use text in Find, you can also use dates to ferret out what you're looking for. Create a list of notes created, or appointments scheduled before, or after, a specified date; tap the list diamond next to "Look for," select "dates before" or "dates after," and write the date you want. Date-based searching doesn't work in the Names file. Also, you can't combine dates and text in a search, you must choose one or the other.

Move along, little data

While working with a large number of records isn't always easy in Newton, there is a trick or two that you can use to move or remove a large number of files without having to manipulate them one at a time.

Let's say you want to move a list of all your *MacWEEK* contacts from one PCMCIA card to another and you don't want to use Newton Connection to do it. You also want to avoid moving all the notes you've taken that mention *MacWEEK*.

Do a Find from within the Names file with "MacWEEK" as the search string, only Name items will be returned. When Newton displays the resulting list, tap the Action button at the bottom of the list window. Now, tap "Move from Card."

It might take a few minutes, but if there's room, Newton will move all those *MacWEEK* name cards to internal RAM. Pop out the storage card you were using and plug in the one on to which you want to move the *MacWEEK* contacts. Perform the same search in the Names application, again. Tap the Action button and then tap "Move to Card." That's it! A few minutes later, the records will be safely ensconced in their new home (see Figure 6.5).

You can also delete a large number of records using this method, or move them to a new folder (tap the Folder button instead of the Action button and select a destination folder). All it takes is a keyword or a range of dates in common and you can ship items around as if you were the digital Federal Express.

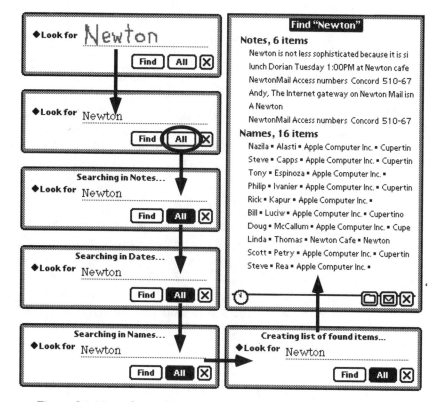

Figure 6.5 *Using the Find list to corral your data.*

Your Assistant

You've probably already had some experience with the Assistant, that part of Newton which can execute commands by interpreting sentences with certain verbs in them. We like to think of the Assistant as a virtual menu, a way to access any command from anywhere in Newton without the need for unsightly menu bars.

The real question to be concerned with isn't how the Assistant works. It works quite reliably, if somewhat slowly at times. The question is when does it make sense to use the Assistant?

We've found the Assistant most helpful when we want to move text we'd already entered into the Notepad. It also proved useful as a shortcut mechanism, by-passing several steps with a tap or two and a scribble. We've also found the Assistant useful for setting up To Dos and appointments, especially because it helps us avoid writing in the cramped calendar interface. In fact, after a certain point we had to use the Assistant to create new To Dos; we had so many that the application wouldn't let us add anymore. But the Assistant could still do it (the Assistant is the only way we know to call up the To Do slip).

Also, the Assistant shows its smartest smarts when scheduling a meeting or To Do. You can write a limited range of variables into the command sentence (such as a date and person to meet with) and Newton will sort it all out, filling in the appointment or day note confirmation slip accordingly. (The Assistant requires confirmation on all verb commands, except time, before executing them.)

Of course, it would be nice if the Assistant could schedule appointments with multiple data points, like several names and a location. After all, at least some of your meetings will probably include more than one other person. But, if you enter something like "Meet Joeseph and Barry Friday 3:00PM at Apple" the results will range wildly. (We've even seen Newton take a command sentence like this and schedule the appointment with an entirely different person. The only thing it gets right is the date.) We know for sure that this command sentence won't get the results you were looking for.

The kind of things we don't like using the Assistant for are faxing, printing, and mailing. While it can save you the trouble of filling out a mail slip, the command sentence will appear in the message if you write it on the note. You can, of course, write it in the Assistant slip (see Figure 6.6). But, really, faxing, printing, and mailing are pretty simple tasks to begin with. The Assistant really doesn't add much value here. At least, it won't add real value until it can recognize that a command sentence should be stripped out of a fax or printed document.

The only other things you need to know about the Assistant are the command verbs syntaxes. You can combine verbs in some sentences, like "Remember to call Bob." Newton is smart enough to figure out from the first recognizable verb (Remember) that it should ignore the second (call). Otherwise, Newton will understand the meaning of most verbs even if they don't come first in the command phrase. So, "Mail Joanne" and "Joanne

Mail" both will call up an e-mail slip with "Joanne" already written into the Name field for you.

Newton comes with support for 47 verbs in eight verb groups. Most command verbs are synonyms of other verbs, that is, they have the same effect. It's just a matter of which word you prefer to use. It also means you don't have to remember a precise command language, several different words can be employed to perform the same task. If you can't remember any of the command verbs for what you want to do, tap Assist and then tap the list diamond next to the "Please" field for a listing of the primary verbs.

Here are the verb groupings:

Verb: Call
Synonyms: Ring, dial, phone
Example: "Ring Steve Capps" opens a dialer slip with Steve Capps already selected.

Verb: Fax
Synonyms: None
Example: "Fax 555-1212" opens a fax slip with the phone number 555-1212 already entered.

Verb: Find
Synonyms: Locate, look for, search for
Example: "Look for Bill Luciw" opens a Find slip and enters Bill Luciw's name.

Verb: Print
Synonyms: None
Example: "Print" opens a print dialog box with the current note or name card (the one showing) selected.

Verb: Remember
Synonyms: Remind, remind me, to do
Example: "Remind me pick up laundry" would create a To Do with "pick up laundry" entered in it. You have to tap the "Do" button in the confirmation slip to add the To Do item.

Verb: Schedule
Synonyms: Meet, Meet with, see, talk to, talk with, Breakfast (7:00 am), brunch (10:00 am), lunch (12:00 PM), dinner (7:00 PM), holiday (calls a day note rather than an appointment slip); birthday, b-day, bday, anniversary (all call a day note that repeats every year)

Modifiers: Days of the week, tomorrow, time
Examples: "Lunch with Dorian Tuesday 1:00PM" would create an appointment confirmation slip for next Tuesday at 1:00 PM with "lunch" as the subject and "Dorian" in the Who field.

If it is before noon, the command phrase "Lunch Dorian" would open a slip with lunch that day at 12:00 PM. If it is before 2:00 PM, the time would be a half hour from when you scheduled the appointment. After 2:00 PM and the Assistant assumes lunch is for the next day.

Verb: Time
Synonyms: Time in
Example: "Time San Francisco" would open Time Zones in the Extras drawer and select San Francisco as the destination city. This is the only verb where Newton doesn't call a confirmation skip.

Expect to see more Assistant verbs coming in the future as third-party developers define their own verb groups.

Easter egg...Hall of Fame

It's something of a tradition around Apple. Invent a whole new way of computing, get to put your name somewhere on the first models that come out. The original Macintosh team got to have their names inscribed on the inside of the original Mac's plastic shell. Well, the Newton Team, dealing with an altogether more refined technology, found a much more subtle way to have their names etched for posterity.

The signatures of the entire Newton team are recorded in electrons buried somewhere deep down inside Newton's ROMs. The only way to get at them is to write "About Newton" on the Notepad, select the sentence and then tap Assist. Newton will play a short movie of the Team's names. You can't stop it from playing, just let it run its course.

The last part of the movie is perhaps the saddest and most poignant. We're speaking of a memorial to Ko Isono, a young engineer who worked on the digital ink technology in Newton, committed suicide at Christmas time in 1992. May he rest in peace.

CHAPTER
7

LIFE'S LITTLE EXTRAS

The Extras icon in the Permanent Menu acts as a repository for all applications and utilities which didn't get their own permanent menu icon, as well as for third-party applications.

When you load a new application into your Newton, whether the destination is the main RAM or a storage card, it lands in the Extras drawer. Items stored on a card will be visible in Extras only when that card is inserted. Likewise, there are some applications, like Connection and the Card viewer application, that cannot be removed from Extras because they are hard-wired into Newton's ROM.

Slider controls for the volume and screen contrast are available in the Extras drawer as well. The contrast control is the only one in Newton, but you can set the volume in two places in the Extras drawer—the main window and the Sound Preferences window. In System Update 1.04 and early ROM patches, the sound settings in the Extras window gave the appearance of conflicting with the Preferences settings. For example, if you changed the volume setting in Sound Preferences, closed Preferences and checked the sound slider in the Extras drawer, it appeared to be set to a different volume. But if you closed and then opened the Extras drawer again, the slider would have changed to the setting in Sound Preferences. If Apple hasn't fixed this, or you have an older system, just keep in mind that the most recent change (to either slider) is what takes precedence.

Keep in mind where the Contrast slider is located. Somewhere along the way someone might turn it all the way down, which makes your screen look like Newton is asleep. If this happens, tap the Extras icon and feel around with the pen, tapping and dragging in the vicinity of the contrast slider, until you get hold of it and can turn up the screen. The sliders can be manipulated by the pen, even if it is as much as one-eighth of an inch above or below the slider diamond.

The Extras drawer will hold 30 icons, and you can install as many applications as you like beyond the drawer's capacity. However you can't scroll through the Extras window. Applications that install icons below the bottom of the window cannot be viewed, so you can't open them. The Connection application will not let you load an application twice, so don't worry about wasting space in Extras. (Apple swears they'll fix this non-scrolling Extras drawer in the next Newton.)

The Out Box

Managing information is easier when you have an identifiable interface with the outside world. Most desks in an office have an In/Out Box shoved off to the corner, beyond the coffee cup full of pens, folders full of project data and pictures of the kids. If you don't take some time each day to manage the In/Out flow, it will get out of hand and contribute to the confusion you are trying to control.

The same goes for Newton's doorsteps to the outside world, the In Box and Out Box applications stored in the Extras drawer.

When you tap open the Out Box, you'll see the names of four categories of Newton communications, Print, Fax, Beam, and Mail (others, such as "Wireless," will be added in future, cellular Newtons, or by third-parties). The Out Box is connected to the Action button in the Notepad, Dates, and Names files, as well as third-party applications. Tap one of the actions, and the message is shunted off to the Out Box, where you must give the command to send.

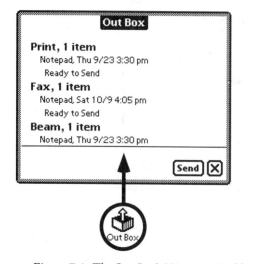

Figure 7.1 *The Out Box's View to a World.*

Beside each communications method, you'll see the number of items of that type waiting to be sent. If you cannot see the messages that are waiting, tap the category name; the list will expand to show items.

Remember that each communications method requires a different connection:

Print. There are two connections you might use to print documents, a direct serial or network connection to Apple LaserWriters, StyleWriters, or through Apple's Print Pack cable to parallel printers.

By the time a message arrives in the Out Box, it's already been "addressed" to a particular printer (see Chapter Ten—*In the Out Door and Back In Again* for more). To finish the job, just tap the send button and choose Print from the pop-up menu that appears. Newton will then look for a connection to the printer and process the message.

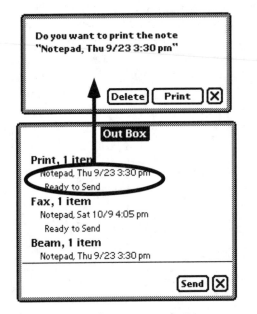

Figure 7.2 The Last Resort for Printing

You can also tap the name of the item to open a print dialog. Just tap the Print button to send the message (you're always two taps from a printer in the Out Box), or the message can be erased by tapping the Delete button. If you want to get rid of a print job, this is the dark alley to head down with your victim.

Fax. The Apple external Fax Modem or a third-party fax modem must be connected to the Newton, via the serial port or the PCMCIA slot, before you can send a fax.

Tap the Send button and select Fax to initiate a connection. Newton will dial the fax number you entered and send the message. If you have multiple messages waiting to be faxed, tapping the Send button will cause Newton to send all of them, one after the other. Several faxes addressed to the same fax machine will be treated as separate messages, rather than gathered into a single transmission.

If you want to send only one message in a long queue of faxes, tap the name of the message in the Out Box window. This opens a Fax-or-Delete dialog. Tapping the item is also the only way to delete a fax once you've sent it to the Out Box.

Beam. The Out Box opens after the Newton has begun to search for a receiver—you've presumably told someone to aim their infrared port at your Newton. It displays a "Looking for receiver..." message and relates beaming progress. Should it be unable to complete a beam, the Out Box retains a copy of the message, which you can send later.

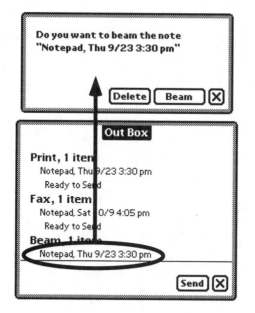

Figure 7.3 Beam Me Up, Newton

Let's say you remember early in the day that you need to beam John a copy of your notes from a sales meeting. Tap Beam in the Action menu of the Notepad, and let the transmission fail—it will take two minutes—so that the Out Box catches the message. Later, when you bump into John, just open your Out Box and tap the item under Beam. A Beam-or-Delete slip will appear. Tap beam and take aim at John's Newton.

You can also resend failed beams *en masse* by tapping the Beam item under the Send button in the Out Box. Newton will send all the stored messages, one after the other.

Mail. Your mail queue might get mighty long as you work during the day, but there's very little management of messages required. All of them will be sent at one time to NewtonMail when you tap the Send button and select Mail from the pop-up menu.

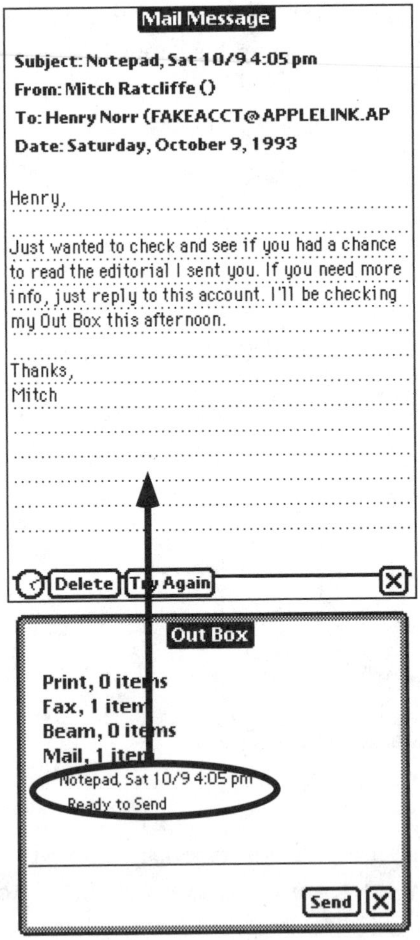

Figure 7.4 Last Chance to Edit!

The Out Box will also let you view and modify the textual information in a message, but ink-based drawings are out of reach once they are sent from the Notepad. Tap the name of the message you want to view to open a text document; the contents can be edited and appended. At the bottom of the document there will be Delete and Try Again buttons. Tap Try Again to connect to NewtonMail. And Delete, well, you know what that does.

The Out Box always sends all the messages in a queue, in the order they appear in the list, when it connects with NewtonMail. If you're one of those political animals who composes a series of messages that must be delivered in a particular order and pace to achieve the greatest impact on your antagonists, make sure they appear in the Out Box in the right order. You can tap the Stop button to terminate the NewtonMail connection after the first message is uploaded to the server (that's computer talk for delivered to the computer that controls NewtonMail).

Assist...Where in the RAM is the Out Box?

Messages sent to the Out Box live in the portion of RAM set aside for its use, even if you have a memory card and have set Newton to save new items to it. If the object you are sending is stored on the card in the first place, Newton makes a copy that is placed in internal RAM. This places a limit on the total capacity of the storage available in the Out Box, but it also plays an important part in Newton's support for PCMCIA communications cards.

Imagine that you are a Newton (a stretch, we know): Your owner has you set to save all her notes directly to the Flash RAM card in your PCMCIA slot (it's roughly where your brain is; sometimes your owner jerks that part of your memory out, and stuff is just, like, gone, man!) She writes out a note, which you save to the card, and taps the Action button to select the Fax function. Now, let's say that you *don't* have the ability to place the fax message into the front of your little electronic brain, the part of RAM that's always there, and she goes ahead and pulls the memory card out of the PCMCIA slot, to replace it with a Megahertz modem.

(continued)

Assist...Where in the RAM is the Out Box? (continued)

You don't have the information she needs to send when it comes time to transmit the message over the modem, because the modem is where that memory used to be. Now, what are you going to do? (Probably display an "Out Of Memory" error message. Yeah, that's the ticket! Distract her from the real problem.)

Luckily, Newton is able to hold a copy of a message in RAM and send it through the PCMCIA modem. This capability will also be important when you start using PCMCIA network cards to communicate with network E-mail services and databases.

The In Box

Every beam and mail message that goes out of another Newton's Out Box lands in an In Box somewhere. First-generation Newtons come with an In Box that's ready to catch beams, mail, system enhancements (read this as system updates from Apple), and paging messages collected by the Messaging Card, when it is installed in the PCMCIA slot.

The In Box takes care of itself, for the most part. It opens automatically when Newton receives a message, and, like the Out Box, displays the number of messages you haven't dealt with. Tap the category name to see an expanded list of the items, and tap the individual item to view its contents.

Beam. The infrared is the most schizophrenic of the communications method listed by the In Box. Depending upon how you have set your Beams Preferences file, the In Box may or may not open automatically when you receive a message.

If you want your In Box to open automatically when Newton receives a beam, select both the "Receive beams automatically" and "Open In Box while receiving" boxes in Beam Preferences. Turning on "Receive beams automatically" consumes a lot of battery power, since Newton will be sending "I'm ready to receive" messages out the infrared port every few seconds, all day long.

Saving power is important, so we suggest that you do not set the Preferences to receive automatically. When someone says "Hey, have I got a beam for you" open the In Box and tap the Receive button, then choose Beam from the pop-up list. This sends the "I'm ready to receive" message, and the In Box will then report the progress of the transfer.

The other preference setting that will have an effect on the In Box is the "Put away beams immediately" box, which, when checked, lets Newton look at the type of object it has received and store it in the associated application; notes to the Notepad, cards to the Names file, and so on.

Checking the "Put away beams automatically" and "Receive beams automatically" boxes and an unchecked "Open In Box while receiving" will allow people to send beams to your Newton without your ever knowing it. Incoming messages will be grabbed and filed, with no record of the transaction.

If your Newton leaves the management to you, the In Box will hold onto incoming messages until you tap the name of the item. Tapping opens a filing slip that asks if you would like to put away the beam (all Newton does is wait for your permission to file a message, you can't view it first). You can also erase the beam without filing the contents by tapping the Delete button in this slip.

Enhancement. Apple will update your Newton system software occasionally (hopefully not too often between the time we finish writing this book and when it reaches the bookstores). The Enhancements category in the In Box is your catcher's glove for this service.

Tapping Enhancements will not produce any results, but if you tap the Receive button and select Enhancements from the pop-up menu Newton will open a slip with a phone number field. The number to enter is (800) NEWTON9.

Apple will occasionally send you a message offering some cool new capability, like the ability to capture news from an on-line service, which you can get by dialing the Enhancements hot-line. Of course, this is going to cost you money, but remember when you entered your credit card number in Mail preferences? Newton will be able to hand off that information at the tap of a button, so you can get your hands on more digital toys.

Enter the Enhancements hot-line number in the telephone field of the In Box slip and tap Call. Newton will upload the necessary data and download self-installing software. Once an Enhancement has landed in the In Box, just tap it to open an Installer slip.

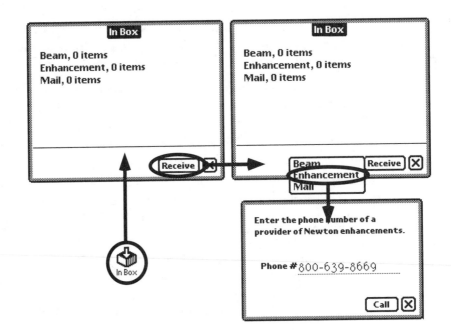

Figure 7.5 Enhancements Dialing

Mail. NewtonMail messages will collect in the In Box in the order they are received. They will not go away until you have given Newton instructions about what to do with each of them.

When you tap the name of an item, the In Box displays a text-only version of the message. Dates and Name records will appear intact, though they will not have quite the same appearance you are used to in those applications. Tap the Put Away button and Newton puts them into the proper format and stores the message.

Notepad messages appear in the In Box message viewer without any graphics. A message that is nothing but a drawing will appear blank. Tap the Put Away button to store the message in the Notepad as an unfiled note.

Version 1.03 of the In Box required that you tap Open and select the Delete button before the message would disappear from the In Box. Keep in mind that In Box messages are stored in the Newton's main RAM, not the card. Keep your In Box queues short to save memory for other functions.

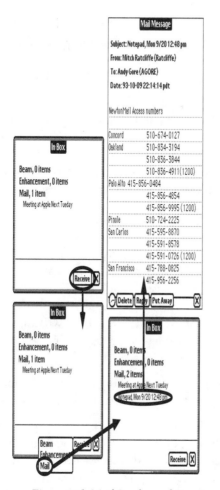

Figure 7.6 Mail Reader and Put Away option

Pages. This category appears only when you have the Messaging Card in the PCMCIA slot. The items displayed are those pages that you have not read. If you typically carry the Messaging Card seperate from your Newton, you can tell if you have a message by looking for a flashing green light to the left of the power switch.

Inserting the Messaging Card causes the In Box to open automatically. Tap the items to view the contents, which are usually very brief. Currently, the pager system used by the card supports messages of less than 240 characters.

Messages are displayed in a full screen window, with an Options button and Action button at the bottom. You can do only two things with a pager message, both choices are listed under the Action button. Pages can be imported into the Notepad as unfiled notes or you can delete them.

The Options button is actually a preferences file for the Messaging Card. The button opens a dialog window that displays the number of messages stored in the card and a checkbox for turning the alert sound on and off. You can also tap pop-up lists of the sounds Newton will play when a message arrives (Double Beep and Chirp), the typestyles in which the message can be displayed (Simple and Fancy), and the text size.

Connection

This is Newton's network viewer. Tapping this icon opens a connection slip that lets you choose serial links to a Mac or to a PC, or a LocalTalk network connection to a Macintosh. As of our publication date, the Connection application on Newton must communicate with Newton Connection software. Later, when third-party developers write applications that send and receive Newton-savvy network packets, Connection will be able to communicate with other software.

Tapping either of the serial connection buttons—Windows PC and Macintosh serial—initiates a straight-forward, hands-off, communications session with a Mac or PC.

The Macintosh LocalTalk button opens a network browser called the Chooser; the first window you see lists the last two Macs to which you've connected with Connection, just tap the one you want to begin synchronizing, restoring or installation of a package. If you don't see the Mac you want, tap the More Choices button. Newton will search the network. If you are connected to a multi-zone network, the Chooser slip will display a "Zones" button along with a list of Macs that live in your zone. Tapping Zones will display a list of Macs in other parts of the network. When the list exceeds the size of the window, arrows appear to the right of the window that allow you to scroll up and down.

If you're a Mac user, don't confuse Newton's Chooser with the Mac Chooser. All this network viewer can display is a list of Macs. For complete information about the way Newton relates to network services, turn to Chapter Three—*The Invisible World.*

Easter Egg... The Serial Debugger

Hidden in the Extras drawer is a programmer's tool for testing serial port activity. It's of absolutely no use to the ordinary user, but it's there.

To open the Serial Debugger tap just inside the upper-left corner of the Extras drawer—a square three-by-three pixels large will turn black for a moment and Newton will generate a click sound. Then tap just inside the upper-right corner of the Extras drawer, a square will highlight and Newton will click again. The Extras drawer closes and the Debugger will open.

It's a window that looks very much like the Connection options window, but it lists three choices you haven't seen before: Built In LocalTalk; External Serial; and Serial Debugger. Just take a look.

The Debugger doesn't communicate with Newton Connection software, only the special Newton-on-a-card developers use to build applications. However, tapping the Serial Debugger option can crash LocalTalk connections between Macs on your network. So, don't tap it if you are connected to the office network, or you can bet that the guy who runs the network is going to come looking for you.

Sharp

Newton's Sharp communications utility is wrapped in a neat package that lets you configure Newton to accept data from Sharp Wizards. For complete instructions on importing Wizard data, turn to Chapter Eight—*Ready, Set, Load!*

Card

Each storage card you insert in Newton needs to be told how to handle the information you enter. You can open the dialog box for doing this from the Card utility in Extras.

The card slip displays the current amount of information stored on the card, the available space for more data, and several buttons. Tap the Card icon to use this slip.

Memory in use. This figure, expressed in Kilobytes, shows the amount of space currently in use by data, in compressed format, on the card. When Newton accesses the data, it will be decompressed as it enters the ARM processor and recompressed as it flows back into the card.

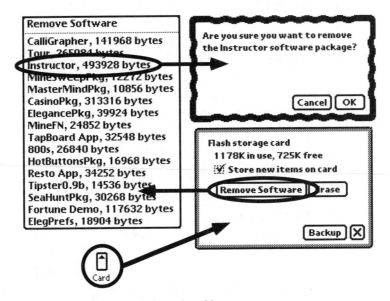

Figure 7.7 Put your cards on the table.

Memory free. The amount of RAM available for use by Newton.

Remove software button. You can tap this button to activate the Card dialog's erase function. The button opens a list of all applications on the card, and how much memory they consume when uncompressed (i.e., if you remove a 36 Kbyte file, only 21 Kbytes may be shaved from the memory total).

Tap the name of the application you want to delete. A dialog will open: Are you sure you want to remove the software package? Tap the OK button to completely erase it (see Figure 7.7).

Erase button. Tapping this button raises a warning that you will delete all the data on the card if you proceed. If you really want to do that, tap OK. Otherwise, tap the Cancel button.

Backup button. You can back up to a storage card the system updates, user dictionaries, applications, and data stored in Newton's internal RAM.

A tap on the Backup button begins a process like the Synchronization performed by the Newton Connection application, only the whole process takes place between Newton and the storage card.

When you insert a card that contains a backup file, the Card application will add several additional items to the storage card slip, including the date and time of when the backup file was created, a Restore button that places the backup file back in the Newton's main memory, and a Remove button.

Newton's Card application also lets you format new storage cards when you insert them for the first time. It senses the capacity of the card automatically and builds a Newton-compatible file system in the memory. You'll also see a Card interface when you insert communications or application cards; it opens a dialog confirming the type of card in the PCMCIA slot.

Calculator

A simple four-function calculator. Unfortunately, you cannot pull this sucker out. But we still suggest installing a third-party calculator for all but the simplest of ciphers. Take a look at GoFigure from Dubl-Click Software, a versatile calculator that handles everything from typesetting figures to kitchen conversions, statistics, and hexadecimal calculations. Howard Oakley's "more than a four-function calculator" is a useful shareware scientific calculator.

Formulas

If Apple put anything in the Newton that you'll find of practical use, it's the metric conversion, currency exchange, loan payment, and net present value worksheets in the Formulas application. You'll see: the next time you're at a car dealership or bank negotiating a loan, this application will be open and arming you with data.

Time Zones

As strange as this may sound at first, the Time Zones application is tied to the performance of Newton's automatic dialer and system clock. Even before you set the time on Newton, you should open Time Zones and tell Newton where you (and it) are. You can also tap the locations of various cities to determine the distance (and time difference) between where you are and the Champs de Elysée, for instance.

Tap the Time Zones icon to open a map of the world. Beneath the map you'll see the names of two cities (San Francisco and Tokyo the first time you open the application) and the time and date in those cities. A scale that indicates the distance between the two cities lies between a circle and square beneath the map, and an I'm Here button let's you tell Newton your current location.

The map includes the names and coordinates of 97 cities. Tap the Overview button in the permanent menu to view a list of cities. If your town is included, or if a city close to yours is in the list, tap the name of that city in the list. The city's name and the local time will appear above the I'm Here button; tap the button if you want to set Newton's clock to this time zone. You can also tap around the map to locate a city, but getting Newton to distinguish between Cupertino and San Francisco can be a bitch.

In all likelihood, your home town isn't listed in Time Zones. If you just can't stand having the wrong name appear as your home, you should download Pensée Corp.'s Place Settings application from an on-line service. This handy application installs in the Extras drawer and lets you add your city to the Time Zones cities list. After you've chosen the nearest city on the Time Zones map, tap I'm Here and close the map. Open Place Settings, you'll see the name of the city you chose in Time Zones and its latitude and longitude. Scrub out the city name and write in the name of your home town. Don't mess with the latitude and longitude, unless you know them—close is good enough, at least you've got the right name and time zone now.

Now that the time zone is set, you can turn to Preferences to set your clock.

Preferences

Newton's personality is a reflection of the settings you give it and Preferences is the mental screw you turn to shape those settings. Here's the mental breakdown:

Personal. This is where you tell Newton who you are. You'll be able to figure this form out. If you've ever been to the doctor, you've written down all this information before. The Set Password button is an important topic which we'll discuss below.

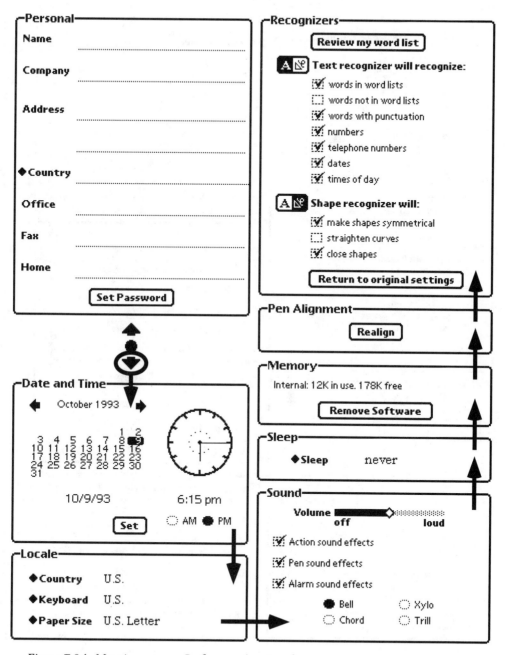

Figure 7.8A Mapping out your Preferences. (continued)

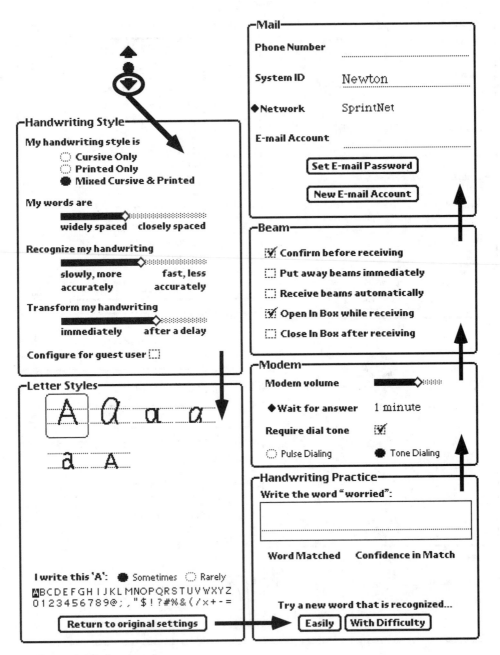

Handwriting Style

My handwriting style is
- ○ Cursive Only
- ○ Printed Only
- ● Mixed Cursive & Printed

My words are

widely spaced   closely spaced

Recognize my handwriting

slowly, more   fast, less
accurately   accurately

Transform my handwriting

immediately   after a delay

Configure for guest user ☐

Letter Styles

A A a a

a A

I write this 'A': ● Sometimes ○ Rarely
ABCDEFGH I JKL MNOPQRSTUVWXYZ
0123456789@;,"$!?#%&(/×+-=

Return to original settings

Mail

Phone Number ....

System ID   Newton

◆ Network   SprintNet

E-mail Account ....

Set E-mail Password

New E-mail Account

Beam

☑ Confirm before receiving

☐ Put away beams immediately

☐ Receive beams automatically

☑ Open In Box while receiving

☐ Close In Box after receiving

Modem

Modem volume

◆ Wait for answer   1 minute

Require dial tone   ☑

○ Pulse Dialing   ● Tone Dialing

Handwriting Practice

Write the word "worried":

Word Matched   Confidence in Match

Try a new word that is recognized...

Easily   With Difficulty

Figure 7.8B (continued)

Easter Egg... We all will be received in Graceland

The influence of the King of Rock n' Roll is thick in
the Newton. If he isn't dropping into the cities of the
world (see Chapter Six—*Info Surfing* for more), he's
inviting you home to Graceland.

In the Personal Preferences, write "Graceland" in the Country
field. This will change the Newton startup screen from the light
bulb logo to a dancing newt. Yes, that's right, claim Elvis' home as
your country of origin and you can begin every Newton session
with a brief glimpse of a Newt doing the Frug. (Note the Morse
code in the tail: someone snuck their initials into the image as
well!)

Be warned, however. There's always a downside to clever little
hacks hidden in the ROM by sneaky programmers at the last
minute. (This particular Easter Egg arrived in the last ROM build
before Newton shipped, and after anyone could do anything
about it.) The Graceland trick causes Newton to get confused
about what area code to dial when you use the modem for faxing,
NewtonMail, or to dial a phone number. See, as far as Newton can
tell, Graceland is another planet, and because it has left the Earth
it always adds an area code to dialed numbers, even when you're
making a local call. And there's no getting around it.

If you enter a local number without an area code, Newton will dial
it correctly. Another thing Graceland zaps is the ability to tap a
phone number on a Name card to dial it. So, don't go to Graceland unless you want to wrestle with strange dialing.

Date and Time. After you've set your location in the Time Zones application, open the Date and Time Preferences to give Newton its specific
chronological bearings.

The date the calendar opens on is controlled by the date set in this slip.
If you want to change the month you are viewing, tap one of the direc-
tional arrows on either side of the month and year.

Setting the clock to the minute is a little tricky, since you must either draw the hands of the clock to match the current time or tap around the clock face. Be sure to tap the AM or PM button, then tap the Set button.

Locale. These preferences let you customize the output of your Newton. You can choose a country from among U. S., Canada, and French Canada (for you Quebecois out there), as well as Britain and Australia, which peppers the interface with characters and formats unique to those countries.

Two keyboards are available, U. S. and British.

Locale also describes your relationship with printers. This is where you choose the standard paper size to which Newton will format letters. Your choices: U. S. Letter and A4 Letter.

Sound. This is where you tell Newton how and when to play sounds. You can set your MessagePad or Expert Pad to make cheerful chirps, doleful trills and zany xyloes as an alert sound, as well as enable or disable the action and pen sound effects.

Sleep. Well, Newton's got to get its rest. You can set it to doze off after you leave it idle, or force it to stay awake no matter what. It's best to leave sleep enabled after a short idle time, this will help extend battery life. Leaving the Newton on for more than 24 hours can temporarily damage the screen, causing images to "burn in" as shadows. Turning the Newton off for a day or two will clear up this problem.

Memory. Like the Card application that gives statistics on memory in a storage card, the Memory Preferences reports on internal RAM usage. If you've installed an application in internal RAM, it can be deleted by tapping the Remove Software button.

Pen Alignment. You saw this when you turned your Newton on for the first time, or after a cold boot. It's the progression of "X"'s you had to tap before the Notepad opened. If you haven't aligned the pen, do it now. This allows Newton to account for the way you hold the pen, correcting stroke information to the intricacies of left- and right-handedness.

Recognizers. These preferences allow you to select what parts of your handwriting Newton will translate. For instance, you can set the recognizer to convert dates and phone numbers, but not punctuation. Turn to Chapter Four—*The Written Word,* for much more detail.

Handwriting Style. The interface for selecting the handwriting style you use, whether it's cursive, printed or a combination of both. Again, turn to Chapter Four.

Letter Style. Here's another group of settings that let you tailor handwriting recognition. Letter Styles will let you control the shapes Newton will associate with certain letters. Another Chapter Four item.

Handwriting Practice. A forum in which you and Newton can come to terms with one another. You write a word in a space, and Newton shows you its top three guesses and how confident it is about each (expressed as a percentage). Turn to Chapter, oh, you know.

Beam. The infrared port is the only communications mechanism that you can script. This Preferences window sets the In Box to put away incoming messages without your intervention, or to receive beams at any time. Turn to Chapter Three—*The Invisible World,* for a discussion of beaming preferences.

Modem. For the most part, Newton's modem settings are embedded in the ROM. But you can control certain aspects of the connection routine, if only for your peace of mind. The modem volume slider tells the external Apple modem to raise or lower the volume of its speaker, so you can listen in for a dial tone and the dialing sequence. Third-party modem speakers are not affected by this control.

The "Wait for answer" list diamond lets you tell Newton how long to wait for a fax tone before hanging up. Since some folks have a fax machine on their voice line, which they must switch on after hearing a tone, this control gives you and them some leeway. Your choices are 30 seconds, one minute and two minutes. One minute should be more than enough time.

You can tell Newton to dial the phone even when it doesn't hear a dial tone, allowing it to call on some digital phone systems or a cellular phone, when combined with the right adapter. The Pulse Dialing and Tone Dialing buttons adjust the type of tone Newton will send when calling a number.

Mail. Last, but not least, are the NewtonMail preferences. When you have obtained your mail registration information, after sending a response card or opening the Mail Starter Kit in the MessagePad packaging, go to this slip.

In the kit you'll find a list of local access numbers for the SprintNet system that supports NewtonMail. Find the number for your city, preferably the one that has a 2,400 bps connection, and write it in the Phone Number field.

The System ID is "Newton." Write it in, if it's not already there. The only network choice is SprintNet. In the future, Newton will support other networks and services which will appear in the Network list.

Tap the New E-mail Account button and fill in the Certificate Number and Certificate Password; most of the fields will be completed already based on your Personal information in the Preferences. The last field, Password Verification, will be uploaded to Apple's network where they will use it to confirm your identity during support telephone calls—it is not your electronic mail account password!

Tap the continue button. In the next form, enter your credit card information after picking the type of credit card you want to use from the list. Tap the Continue button, which logs you on to the NewtonMail system and takes you to the account information.

Remember that the dialing options slip you fill out for faxing will not make the jump to your mail account. Instead, you must enter prefix and access codes manually when dialing for mail.

Enter the word you want to use as an electronic mail address. This is your virtual face, so think about it for a moment. Do you want to be mysterious, humorous, wicked or staid? Will you want this word on your business cards, would you mind if it appeared in the *New York Times* (Mitch's closely-held Internet address did recently, much to his surprise, though he rather enjoyed explaining to several people where the name "godsdog" came from). You've got up to twelve characters with which you can work, and you can mix letters and numbers, if you like. What you enter here may not be accepted because of a conflict with another address, so don't print up new cards until you receive confirmation of the address.

The last field is your account password. Choose wisely, and see below for a brief discussion of password strategy. (For more on filling out and registering for NewtonMail, see Chapter Three—*The Invisible World*.)

Assist... A word about your password

For thousands of years secrets have been protected by passwords. Sentries have called them into the night, and spies have shouted back stolen responses to gain entry to the general's quarters. Now you need to pick the best possible password you can to avoid having someone drop in to read your mail.

Why the paranoia? Well, it's simple really. You hand out one-half the information needed to crack your mail account when you give someone a business card with your NewtonMail address. The other half, the password, is merely guesswork, or more likely, a matter of making a phone call to you and pretending to be a friendly NewtonMail representative who just needs to check what your password is. People's accounts are cracked all the time, and as more business is transacted via electronic mail, there's a burgeoning market for people who can gain access.

NewtonMail passwords may be up to eight characters long. Use them all, mixing letters with numbers. Use a nonsensical combination no one could guess by listening for the names of your children or spouse (a common password strategy that's commonly broken).

More important than protecting your mail account is the information on your Newton that you really want to guard against prying eyes. If you want to add a password that must be entered before Newton will power-on, tap the Set Password button in Personal Preferences.

We recommend that you use as a word or combination of letters and numbers that is not in Newton's 10,000 word dictionary. If you are an executive who might be carrying valuable information, all a competitor need do is get hold of your Newton and type each word in the dictionary into the password screen. Sooner or later they will get it. *(continued)*

Assist... A word about your password (continued)

Choose eight letters and numbers, and mix them up good. For added security, don't put the word in your personal word list. Instead, when you power up your Newton, double-tap the password field and use the keyboard to enter your code. Newton will recognize a typed password, even if it isn't in the dictionaries. This eliminates the possibility that someone would obtain your password by browsing your word list.

Is this paranoid behavior? Well, if you think so, consider the fact that a cracker recently broke into Mitch's account on the WELL, a well-known Internet hang-out. For more than a month the cracker used Mitch's account, gaining complete control over his account—Mitch's bill didn't even reflect the hours this cracker was spending disguised as Mitch. The mistake that tipped Mitch and The WELL staff off was a pile of files saved to his account.

What was the password that got cracked? "BigWord2." So, you see, even a relatively unusual phrase can fail as a password.

One other note about Newton's internal password. It is saved in internal RAM, so, if you store your most valuable information on the PCMCIA card, all a data thief need do is steal your Newton, remove the card and plug it into their Newton. There's nothing you can do to protect yourself from this data bait-and-switch short of putting all your most valuable files into internal RAM.

Styles

Newton offers very few choices in the way of fonts. Of course your paper notebook has never let you change the typestyle of a note. The Styles icon in the Extras drawer provides a limited palette of font and ink options.

Newton ships with three built-in fonts, the 9, 10, 12, and 18 point Simple and Fancy fonts, and a hidden font, called Espy, which you cannot access that the Assistant uses when entering Notepad information into the calendar. Apple will not be shipping additional fonts for the MessagePad, but third-parties will be able to offer font packs which install into Newtons. (Elegance, a must-have utility from Tanis Development, allows you a

greater range of font sizes and access to the mysterious Espy font. You can also add things like shadow effects to type, if you want.)

The MessagePad and Expert Pad use bit-mapped fonts to render text on screen and when printing to TrueType-compatible printers. When you send a document to a PostScript printer, Newton uses PostScript versions of the Plain and Fancy fonts.

Select the font, size and style (Plain, Bold, and Underline) Styles palette by tapping the appropriate buttons. After you make the changes and close the Styles window, all text you enter in the Notepad will appear in that font style.

You can also change existing text by selecting it. For instance, say you want to make a single sentence larger and bold so that it stands out. Tap and hold the pen until you hear a mouse-squeak and the ink beneath the pen becomes very thick, then highlight the text you want to change. Open Styles and make the changes to the font description. When you close Styles, the selected text will have changed, but further entries to the document will appear in the standard font.

Styles also lets you change the thickness of the ink produced by your pen. A thicker line, for example, might make your untranslated ink notes easier to read.

Ink thickness has no bearing on the performance of your handwriting recognizers. They collect only the stroke information, and any kind of ink line can be layered on top of the vectors of a stroke without affecting Newton's perception of the input. Want proof, change the ink settings to the thickest line and write a word in the Notepad while the recognizer is turned on. Then, double-tap the translated word; the ink choice just above the keyboard in the pop-up list will appear in a fine line. Tap the ink choice and Newton draws the word in the original thick ink—same vectors, different ink lines.

Connecting Newton

The Third Law: The closer to the speed of light an object travels,
The more likely it is to be traveling on an optical phone line.

Corollary II: The true philosopher never stops at a busy signal.

Dial 1-900-4NEWTON

Newton networking isn't so much about cables and serial ports as it is about how information is transferred between the PDA in your hand and a world chock full of information you might find useful, if only you could reach it. Information connections are made by the applications that run on your Newton, desktop computers and company and public networks, like NewtonMail.

Many of the questions dominating the on-line forums in the months after the first Newtons shipped had to do with the Newton Connection software from Apple, a software tool for linking Newtons to Macs and PCs. When would Connection be widely available? How did the early version of Connection for Macintosh, which was given free to Newton buyers, work? Which version, Newton Connection or Newton Connection Pro, did people need if they wanted to import data from their existing desktop applications? These were some of the queries frequently seen on the online support forums.

Then Apple announced that Pro would never ship. Instead the company would fold the advanced features promised in Pro into Newton Connection 2.0, which was due out in November, 1993.

Although not as common, other communications-oriented questions included things like when would NewtonMail be available? How can I receive a fax? (You can't.) Where do I find a Newton Messaging Card? Although there were the typical blazes over sloppy handwriting recognition and regular meetings of the Newton "bug of the month" club, discussions about communications dominated the online banter—as it should be with a "Personal Communications Assistant."

This section will take you by the hand for a journey through the Newton Connection software, Sharp Wizard translators, faxing, electronic mail, the MobileComm paging network, and printers of all ilk. We'll take a look at the strategies you can use to transfer data, create custom archives that address different situations, and how to put what you learn to use in your Newton-enabled life.

CHAPTER
8

READY, SET, LOAD!

The best place to start our digital data voyage is with the capabilities of the Newton Connection, the software you'll use to get your data back and forth between a desktop computer and the Newton.

Connection, the Newton Side. When opening the Extras drawer, you'll see an application called Connection. This is the application that hooks your Newton to a desktop computer running Newton Connection software (see Figure 8.1).

The Connection application looks around your Newton's internal and card-based memory and, at a cue from your PC, sends a copy of everything it sees to the desktop machine; it also catches data sent by the desktop computer, determines where it belongs, and installs it into the appropriate place in Newton's RAM or on a card.

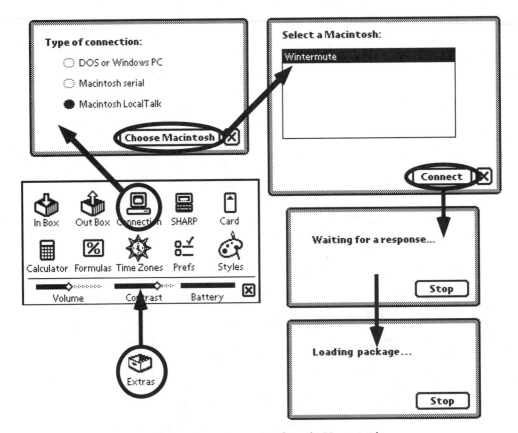

Figure 8.1 *Starting a Newton Connection session from the Newton side.*

Connection, the Computer Side. The Newton Connection for Mac or PCs, which you must purchase separately, creates an exact copy of the information stored in your Newton, a record of all the changes you make and the information you delete, and allows you to edit Newton data in windows that mimic the Names, Dates and Notepad applications. You'll also need Connection to install Newton applications, system updates and restore archives. And you must hook your Newton to the Mac via either a LocalTalk or serial connection (LocalTalk is faster) or to your PC via a serial cable (see Table 8.1).

Table 8.1 Two ways to make your connection.

Connect Newton to:	*Via:*
Macintosh running Newton Connection	1. Serial port and serial cable. 2. Serial port and LocalTalk connector or serial cable.
Windows PC running Newton Connection	Serial port and serial cable.

Newton Connection 2.0, which should be out by November, 1993, adds to the basic backup, edit and restore features of the application. It will include special translators that let you export data and graphics from desktop computer applications (see Tables 8.2 and 8.3).

Be sure to purchase the version of Connection that runs on your computer. Apple and Sharp will offer a Mac version, and one that runs on a Windows-based PC—there's no particular benefit to running Connection on either platform—the applications are functionally identical. It's just a matter of where your data's at.

Mac users: make sure that you are running System 7.1 or later. By the time you read this, there will be a second name for the Mac operating system, System 7 Pro, an enhanced version that includes collaborative capabilities that are part of the Apple Open Collaboration Environment. But under the pretty duds, System 7 Pro is basically System 7.1.

Windows users must be running Version 3.1 of Windows or Windows for Workgroups.

Table 8.2 PC Data Export/Import Translators available in Connection 2.0.

To/From Newton Notepad	To/From Newton Name File	To/From Newton Dates
Lotus Development Corp. Lotus Organizer	*Lotus Development Corp.* Lotus Organizer	*Lotus Development Corp.* Lotus Organizer
Polaris Software Inc. PackRat	*Portfolio Software Inc.* Dynodex	*Polaris Software Inc.* PackRat
Contact Software International Inc. ACT!	*Polaris Software Inc.* PackRat	*Contact Software International Inc.* ACT!
Lotus Development Corp. AMI Pro	*Contact Software International Inc.* ACT!	*Microsoft Corp.* Works
Micorosoft Corp. Word [1]	*Micorosoft Corp.* Works	*Micorosoft Corp.* Excel
Microsoft Corp. Works [1] Rich Text Format (RTF) files [1]	*Microsoft Corp.* Works	*Lotus Development Corp.* Lotus 1-2-3
WordPerfect Corp. WordPerfect [1]	*Microsoft Corp.* Excel	SYmbolic LinK (SYLK) files Data Interchange Format (DIF) files Tab Separated Variables (TSV) files Comma Separated Variables (CSV) files Tab-delimited Text files
	Lotus Development Corp. Lotus 1-2-3	
	SYmbolic LinK (SYLK) files dBASE format (DBF) files Data Interchange Format (DIF) files Tab Separated Variables (TSV) files Comma Separated Variables (CSV) files Tab-delimited Text files	

(1) = Embedded graphics translated: WMF <-> Newton Graphics

Table 8.3 Mac Data Export/Import Translators available in Connection 2.0.

To/From Newton Notepad	To/From Newton Name File	To/From Newton Dates
Contact Software International Inc. ACT!	*Power Up Software* AddressBook Plus	*Aldus Corp.* DateBook
Claris Corp. MacWrite II [2]	*Portfolio Software Inc.* Dynodex	*Contact Software International Inc.* ACT!
Microsoft Corp. Word [2]	*Contact Software International Inc.* ACT!	*Now Software Inc.* Now Up-to-Date
Microsoft Corp. Works	*Microsoft Corp.* Works	MS Works SS
Nisus Software inc. Nisus [2]	*Microsoft Corp.* Excel	*Microsoft Corp.* Excel
Rich Text Format (RTF) files [2]	*Lotus Development Corp.* Lotus 1-2-3	*Lotus Development Corp.* Lotus 1-2-3
	SYmbolic LinK (SYLK) files	SYmbolic LinK (SYLK) files
WordPerfect Corp. WordPerfect [2]	dBASE format (DBF) files	Tab Separated Variables (TSV) files
WriteNow	Data Interchange Format (DIF) files	Comma Separated Variables (CSV) files
	Tab Separated Variables (TSV) files	Tab-delimited Text files
	Comma Separated Variables (CSV) files	
	Tab-delimited Text files	

(2) = Embedded graphics translated: PICT <-> Newton Graphics

Get Info... Pro no more

Apple contributed to a good deal of confusion about how people would be able to import data from their existing electronic records, when it first announced and then canceled Newton Connection Pro.

Pro was supposed to make the Connection application truly useful, because, let's face it, entering names and addresses by re-typing them into plain-vanilla Connection is just a pain. But, for some reason, that was all the Newton Connection buyer was going to get.

On-line forums were a-buzz with tips for cutting and pasting between Mac applications and the Connection Names file, which reformats data incredibly slowly once you have more than a couple dozen records in it. One tip advocated importing the names to Newton in a single chunk (Name, address, phone number, title—everything—as a single field) and separating the data once it was in the Newton.

But it was clear that people who were about to spend $199 on Newton Connection would shortly reach their frustration level with that program and be forced to spend a little more on Pro. Dumb.

Fortunately, Apple recognized that it was about to ask a premium for a feature that everybody expected—after all, why shouldn't a personal digital assistant be able to read existing computerized data? They decided to delete Connection Pro and put these much needed import/export capabilities in the second edition of Connection, Version 2.0 (which, in reality, is Pro). Folks who bought Connection would get the upgrade for free, and everybody gets happy.

But the story doesn't end there. Think for a moment about how you use, or intend to use, Newton. It should be the only interface you need to learn to manage your personal information, whether you are writing on the MessagePad or Expert Pad or typing on a computer.   *(continued)*

Get Info... Pro no more (continued)

Connection can't quite keep up yet, since the desktop application can communicate only with Newtons, not other computers on the network.

Now, remember what we said about System 7 Pro? There's an eerie familiarity to that name, *Pro,* isn't there? The basis of the new Mac OS bundle is that it can communicate with applications, other Macs and even PCs. It can send calendar items, messages and just about anything else from computer to computer.

Just imagine a future version of System 7 Pro that includes Newton Connection with the added capability to allow a Mac user to share Newton data with other computer users. You'd be able to schedule a meeting on your Mac, check in with the people you want to have attend the meeting, share a proposed agenda, and have the appointment entered automatically on everyone's calendar, which could be exported to your Newtons, as well.

Pretty slick, and we hear that this is an idea whose time may come. If so, the Connection Pro will be back, maybe in "C3, The Network Terminator" (ouch!).

The Fetch Connection (Mac or PC to Newton)

When you open your Newton Connection box, you'll find a manual and two diskettes that contain the software. Apple includes an Installer program on Disk One that automates the placement of all the necessary files on your computer. Here are the steps for installing Connection on each type of computer:

Macintosh Installation

1. Click on the Install Connection icon in the window that opens when you insert Disk One. This launches an application that lets you install all the files on the two disks, or just the application itself *sans* user help files. To save some disk space, skip the help files.

2. Sit back and let the Installer do its work (it'll prompt you for the second disk when it needs it). What happens now? The Connection application is installed in a folder, called Newton Connection, on your startup hard drive; a sample archive that represents the contents of a Newton and a ReadMe file with notes about the most recent version of the application are also placed in this folder.

Meanwhile, the Installer puts a new AppleTalk ADSP Tool in your System Folder. It works with the standard Macintosh communications utility, the Communications Toolbox, which is part of System 7. Essentially, you've just added a new extension that links the Mac OS to your Newton over an AppleTalk network. Third-party Mac applications that want to communicate with Newton will also talk through this tool.

3. Launch Connection by double-clicking on its icon. Then click on the Edit menu and select Preferences, which opens a window that lets you tell the Mac where and when to look for a Newton connection (see Figure 8.2). If you are using a LocalTalk network, check the "Connect via Network" box. When you choose a serial connection, you'll need to click the "Connect via Serial Port" box and tell the application to which of the two serial ports on the Mac the cable will be connected.

The "Always ready to synchronize" button is somewhat misleading, because Connection can synchronize its database with a Newton only when it is actually running. Many applications, like screen savers or file compression utilities, operate whenever the conditions on the Mac are appropriate—the machine has been idle for a preset number of minutes, so the screen saver goes to work. You can launch Newton Connection and leave it running in the background while working in another application, but the performance of other applications will slow to a crawl during synchronizations.

You don't have to open the Preferences window to see if your copy of Connection is set to accept synchronizations at anytime. Look at the main Connection window, which presents oversized icons for the Synchronize, Restore and Install Package functions. If the Synchronize button is highlighted (black), Connection is ready to synchronize anytime it receives a signal from a Newton.

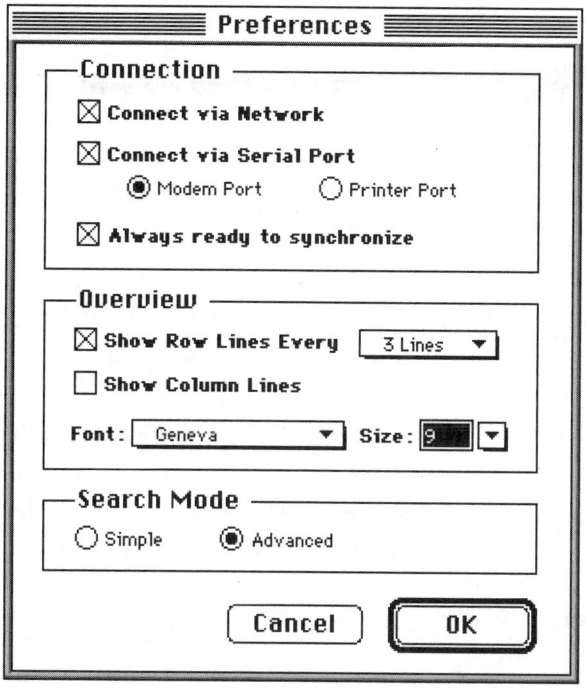

Figure 8.2 *Express Your Connection Preferences.*

The other settings in the Preferences window control the look of Connection's mimic'd Newton applications. Try them in various setting until you find what feels right.

Windows installation:

1. Insert the Newton Connection Kit for Windows Disk One into the floppy drive and launch the Installer application. You can install Connection and help files; we told Mac users to ignore the help files, but since you are a Windows user, you'll probably want to install them—you people seem to like documentation. We don't know what it is about you! (Just kidding. Feel free to ignore the help files if you want.)

2. Since the Windows version of Connection relies on the serial port to link to a Newton, all the Installer puts on your hard drive is the Connection application itself and the sample archives.

3. After the Installer is done with its work, open the Connection application and select the Edit menu, click on Preferences. The only choice you have to make here is which serial port you'll use, and whether you want your PC to be ready to synchronize at anytime. The Synchronize button in the main Connection window will be displayed in black if the "Always ready to synchronize" box is checked in the Preferences window.

The rest of the Preferences settings control the look of Newton application windows within the Connection interface.

Synchronized Swimming

Now that Connection is installed, it's time to create a backup file of your Newton's personal data, preferences, and changes in the adaptive handwriting model. The Synchronize function takes care of this, weaving together the data stored in the Newton's internal RAM, and any PCMCIA storage card inserted at the time, with Connection's own archives like two swimmers performing an Olympic-competition water ballet—a klutzy sport if ever there was one.

What you get when Connection is done with its synchronizing performance are three files: the backup file of the most recent data on the Newton (Connection uses your personal information to name these files, for instance, the most recent backup is called "Mitch Ratcliffe's Newton"); the previous backup file (i.e., "Mitch Ratcliffe's Newton Backup"); and a record of all the information that has been deleted from your Newton, the archive (i.e., "Mitch Ratcliffe's Newton Archive"). Connection also creates a set of backup files for each storage card it finds in the PCMCIA slot; it will open a new set each time you Synchronize with a different card.

What good are all these files? Well, let's say your MessagePad's batteries didn't have such a good day and the contents of its internal RAM were lost. This is a remote possibility, but one for which you should be prepared. All of a sudden, you've plummeted into the pre-historic era of Newton Version 1.0, all the learning about your handwriting Newton piled up is gone, your personal dictionary has pulled up stakes, Newton's as dog-stupid as the day you got it. Data stored on a RAM card is still good, so your Names list, applications and the like are okay. But you never bothered to backup your Newton's internal RAM to the card. If you've synchronized with Connection recently, a fresh copy of the operating system, your handwriting files, and settings are waiting to be restored.

Assist...Connection at the Company

An office making the move to Newton platform will probably want to provide some kind of centralized Newton archive. Just one copy of Connection for Macintosh with a LocalTalk network link can serve the backup needs of an entire office.

Each time Connection synchronizes with a Newton, it first checks the name of the user in its Preferences settings. If it is a Newton that's never dropped in for a backup before, Connection creates a new folder where the synch file, backup and archive for the Newton and cards are stored. As many Newton backups can be managed by one copy of Connection as you have room on that computer's hard drive, though it can synchronize only one Newton at a time (even if they're connecting over the network).

The Mac version of Connection is the ideal choice, since it supports a network interface. If you were to force folks to line up for a serial connection to Connection, there'd be mutiny in the hearts of your crew.

If you do backup your Newton to a central server, make sure that you don't keep another version of Connection on a second computer—or, if you do, be very careful to perform synchronizations to one right after the other, and be sure that you edit data in only one version of Connection—the one you synch first each time. This will prevent changes made to one Connection file from being shuffled into the archive before you update the other, which would lead to seriously contradictory versions of your data on the two desktop computers.

Also, remember that each time you perform a cold boot (factory reset) to clear your RAM, Connection believes it is starting anew with a different Newton. It creates a new folder and ignores your old archive. The best way to avoid the two-folder blues is to restore the last synch'd file to your Newton after a cold boot.

If you happen to modify an existing name record between two synchronizations on both the Newton and in Connection, the update will not be erased. Changes made to Newton take precedence over the information stored in the Connection backup file—so the older version of the name file record will be shuffled down the Connection food chain to the backup or archive file.

Newton precedence can occasionally be the cause of confusion, too. Connection tracks changes on a record level, rather than by following individual fields in a record. So, for instance, if you change the Name file record for Nazila Alasti, altering Nazila's address on your Newton and then her home phone on your Macintosh, only the Newton changes will be reflected after the next synchronization. The Mac changes are relegated to the archive of deleted information in the Connection folder for your Newton. You'll receive a message in Connection that tells you that you changed the same record on your Newton and computer, what kind of record was changed and that the computer version of the file has been sent off to the archive archipelago.

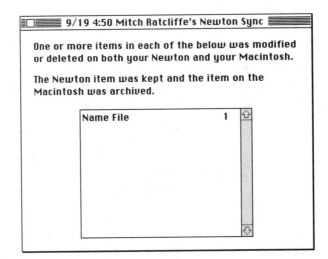

Figure 8.3 Conflicting Message

The contents of notes are backed-up en masse. Changes made within a note, like a list that you have updated on your Newton, are lost during synchronizations. The last backup copy of the note is replaced by the current version of the note.

Assist... What backup?

Everything stored in the RAM of a Newton is backed up, everything. That ensures that when you lose your data and the files that make your Newton personal and functional, Connection can put your Newton back into fighting shape.

The Backup Roster

Connection copies these files to your Mac or PC:

System updates

User dictionaries Recognizer files

Calendar items and notes

Names files

Notepad notes

Application Directory

Files stored in the In Box and Out Box

Repeat calendar items and notes

To Do items

Connection begins each synchronization by copying the last synch file into the Backup file, then it runs through the list of objects above, copying them to the Mac or PC. Then it goes over an installed storage card, copying the information on the card, but not Newton backups stored on the card. Finally, Connection checks for changes in the Connection files on the desktop machine and uploads them to the Newton. You end up with two identical copies of your Newton data, one in the MessagePad or Expert Pad, the other in Connection on your PC.

The Restore button in Newton Connection opens a file dialog box where you select which file you want to install on the Newton. It's not necessary to select the most recent backup file; instead you can install customized versions of your data that fit different situations. See Chapter Nine —*The Information Sculptor*, for more information.

Once you've selected the backup file you want to restore, Connection will ask you to open a connection from the Newton. Tap the Extras drawer icon on your MessagePad or Expert Pad, tap Connection and select the desktop computer link you want to use (Figure 8.1). A window will open on the computer that relates the progress of the restoration.

Restoring replaces all the information on your Newton, including any system updates that have earlier version numbers than the current update in the Newton memory. Use this feature only when you absolutely need to, or when you are sure the backup you are using includes the latest system update and dictionaries.

Naming Names

Extracting names, addresses, and phone numbers from your existing database—whether it's Polaris Software Inc.'s PackRat on a Windows machine or Portfolio Software Inc.'s Dynodex running on a Mac—is made fairly easy with Connection 2.0. But you must understand how your data is arranged in your current application, what happens to it when exported from that application, and how it must be arranged for easy digestion by Newton Connection.

All contact management applications draw on the stultifyingly boring world of databases. We won't bring you to tears with the painful minutiae of database structures, but we will take a bit of sadistic pleasure in introducing you to the Concept of Computer Records and Fields... not to be confused with Newton records and fields.

As we've already explained, the datascape inside Newton can be imagined as standing inside a bowl of soup. You can see data objects, which can be linked in many different combinations, floating around like so much alphabetical pasta (this is a Campbell's-driven fantasy). These objects are arranged in frames, the conceptual order that connects a name to an address, company name, title and phone numbers on a business card, for example.

In a standard database, running on an aging mainframe or your own desktop computer, information is much more rigidly organized. Every database has a column and row-based structure. Columns are lined up next to one another, each designated to contain only first names, last names, phone numbers and so forth. In a contact database, a person is described as a fixed collection of data listed in a single row and arranged in the appropriate columns. So, "Frank at the bank," your father's old friend, is represented in a row thusly:

First	Last	Title	Company	Address	City	Phone
Frank	Cable	Loan	Bank	1 1st.	Tacoma	206...

Even if you usually deal with data in a friendly form, the names, addresses and phone numbers you enter flow right into a row of data arranged in columns. Each field in the form is linked to a particular column in the database; the forms provide a natural way to view and enter data into a single row.

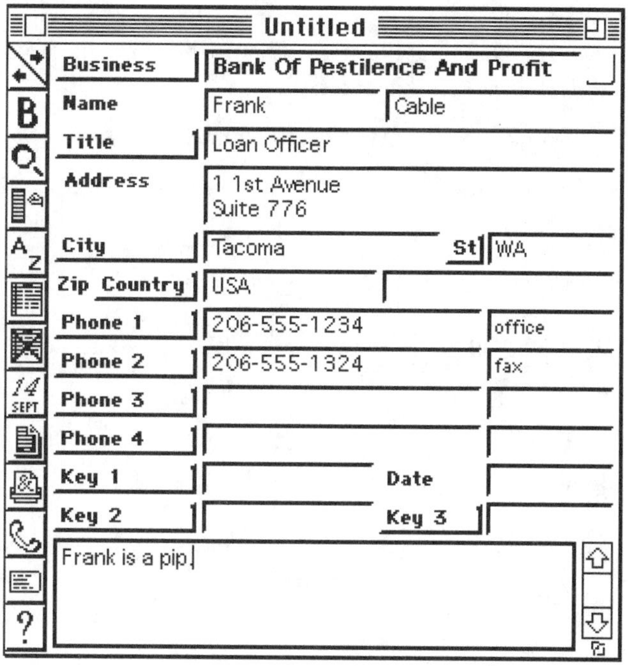

Figure 8.4 *From columns and rows to friendly forms.*

Newton applications, in general, are forms-based. Take the Newton Names file application; it lets you enter data in a form and presents information that has been linked to forms that look like a business card or a list.

Traditional databases are created before the data is entered into them, so the data has to fit. When you move data from one database to another, it must be arranged so that the first names land in the first name column of the destination database, last names in the last names columns, and so forth.

It's an anal-retentive world view, but you have to live with it. Translators included with Connection 2.0 will not deal with organizing your data (You'd think a *translator* could handle that kind of work, but no). They can't look over the data, match the first names in one database to the first name column in the other. Translators simply put it into a form that indicates where one field begins and another ends, so that the data you move doesn't end up in a single field.

When preparing your current contact database for export to the Newton, you should compare the structure of the information with the requirements of the Names application. Export the contents of your database so that the fields match this order:

1. Salutation (Ms./Mr.)
2. First Name
3. Last Name
4. Title
5. Company
6. Address
7. City
8. State
9. ZIP Code
10. Country
11. E-Mail
12. Phone 1
13. Key 1
14. Phone 2
15. Key 2
16. Phone 3
17. Key 3
18. Phone 4
19. Key 4
20. E-Mail
21. Birthday
22. Folder Name
23. Card Style

Look for the help in sorting fields in the export engine of your desktop database application. Whether working with a Mac database like Aldus Corp.'s TouchBASE or a relational database for the PC, like Borland International Inc.'s Paradox, you can specify the order in which fields will be exported.

From Here—a list of contacts records in Dynodex...

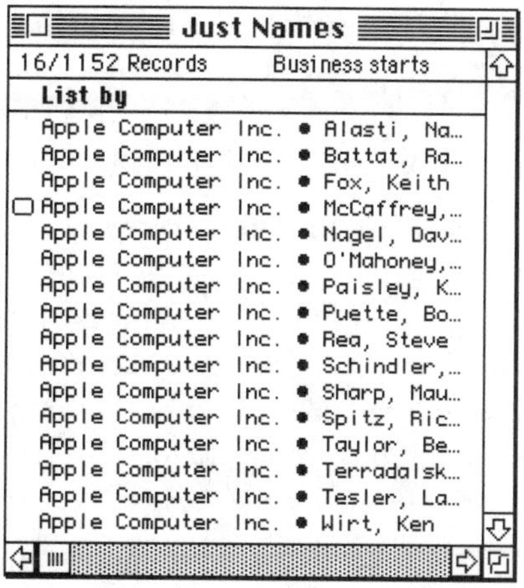

Through Here—the Dynodex export dialog box...

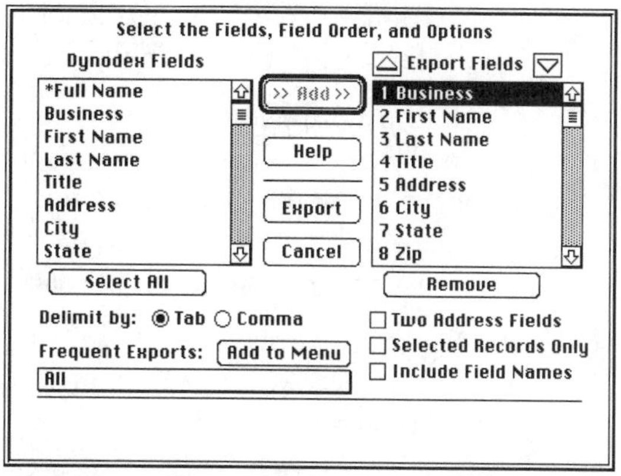

To Here—The Newton Connection Name file list window.

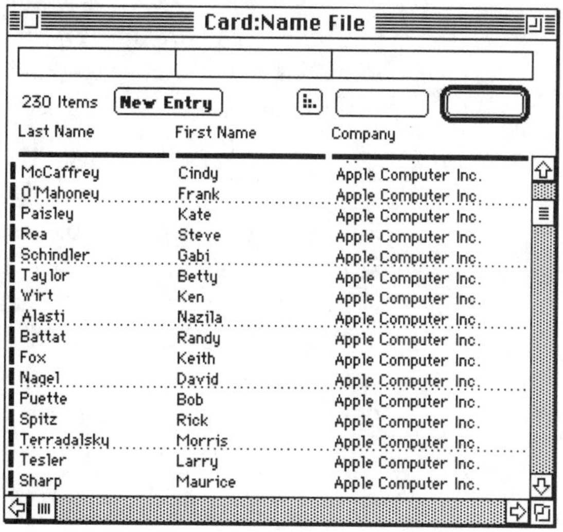

Figure 8.5 *Getting records from a PC to Newton.*

Your database might not have 23 fields for each record, that's okay. Or, your company's database may take up 100 fields that describe in great detail a person or company, and in that case you'll need to decide which fields are crucial and need to be downloaded to your Newton.

The practical limit for a Newton Names entry is 17 fields, because the fields Key 1 through Key 4, the Folder Name and Card Style are dedicated to recording your preferences for the phone fields, filing and display of the record. If you import a record from a database that includes a fax field, Connection can take a cue from the import file and change the name of the phone field into which the data is imported to "Fax" (that bit of data is then saved in the key field associated with the phone field).

When synchronizing Newton data to a third-party database, rather than Connection, you can save the Folder Name and Card Style keys by creating special fields that can contain that information.

Third-party applications, like Portfolio's Dynodex and TouchBASE will eventually bypass Connection and provide direct synchronization with Newtons. Once they accomplish this feat, you'll be able to manage your data on your Newton and desktop computer database in the same convenient manner that Connection enables today.

Did we say convenient? Well, if you were one of the lucky ones whose Newton arrived with Connection 2.0, data management is a matter of three easy steps:

1. Export the data from your desktop database. Take a look back at the file formats supported by Connection 2.0, if you see the native file format of your current personal information management software —for example, the ACT!, PackRat, Excel, or Dynodex formats— then all you need to do is set the fields in the right order and export them.

   If, however, Connection 2.0 doesn't handle your application's native format, you should export data into one of the generic formats, like SYLK or tab-delimited text. These files include markers that separate the fields and records in the database from one another. We recommend the tab-delimited format, it's the *lingua franca* of file translation, not so nearly exotic as the Comma Separated Variable format, for instance.

2. Import the file into Connection 2.0. Now here's something that looks easier than it is. If you repeatedly import the same data into Connection, you'll end up with multiple copies of each entry—a dozen Tricia Chans are no better than the original, in fact they're worse (Tricia, who was the Apple PR person who was the greatest help with Newton inquiries, doesn't eat much, but try taking all twelve of her to lunch—Ow!).

Moving information back and forth from your Newton through Connection to a desktop database requires that you constantly purge the old data from Connection before you import the updated information. Hold down the Shift key and click the first name in the Names Browser Window, then scroll to the bottom of the list and click the last name. The entire list will be selected and you can use the Cut command under the Edit menu to remove them from the Connection database.

3. Synchronize your Newton, the data now appears in the Names application.

This process works the same way in both the Mac and Windows version of Connection 2.0.

Now, let's imagine that you're still waiting for Connection 2.0 (a possibility for the first of you who buy this book). How do you get your data into that $700 MessagePad or Expert Pad sitting there amidst the packaging and bill of sale scattered on your desk?

Let's start with what you cannot do: You can't open the Overview window and paste in an entire row of information. There is also no way to import data from Dynodex, TouchBASE or PackRat directly into Connection 1.0.

So, you have to open the two applications, Connection 1.0 and your database, and copy the data field by field into the Connection Detail window (the form for entering and viewing data). Several macros were developed for finishing this process more quickly. They are available in the software libraries of CompuServe's and America Online's Newton forums. This is the heavy work of the information age, no doubt about it.

Our guess is that Newton loading is going to end up being the work of the secretary or administrative assistant. Can't you just see the ghost of Frederick Jackson Taylor standing over the shoulders of these people as they cut-and-paste their bosses lives into Newton Connection. Truly, there is a new blue collar class coming along, only their hands won't be callused. Instead, they'll all have carpal tunnel syndrome.

If you are one of those unlucky people who has to manage someone else's Newton information, make sure that you keep up on the developments with Dynodex and TouchBASE, which will be the first databases to have direct Newton data links. They'll let you plug in a Newton for an automatic update, as well as allowing you to create custom databases for certain trips the boss takes (an Asia-only database, for example, that you send along on a trip to Japan).

One last, but important, note about importing names to your Newton. Remember that Newton Connection works on dates and judges if the information it contains is more current than the data on the Newton by comparing *both* the last backup date and the date the record was last modified. So, if you have Tony Espinoza on your Newton and in the current Connection backup and you change something in Tony's record on Connection's version of the record, the next time you synchronize your Newton to that file the modified version of Tony's record will replace the Newton's version. The Newton name record only wins out over Connection if it too has been modified since the last backup.

ConTextual Transfers

Getting textual information from your favorite word processor to the Newton Notepad, can also be a bit of a trick.

We were not able to test the translators for Rich Text Format files included in 2.0, which includes the ability to convert a graphic image from the Windows WMF or Macintosh PICT format to the Newton Graphics Format. However, our experience with desktop and other portable computing devices, like the EO Personal Communicators, suggest that making the leap from a beautifully-made word processing document to the small-screen world of Newton will not be easy.

For one thing, a full page of graphics will take considerable squeezing before it'll fit on a Newton's 3 × 5 screen. Tables, charts and specially formatted text are likely to get scrambled a bit.

Text files will quickly run up against the length limit on a Notepad note of 4,000 bytes (and long notes slow Newton down considerably). Until Apple accommodates longer notes, don't expect to translate your novel into

Newton format, unless you intend to become a Newton developer and use the electronic book player in the Newton ROM. There is a tool for the Macintosh code-named Dickens/Copperfield that makes it relatively easy to move text and pictures over to a MessagePad or Expert Pad. Developers, contact PIE-DTS (Personal Interactive Electronics—Developer Training and Support) for more info.

If you need to distribute information to Newton users, or just carry along a set of product sheets, break them up into page-sized chunks before sending them to Connection. The average page of printed matter on a computer contains between 250 and 300 words, just enough to fill a Newton note in a small font. Tag the beginning of each note with keywords; that way the user can search for relevant information using the Find button or by tapping the Overview button to see the first words of all the notes in their Notepad.

Connecting Calendars

Several calendaring applications will get direct links to Connection 2.0. ON Technology's Meeting Maker, Now Software Inc.'s Now Up-to-Date, and Aldus Corp.'s DateBook are among the leading Mac calendaring programs that will be able to exchange information with Newton. On the Windows side of the tracks—the main street of computing—Polaris Software Inc.'s PackRat, Microsoft Corp.'s Works and Contact Software International Inc.'s ACT! will be able to hook onto Connection to update the Newton Dates calendar.

Apple wasn't finished with the calendar features of Connection 2.0 when we went to press. In fact, Apple hadn't specified how calendar information should be formatted. Nevertheless, a couple companies had hacked together their connections for demonstration at the first Newton Expo in September.

Users will first export their calendars to a file. Connection 2.0 will be able to import or install the file directly into the Newton, depending upon how you want to handle the information.

Some sick souls, deprived of better tools like pen and paper, have attempted to keep their personal calendars in a spreadsheet or database on their computer. That's why Apple will also support imported data from Microsoft Excel, Lotus 1-2-3, and the Tab-delimited text file format. At press time, the order in which time, subject, description and alarm fields should be arranged for Newton use were not set.

Look Sharp! Incantations for Wizard data

Newton wasn't the first pocket organizer, and it won't be the last, either. Apple and Sharp Corp., who manufactures the MessagePad and its own Expert Pad, made sure to provide a method for getting data out of the dominant organizer of the last generation, the Sharp Wizard.

You can transfer data in any Sharp Wizard Series 7000, 8000 or 9000 organizer using the RS-422 Level Converter serial cable (which fits the Wizard's flat serial port and the Newton's Mini DIN-8 serial port). It is not possible, however, to export Newton data to a Sharp organizer. Wizard applications that the companies claim can make the journey to Newton are:

- Telephone 1 [N]
- Telephone 2 [N]
- Telephone 3 [N]
- Business Card [N]
- To Do*
- Memo [Np]
- Schedule*
- Anniversary 1 [N/A]
- Period [N/A]
- Alarm*

(N) = imported info to Names application

(Np) = imported info to Notepad application

* = just plain didn't work in our testing with an OZ-8200

(N/A) = not available for testing

We also found that fax numbers stored in the Telephone application didn't make the transition to the Newton; they simply vanished. Fax numbers in the Business Card application did make the leap, and appeared labeled as fax numbers on the Newton.

The import procedure is:

1. Connect the Newton and Wizard.

2. Open the Wizard's PC Link application by typing Shift-Option and "4" in succession.

3. Open the Extras drawer on your Newton. Tap the Sharp application icon. Select the Wizard application from which you wish to import data, and tell Newton where you want to store it (your options are in the internal RAM or on a card). The Wizard is a kind of dumb bunny; it can't do anything but connect, then the computer on the other end sucks the data out like the Wizard was a Slurpee.

4. Now that you've got the data, you have to edit it to fit the Newton application. Things get a little messy here.

Alternatively, if you bump into a friend with an OZ-9600 II Wizard, you can beam droplets of data, such as a single business card. The 9600 must be set to "Direct IR" mode when sending or receiving data. Newton users must open the In Box and tap the Receive button, regardless of how they set their Beam Preferences. You can send only one item at time, so it's better if you have a Wizard and a Newton to use the serial cable when transferring your whole database. Editing the data will take long enough, you might as well save the time it would take to beam every business card in the Wizard's files.

The way the Wizard stores data in the Telephone and Business Card applications is less sophisticated than Newton. The address lines are saved in the Wizard as a single field that holds the street address, city, state and ZIP Code. Once in Newton you can't see the better part of the address, since it runs off the end of the address field. When you tap the address field to open the editing pad, you'll see that the address is truncated by an ellipsis that doesn't seem to want to go away. To separate the data, use the procedure concocted by Robert Wiggins, which he disseminated in the CompuServe Newton Forum:

1. Select the address field to enter the editing mode (a box appears around the text).

2. Double-tap the end of the field (by the ellipsis) to open the keyboard. The insertion point should appear to the left of the ellipsis.

3. In the keyboard, tap the right-pointing direction arrow, then the delete key, and finally the space bar. What you've done is removed the carriage return that forced the ellipsis into the address field.

4. Select the second line of the street address or the name of the city, whatever you want to move to another field, and drag it to the side of the screen (the cut-and-paste procedure). The selected text will shrink and stay glued where you leave it.

5. Select the field into which you're moving the data.

6. Drag the tiny text into the field, where it blossoms into full-size again.

7. Return to the address field and select the next part of the address you want to move. Repeat the cut-and-paste process to get it into the appropriate field. And so on through your entire database.

CompuServe users reported it took two to three hours to get through 150 names. Considering that the Wizard-to-Newton route was the most direct way to import addresses into Newton for the first two months of Newton's life, you can bet that this method got a lot of testing.

Installing Applications and Extras

Connection confusion was amplified at the outset by the fact that the Apple application was just about the only way Newton People could install applications or system updates on their MessagePads and Expert Pads. Weeks worth of CompuServe, America Online, and Internet conversations revolved around when folks would be able to get their hands on Connection so that they could try out the first freeware and shareware applications for Newton. Or, just so they could install the system updates that were flowing out of Apple.

Now, as we settle into the Newton lifestyle, several other installation options are available. But Connection remains a high priority, it's one of the key tools for extending Newton's usefulness.

Let's look at the different forms Newton software might take before it lands on your real or virtual doorstep.

Floppy Disks. You thought you'd never see one of these things again, didn't you? Two words: Absolutely wrong! Floppies are an inexpensive distribution medium for Newton software, just as it is the predominant and desk drawer-filling medium of the PC landscape. You'll need the Connection software to install applications and updates you receive on floppies.

Files on a floppy will arrive in two forms: packages and patches.

The package file (which may or may not appear with a ".PKG" appended to the end) will carry the code needed to add application functions to your Newton. They will be installed into the internal RAM of your Newton, or on a memory card if you set your preferences that way, and will appear in the Extras drawer after Connection is finished.

Patch files include system updates and bug fixes for applications installed in RAM. They install as part of the operating system or an application. So, except for a different version number, they don't necessarily change the look of your Newton.

To install a package or system update, click on the Install Package button in Connection for Windows or Macintosh. This opens a file dialog window that lets you browse and select the file you want to install. When you give it the go-ahead, Connection will link up with your Newton (you must open the Connection application on Newton and tap connect). A moment later, the installation will be complete. Keep the disk in a safe place, because you may need it to reinstall the software if your Newton goes kaput.

Also, beware conflicts when uploading the latest version of an application to your Newton. You'll need to remove any previous versions of an application before uploading an update. Otherwise, the upload will fail with Newton telling you that application is already installed. (Newton can't always tell the difference between two versions of the same application.) This won't be a problem for system updates.

Online Files and Applications. There's a world of free and very inexpensive software out there on the computer networks for those of you with computers and a modem (try the Newton modem with your computer, if you don't already have one). From tip calculators and restaurant bill splitting applications to games and useful utilities, you can be assured you'll find something worth trying out among all the freeware (take it, it's yours) and shareware (you obtain it for free and, if you use it, send the developer a small fee).

Apple has also committed to posting the most recent Newton System Updates on its Internet archive, in CompuServe's and America Online's Newton forums, and its own AppleLink on-line service.

These applications and updates arrive as packages or patches that can be installed through Connection, using the same steps listed above. Tap Install Package, select the package you downloaded and open the Connection application on your Newton and tap Connect. All set.

PCMCIA Cards. Plugging a PCMCIA card with an application stored on it into your Newton is the functional equivalent of installing the software through Connection.

Apple and other developers plan to ship applications on ROM cards, which have very inexpensive read-only memory which contains their software. To give you an idea of what you are paying for in a $100 application, about $70 goes to cover the cost of "burning" the ROM, building the card, packaging, distribution, documentation, and dealer markup; the rest goes to the application developer.

System updates distributed by PCMCIA card will come with an installer application that recognizes when it has been inserted into a Newton running an earlier system update. It will place the system software into RAM and force the Newton to restart. You can call Apple at 800-242-3374 to receive an update card. Apple will include a postage-paid envelope that you should use to return the card. Otherwise, you'll be charged for the unreturned card. That's why Apple asks you for a credit card number when you call requesting the update.

Applications that arrive on PCMCIA cards may have both ROM and RAM memory, which will allow you to save data specific to that application on the same card. For example, Fingertip for Golf, a golf scoring and game analysis application, will ship on a card that includes maps of several golf courses. If you want to add another course, you can upload it directly to the Golf card. As you play, your scores, the clubs you used and distances of each shot will be stored in the card.

Some applications, however, will be shipping on ROM-only cards. An installer application may be included on the card which lets you move the application into RAM, or you'll be able to run the application when the ROM card is inserted. Newton users will be playing the role of Mr. Spock with his data cards, which he shuffled in and out of the PCMCIA slots on the Enterprise. That's actually what those slots were, PCMCIA slots—really.

The problem with placing an application in RAM from a ROM card is, of course, that it pares the available memory for your data. There is no way to move an application directly from RAM onto a storage card. However, several hackers we know have developed ways to bypass the lock that prevents you from beaming applications. Also, at least one developer we know, Tanis Development in New York City, is working on a way to beam applications that aren't secured by their developers (basically, freeware and shareware). It should be part of their upcoming Elegance for Newton utility, which we recommend for every Newton user. (We helped come up with some of the features, so, of course we like it!)

Once you get your hands on a utility, find a friend with a Newton and beam the application to their unit. Make sure that you have your Newton set to save new items to the card, and have your friend beam the application back. It will slip neatly into the card, and you can erase the application from RAM.

We're not advocating that you should beam applications to everyone you meet. People work hard to write these programs, and they deserve the payment for your use of their tools (The League for Programming Freedom, which argues all software code should be free, notwithstanding). There are certainly uses, however, for a utility that allows an application to move from RAM to a card. This would facilitate moving applications to different cards, making it possible to build custom cards that combine information and applications that are most appropriate to the different parts of your life (for more on this, turn to the next chapter, *The Information Sculptor*). This, plus the lower cost of materials, is why we recommend that computer owners get applications on floppies whenever possible. This way, you can determine where an application resides—on a card or in your Newton's main RAM.

Enhancements. The In Box Enhancements feature is a ready-made gateway for installing system updates and applications. You'll need a Newton-compatible modem to use it.

The first Enhancements service is Apple's own 1-800-NEWTON-9, a toll-free number that lets Newton People in the U.S. call in for system updates.

The procedure is as follows:

1. Open the Extras drawer and tap the In Box icon.

2. Tap the Receive button in the In Box, and select Enhancements from the pop-up list that appears. A dialing slip will appear; double tap the phone number field to open a telephone key pad on which you can tap out the number.

3. Tap the Call button. Newton dials the telephone number you entered (you'll see a "connecting" message below the In Box browser window) and downloads the system update or application. When installing a new System Update, you'll see a message, "New system software has been installed. Please tap restart." At this point, according to the In Box status message, the Newton is still receiving information, but go ahead and tap Restart. When it wakes, Newton will be shined up and ready to go with new features (or, more likely, more stable versions of the same features).

Apple and third-party developers will take full advantage of the Enhancements capability in due time. Being able to deliver software to a customer without any packaging, without the intervention of profit-hungry dealers, is like a dream of finding the riches of Crœsus come true. On-line software sales is a marketeer's Eden, they just need you to do one thing: fill out the credit card information in the Mail section of the Preferences file (tap the New E-Mail Account button in the Mail window, then tap the Continue button beneath the account information form, you come to, viola, a credit card form).

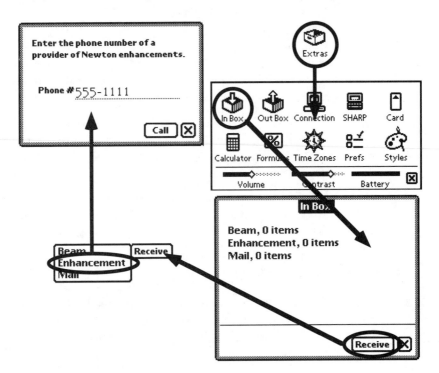

Figure 8.6 *Getting Up-To-Date online.*

Developers will offer new versions of their applications and cool new tools for Newton through direct mail or magazine advertisements. We also expect to see Apple and perhaps other explore the world of "900" numbers to sell software. this way the telephone company can concern itself with collecting your payment, instead of the credit card company. (We can see no reason why Apple would care which it got its money from, with the possible exception being able to net customers reluctant to give over their credit info to a dialog box.)

A word about your privacy in the rugged new market of online sales: You have none. If you look through the Newton documentation and the

Newton interface, there is no guarantee that information you send to an on-line vendor is not going to be sold to innumerable mailing list houses. There's a lot of money in the mailing list business, and selling your name is one way that companies increase their profitability. That's not good, because you have a reasonable expectation of privacy in most sales situations. You can pay cash and avoid giving away any information about yourself; or you can at least ask point-blank, "Are you going to sell my name?"

We suggest that until there is a written explanation of how the credit card information you enter in the Newton will be used, don't go on-line to shop. In this age of information technology that is redefining the relationship of people and the companies or governments with which they interact, it's better to draw the line in the digital sand at your first opportunity. That's how you can retain your personal boundaries.

But enough about installation and backups, it's time to take a look at how you can customize your use of information.

CHAPTER 9

THE INFORMATION
SCULPTOR

Data is by its very nature malleable. It can be used to prove a truth, perpetrate a lie or to cast a question in a more incisive way. When you get data into your Newton it can take on a life of its own, calcifying into useless and troublesome dross when you don't need it or refusing to lend clarity when you need it most, but cannot find it in the mass of information stored in a MessagePad. Now that we've learned how to import, export and backup data, it's time to tackle the surgeries you can perform to tune Newton data and applications to fit the job at hand.

Access to shared data, like calendars and corporate databases, too, is a key to making the most of Newton's information proficiencies. This chapter will also take you on a brief tour of the third-party applications that can be used to add organizational context to the data you own.

Organizing a Newton is not analogous to the annual buying of Day Timer pages for use in a fine leather binder that you'll carry everywhere. Newton is more like your own brain, you have to load it with information, set priorities and memorize facts.

Say you have a slip of paper with three items written on it: Your mother's telephone number, the amount of your monthly car payment, and what you need to pick up at the store. You memorize Mom's number before you put the paper away. About once a month you drag it out when paying your car loan, while the portion with the shopping list will become useless once you make the trip to the Lucky store at the strip mall. So it is with Newton. You'll want some data stored in the Newton's internal memory where you can get at it anytime, other items can be sent off to a storage card that you insert when performing a specialized task. And some items, like a shopping list, you won't save at all.

We're going to go out on a limb and suggest that you should organize your Newton around the tasks you perform and the information that relates to those tasks. Place critical information, like the calendar, into the Newton's internal RAM. Keep a couple of storage cards with customized sets of data for use in the various aspects of your professional and private life (there's no reason that you couldn't use the MessagePad to maintain a Christmas card list; just don't put Uncle Betty and Aunt Jo in the same list with the purchasing managers of your seven largest customers). When you need a list of contacts in the Tri-State area, pop in the storage card that contains those names and the records of your meetings, communications, and reports related to them.

It shouldn't be necessary to buy a dozen storage cards to shape Newton to a dozen different jobs, unless you have twelve distinct and exclusive tasks. Rather, combinations of a few applications, a batch of custom data sets and a bit of Newton Connection savvy should get you through almost any situation.

The volume of storage you'll need to buy should be dictated by the amount of information you need to have at the ready during the day, and the tyranny of your credit line. Since Newton can't handle storage cards with more than 4 Mbytes of data without grinding to a computational halt, you'll need to come up with a mix of one- and two-Mbyte cards (see Chapter Fourteen—*Hot Hardware*, for a list of compatible cards).

We recommend that you carry two cards, if possible, when traveling away from your home or office. Keep a complete data set, which includes your entire Names file and a backup of your system, on one card.

The other card is the one with which you'll get work done in meetings, restaurants and airplanes. You'll be aiming for great performance with Find and Assist when creating the data set on this card. Newton slows down when you enter a thousand, or even a couple hundred, names; it can't keep up in a situation in which you want to write "schedule lunch with David on Thursday" while standing with David at a subway station. Since you're unlikely to need all the names in your database to schedule most of your appointments, use the second card as a repository for the 75 to 200 people whose personal information you really need.

If you're taking a trip to the Seattle area, load the Northwest contacts you'll most likely be meeting with while in the area. You can also get away with a different mix of application software. Leave the programs you use around the office at the office and travel with your RAM storage set aside to support expense reporting, communications, and presentation software you need while sipping Seattle espresso with a sales contact.

Customizing Archives: Mixing a Data Palette

Newton Connection is the place to start. At press time, it's the only chisel you can take to a chunk of Newton data. In 1994, third-party applications will offer direct connections to Newton, allowing you to synch a Names database with a mainframe server or the word processor on your desktop computer. However, the habits you learn in Newton Connection will be valuable throughout your life as a Newtonian pioneer. Time to sharpen those editing skills, everybody!

Fortunately, you never have to operate on a live body of data. Cadaverous backup files will do nicely. In this case, you are both Dr. Frankenstein and Igor, who goes to fetch a fresh brain for his master. Only there's less likelihood that you'll drop the jar containing the good brain (remember, avoid taking the jar labeled "Abby Normal"), if you make a copy of your last synchronization file.

There are three different approaches you can take when creating a custom archive of Seattle contacts on a second storage card.

The Hard Way is the Best Way Method

1. With your main storage card installed—the one with all your contacts and notes stored on it—perform a synchronization of the Newton.

2. Make two copies of the Card file in the Newton folder generated by Newton Connection. Name one of the files "Seattle" and leave the other one alone—just in case.

   To make a copy in the Macintosh Finder: Highlight the Card file in your Newton folder and select the Duplicate command under the File menu.

   To make a copy in the Windows File Manager: Highlight the Card file in the Newton Connection directory and use the Copy command under the File menu.

3. Follow the directions below to edit the Seattle data. Chop up your data, slash names and mess with it until you have a combination of names and notes that fit your typical day in Seattle.

4. Now insert your second RAM card in the Newton (the Seattle card). When you click Restore in the main Connection window and choose the Seattle Card file (not yet!), this blank card will be loaded with the Seattle data. You end up with one card that contains a complete database of contacts and notes, and a second card that contains only that data you need on trips to Seattle.

5. Open Preferences in the Newton Extras drawer. Choose the Personal settings and Change your name to Seattle (or whatever you want to call your custom archive). Close the Preferences and synchronize your Newton using Connection; the program will generate a new folder called Seattle's Newton, which you can use as a backup of the Seattle archive.

6. Remove the Seattle RAM card from your Newton. Put your main RAM card in the slot. Open Preferences again and put your name back in the Personal settings. You can go ahead and work with Newton. The next time you head off to Seattle, you'll have a card for that trip.

7. Return to your desktop computer. You now have two backup folders in Newton Connection (i.e., Mitch Ratcliffe's Newton and Seattle's Newton). When you run Connection it will look at the name in the Personal field of your Newton Preferences and synchronize the Newton to the folder that matches that name. We suggest that you synchronize with your main backup file only. Synching to two different folders can create conflicts that cause Connection to delete data inadvertently.

The Hard Short-cut Method

1. With your main storage card installed—the one with all your contacts and notes stored on it—perform a synchronization of the Newton.

2. Replace your main storage card with a blank PCMCIA card (write "Seattle" on the label so you don't confuse it with the other card). Open Preferences in the Newton Extras drawer. Choose the Personal settings and Change your name to Seattle (or whatever you want to call your custom archive). Close the Preferences and synchronize your Newton using Connection; the program will generate a new folder called Seattle's Newton.

3. Follow the directions below to edit the Seattle data by opening your main archive to select and copy the data you want in the Seattle archive. Now, open the Card file in the Seattle archive, open the Names file and paste the data you copied from the main archive. You can open both your main and Seattle Names files side-by-side on screen to make moving the data easier.

4. With the Seattle card still in your Newton, perform a synchronization. You now have a main archive that is the picture of your Newton when working in normal circumstances, and a Seattle archive
   that mirrors your Newton when working in Seattle.

5. Remove your Seattle card from Newton, return your main storage
   card to the slot and put your name back in the Personal file in Preferences. Connection thinks it is synchronizing two different Newtons.
   You can still use the Seattle card without changing the Newton's preferences to "Seattle." Be sure you synchronize very carefully: it's best
   to synch only to your main archive. But if you are feeling daring, go
   ahead and try to maintain a Seattle archive separately from your main
   backup—just be sure that you have your main archive up-to-date before switching to Seattle mode, and keep your Calendar in the Newton's RAM, not on the card.

If you made a copy of a Newton Connection file in the Finder or File
Manager, all the data it contains will appear in the file when you open it in
Connection. You can take a short-cut to the copied data by double-clicking
the copied file's icon on your Mac desktop or the Windows File Manager.
All you have to do when editing a custom archive is cut the rows that don't
fit your needs when traveling to Seattle, for example.

Newton Connection, by contrast, can generate copies of the applications in an archive, but not the data those applications contain. Connection copies are empty templates for building a custom archive. You must
paste data into this window—it's like starting from scratch.

But it gets weirder still. There's a certain uncoordinated panache to
Connection. The application can synchronize or restore only the authentic
backup files and copies made by the desktop computer's operating system,
but it cannot synchronize nor can it restore the copies of those files that it
makes. So, you have to do your data surgeries on the authentic data—we're
right back in a situation where, if Igor drops the good brain, all is lost—
unless you use the copy of the archive as a repository for your data.

Here are the steps for creating a custom card, using Connection to create a copy:

The What the Hell??? Method

1. With your main storage card inserted in the Newton, do a Connection synchronization.

2. Select the New command in Connection's File menu to begin making a copy of an archive. Connection will open a file dialog box in which you can pick the particular backup file you want to copy.

3. Highlight the Card archive in the file window and click the Open button. Connection will copy all the Newton applications in the Card archive, including third-party applications that appear in the Connection overview window.

4. A third window will open, in which you can name the copy—again, make it a recognizable word, like "Seattle." Because it takes a while to copy the applications, Connection displays a message telling you to be patient while it works.

5. Now, open the Names application in the Seattle archive and in the original Card archive.

6. Select all the data in the Card archive and copy it; use the Select All and Copy Name File Item commands in the Edit menu.

7. Paste the Card archive data into the Names application in the Seattle archive—this is the backup copy you'll need to use when restoring your Card archive at the end of this tedious process.

8. Follow the directions below for editing the data in the Card archive.

9. Once you've got the Seattle data the way you want it, close the Name File and make any changes you'd like to the Notepad.

10. Insert the RAM card you'll use as your Seattle archive into the Newton and use the Restore command to load the modified Card archive. Now, you have a Seattle card and a main data card.

11. Go back to Connection and open the Seattle file and select all the data you stored there (Yes, it's time for the Select All command, again.) Copy the data.

12. Open the Card file, select all the items in the Names browser and choose the Paste Name File Item command. Your original data will flow back into the browser and that nasty customized Seattle data

will go the way of the buffalo. Do the same to restore the Notepad files on your main card.

13. Remove the Seattle card from your Newton and insert your main storage card. Click Restore in Connection to reinstall the original card data. You may be thinking, "Wait a minute, my original data is already in the card." If you don't restore the data now, the next time you synchronize your Newton, Connection will load all the names into your main storage card a second time, and you end up with two of everything.

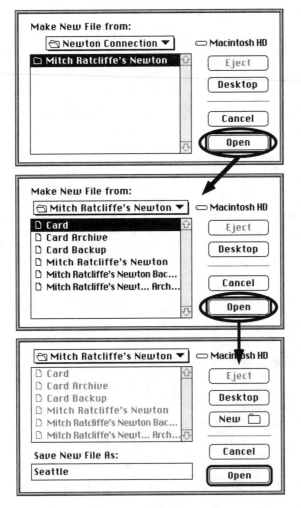

Figure 9.1 *Moving to Hell. First, make a new Connection file called Seattle and open it.*

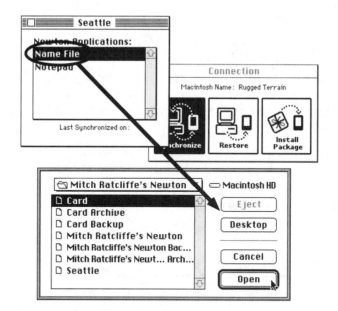

Figure 9.2 *Next, open Seattle's Name file, open the Card synchronization file and then open the Card's Name file (Seattle's browser window should be empty).*

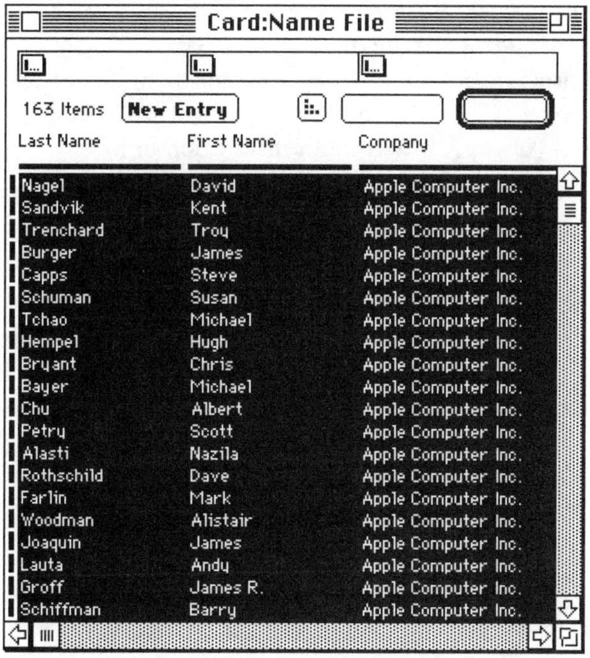

Figure 9.3 *Now, select all your names in the Card Names file browser and copy them to Seattle.*

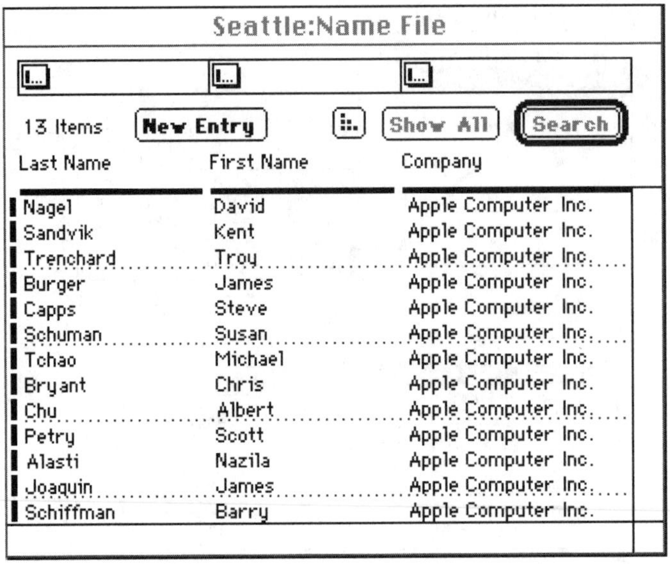

Seattle:Name File

Last Name	First Name	Company
Nagel	David	Apple Computer Inc.
Sandvik	Kent	Apple Computer Inc.
Trenchard	Troy	Apple Computer Inc.
Burger	James	Apple Computer Inc.
Capps	Steve	Apple Computer Inc.
Schuman	Susan	Apple Computer Inc.
Tchao	Michael	Apple Computer Inc.
Bryant	Chris	Apple Computer Inc.
Chu	Albert	Apple Computer Inc.
Petry	Scott	Apple Computer Inc.
Alasti	Nazila	Apple Computer Inc.
Joaquin	James	Apple Computer Inc.
Schiffman	Barry	Apple Computer Inc.

Figure 9.4 Finally, use the paste command to copy all the records you selected in the Card Names file into Seattle's Names file browser window.

Seriously, folks, there's got to be an easier way. We're talking dippy information management here, the kind of all-consuming tasks that small consulting firms are built on. We can only pray that the third-party developers of the world will quickly solve these problems. Then, we'll write a second edition of Newton's Law without this section in it. Anything is easier.

Until then, however, here are the details of the editing process in Connection. These instructions will be useful when you are moving data between Connection and third-party databases and spreadsheets, as well. So, if you're planning on using a desktop application other than Apple's Newton Connection, you'll want to look this over.

Step-by-Step in Data Hell

Let's say you want to cut and paste data from one archive to another after one of your main contacts moves to Seattle; you want her to appear in your custom archive. On your PC or Mac, open the regular Connection file and the Seattle archive. Click on the Name File in each Overview window, so that both browser windows are open and viewable.

In the main synch file, click on the heavy black bar to the left of the name of a person whom you want to add to the Newton Names file. The entire row will turn black. You can now copy it by selecting the Copy Name File Entry command under the Edit menu.

Now, click on the Newton Names browser window to make it the active window. Select the Paste Name File Entry; the row is added to the Newton Names file. You can now click on that row to open a detail window where you can edit the person's name, address, and phone number.

Aren't these the most compelling instructions you've ever read? Well, you can live that experience over, again and again as you cut and paste Name entries. You can cut down on the cutting and pasting by selecting multiple rows. Hold down the Shift key, click on one row and then move to the next row and, still holding that darned Shift key, click that row as well. Both will be highlighted, and you can choose the Copy command to move the information into another archive.

If you're a Mac or Windows user (in the File Manager), the Shift key has long been a means of selecting multiple items on a screen, even if you did not select some intervening items. It's a very easy and natural way to grab a whole lot of stuff for copying, cutting or dragging. But in the version of Connection we tested, the Shift key forced us to select all the items between two points, rather than leaving some items behind. This means you have to go back and forth between the Connection browsers instead of selecting all the rows you want and copying them in one fell swoop. Apple should fix that.

Conversely, however, if you started with a complete copy of your data which you made in the Mac Finder or Windows File Manager, you can avoid all this cutting and pasting. Just open the copy of your synch file and select the rows you want to remove, then use the Cut Name File Entry command under the Edit menu to excise them. You'll end up with a tailored data set much more quickly.

Notes can also be customized. You can use the same cut-and-paste approach to editing the data by opening the Connection-generated template and moving data from the main backup file into the empty Notepad browser window. Or, if you are working with complete copies of the data, go ahead and open the Notepad in the copy, select the rows you want to remove and use the Cut Note command in the Edit menu.

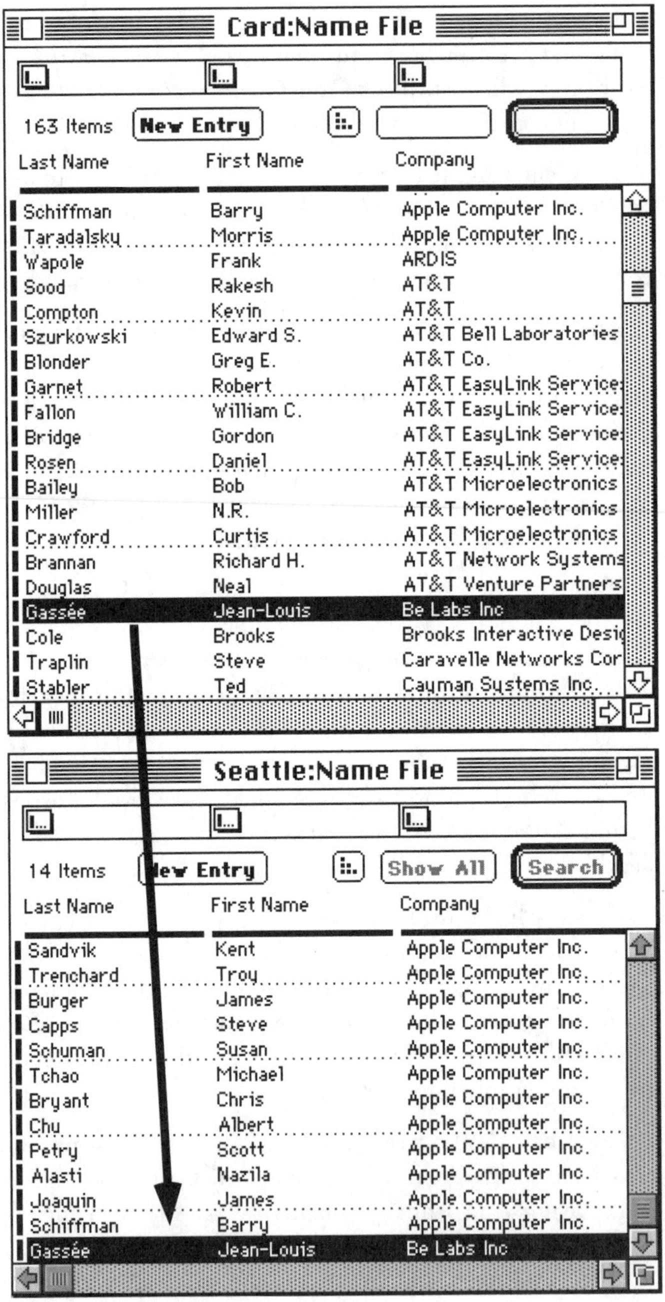

Figure 9.5 One by one, customize Seattle by moving individual records.

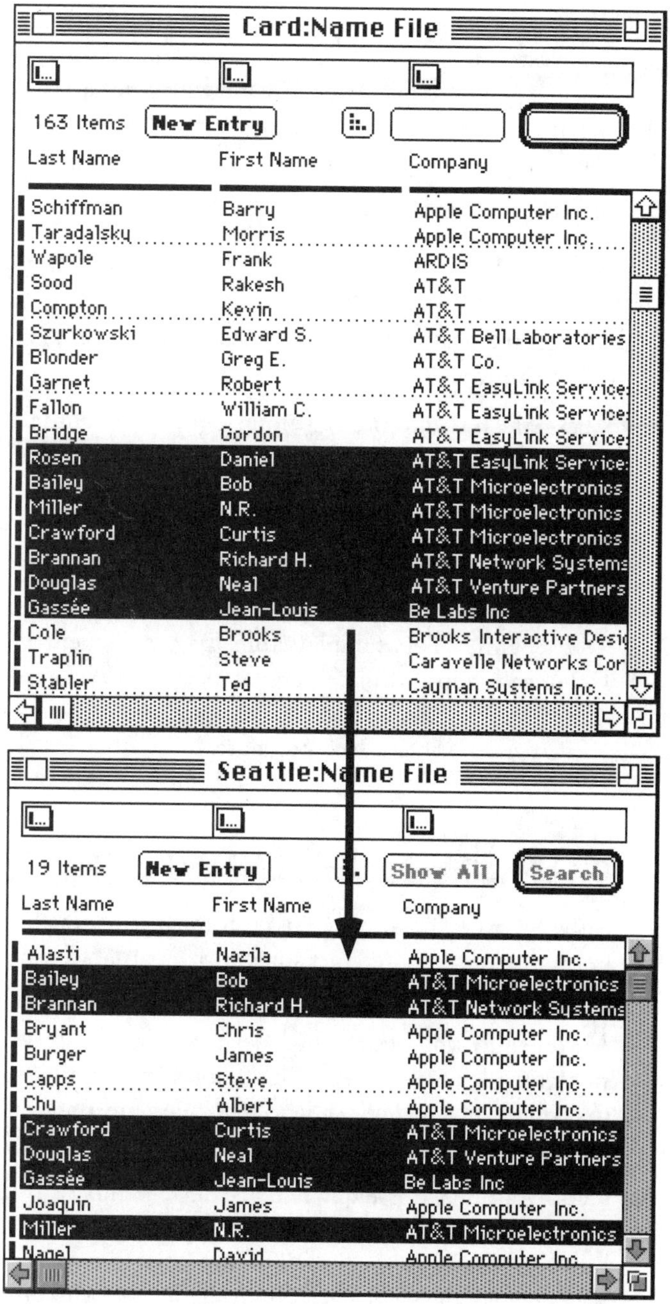

Figure 9.6 Multiple row selections: Convenient, but kind of a pain in the butt, too.

One nifty aspect of the Notepad application in Connection is that you can copy text from a regular word processor and paste it into a new note. This is a handy way to load your Newton with price lists, reference materials and letter templates (you just change the address and key words on your Newton before printing, faxing, mailing or beaming).

The process takes three steps:

1. Select the text in a word processor application and copy it using the standard copy command.

2. Open the custom archive Notepad application and click the New Note button.

3. Paste the text into the new note. Connection automatically formats the text using the font and font size you have selected, and adjusts the line lengths to conform to the narrow margins of a Newton note. When you fax this note from your Newton, the text will flow back into the layout appropriate to a business letter.

The Notepad in Connection will break long text files into Newton-sized chunks. For example, a three-page document will appear in the Notepad as approximately three separate notes. Graphics are beyond the reach of Connection 1.0, but Version 2.0 will support pasting PICT images into a Notepad note.

Get Info... Calendars are a RAM kind of thing

Although we've made much of customizing names and notes, you never want to get stuck with a partial view of your calendar. So, keep your calendar entries in RAM.

As you know, you can set your Newton to store all new items on a storage card. This includes names, notes and dates, if you happen to open the Dates application to schedule a meeting while the card is inserted and Preferences are set to shunt all new data to the card.

Getting around this requires that you remember to turn off the save new items to card setting when you open the Dates application. This will force calendar items into your Newton's native RAM, where they will always be available, regardless of what card you have inserted in the PCMCIA slot.   *(continued)*

Get Info... Calendars are a RAM kind of thing (continued)

Big hassles, yes, but this is one of the prices of power usage. If you want a different view of your data each day or every hour, and you also want a comprehensive view of your calendar, you've got to do this. Heck, you already went through the pain of creating a custom archive, this is cake.

Two possible shortcuts are Pocket Science Co.'s KwikPrefs and Tanis Development's Elegance. These utilities will automate changing the "Save new items to card" preference with a single pen tap.

KwikPrefs is a Newton utility that lets you create unique groups of preference settings for use in different situations. The first version doesn't include the ability to save settings for different cards, but we're sure they'll get it into a future revision.

Elegance is a utility that places a floating palette of preferences buttons on the Newton screen. It will allow you to tap a button to reach the "Save new items to card" setting instantly.

Once KwikPrefs and Elegance let you toggle between saving data to the card and saving data to RAM, you'll be able to tap a floating button on the screen or an icon in the Extras drawer that changes the setting for you. That will cut down on the hassles, and the real benefits of this strategy will begin to shine through.

From here to third-party data paternity

Connection is only the first step toward working with data on both your Newton and a personal computer; if it were the last step, Newton would be doomed. Apple has a long history of doing applications on its own that blaze a trail others follow. And, to be fair, Connection does a much better job of integrating desktop data into Newton than any other PDA link out there. The EO Personal Communicator's DOS-only desktop data connection is a pathetic pretender to the welter-weight title by comparison to Newton Connection's heavy-weight contender status.

It's the third-party applications that open new data vistas to your Newton which will really take the PDA to new heights. Granted, this is an evolutionary process, but its a long road that could be very well worth the trip.

Before anything really powerful can happen, it will be necessary for someone to come up with a means of synchronizing data from multiple applications, because people by their very nature scatter their valuable information all around them (it's a habit we picked up when burying meat to keep the saber-toothed tigers away from the clan's food supply; a bone here and there in the forest could feed a family for the winter). Apple's support of Apple Events, the inter-application communications feature of System 7, could provide the hooks that fulfill the need for links to many applications. Apple Events let two programs exchange information in the background, without being told to, so they might be used to synchronize the Newton Connection Dates file to a shared calendar application on the corporate network in your office, for example.

On the Windows side of the house, Apple must provide support for Microsoft's Object Linking and Embedding (OLE) technology. OLE works much like Apple Events, linking applications together so that they can communicate so you don't have to. But when you get into a situation where you have a Mac, but the corporate database runs on a PC, the going gets weird (and there aren't nearly enough weird people to deal with weird goings-on in a big company). Suddenly the Mac version of Connection has to know OLE. Nothing is clear-cut in a cross-platform data network; there are no easy solutions to OLE-Apple Events problems. It is going to be an interesting year, as Newton grows up and Microsoft starts introducing its own PDA designs.

Here's a brief synopsis of the capabilities you'll be seeing in Mac and PC applications with Newton communications features. For a more complete description of these applications and others, see Chapter Fifteen—*Cool Software*.

Calendars and Scheduling. At least two people have to attend a meeting. Since Newton's Date Book helps you, and only you, remember an appointment, there's always a chance you'll have no meeting at all when your companions forget the place or time.

Group scheduling applications can ensure that, at least, there are no excuses for missing a meeting. These programs run on Macs and PCs to let a group of folks share appointment information, invite one another to a meeting, or distribute agendas.

Two Mac-to-Newton calendar applications will work from the get-go.

ContactPad, a Newton business organizer application from Pastel, will let you exchange Date Book items with its own DayMaker organizer for the Mac. The Newton connection will be made a system extension that installs in the Mac's System Folder to translate Newton data into useful information in DayMaker.

ON Technology, which makes a cross-platform (Mac and Windows) scheduling application called Meeting Maker, will offer one-way connectivity to Newton. You'll be able to keep your calendar and make appointments on a Mac and export the latest version to your Newton through Newton Connection 2.0. The return route, sending Newton calendars to Meeting Maker, will be a while in coming.

The same capability for PC users will have to wait for someone, perhaps ON, to design a Newton communications utility for Novell NetWare networks. The Meeting Maker XP client for Windows runs only on the IPX (Internet Protocol Exchange) protocol used by NetWare, so there's currently no way to export a calendar to the AppleTalk-only Newton.

If an IPX communications utility does ship for Newton, ON will also be able to enable a "true client" application for Newton, which would allow MessagePads or Expert Pads to export their calendars to Meeting Maker.

Scheduling doesn't necessarily turn on the ability to get two people together at the same time. Just as important for a professional who has to manage a large number of contacts each day is the ability to load into Newton a list of the times and people they need to keep up with. Doctors, salespeople, and other professionals have been looking for these features in a portable device for years. Why do you think the Sharp Wizard is so popular?

Pastel's ContactPad application for Newton will include a set of forms for doctors, lawyers, salespeople, real estate dealers, and managers that blend appointment information with data about the people they meet. For example, a doctor will be able to tap an icon, called a Paper Clip (it even looks like a paper clip), to view patient records before entering an examination room.

More to the point for doctors is the Hippocrates electronic medical assistant. Designed by HealthCare Communications to supplement its own MacHealth software, it allows doctors and their staffs to download to Newton a complete patient schedule for conducting rounds in a hospital or clinic, regular appointment information, records and prescription information. A physician can start each day with a Newton primed for the specific schedule they need to keep.

The Hippocrates application also works as a distribution system for any medical management software that can export data in the ASCII text format. You will need to import ASCII files into Connection 2.0, then export them to the Newton.

ProMED, another medical application with scheduling features, will be offered to large medical organizations by KPMG Peat Marwick, one of the big computer consulting firms. Because it is keyed to a large information management system, this is probably not the application for the medical clinic or individual doctor who wants to go digital.

Sales managers will want to take a look at CorNet Inc.'s electronic territory management application for Newton. This system will let managers build sales call schedules, attach information about each account, and distribute it to Newton-using salespeople.

Electronic mail. We'll spend a considerable portion of the next chapter on the subject of electronic mail, but it bears mentioning here. Newton's AppleTalk network and modem support will give you ample access to the flow of information inside your own company or the messages rushing between individuals and organizations on global computer networks.

In offices with CE Software Inc.'s QuickMail, mail systems based on Novell's NetWare Message Handling Service (MHS) or Apple's Open Collaboration Environment (a big name for an overarching technology included in the new System 7 Pro), Newton will be able to access a network mailbox using CE's QuickAccess mail extension.

QuickAccess installs on a mail server (the computer where the mailboxes reside) and in Newtons to allow the Newton—with its relatively brain-dead, one-direction-at-a-time AppleTalk Data Stream Protocol connection to network services to exchange mail with other networked computers. Newton users will be able to tap a button that sends all stored mail to CE's QuickMail server or MHS and AOCE gateway products, and then receives all incoming messages stored in their mailbox—a file that acts as their address, even when the Newton isn't connected to the network.

Ex Machina's PocketCall will give you access to global networks, not the local mail server. It will provide some nifty client software for Compu-Serve, GEnie, the Dialog Information Service (for the data junkie with a

$125-an-hour habit), MCI Mail, AT&T EasyLink mail, Official Airlines Guide (need to know when the next flight to Phoenix takes to the sky?) and cc:Mail Remote.

The cc:Mail connection is the one that fits the current discussion. If your office doesn't operate on CE Software's QuickMail or the MHS systems you can get to through QuickMail, it may very well be a cc:Mail environment. PocketCall will let you dial into your office network from almost anywhere (there's always an "almost" in telecommunications) to send and receive mail to your colleagues.

Accounting data. We all hate doing an expense report. If you're anything like we are, filling out the paperwork needed to recoup the money you spend on travel and other business activities takes a day and a half, not to mention a goodly parcel of patience. (One of us is currently nine months behind on his expense reports; we won't say whom). Newton can wipe those hours of suffering from your life in one fell swoop.

Several applications will let you collect and process expense report information with a few taps.

State of the Art Inc.'s Expense It! application for Newton will let you enter your travel, parking, restaurant and hotel charges in a form that tracks the category of each expense and maintains a running total for a single trip or an entire month. When you are ready to submit your expenses, you can review the entries, make changes, and send the resulting report to a Mac or PC running a database, forms or spreadsheet application. State of the Art also offers minicomputer-based accounting applications that can accept a Newton report over AppleTalk networks.

Slate Corp.'s Day-Timer Expense Assistant will provide forms and communications to PCs that let you enter expenses, categorize them and upload the results for processing in a desktop spreadsheet application.

Great Plains Software, which makes a line of accounting products for the PC, Macintosh and other computing platforms, will introduce an expense reporter in 1994. For now, they have announced an application, Personal Time and Billing, which lets you upload data that describes the time you dedicate to each of your clients for use when billing for professional services.

Information collection. Great Plains time and billing software is an excellent example of how a forms-based Newton application can streamline the headaches out of a paperwork-dependent organization.

Personal Time and Billing is enabled by entering information about how much you bill per hour and the clients you work with in an application stored in the Extras drawer. Henceforth, when you make an entry in the Dates calendar that refers to a client, Newton automatically racks up the time you spend against the client's account. It also lets you note billable and non-billable items, special charges and taxes associated with each client.

At the end of the month, when the accounting department calls to bug you about your activity reports (even if they bellow across the room in a three-person company), you just tap an upload button that assembles the client billing data and sends it off to Great Plains' Dynamics software running on a Mac or PC.

The medical applications, Hippocrates and ProMED, also provide a high level of information collection power, allowing doctors to record the results of examinations, prescribe drugs and order follow-up tests for patients that can be uploaded to the office network. Medicine, like the law, is the organized collection of data for use in subjective analysis. What more human process is there, and it's one that has been keening over the agonies of information management for centuries.

Teachers will also get access to institutional data systems with Newton. Chancery Software's CSL Profiles In Hand, a Newton application that helps teachers collect information about each of their students that can be saved on a network server for use when grading at the end of the quarter, semester or school year. This kind of information gathering, which puts the student's performance into the context of a long period of personal contacts rather than the answers to a single test, could eventually obsolete the rigid grading structures schools resorted to when asked to handle the education of millions.

Teachers will make notes in a form on their Newton. At the end of the day, they'll plug the Newton into an AppleTalk network to upload their observations to Chancery's CSL Profiles application running on a Macintosh.

On the simple end of the spectrum, beyond the strictures of forms-based applications, is the need for sharing notes, agendas and documents with our co-workers.

Portfolio Software's Dyno Notepad, an outliner application, provides a useful format for creating lists, collapsible topics within a note (so that the bullet-items that describe the agenda of a meeting are indented beneath a topic), and schedules for goals and projects. When you are finished with a note, it can be exported to the Mac or Windows versions of Dyno Notepad, or to word processing applications, like Microsoft Word or MacWrite Pro.

Remote access to information. Mobile computing still seems an exotic practice for most companies. Something like severe physical shock comes over a company when its executive staff starts logging onto the corporate data network from Paris, Tokyo and Moscow, simultaneously. All the old boundaries that delivered a sense of security against deadlines—The boss won't be back until Friday, the report can wait!—fall before the virtual presences of mobile computer users.

Newton takes things a step further.

Imagine that your organization, whether it's a one-woman business that runs on voice mail and a database or a multinational corporation, is nothing more than a television with a VCR. It is designed to distribute information to people who use knowledge to make decisions and shape policies, and depending upon who is watching, it presents that information in a different way.

Newton (maybe not the first models, but the third or fourth generation devices) is the most powerful remote control for manipulating your organizational TV/VCR. With a properly scripted application, you can send commands to a database, a voice mail system or a calendaring application that lets you inside the collective mind of the company from anywhere, at any time. This is the future, whether Newton or some other handheld device actually ends up being the tool that ignites the remote worker's virtual lifestyle.

The first wave of Newton applications includes several remote work programs that demonstrate that the potential is more than a fool's dream of working in pajamas in the kitchen.

CTM Development SA, a Swiss software company that makes a voice mail management system for Macintoshes, has introduced a remote control application that runs on the Newton. Voice mail systems are like actors, you can hand them almost any script and they'll change their character to fit the new show. CTM's VoiceAccess Mac software lets you set up the system to reply to incoming calls differently, based on the time they are received, who is calling (if your state allows Caller-ID information to be transmitted on the phone line), and where you are. For instance, it can be configured to recognize your partner's phone number when he calls and immediately write and send a pager message to the Newton Messaging

Card you carry on trips. It can also schedule voice mail service to start and stop at certain times of the day.

All these features can be controlled with VoiceAccess Remote, the Newton application. Using your pen, you can tap selections in pop-up menus that are added to a script which is uploaded to the Mac by modem. For example, you can choose to have calls forwarded to your mobile phone number for two hours on Thursday, when you'll be driving from New York to Allentown, Pennsylvania. With a line splitter on the telephone jack, you can plug both the Newton and a telephone into the one line so that you can control the playback of voice messages using VoiceAccess Remote while you listen on the handset.

Data can be as powerful as a voice message, and even more important when the information is timely. One example of the power of knowledge will be provided by a real estate application that lets agents using Newtons query a Multiple Listing Service database of home and business property listings. Integration Systems Inc.'s Portable MLS will make its debut in late 1993.

Portable MLS will work with a modem to provide instant access to a Multiple Listing Service database from a Newton. So, let's envision Sally Realtor® (did you know "Realtor" is a registered trademark? Ridiculous, next it will be "Your garbage, disposed of by the Sanitation Engineer®."). Sally's got a family of four in the minivan, and she's hot on the trail of a four-bedroom-with-a-view, but the Prospect family hasn't been jazzed over anything, even the brick-with-cedar-roof-and-out-building on Larchmont Drive.

While the Prospects wander around someone else's home, Sally plugs her Newton into the phone line. She already entered the size of the home and price range before she left the office. With a pen-tap, she tells Newton to logon to the MLS computer and look around for a few more homes in the area that match up with the Prospect family's requirements. Newton does the work, since this is a scripted call. Sally just waits until Newton says it is finished. Now she has a complete list, with tax and deed transfer information, of six more houses she can show; all the data is stored on the PCMCIA card in her Newton.

This kind of access to data can slash the time people now put into driving to the nearest office. Look for many more remote access applications that are capable of funneling a tremendous bounty of data into the Newton.

Oracle: Glue you to your sets

A major development in the race to improve Newton's access to data came when Oracle Corp. announced it would build a bridge between Apple's PDA and its own relational database servers. Oracle databases are among the most sophisticated on the planet, and the company has made several key alliances that put it on the cutting edge of the information age. In 1995, for example, Oracle and Baby Bell telephone company U S West will unveil a national electronic mail and information distribution system —Newton will be one of the first devices that can tap into the data they will offer.

What Oracle does that no one else is succeeding at is massive parallel computing on personal computer platforms. The Oracle7 database management system can run on 200 networked PCs, all of them holding a part of a data set that appears to the server software as one big pile of ones and zeros. When a user asks a question, the server software tells every one of the 200 PCs running the Oracle software to look for the answer, even if the question asked for the relationship between information stored on 120 different computers. First, all the computers look for the data, answering the server when they find some. Then, the server collects the data and determines the relationships between all the pieces to generate a response to the user's query.

Compared to a mainframe or minicomputer, the "distributed" system Oracle uses (meaning that it uses the processing power of many computers) is screaming fast. A single computer, even a powerful mainframe, must look at all the data one piece at a time while the distributed system of 200 computers can look at 200 pieces of data at a time. On a cost basis, it's much cheaper to buy 200 PCs than it is to buy one mainframe with 200 processors (a massive parallel computer). So, Oracle has something pretty special, and they're selling the hell out of this stuff.

Lots of organizations are standardizing on Oracle software. Many others that run another database application are buying Oracle7 for its ability to tie together disparate data sources.

With its announcement that Newton would be added to the list of computers supported by Oracle Glue technology, Oracle gave corporate and third-party developers a powerful tool for building Newton applications that can tap the power of a relational database.

Glue is an application programming interface, or API, which is—more than anything else—a kind of pipe. When a programmer is making an application, she sometimes has to get access to a function in the operating system, and that's the time to "make a call to an API." In other words, the API is a collection of pre-programmed capabilities that applications can use, a pipeline to useful features or a network connection or a database.

Glue is a super-API, it includes conversion features that change database queries from one language to another, so that not everyone accessing a database must know the way to talk to that database. They just have to know how to talk to their own computer. The programmer is supposed to have taken care of the rest. Glue also includes messaging capabilities that let computers hold on to information the way an electronic mail system does, so that a Newton can send a database query and then reconnect later to retrieve the answer.

This is not meant to trivialize the complexity of using Glue. If you ask your company's programmers to build a Newton-to-Oracle application, they're in for a lot of hard work. But if they have already built a Mac-to-Oracle application, half the battle, or more, is already won.

The way Oracle envisions the Newton's place in the Glue architecture is as an appendage to a Macintosh that's actually connected to an Oracle database. Using an AppleTalk Data Stream Protocol (ADSP) connection, a Newton application will send a question to the Macintosh. Then, if the Newton user has other things to do, he can disconnect his Newton. The Mac will take the Newton's question and pass it on to the Oracle server using Glue. While in the Glue pipe, the structure of the query may be altered to conform to the way the Oracle server processes questions and answers.

Once it hits the server, the Newton's query will be answered, and a reply will be composed by the Oracle software. The answer may include data—like formatted text, tab-delimited fields or graphics—which Newton won't recognize, so back into the Glue API the reply will go. Glue, or the Macintosh that is acting as the Newton's agent on the network, will convert the reply into Newton text or graphics, as appropriate. The answer will wait on the Mac until the Newton connects once again, when it will be downloaded over the network to the In Box or an application.

Oracle will also let Newtons upload a soup full of information for analysis by the database server. This means you may be collecting information about a group of people whom you interviewed in the local mall, sending that data off to an Oracle server through Glue, which will convert the soup into the rows and columns used in databases, and receiving a report that includes analysis of the factors that influence shopping at Victoria's Secret. Because the contents of every field in Newton can be treated as a discrete object, the complexity of analysis can be extraordinary.

What's all this mumbo-jumbo mean for you and your company? Well, databases are a means for controlling the flow of information in a company, not just a tool for analyzing that information. The mall shoppers report mentioned above could be automatically routed by the server to different departments based on the outcome. You don't always have to have your hands on the rudder.

Glue makes Newton a comfortable player in inventory control systems, sales automation programs, workgroup environments where data is flowing between people automatically, and in companies that treat their human resources as distributed nodes in a collective mind.

The question you have to ask is "How much flexibility do we want and to what extent are we willing to hand over decisions to machines?" Companies that come up with answers combining more freedom for their workers with pragmatic use of database technology might discover a new organizational architecture that unleashes employees' mental capacity for more creative and profitable work.

CHAPTER
10

IN THE OUT DOOR AND
BACK IN AGAIN

Communications is a two-way street. Newton offers access to a rich blend of messaging media, from the phone line to the airwaves, but only Newton-Mail offers bi-directional communications. You'll need to take several different roads when exchanging messages with the world at large.

We've already covered the simplicities and complexities of the In Box and Out Box. In this chapter we'll take a look at how to format and address messages in the Notepad, Names, and Dates applications for delivery by fax, electronic mail and in printed documents. Gathering information from various sources, including electronic mail and paging networks also takes a bit of savvy, and you'll find that here, too.

Fax: Telecommunications for the masses

Without a doubt, fax is the most democratic of telecommunications technologies. It helped topple the Soviet government, threatened the authority of China's despotic leaders, and made mincemeat of the U.S. Postal Service. Grandmothers and grandchildren can use it with ease (it's about as hard to use as dialing a telephone) and it has found a foothold in almost every business, large and small, in the United States. Fax is your means of taking digital information to the analog masses.

Unfortunately, Newton's fax features don't let the analog masses slip a sheet of paper into a fax machine and send it to you. Fax-receive capabilities will come from third-party software developers and in future Newtons. The factor that prevented Apple from including fax-receive in the MessagePad and Expert Pad was the lack of memory to hold the large amounts of data necessary to recreate a fax image. The company would have had to double or triple Newton's built-in RAM to support fax-receive, a move that would have boosted the price, and perhaps the size, of the first PDAs.

Since you won't have the benefit of conducting a dialog by fax, you'll have to make sure that you send the most compelling package of information each time you fax. There are, of course, limits to what you can send in a single message. Newton lets you send only one note, a single calendar item, as much as a week's schedule, or business cards. While this is useful, you can't easily combine these documents to, for example, send an agenda for a meeting with the business cards of all the attendees.

But a devious mind can work out solutions using the basic Newton fax features; you don't have to wait until a third-party developer markets an improved fax application (though, a better fax manager wouldn't hurt).

Here are the documents you have to work with (you can print these, too):

- Single Business Card
- All Business Cards
- All Business Cards and Notes
- A Summary of All Names
- A Single Day's Agenda
- A Daily Calendar
- Five-Day Calendar
- Seven-Day Calendar
- One-Week Agenda
- Notepad Note
- A Letter
- A Memo
- A Week's Notes

Fax formatting is taken care of automatically when you chose a particular style in the fax slip. For example, if you tap the Format menu in the Fax slip for a Notepad note, you are given a choice of a plain note, letter, memo or weekly summary. Tap plain note or weekly summary, and Newton formats the fax to look exactly like the note you see in the Notepad window, including the time stamp line (see Figure 10.1).

Tap the letter format to create a document that includes your name and address centered at the top of the page; the fax slip will open a window that lets you enter the name and address of the recipient (if the name is in your Newton, the address will flow into the slip automatically). The address will be placed at the top-left corner of the fax page (see Figure 10.2).

Calendar items are formatted as a list (Day's Agenda or Week listing) or a standard calendar page (1 day, Next 5 days, and Next 7 days).

You can also add a cover page to any document that you send (see Figure 10.1); tap the Notes button in the Fax slip to add notes to the cover page. The Newton cover sheet includes an address field for the recipient, your name, title, and phone numbers; any notes you write in the Cover Sheet Notes slip appear on this page as well. A cover page also includes a heading in the top margin of the page that tells the time the fax was sent, your name and phone number, and the number of pages in the document; faxes sent without a cover sheet do not include this information anywhere in the document.

Unfortunately, Newton provides no utility for creating your own cover pages, letterhead, or memo layouts. A third-party application will probably provide more choices for fax output, but no one had come up with firm product plans before we went to print. Pocket Science, which makes Kwik-Prefs, said it is planning a fax forms application.

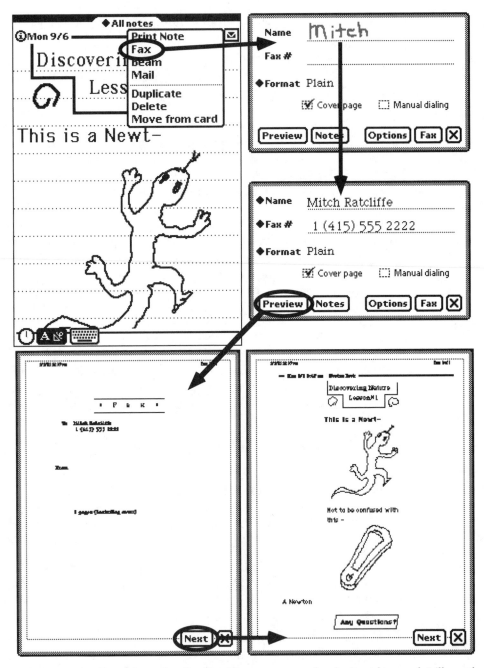

Figure 10.1 *From Notepad to Out Box, Newton sets up a fax that's ready to send. It'll even let you preview what the fax will look like when it comes out of the receiving fax machine.*

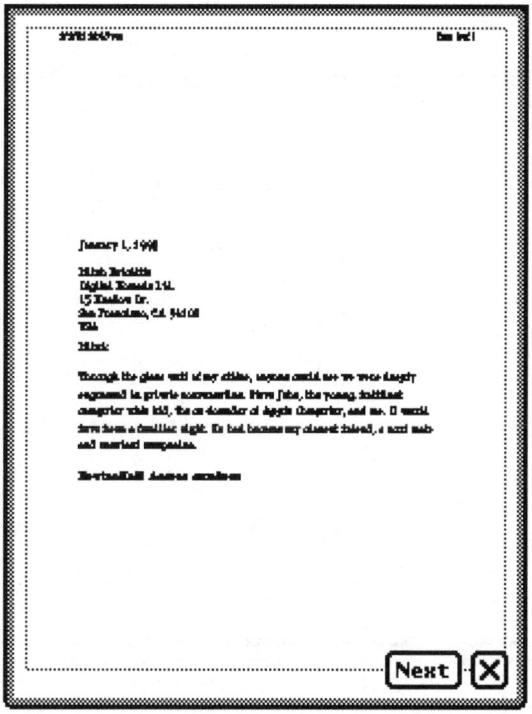

Figure 10.2 *What the letter format looks like.*

Let's get back to a practical situation and making the most out of a relatively rigid interface for faxing.

A meeting is scheduled for the last Thursday of the month, and several new hires need to be invited and pre-briefed on the agenda. You have complete notes from the past three meetings, which were transcribed on and downloaded from a PC through Newton Connection. There are also three product descriptions stored in your Newton with which these new people must be familiar by the time the meeting rolls around. You'd also like to have them get in contact with the other attendees, if they have questions. Oh, and did we mention that the new hires work in three branch offices scattered around the country?

Good thing you have a little time on the flight out of town to prepare. You're going to need a little time to compose an introductory letter.

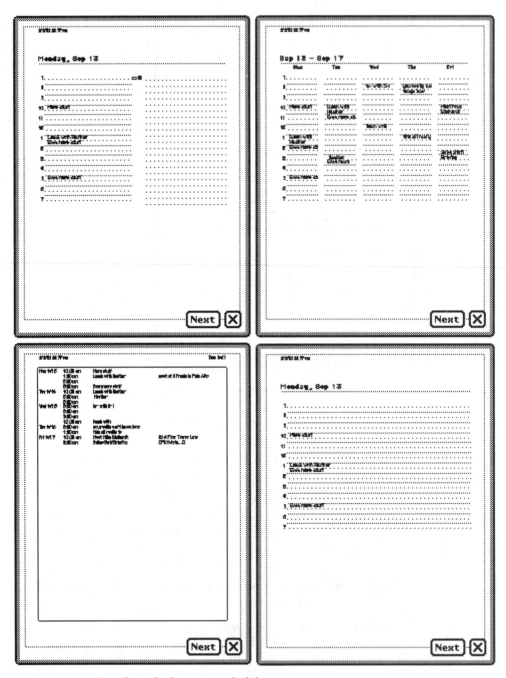

Figure 10.3 Four forms for faxing your schedule.

Now, we've already established that you cannot send all these documents in a single fax. Instead, you're going to create in the Notepad a custom cover sheet that describes all the documents you'll be sending. When you are ready, send that "cover sheet" fax first, then all the separate faxes that constitute the information package. Here are the steps, follow them for each addressee:

1. Write a cover sheet in the Notepad. Include a complete list of the documents that you'll be sending, and mention that they will arrive in a series of faxes. Tap the Action button and select Fax. In the Fax slip that opens, tap the Format diamond, and choose the Letter format from these options:

   - **Plain.** This sends the note you wrote in a format that looks exactly like the Notepad interface, including the date and time when you created the note. This is inappropriate for a business letter.

   - **Letter.** The letter option opens a slip in which you can enter the name and address of the recipient, which are incorporated into the note layout with your own name and address. The result is a finished, professional-looking business letter, apparently on your own letterhead (Apple really should build in a means for entering your company's name, address, phone, and logo.)

   - **Memo.** This option formats the note as part of a memo that includes the recipient's name and a subject line, which you enter in a Memo header slip that opens below the Fax slip, as well as your own name and the date. If you need to assert a little authority or have a penchant for politicking, this may be the format for you.

   - **Week summary.** This option sends all the notes you've made in the last week in the standard Notepad format, with creation dates and times, and lines separating the items. Bad choice for the executive on the go who wants to create a professional impression. It's a good choice for a later step in this process, when you collect the product descriptions.

As we said, for this step, choose the Letter format. A second slip will open; write the first name of the first addressee in the Fax slip, not the addressee (the second) slip! After the name is translated, Newton will let you choose from a list of all your Name records with the same name. To actually see the addressee's information in the addressee's slip, change the format to plain and back to letter. Don't ask us why this is necessary. Even if you don't toggle formats, the addressee's address will appear in the letter. If you enter the name in the addressee's slip, you'll get the list diamond and you won't have to toggle formats. However, you'll have to add the name twice as, for some reason, it doesn't appear on the Fax slip, although the fax number does (strange!).

Make sure the Cover Sheet and Manual Dialing boxes are un-checked, and tap the Fax button. The document will be transferred into your Out Box, which will open on the screen. Tap it closed and move to the next step.

2. Now, you want to introduce the new hires to all the people who will be at the meeting. Tap the Folder button followed by the Edit Folders button; create a new folder called Thursday Meeting. Open the Names file and file all the cards belonging to people who will attend the meeting in the Thursday Meeting folder. When finished, tap the Folder list diamond at the top of the Names file form and select the Thursday Meeting folder. This gives you a list of all the people attending the meeting that you can send as part of a single fax.

3. Tap the Action button at the bottom of the Names screen that includes the list of Thursday Meeting attendees. Tap "Fax" to open the Fax slip. You have several options to choose from in the Format menu:

   • **Single Card.** This sends only one card; you don't want to tap this option when sending a list.

   • **Cards.** This sends a print-out of all the cards in the current folder (Thursday Meeting). If you just want to let folks know who will be attending, this is the way to go.

   • **Cards and notes.** Say you want to do a little bit of explaining about the role of each person in the Thursday meeting. Go back to the Names file and write notes about each attendee in the Notes field of their business card. Then follow the steps for faxing the Thursday Meeting names and choose the "Cards and notes" format, which will send both the cards and your explanatory notes. They print out side-by-side on the recipient's fax machine, so there is no confusing which cards and notes go together.

   • **Summary.** This option sends a different view of the information about the people in the Thursday Meeting folder, showing data in the same field-based format as the data entry window in Names.

Once you've chosen the format for the cards, make sure the Cover page and Manual dialing boxes are not checked and tap the Fax button. The Out Box will open again. Close it.

4. You've come to the most complex step, and Phoenix is just arcing away beneath the wing of the 767, only an hour more to go before the plane lands and you want to fax these notes.

   The notes from past meetings and product descriptions you need are spread all over your Notepad. Meeting notes will probably be broken into several Notepad notes, because they exceed the 4000-byte limit of a single note. You want to collect them into a single week by creating new notes and pasting the contents of older notes in. If you happen to have downloaded all the data from your Mac or PC before beginning this process (given that you pasted these notes into Connection immediately before hopping the plane), then all the data will appear to have been created within the last week.

   Once all the notes have creation dates within the last week, file them in the Thursday Meeting folder. Now, tap the Action button and choose Fax. Tap the format diamond and select the Weekly summary option. Newton composes a super-message that contains all the notes you've created within the last week which are filed in the Thursday Meeting folder. Write the recipient's name in the Name field of the Fax slip, make certain you have not enabled the Cover page or Manual dialing options and tap Fax.

5. Finally, you want to let everyone know where and when the meeting will happen. It's already entered into your calendar, so tap the Dates icon and turn to that fateful Thursday. Write the location of the meeting next to the time, if you haven't already done so. Tap the Action button, select Fax and prepare the message for your colleagues by choosing from the following format options (also see Figure 10.3 for a look at four of the five formats):

   • **Day's Agenda.** This option provides a two-column view of your day's appointments and To Do items.

   • **1 Day.** Delivers a single column of appointments for a day, from 7:00 AM to 7:00 PM (all calendar views present this time frame), but no To Do view. This is the choice you want to make, if all you need is to convey the Where and When of the Thursday Meeting.

- **Next 5 Days.** Provides a five-day view of your appointments, from the date of the item selected. We recommend this if you want the recipients to know how to find you immediately after the meeting. You can orient this view by selecting a different day as a starting point, so people can find you before the meeting, too. Of course, you should think a little about your own privacy.

- **Next 7 Days.** Seven days, just like the five-day option, of your appointments.

- **Week listing.** Instead of a calendar view, the week listing generates a list of your appointments by date and time. Not the right choice, unless you are providing someone with an itinerary.

With the calendar message formatted, you simply enter the recipient's name in the Name field and tap Fax.

7. When you've repeated this process for each attendee and landed in Dallas, find a phone and some time to send all these messages. Open the Out Box and tap the Send button, choose Fax from the pop-up list. This initiates the sending of all the messages in the Out Box fax queue. If you tap the first message in the queue, Newton will send only that fax. It's easier to tap Send and get to work on something else. Make sure your Newton's AC power is attached and plugged into a wall socket; you really don't want to run out of power while faxing or printing.

Get Info... The Cold, Hard Fax

A Megahertz Corp. PCMCIA data/fax modem can be a mighty handy tool, but Newton's 640-Kbyte memory capacity is a bit too skinny to handle a lot of faxes in the Out Box when running this slot-based modem.

If all your data is stored in internal RAM, then the PCMCIA modem will work just fine. The items in the Out Box are, after all, just pointers to the real file in RAM; they take up only a few bytes of storage. On the other hand, if you fax documents stored on a PCMCIA RAM card, which must be removed to accommodate the Megahertz modem, the Out Box must hold a copy of the real file. *(continued)*

Get Info... The Cold, Hard Fax (continued)

There simply isn't room in the RAM to hold a lot of fax documents, so you're stuck using an external fax modem.

The other problem with faxing through a PCMCIA card when most of your data is stored on a RAM storage card is the Names and Dates applications' duplicitous faxing habits. These applications do not send a complete copy of summary and full-week schedules to the Out Box at any time (they do send a single business card or a Day's Agenda to the Out Box).

Instead, they send a pointer to the complete file that you want to send. Once the fax connection is established by the Out Box, it tries to access the file in Names or Dates. If those files are stored on a RAM card which you have removed to make room for the PCMCIA modem, the Out Box will kill the connection and raise a message that says the file could not be sent.

All that's Fit to Print

Of course, one sure fire way to get around Newton's fax limitations is to print out what you want to fax and then use a regular desktop fax machine. Okay, we're just kidding. Really!

But getting a message to the right printer is the first and foremost problem you'll face when transferring your ideas from the digital realm to paper. It's also the least of your problems, unless you don't happen to have one of the printers Newton supports.

Apple built support into Newton for three kinds of printers, their Personal LaserWriter 300, the Apple StyleWriter, and networked LaserWriters. It strikes us strange that Apple won't let you print to all the members of the LaserWriter family, they sell them, after all. Nor does Newton print to all third-party printers that emulate the LaserWriters which are compatible with Newton.

Table 10.1 and 10.2 show the Newton-to-Apple-printer equation breaks out.

Table 10.1 Apple Printers and Newton

For this Model...	choose this driver in the Print slip
StyleWriter II	Apple StyleWriter
Portable StyleWriter	Apple StyleWriter*
Personal LaserWriter 300	Personal LaserWriter 300
Personal LaserWriter LS	Personal LaserWriter 300
LaserWriter IIg	Network printers
LaserWriter IIf	Network printers
LaserWriter IINTX	Network printers
LaserWriter IINT	Network printers
LaserWriter IINTR	Network printers
LaserWriter	Network printers
LaserWriter Pro 600	Network printers
LaserWriter Pro 630	Network printers

*Requires the Portable Style Writer cable—but you must select the Canon Bubble Jet driver in the other printers menu.

Table 10.2 Apple printers that don't work with Newton.

Model
ImageWriter II
ImageWriter LQ
LaserWriter Select 300
LaserWriter Select 310

The Newton-to-PC printer relationship is fantastic, the MessagePad and Expert Pad can connect to 545 different models of parallel printers using Apple's Print Pack intelligent printer cable; it also works with an additional several hundred printers which emulate the features of supported printers. The Print Pack is a serial-to-parallel port cable with a memory chip and circuitry that converts the signals sent by the Newton serial port into a form understood by parallel printers.

GDT Softworks Inc., which makes an excellent package of drivers for the Mac, developed the Newton cable. Because the Print Pack drivers are drawn from GDT's Mac product, they are the most-tested software in the Newton suite of add-on products. It works darn fine.

When you choose a printer driver in the "Other printers" menu shown in the Print slip, Print Pack will automatically load the driver into your Newton.

It is worth noting, however, that if you own a Mac-compatible version of any of the printers on the Print Pack list, it probably will not work with the Newton in Mac emulation mode . Most notably, the Hewlett-Packard DeskJet printers for Mac don't seem to function properly when emulating a Mac network printer, although in PC mode the DeskJet works fine. A complete list of the parallel printers supported by Print Pack is included with the cable. Ask your dealer to show you that your printer is on the list before buying the Print Pack; it also shows which driver you need to select in the Print slip.

Before you turn on your Newton, plug in the serial cable, which is what you'll use to connect to a StyleWriter or Personal LaserWriter 300 or LS; a LocalTalk cable, which is what you'll use to connect to a networked Laser-Writer; or the Print Pack, for parallel printers. With the Print Pack, in particular, Newton will not be able to see the drivers for parallel printers available unless the cable was plugged in before you tap the Action button to begin the printing process (that's when Newton looks for the drivers).

Also, be sure that you don't disconnect the printer cable while Newton is printing. Newton's serial port controller can scramble the contents of messages in the Out Box if it gets cut off in mid-print. The MessagePad and Expert Pad will not go to sleep while documents are printing, even if you leave the device idle for longer than the Sleep preference time limit, in order to prevent damage to Out Box files.

Easter Egg... Background printing, faxing and mail

The In Box and Out Box don't have to be open while they work. Once you've tapped the Send or Receive button and selected the type of connection, you can close the In Box or Out Box. Newton will handle sending and receiving of messages in the background while you continue to work.

(continued)

Easter Egg... Background printing, faxing and mail (continued)

Our testing showed that the performance of applications, hand-writing translation and searching is not impacted upon too seriously by communications happening in the background. The only annoyance you'll have to endure is the In Box's habit of opening when it begins to receive mail. Also, if what you're sending requires a lot of RAM, like a Fax with a lot of graphics in it, there may not be enough memory left for handwriting recognition to work properly.

Once you've established that you can print to your printer, these are the kinds of documents that Newton can put on paper:

- Single Business Card
- All Business Cards
- All Business Cards and Notes
- A Summary of All Names
- A Single Day's Agenda
- A Daily Calendar
- Five-Day Calendar

- Seven-Day Calendar
- One-Week Agenda
- Notepad Note
- A Letter
- A Memo
- A Week's Notes

Assist... Printers that hang around

The first time you tap the Printer list diamond, you'll see the Apple StyleWriter driver, as well as the "Network printers" and "Other printers" options. Newton will add the names of the last Print Pack driver or networked printer to the ready-at-a-tap list. For example, if you've printed to a networked printer called "Wonder Printer," it will appear below the Apple StyleWriter driver the next time you open the print slip.

If you want to change the printer listed next to the Printer list diamond, just tap the "Other printers" or "Network printers" options and select another printer. It will be the first item in the list the next time you open the Print slip.

Some folks like to put together a paper view of their week. They buy special paper for their Day Timers and Day Runners which they can run through a laser printer to grab an inked rendition of their schedules and contacts. At least, that was the habit they got into with a personal computer organizer, which is hard to check when you're standing in the subway.

Unfortunately, you cannot set the paper orientation when sending a document from Newton to a printer. It cannot handle the little pages and calendars can't be printed in landscape (horizontal) orientation so that they can be folded into a booklet. Basically, you're out of luck.

Newton also scales the image to fit the paper, rather than preserving the smaller than life view you get on a MessagePad screen—business cards are centered on the page, the text of notes and calendar items fill the page to the normal margins used in a business letter. That means laser printers, which send all sheets of paper through in a standard portrait orientation, will not let you mess with the position of the paper in an effort to line up the cards with the edge of a page. There's also no means for creating mailing labels.

We expect that a third-party developer, perhaps Pocket Science or Pen-Magic Software Inc. (which already makes a fine word processor for the EO Personal Communicator), will deliver additional formatting options.

So, how do you make these wondrous forms appear? Well, here are a few examples:

- **A single business card to a LaserWriter LS.** Open the Names application and select the card you want to print. Tap the Action button, followed by Print Card.

  The Print slip will open on your Newton screen. Tap the Printer diamond and choose the LaserWriter 300 driver. In the Format list, you'll already see the Single Card option selected. If you want to change to a view of all the data in the Names file, tap the Format list diamond and select the form of the report you want to generate.

When you are finished, tap the Print button.

- **Print a single day's agenda to an HP LaserJet III.** Connect the Print Pack cable to the Newton serial port. Open the Names file to the day that you want to put on paper. Tap the Action button.

You'll see the Day's Agenda format selected, that's the default in Dates. If you want to print a five-day calendar, you must tap the Format list diamond and select that format.

Newton needs the LaserJet III driver in Print Pack to output to the H-P LaserJet series. Tap "Other printers," a dialog box will open that lists all the drivers available to the Newton. Tap the LaserJet III driver, then tap the "Use printer" button. Tap the Print button to send the document to the Out Box.

Assist... You can't take a print driver back

Newton makes it incredibly easy to send a document to a printer, but what happens if you arrive at your destination and there's no printer that matches the driver you chose?

First off, remember that the Print Pack cable has to be connected if you want to choose a driver for a parallel printer. But overall, Newton does give a broad range of choices in printers. You can select a driver, which is attached to the document when it travels that short virtual distance to the Out Box, even when there's no printer attached to your Newton.

If, when you waltz into a client's office with a Newton Out Box full of dazzling documents to print, you find the LaserWriter you anticipated is, in fact, a Kyocera F-3000A, you've got to go back and recreate all those documents. There is no method for changing the driver that's attached to a document.

Apple or a third party should come up with a better Out Box manager, which would let you modify the driver, or even the output methods, so that a print job could become a fax in a pinch. Even if we can't offer a work-around, at least we can offer a suggestion.

Gutenberg's Notepad: A word about formatting

Newton's no lush canvas for your creativity, it's more like a Rosetta stone. It can't do anything but get better. That doesn't mean that you can't make a damn fine looking business letter with the MessagePad.

When you print or fax a note, Newton takes the text and puts it into a full-page format before sending the document. Should you want to check the look of your message, tap the Preview button in the Print or Fax slip to see a very tiny representation of the way the document will look on paper.

The Preview button isn't a lot of help with proofing your letter (unless you've entered incorrectly spelled words into your dictionary, there should be no misspellings—grammar's your problem). But it does let you keep an eye out for "widows," words all by their lonesome on a line at the end of a paragraph. If you see a widow, you can go back to the Notepad to cut out words or add spaces in other lines to eliminate that lonesome meme (see Chapter Five—*Newton 101*, for more on formatting text in notes).

Preview also lets you see how the text fits on pages, so that you don't send a letter that contains all but your signature on a single page. In any case, it's less work than old Johannes Gensfleisch Gutenberg had to put in on getting his 42-line per page Bible finished. He actually quit before completing the first Gutenberg Bible, got himself sued, and had to start on a second Bible with his own press. Now, of course, we're back to scribe-based technology!

Electronic Mail, your thoughts a byte at a time

Measured by the potential for reaching the most people, NewtonMail is perhaps the most powerful communications feature in the MessagePad and Expert Pad.

Electronic mail has given birth to a new organism, a human community that spans the globe on the digital spines of thousands of networks that stretch around the globe. Newton plugs you in to this creature comfortably, allowing you to send and receive messages even when you aren't connected to a network. Notes are stored in the Out Box until you plug in the modem and dial the local network access number, at which time they are delivered and incoming messages are loaded into the In Box.

A network is a marvelous thing, it gives you the ability to project yourself into distant places, libraries, even the Library of Congress, and it lets you join discussions about thousands of topics. Apple has Big Plans for its mail system, the executives who envision profits in the trillions of dollars are hoping to turn Apple Online Services, which offers the AppleLink information network in addition to NewtonMail, into your source of news, software and friendship. The simple messaging offered in Newton is just the beginning.

We've already discussed how to register your NewtonMail account, and how to send and receive mail with the Out Box and In Box, respectively. Now, we'll hit you with the limits and limitlessness inherent in the hand-held mailbox that is Newton.

The mailing capabilities in Newton are somewhat limited compared to the printing and faxing features. You cannot, for example, send multiple business cards in a single message. Here's what you can do:

- **Notes.** When sending mail to another Newton user you can include drawings so that the message will appear with exactly the same graphics as it does on your MessagePad. Messages to personal computer users with access to a network which is connected to the NewtonMail network are confined to text-only contents. Drawings and other graphics are stripped out of these messages when you check the Text Only box in the Mail slip.

  You can send a single note or a week-summary that includes all the notes made in the last seven days.

- **Names.** Business cards can be sent as text with information about the card type you use to another Newton, which will display the data in a format identical to your own Newton. Personal computer users will receive the data as a series of field names (i.e., Company and First Name, followed by the contact information).

  Newton can mail a single card with or without your notes data for that person. Cards cannot be grouped for mailing, nor can you send a summary of all the data in your Names file.

- **Dates.** This is the most robust interface for mailing information. Like the Fax and Print options, Mail can generate several different versions of your calendar. In addition to a single day's agenda, a five- or seven-day calendar and a week summary of appointments, Mail can also send a single calendar item.

To send information about a single appointment, open Dates to the appropriate day and tap the Action button. The Mail slip will open with two list diamonds, a Format list that appears with One Item as the default option and a Meeting list (see Figure 10.4). The Meeting list will appear only when you set the format for a single item, tap it to display a list of the meetings that day (not the To Do items). Select the appointment you want to mail, fill out the Name and Address fields, and tap the Mail button.

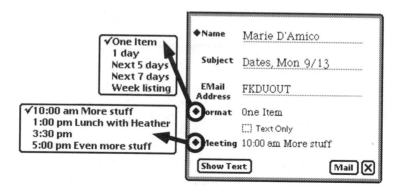

Figure 10.4 Mail your agenda through the electronic ether.

The item will be on its way to a colleague the next time you connect to NewtonMail. If the recipient is a Newton user, do not check the Text Only box in the Mail slip to give them the option of importing the meeting into their own Dates calendar. Check the Text Only box when sending the item to PC or Mac users.

Assist... Our Solitary Beaming Note

While we're at covering the all-electronic world of mail, here's a couple key pieces of knowledge about the other digital communications option. Beaming is easier on the wallet and your nerves than any other Newton communications technology. It's just point and shoot.

The types of documents that can take a trip on the high-frequency highway are:

- A single note in the Notepad
- A single Business Card in Names
- A single appointment in Dates

The Beam slip does something special in the Dates application that is available to none of the other communications mechanisms. You can select a day or an entire week in the calendar, tap the Action button and then "Beam" from the pop-up list, and Newton generates a list of all the meetings during the selected day or days from which you can choose the one you want to beam.   *(continued)*

Assist... Our Solitary Beaming Note (continued)

Beaming is, of course, instantaneous. Too, it is the most personal mode of communication, since you have to stare at the person while your Newtons do the talking. Not a wooden stare, not an Al Gore stare. Actually, you can talk when beaming. It is permitted.

Several folks have asked for a bit of etiquette advice. Here it is: Is it polite to beam a business card or note that has been filed in a particular folder? Not to worry, our Miss Newton Manners tells us, the folder assignment doesn't go with the document, so it will appear as an unfiled note or card in the recipient's Newton (just in case you filed someone's card under "Miscellaneous").

Now, it's one thing to say that Newton users can communicate with one another over Apple's NewtonMail network, but it's quite another job altogether to get it talking to that retrograde slab of the population that hasn't gone PDA crazy (John was our favorite PDA, even though our wives think Paul is cute. Okay, that was just plain weird.)

NewtonMail is a small slice of a larger network owned and operated by Sprint and BT North America. Apple is merely a tenant on that network who has set up a nursery for its new little Newton. Sprint uses its network to deliver mail, faxes, news clips and digital conference rooms to businesses, government and individuals. In fact, if Newton could ever work the door to its NewtonMail nursery open a little bit, it would see and hear the most extraordinary conversations. That revelatory service is coming, but not quite with Sprint's cooperation—more on that later.

In the meantime, just understand that the reason NewtonMail runs on the Sprint/BT network is that they have local access points—computers with modems—in just about every locale in these here United States. By contracting with these companies, Apple avoids the expense of placing its own access points in habitations as large as Los Angeles or small as Los Alamos. (Expect BT in Europe to supply EuroNewtonMail, which we hope will be more socially acceptable than Disney's venture.)

When Newton dials into a network access point, it is communicating with a special kind of computer, called a router. These routers are all connected to one, two or more central computers by very fast dedicated telephone lines that carry nothing but data, and which are connected and active at all times. Once your puny little modem makes the connection to the router, you're on the fast lane (you don't see it, because the 2,400 bps Newton modem is a digital Volkswagen).

Mail is stored on these central computers, called servers, and each user has a file on the computer known as a mailbox. Newton is tuned to take a look in the mailbox for new messages, if it finds none, it logs off.

When Newton sends a message, it communicates with a program on the server that takes messages and delivers them to the correct mailbox in the system. Think of it as an automated postal worker, but made of electrons and with no inclination to slaughter its co-workers.

What happens if the mailbox described by the address isn't in the local network of computers? Well, depending upon whether your network is connected to other networks, two things can happen. If there are no connections to outside networks, the mail server sends a message telling you that the address is not valid (it appears in the In Box, under the Mail item in the Send browser window).

On the other hand, if there are connections to other networks with mail servers of their own, the NewtonMail server looks around to see if any of those networks match the network in the address and hands the message off to the one it thinks contains the destination mailbox. If the mailbox is not there, that mail server tries to pass the message on to another network or it returns the text with an error message attached to it. These network-to-network error messages aren't generated instantaneously, you don't usually see them until the next time you log on.

The gateways between two networks that let mail servers talk are called, coincidentally enough, gateways. Networks can have mail gateways and printing gateways and calendar gateways, all special types of software that watch the interconnection between themselves and other networks for the particular kind of data they are able to translate. It can be a very messy business or quite elegant, depending on how it has been implemented.

NewtonMail has a single, terribly important gateway that connects it to virtually every other significant network in the world, including Apple-Link, CompuServe, MCI Mail, SprintMail (yes, you need a gateway to get there, too), and AT&T's EasyLink Global Mail Network. That super gateway is a doorway to the Internet, the much-hyped, much-used network of networks that Al Gore and Bill Clinton are pointing to as the Great White-Light Hope of the 21st Century. You've heard about it and read about it, now you can use it.

Addressed for Success

Let's step back a moment and consider the humble E-mail address. When you subscribe to NewtonMail, you'll receive a one-word address, probably your last name; in many cases it will be your first and last name. There might be a period somewhere in the address but never any spaces. This is your local address.

Now, imagine that you were trying to describe your local address to someone who had never heard of E-mail or Newton. You'd say something like "My address is RATCLIFFE on the NewtonMail network." Simple, elegant, and approximately how you describe you address to a computer—only with the computer you abbreviate the sentence into a single polysyllable: RATCLIFFE@online.apple.com, which is digital insider talk for "the mailbox called RATCLIFFE at (hence the "at" sign) the Apple Online Services network, which is part of the Apple commercial network connected to the Internet."

So, if your NewtonMail address is SWEENY, you can tell other Newton users to send mail to SWEENY. Because you and they are on the same local system (even though you are dialing into routers on opposite sides of the globe, it's all NewtonMail), the mail will be delivered based on that address alone.

When you meet a CompuServe user who wants to keep in touch by E-mail, you would tell them to send your mail to sweeny@online.apple.com.

The reason you see all this .apple.com stuff is the Internet's decidedly experimental bent and the fact that it is a "backbone network" to which different types of networks—governmental, commercial, academic, and non-profit—are connected. Originally exclusively funded by the federal government, the Internet has established clear guidelines for the use of the network backbone by each type of network user. You can tell a lot about what kind of person someone is by the last three letters of their Internet address (the address that describes their mailbox from the Internet perspective), which identifies what kind of local network they live on. Here's the key to deciphering the network type:

Table 10.3 Three characters tell all on the Internet.

if the end of the address is:	*then the receipient is part of a network operated by:*
.gov	Government agency
.edu	University
.com	Commercial or corporate
.org	Non-profit organization
.mil	Military
.net	Telecommunications network

All you need to know to send mail to someone is their Internet address. Anything connected to the Internet is connected to NewtonMail through the systems' Internet gateway.

All you can send back and forth with an Internet companion are plain text messages. There's no reason that your having to resort to the English language should prevent you from accomplishing considerable business and personal transactions. After all, we've only suffered from the graphical user interface these ten years now, and we're not mute yet.

Table 10.4 shows the formats for sending and receiving mail from popular networks, using the authors accounts on various systems as examples. You'll neet to check with your network about how to access an Internet gateway.

As you can see, there's not much that's very convenient about Internet addressing, although it is fairly consistent. The secret to handling your E-mail efficiently is a third-party application that lets you log onto many different networks, or which grabs the address off an incoming mail message and adds it to a directory of addresses that you can use when sending a message—anything is easier than writing "internet!online.apple.com! RATCLIFFE" with a pen. Unfortunately, such a program doesn't exist, yet.

Table 10.4 Addressing e-mail for a quick ride through the Internet.

Network Name	Local Address	Send from a Newton	Send to Mitch's Newton from network
NewtonMail	RATCLIFFE	RATCLIFFE	RATCLIFFE
AppleLink	MRATCLIFFE	mratcliffe@applelink.apple.com	ratcliffe@online.apple.com
America Online	MW ANDY	mw_andy@aol.com	ratcliffe@online.apple.com
AT&T EasyLink	RATCLIFFEM	ratcliffem@attmail.com	internet!online.apple.com!RATCLIFFE[1]
CompuServe	72511,274[2]	72511.274@compuserve.com	ratcliffe@online.apple.com
MCI Mail	243-3516[3]	2433516@mcimail.com	ratcliffe@online.apple.com

1 AT&T EasyLink uses the X.400 addressing protocol, an awful, but very accurate, system.

2 Mitch's CompuServe address.

3 A made-up MCI Mail address.

What should you do about accounts?

Well, it makes a lot of sense to have more than one account in this day of fragmented E-mail connectivity. Oft-times we find ourselves subscribing to networks that have Internet connections just to make the people with whom we communicate on those network more comfortable; they don't know how, and don't want to learn, to handle sending mail through the Internet. PocketCall is an almost ideal solution for folks who make this decision, because it lets you participate in conferences on America Online, CompuServe, and other systems. You'll still need to use the In Box and Out Box to check your NewtonMail account.

On the downside, a whole bunch of on-line accounts costs a whole lot of money every month. NewtonMail will give you approximately five minutes of on-line time a day to check your mail, according to Apple, then the company will begin to charge you for your additional use. Pricing had not been set when we went to press.

Third-party applications, particularly a future version of PocketCall, will add directory capability. Once the ability to save addresses is built in to tele-communications software, preparing messages for delivery over the Internet will be substantially easier.

There is a solution available today, but it will cost you a precious slice of your Newton's internal RAM.

The In Box saves mail until you either put the message away in an application or delete it. When you open a message by tapping it in the Receive browser window, you'll see a Reply button at the bottom of the form. But, wait, don't tap that button, yet. You've got to edit your reply first.

Scrub out everything in the message that you don't want to refer to in your reply and write the text you want to send. Then tap Reply, the new message will be sent to the Out Box, and another copy will stay in the In Box, ready to act as a Reply form, again.

So, you see, you can save messages which can be used as pre-addressed message templates for your mail to the important people in your life. Re-grettably, messages stored in the In Box reside in the Newton's main RAM, rather than a storage card. The more messages you keep at the ready, the smaller your PDA's available memory for other processes.

Get Info... The Internet libraries and salons

The Internet is more than a conduit for your mail, it is also the home of thousands of discussion groups and archives of software and information that can be retrieved by electronic mail.

More than 5000 newsgroups conduct debates and keep people informed through the Internet.

You can join a discussion on almost any topic—from Slavic culture to carnal explorations with a collie and spanning the political spectrum from the Libertarian to the Socialist—by sending a message to one of various list servers that control access to these communities.

Newton discussions sprung up almost immediately after the Macworld introduction. Send a subscription request to:

Newton.Announce-request@umich.edu

to begin receiving the latest information about Newton on your Newton.

Archie, an electronic librarian, can help you dig up information from computers around the world. Send E-mail to:

archie@cs.mcgill.ca, include the phrase "prog Archie"

in the body of the message, for a complete run-down of the service. It's free.

And you can send mail to President Clinton or Vice President Gore at:

PRESIDENT@WHITEHOUSE.GOV

and

VICE.PRESIDENT@WHITEHOUSE.GOV, respectively.

Keep in mind that the more mailing lists you subscribe to, you're likely to run into overtime on your NewtonMail account and be billed by Apple.

The future of NewtonMail

What if your E-mail network was smart enough to examine, categorize, and file your mail by the contents of the messages or the names of the people who sent it to you? There'd be a lot less hassles in managing your communications with the world. The networks might even be smart enough to cooperate with one another, so that all the mail sent to your different accounts landed in a single mailbox accessible through one phone call.

Somehow, we need to find a way to control the network when our computers are not connected to it. The mechanism that will deliver on that idea is called a software agent.

An agent is a kind of program that you upload to your mailbox on the network. Once it lands on the network, the agent can sit at the ready to control the way messages and other information are handled by the mail system. It can be a simple agent that merely watches for mail from your best customer and forwards it to a paging service that will send the text to your Newton Messaging Card, or it can be a complex set of instructions that are wrapped around a file—other agents, sent by different users, can ask to see the contents of the enclosed file and even pay for the right to open the file—and you can send many agents to your mailbox to manage many different tasks.

Apple is working with AT&T and a small Silicon Valley company named General Magic to create a software agent-based service that is now known by the code-name Main Street. One of the largest side-streets leading to Main Street will be Apple Online Service's network. Newtons, devices made by Motorola, Sony, and Macs or PCs will be able to run General Magic-authored software for creating agents which will roam Main Street to do your bidding.

Main Street is only one of many agent software projects. Microsoft is working on a competing technology, as are several other companies. But we think the vision stated by AT&T and General Magic is the most interesting in this horse race. And the first version of the technology will be in place on AT&T's network by the time you read this book; the service will start-up during 1994. A second- or third-generation Newton will be among the first to have access.

You may see, or might already have seen, a major announcement about Apple and AT&T collaborating to extend the forms of mail and files that the General Magic technology will deliver. There is always a possibility, too, that AT&T will eventually acquire all or part of Apple.

If the NewtonMail connection to Main Street plays out during the next five to ten years, you will be able to open a form on the MessagePad that offers a series of choices that, taken collectively, tell the agent how to deal with a particular situation. That form might have a single address field, in which you'll write the E-Mail address of a friend or colleague, and a series of check boxes, including "Forward to pager," "Forward to NewtonMail," or "Throw away, I never want to see a message from this person."

Another interesting, and possibly more immediate, future in the plans for NewtonMail are transaction services. The way these work is you send a request in the form of a message to a special service account. The account processes the request and sends back a message to your Newton telling you it did what you wanted it to do.

For example, let's say you want to send flowers to your spouse for his birthday (role reversal? We don't know about you but either of us would be more than pleased to receive flowers on our birthdays!) You send a note with his name and the address where you want the flowers delivered plus a price limit, flowers you want and a message for the card to Newton Flowers. The receiver account checks with the NewtonMail server to get and verify your charge card information and sends the request to a local florist. The next time you sign on, you'll get a receipt. And we're sure you'll get a grateful kiss from your husband once the flowers arrive.

That's it, the future, and you can expect that it will arrive not only in your Newton, but also in the telephone, television and your car radio. Newton may show up in all these places, too.

Turning a New Page

Wireless messaging is the last great frontier you'll enter with a Newton. The first tool for grabbing data from the ether is Apple's Messaging Card, a Motorola NewsCard pager grafted onto a PCMCIA 2.0 card. It can receive messages sent over the MobileComm national paging network.

At 240 characters per message, the Messaging Card is certainly the medium of succinct communicators. However, that's plenty of characters to convey a short message that includes a meeting place, time and confirmation number. The Messaging Card has 128 Kbytes of internal memory that can store hundreds of messages of 240 characters. When the card is full, the oldest message is erased to make room for the newest message.

The card makes a tone when a message arrives, and displays a flashing green LED to let you know that you have un-read messages. Thankfully, you can turn it off. Messages stored in the card are preserved while the pager is off.

The card we tested operated reliably for three-and-a-half weeks on a single AAA battery.

MobileComm offers three grades of service: Regional, National and Roaming. A regional service contract can provide paging within a metropolitan region or several states; national coverage will put a message into your card wherever you happen to be in the U. S.; and roaming service lets you "forward" your messages from one region to another, depending upon where you are. Regional service will cost between $18 and $30 a month, while national paging can run up close to $70 in monthly charges. The roaming service falls in the middle, but you must manage the connection, phoning in to change your location when you leave a region. Complete details will be available from MobileComm when you buy your Messaging Card.

Most folks don't have their paging service with MobileComm, and many receive messages over private networks, like a hospital's paging system. The Messaging Card could be made to work with these other systems, but Apple currently isn't willing to share the software that will let these organizations offer their services to Newton users. Developers speculate that Apple will license the pager code to larger organizations which want to use the Messaging Card for their own applications.

Apple cut a deal with MobileComm, a nationwide paging company that provides the only Messaging Card-compatible alphanumeric pager service. The card is tuned to the specific frequency used by MobileComm, 931. 8875 MHz, although it can listen to any frequency between 929 MHz and 932 MHz. The pager would have to be reprogrammed to accommodate another service, and you'll need to get your hands on a PCMCIA programmer device that can rewrite the memory in the card.

Two functions in the card must be changed to make it work with foreign networks: The frequency the device receives must be altered, and you must make sure that the card is set to receive data in the format the system uses. Because MobileComm has a lock on the frequency used by Newton Messaging Cards, it seems they'll be the only general-use paging game in town, or the nation, for some time to come.

We've already discussed how to open, put away and delete paging messages in Chapter Seven—*Life's Little Extras*, so let's look at what you can do with a service like MobileComm's.

Incoming!

A pager is a lot cheaper than a cellular phone, and it can be just as effective for keeping in touch as a voice telephone connection. A toll-free number and your individual pager PIN (personal identification number) on your business card can serve as a link to people and computers anywhere in the U. S. In 1994, Apple will announce relationships with paging vendors in other countries who will be able to deliver their messages to the Newton's PCMCIA slot.

These are the types of connections you'll have:

- **Numeric paging.** Callers can dial the MobileComm access number and, at a tone, enter their phone number by dialing it on their keypad. The number arrives in a message that you can open, read and store on the Messaging Card.

- **Alphanumeric paging.** When a caller dials MobileComm, an operator will take a short text message and their telephone number, which are typed into a computer and sent over the pager network. The MobileComm operators are fanatics about abbreviation, messages can be converted into cryptic codes. But, hey, for the people out there without computers who demand that they can send you a detailed message, it works.

- **Computer-to-pager.** A variety of software applications for PCs and Macs can send messages to the MobileComm network for distribution to pagers. These programs look a lot like a standard electronic mail package, but instead of a network address you use the pager access number and a PIN number when addressing the message.

This pager-savvy class of software is the most interesting means for linking your Newton to a desktop machine, since there is no need for a physical connection. Data can flow from the desktop to the Newton when necessary, not just when you manage to find a wire between the two. It requires much less planning, no orchestration other than choosing the right software and pager service (you've got no choice with the Messaging Card). It's an ad hoc method of communicating, very like how we begin to talk when an idea strikes.

The character of pager messages is like those sent through the Internet to NewtonMail accounts, just a text message. The Messaging Card interface lets you import messages into the Notepad, but not Names or Dates. Eventually, it will be possible to send Newton frames that will automatically update the calendar or your address database when they arrive. What must happen before this becomes a reality is an agreement among paging network providers, hardware makers, and software developers on a standard way to increase the number of characters in a single message. Then, look for companies like Ex Machina to incorporate frames into their pager software—Ex Machina already provides a similar update capability for PowerBooks and H-P 95LX and 100LX computers in a product called Update!

Your paging options for the desktop are:

- **MobileComm** makes its own DOS, Windows, and Mac software, called MobileComm Messaging Software. It's a very inexpensive package, because the company is interested in selling paging services filled with messages generated by the software. It works, but the interface is pretty klunky, providing very little feedback about the progress of your paging message.

- **Ex Machina** offers several variations on its Notify! paging product. Individual users with Macs and PCs should check out the Notify! Personal Edition for Mac and Windows, respectively. It provides a useful directory of pager addresses and can pass on to the paging network messages sent from other applications running on the computer. For example, you can have your desktop calendar send reminders of meetings to your Messaging Card through Notify!. Network users can share a Notify! server for Macintosh, which lets individuals compose messages and send them to a Mac equipped with a modem.

- **Information Radio Technology Inc.** makes a Mac pager messaging application, called AlphaPage.

- **Wolf Creek Technologies Inc.** makes a gateway application, QM-Page, which runs on QuickMail electronic mail servers. The advantage in taking this approach to paging messages is that users don't need to learn anything new to send a page, and all their communications happen in a single interface, using the QuickMail directory as a centralized list of addresses.

- **Caravelle Networks Corp.'s** PagerPro software for Mac offers the same basic functionality as Notify!, such as the ability to send and forward messages from other applications on the computer. On top of that, it gives you a nice scripting and scheduling feature that lets you compose messages that will be sent later, when you're out of the office.

- **Fourth Wave Technologies Inc.'s** WinBeep is a Windows paging application that lets you compose and forward messages sent over Microsoft Corp.'s Microsoft Mail or Lotus Development Corp.'s cc:Mail electronic mail networks.

Information on tap

News, sports scores, and stock prices will be winging their way to Newton's Messaging Card in the very near future. MobileComm will introduce a service in early 1994 that delivers information for an added monthly fee.

But the information age won't stop at the relatively short messages the Messaging Card can deliver. Look for new services offered by Motorola, IBM, and Apple next year, as well.

External adapters for Newton will appear that give it access to the EMBARC paging network, which already offers news and financial information to its users. EMBARC distinguishes itself from other pager-oriented communications by the sheer length of its messages—it supports up to 30,000 characters of data, more than enough to ship the contents of a Wall Street Journal story to your Newton (now, if your Newton only had the RAM to hold it). Motorola also makes the EMBARC receiver, a pager-like gadget that connects to the serial port of a computer. You'll install a special application in the Extras drawer that can recognize and import information from the EMBARC receiver.

Motorola in 1994 will also roll out PCMCIA wireless modems, a fancy radio that acts as an interface to a network of antennas which can pass network packets between two devices, including Newtons and mainframe computers. These packet radio networks, as they are called, are very effective, low-cost connections. At least, they're getting less expensive all the time. The Motorola transceivers will connect Newton to the RAM Mobile Data Network and the ARDIS network, a wireless network launched by IBM and Motorola in 1991.

You'll need a different Motorola card for each network, but the company promises two-way communications in more than 400 cities and towns in the U. S., coverage that's as good or better than cellular. Prices for these services average between $50 and $90 a month, depending upon your usage.

The real break-through network may come out of nowhere. Metricom, a company that made its name selling packet radio modems to electric utilities, is planning to blitz the wireless market with very inexpensive radio that is billed not by usage, but by the speed of your access. Unlimited use of a 2,400 bps connection will cost as little as $2.95 a month. A 14,400 bps link will be $9.95, and so on up to $19.95 for a 56,000 bps link. Even after you factor in the cost of the radio modem, the total expense of a Metricom account is considerably less than the competition's, and the performance is better.

What's the catch? Well, someone has to put the radios that will tie together Metricom-equipped Newtons and computers. Right now, Apple has covered the Silicon Valley with these things to allow their employees with power to log into the company's AppleLink service at high speeds, but that has to happen everywhere for this to become a winning technology. However, the Metricom base stations, which can be nailed to the top of a phone pole, are very inexpensive. If the utilities that are already using them to monitor the power grid get wind of the profit opportunity in selling access to their radios, wireless connectivity could become a trivial expense in just a year or two.

Get Info... Wireless, The Next Generation

Paging's one-way messaging is only the first step toward a world in which our PDAs and computers are seldom connected via wire, but always on the prowl for data sent over the airwaves.

Cellular telephones are getting smaller all the time, and it will be a matter of months after this book ships before a PCMCIA digital cellular transceiver that plugs into the Newton serial port is introduced. This new cellular unit will rely on a new technology, Cellular Digital Packet Data (CDPD), an emerging standard for sending both voice and data over the cellular net.   *(continued)*

Get Info... Wireless, The Next Generation (continued)

CDPD billing will be based on the number of the packets you send, rather than the time you spend connected to the network. Your Newton will be able to maintain a "virtual circuit" all day, sending and receiving data as it is generated. No dialing the phone, no waiting for the modems to handshake, just connectivity —according to the hype. It remains to be seen whether CDPD will really work; the first real world use of the technology was demonstrated in Las Vegas during the summer of 1993.

Las Vegas... Banking on CDPD as your wireless network of choice may be a bad bet.

You can connect to a modem using a standard cellular telephone and a special adapter that attaches to the Newton modem. The adapter will generate a dial tone, which cellular phones don't need but modems do. It also appends a "send" tone at the end of the dial string sent by the modem, which modems don't normally do but cellular phones desperately require.

Applied Engineering's Axcell Cellular Interface is a proven adapter that works with several manufacturers' phones. It also adds an additional error correction protocol for cellular connections, MNP-10, on top of those supported in your modem. The result is a functional, if not entirely reliable, connection to fax machines and NewtonMail services. The problem with cellular is not the hardware. It's the network which still affords spotty coverage—drive beyond the wrong hill and you'll lose your signal.

Motorola also makes a family of adapters for its own phones, with which users on CompuServe reported success in faxing. However, at least one person on the Newton Team who uses this adapter claimed it wasn't reliable for e-mail.

Newton, unlike most personal computers, can be set to initiate a modem connection in the absence of a dial tone. This is obviously an orphan feature that's waiting for the first cellular Newton or an adapter. Open the Preferences and select the Modem settings. You'll see the phrase "Require dial tone" and a check box, leaving the box un-checked lets Newton dial without a tone.

Finally, the phone

Newton can dial your analog phone for you, if you have both the PDA and the phone plugged into a line-splitter. You can also hold Newton's speaker up to the microphone of a telephone, it will dial the phone.

Keep in mind that you may have trouble with some digital telephones in offices or hotels. Many companies block external dialers to prevent abuse of voice mail systems.

The really cool thing about Newton's dialer is its ability to convert hokey telephone numbers that spell something into the numbers you want to dial. So, you can write 1-800-NEWTON9 in a phone field and Newton will dial 1-800-639-8669, the correct number.

Practically speaking, the most convenient function of Newton might be its ability to dial a number and your telephone credit card number. To set these numbers, tap the Options button in the Dialing slip. You can get the Dialing slip by either tapping the phone number on someone's card from the Names file or by writing "Call Your Name" on the notepad, selecting it and tapping the Assist icon.

The Area Code field is your current area code, based your location in the Time Zones application (The I'm Here button is linked to your area code setting). The Prefix field should hold the number you need to dial to get an outside line on the phone you are using.

If you must dial an access code to reach your long-distance provider, enter that number in the Access Code field. After it has dialed the prefix, access code and telephone number, Newton will wait a few seconds to dial the number in the Credit Card field. Many credit card numbers are actually a progression of numbers separated by pauses. You can add pauses to the credit card field by typing commas. Each comma adds a two-second pause (see Figure 10.5).

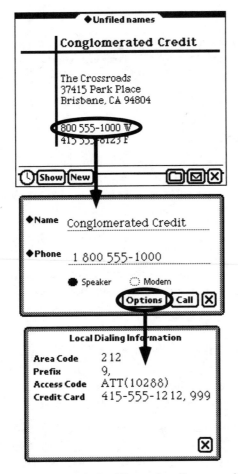

Figure 10.5 Let Newton handle your credit card calls.

Where's Newton?

The Fourth Law: E = MC^2, an address somewhere in Tokyo.

Goin' Mobile

The quality of life is determined by little things. No single all-encompassing convenience can make up for an accumulation of timely assistance. In the end, we remember most the moments when life seems effortless. When we create, not for our boss, or our spouse, or our children, or posterity, but only for ourselves. Those moments when we produce a sentence, a carving, a drawing or whatever pleases is an expression or our selves.

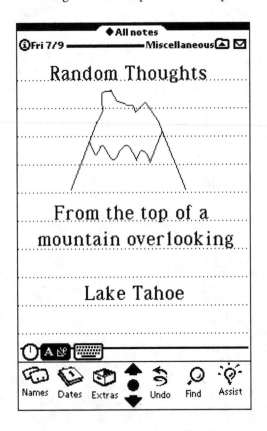

Over the years humanity has created many tools for capturing ideas. From clay tablets to movable type, as the accessibility of man's tools of expression has grown, so has the complexity, the depth, and the sheer variety of the ideas that have gained voice through those tools. Never has this seemed more true than with the advent of personal computers. These relatively inexpensive devices promised to be a boon to the creative output of mankind, but they actually resulted in an average increase in work of eight hours a week per person since 1980. However, they've also made technologies previously reserved for the print shop accessible to us in our homes and offices. If you take the time to learn to use a word processor or a page-layout application, you have the power of the press on your desktop.

Two variables define creative accessibility. The first—easy access—desktop publishing and word processing fulfilled admirably. The second—ready access—has only just begun to be realized, through portable and notebook computers that allow us to bring the power of our tools with us where ever we go. But, lest we give the impression that this is All Good, society has not succeeded in making these tools available to everyone who might benefit from them.

If you must constantly be aware of things like how much longer you have left on a battery charge, finding a comfortable place to work, and having this heavy thing hanging off your shoulder like an electronic marsupial, you are less likely to use it whenever and wherever the creative mood strikes. Anytime, anywhere computing only works with devices you can use anytime and anywhere.

Thus enters Newton.

In some respects, Newton is a perfect mobile computing device. It's built around communications capabilities—one of the key functions users need while on the road. It's instantly accessible—nothing could be more convenient than always being a tap away from any application. It's small and light enough to work with in an elevator or a parked car—who wants to hunt down a table and chair every time they want to create? Newton will go a full day on a battery charge—there's nothing more frustrating than a low battery warning just one hour after sitting down on a five-hour plane flight.

You might not be able to write long memos or render precise schematics on your Newton, but you can get organized, draft mail, check out some numbers, and entertain yourself, all from the palm of your hand. For many users, Newton won't replace the portable computer. But in a one-pound, pocket-sized package, it seems likely that portables will be spending a lot more time in hotel or motel rooms while their masters are out with Newton in hand. Newton is a data peripheral, it works independently of your computer in order to feed data into that computer.

In this section, we'll briefly explore some of the preparations you need to make when taking Newton on the road; Finding a modem connection in hotels; What any good Newton Traveler will want to carry with them; and How to get the most from your PDA's power packs. At the end of the section, we'll provide some quick tips on caring for your Newton and a trouble-shooting guide, in case something goes wrong while your away from home.

CHAPTER
11

THE POWER OF NEWTON

It's pretty incredible. All that Newton technology can fit in your pocket and can run all day on power barely adequate to make a flashlight work. Newton's ability to manage its electrical appetite is quite good—shutting down and cranking up the processor from moment to moment, activating ports only when they're needed, built from low power components that demand but a trickle of current. No doubt about it, Newton was designed to save power while delivering maximum performance.

Why this obsession with power frugality? Well, in most portable computing devices the batteries represent as much as half the weight. If Apple could find a way to use the tiniest, lightest power sources and still meet the runtime requirements of the average user, the company could construct a device well suited for the mobile life. They did it, using the smallest of standard power cells, AAA batteries, which can keep a Newton going anywhere from two to sixteen hours without need of a recharge or fresh cells.

Certainly, in comparison to Apple's other portable products, the Power-Books, a two to sixteen hour runtime is impressive. Depending on the model and how it's being used, PowerBooks get as little as an hour's worth of life from a fully-charged battery. However, it should be noted that in the PDA arena, the MessagePad and Expert Pad are power hogs. Devices like Casio's Zoomer claim 100 hours of active use before needing new batteries. Runtimes of this length are also not uncommon with Newton precursors like the Sharp Wizards. Even some PC notebooks claim battery life of eight hours or better. It seems that when it comes to portable power, Apple products will always perform toward the lower-end of the spectrum.

Despite this, we do feel that Newton supplies more than adequate battery life for most users. And carrying an extra power pack shouldn't prove a great inconvenience for those who need more power. Also, when it comes right down to it, if the choice is using a Wizard for a hundred hours or Newton for eight, we know which we'd choose.

There are things you can do to extend a charge and the life of your batteries. Granted, you don't have the option of turning the hard drive on and off like you do in most portable computers—there is no hard drive in Newton. But there are measures you can take to make sure you're getting the max from your power packs.

Powers That Be

As we said in Chapter Two—*Your Information Surfboard*, Newton can use three sources of power: The AC power supply which will run Newton while its plugged in, even if the PDA's power pack is completely depleted. The two internal power sources—the Alkaline power pack which delivers longer, although not restorable, runtimes and the NiCad power pack which, although it can't match battery life with alkalines, can be recharged hundreds of times before its usefulness will be at an end.

Then there's Newton's emergency backup system, the coin cell, which, although it won't supply enough power to run your Newton, can keep your data safe when all else fails for up to twelve weeks.

In this section we concern ourselves primarily with your NiCad power pack, which we hope you'll invest in. In fact, we hope you'll buy or have already bought two packs, not because we have stock in a NiCad manufacturer, but because it always pays to have at least one spare on hand, just in case you get caught short (no power puns, please!).

There are good power habits you should cultivate in your day-to-day Newton usage, just to be safe and sure you'll have a charge whenever you need it. Follow these tips and you'll never have to worry about power for your PDA.

Power Tip #1: Stay Plugged In. Whenever possible, leave your Newton plugged into the wall. Not only does this keep you from using up your batteries, it helps keep them fully-charged. Your Newton will trickle-charge the power pack whenever its plugged in (and Newton isn't running). The power supply is so small and light, you'll hardly notice the extra weight in your briefcase. But you'll certainly notice the extra power when you need it.

Power Tip #2: Keep Your Alkaline Pack handy. One of the great things about a device that can use both an exotic, but convenient, power source like NiCads and more commonplace batteries like Alkalines is, if you're ever in need, you can find AAA batteries at almost any drug or convenience store. (Buy only alkalines. Mixing standard cells with alkalines in the pack could damage your Newton.) But if you forget the Alkaline battery holder, easy access to batteries won't do you a bit of good.

Use Alkalines as the last line of defense. Although you'll likely get twice the battery life from an Alkaline pack, your Newton is tuned to NiCads and, therefore, works more reliably with them. For example, the battery status meter at the bottom of the Extras drawer will almost always give a false reading with alkalines. Also, your screen is likely to flicker and dim occasionally when alkalines are running low (below half-charged) on power.

You can also experiment with AAA lithium cells available in stores like Radio Shack. One Newton user we know tried them out and said they worked fine, powering their PDA for several times longer than Alkalines. However, before you run out and buy lithium cells we should warn you that they may not agree with Newton's power manager, seeing as they aren't what the system was intended to be used with. Problems caused by lithium cells could be as minor as false battery status readings or as major as overheating and damaging power circuitry. We haven't tested it so we just don't know.

Power Tip #3: One to Go and One to Glow. The minimum battery purchase for any road warrior is one NiCad power pack and one NiCad recharger, which comes with a power pack. Keep one pack in the charger and the other in your Newton. At the end of the day, swap the packs. This way, you're always sure of a fresh power pack every morning.

Power Tip #4: Store Plugged In. If you're not going to use your Newton for a while, make sure you store it someplace where it can also be plugged in to a reliable power source. There's nothing worse than coming back from vacation to find your batteries dead and your data and settings expired.

Power Tip #5: Change Your Backup Often. An insurance policy is no good if it lapses. The same is true of backup batteries. If you think you're Newton has spent a lot of time on the coin cell, or if its been about a year since you last changed it, replace it. Newton will display a warning when the coin cell is almost empty. But, coin cells are cheap enough so, better safe than sorry.

Power Tip #6: Run It Down. Once every so often, instead of running to an outlet when you get the "Battery Low" dialog box, just keep on using your Newton. Eventually, the PDA will just shut itself down, refusing to start up until plugged in. When this happens remove the NiCad pack and mount it in the external recharger (don't forget to plug your Newton in as well!) You can also plug-in your depleted Newton to trickle charge, if you're willing to leave it undisturbed for at least 12 hours. This will help guarantee that your battery pack is performing at maximum efficiency at all times.

Power Tip #7: Set Short Sleep Times. It's easy enough with a Newton to forget its on, considering the fact that you're probably turning it on and off all day. But letting it run when you aren't using it just wastes battery power. To prevent this, go to the Sleep Preferences and set your Newton to turn itself off automatically after either one or five minutes of idle time (five minutes should be sufficient). Your Newton is idle if you aren't writing on it and it isn't involved in either a communications session (over the modem or network) or processing a request.

Changing the Battery

To mount either the Alkaline or NiCad power packs, first make sure your Newton is switched off and plugged in. Then, flip the unit over so that it's face down on a flat surface, preferably on a soft, clean cloth. Now, pull the battery cover down and off (look for the little thumb guide and arrow etched in the plastic.)

Once the cover is completely off, you'll notice two areas for putting your batteries plus a brightly colored switch on the left (see Figure 11.1). The switch has three settings: Replace Main, In Use, and Replace Backup.

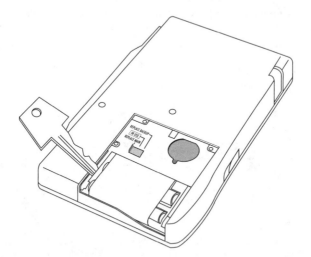

Figure 11.1 Replacing the main battery.

If you're replacing the coin cell, push the switch to "Replace Backup." This will unlock the coin cell so it can be removed. You'll probably need to pry it out with the tip of a small screwdriver placed in the notch at the bottom of the battery. The coin cell has a tendency to get lodged in its hole.

Once you have the old cell out, drop the fresh battery in so that the positive terminal is facing up (you may need to press the cell into place). That's all there is too it.

If you're replacing the battery back, move the colored switch to "Replace Main." Then, take the tip of a key, a coin or screwdriver and stick it into the slot on the left side of the battery pack. The pack should pop out (see Figure 11.1). Don't forget to move the switch first, jamming a key into the crack when the switch is set to Replace Backup or In Use could damage your Newton.

When you're done changing batteries you can push the switch back to In Use or leave it where it is. The switch only prevents the batteries from being accidentally removed, it doesn't stop your Newton from running. It is a good idea, however, to leave the switch set to In Use when the Newton's, well, in use.

I Get A Charge Out Of You

Newton gives you only one meter for telling where you are in a battery charge. You can get at it either by tapping the clock button or by opening the Extras drawer (see Figure 11.2). While the meter does a better-than-average job of displaying an accurate account of the charge left in the power pack, because your Newton will consume power at drastically different rates depending on what you're doing, the level shown is hard to equate to a specific runtime.

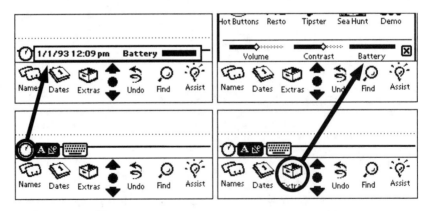

Figure 11.2 Two ways to see your power.

Another problem with the meter is that it doesn't display battery status while Newton is plugged in. You can have a completely depleted power pack in your PDA, plug it in and, a moment or two later, Newton will try to tell you the battery is fully charged. Don't believe it. It takes a minimum of three hours to recharge a NiCad with the recharger and about four times that long if you charge the pack inside your Newton. Keep in mind that when your Newton is running your battery isn't charging.

Beyond the status meter, Newton also includes an early warning system that alerts you if the battery charge gets low. Actually, the MessagePad and Expert Pads we tested were tuned a bit too conservatively. The battery warning came up when there was still 25 to 30 percent of the charge remaining. We continued to use our Newtons for hours beyond when the first warning came up. The fact is, if you have a power supply and outlet or a fresh power pack at the ready, you can safely use your Newton right down to the bottom of the battery's charge. The PDA will shut itself off and refuse to turn back on once the current drops to near zero. However, there's no danger of data going away, unless your coin cell is depleted. Just swap power packs or plug your Newton in and press the power switch. You may get a dialog box that says power was interrupted. Ignore it. It just means current ran too low to restart the system.

When you do go to refresh your power pack in the recharger, be careful that the power pack is really drained. The recharger uses a fast charge method which blasts the pack with current for four hours while plugged in. At the end of four hours of hanging on a wall socket, the recharger automatically shuts itself off, even if the pack isn't fully charged (don't worry, it is). This is a good thing. If it didn't shut itself off, the recharger could damage the battery by overcharging it. That's why it's important not to put a fully charged, or even an almost fully charged, power pack in the recharger.

Conditioning. All NiCads can suffer from power memory which will significantly curtail the length of time your Newton will run on that battery. If your battery normally gives you about four to six hours of use before needing a charge and then one day it'll only power your Newton for two hours, you could be suffering from this syndrome.

It's caused by shallow-charging and discharging the power pack over and over again. After a while, the battery gets stuck at the shallow level to which you've been recharging it to, which could be much below its real capacity.

The cure for this problem is simple. Just run your Newton on the power pack until it shuts itself off and refuses to restart. You can do this by setting sleep in the Sleep Preferences to "never" (if you're using Elegance, use that utility to quickly change the sleep settings) and just letting your Newton run down (see Figure 11.3). This could take several hours depending how much of a charge is left in your battery. Then, either put it in the recharger for the full four hours or plug your Newton in, and don't use it for at least 12 hours. That's how you do the battery conditioning hokey-pokey.

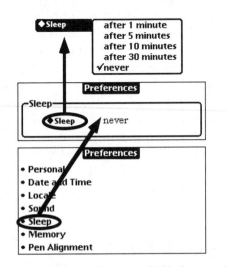

Figure 11.3 *Setting up beddy-bye time for your Newton.*

If a conditioned battery continues to show signs of limited capacity, try conditioning it again, only this time, if you can, take the battery pack out and leave it on a shelf for 24 to 48 hours (this would be a good time to have a second power pack, wouldn't it?) If you don't have a second power pack, don't forget to plug your Newton in so you don't run down the coin cell.

If after this second conditioning session the power pack still delivers only limited power, it may be the first signs of old age.

It's a good idea to condition your batteries regularly, at least once every 50 cycles (charges and discharges). This not only prevents power memory from occurring, it'll extend your power pack's useful life.

End of life. Everything dies, even batteries. NiCad packs are usually good for about 500 charge and discharge cycles (although we've had some packs last considerably longer and a few have died much sooner) and then they start losing their ability to hold a charge, sometimes quickly. If conditioning the battery doesn't seem to restore its vim and vigor and you think it's a relatively old battery, the time to get a new pack has come. Please, if you can, be kind to the planet and take your pack to a dealer, who can have it recycled.

SRAM Cards. Unlike Flash RAM cards, which don't need current to maintain data, SRAM cards have their own built-in power sources to protect the contents of memory. Some cards have the ability to "parasite" your Newton, drawing on the PDA's power to recharge its own source. Others will require you change the battery. Follow the directions that came with your card on how you can do this without losing the contents of the card. You may not be able to, in which case make sure to backup the card before attempting to charge the battery.

As to when you'll need to change SRAM card batteries, with most cards Newton will let you know when the card's power is low.

Assist... Battery labels

If you're using multiple NiCad packs, it's a good idea to label them so you'll know one from another.

Because NiCads have a limited number of recharges before they lose their ability to hold current, it's important to know when you bought a battery so you can guess if it has reached the end of its usefulness. If you also number your batteries, you can use those numbers to even out usage by rotating packs.

Unlike portable computers, which are mostly used when away from home base, Newton is the kind of tool you'll use every day— at the office, in meetings, over lunch and at home. For this reason, you're likely to go through power packs much quicker than with a portable computer. So, it behooves you to make sure you rotate power packs insuring you'll always have a rough idea of how much of a useful life is left in the pack. Nothing's worse than going on a trip with a pack you think is good, only to find it's shuffled off this mortal coil during the plane flight.   *(continued)*

Assist... Battery labels (continued)

Any standard mailing label, cut down to size, should do. Write two things on it: the date of purchase and a number. Make the first battery you buy number one, the next number two, and so on. Then, make sure you rotate the packs each evening. One should go into the recharger while the next battery in line should get plugged into your Newton.

Another thing you can keep track of on the label is the last time you conditioned the NiCad pack. Write the last date in pencil. Then, the next time you condition the battery, erase the old date and write in the new.

With labels in place, the next time your power pack doesn't seem to have its usual vim and vigor, a quick check of the dates on the back will tell you if it's time to condition it or bring it into your dealer for recycling.

Power States

Your Newton operates in three power states that require gradually increasing electrical current. It's never really off, although it may seem that way at times. Unless it's broken or you've allowed all the batteries to die, your Newton always draws at least a modicum of electricity to keep the contents of internal RAM intact.

Sleep. When your Newton is "off" it's actually asleep. That means the screen, processor and all ports are shut off, but RAM is being powered. This way, if you press the power switch, Newton will bring you back to exactly where you left off when it went to sleep. Your Newton draws only minimal power while asleep. A fully charged NiCad pack can protect memory for weeks.

Idle. The screen is on, but the processor and ports are temporarily shut off. Although Newton draws much more power when idle than when it is asleep, it's still uses much less power than when the unit is active. A Newton can stay switched on for many hours in idle mode, if you have sleep set to "never."

Active. The processor or ports are busy executing commands or communicating. This is Newton's power high ground. An active Newton can go through a fully-charged NiCad pack in a matter of a few hours.

The Battery Killer Gang

The following is a list of Newton's components that drain power while active. This list should help you avoid using power-hungry facilities, where you have the option.

- **CPU.** When active, it sucks current like it's fine champagne. Luckily, it's only active when it's got something to do.

- **Internal RAM.** Static RAM is pretty power-frugal. But even if it wasn't, you still need to keep it powered to run your Newton, so there's no point in worrying about it.

- **SRAM Cards.** Same as above. They will draw current while plugged into the Newton's PCMCIA slot, but not much.

- **Flash RAM Cards.** Flash RAM cards only draw power to read or write data. Otherwise they draw no power to maintain the contents of memory.

- **Device Cards.** These suckers are big power hogs and drain a Newton's power pack in practically no time, if they don't have their own power source. It's probably a good idea to only use a modem card, for example, while Newton is plugged in. Other cards, like the Messaging Card, have their own power sources and, therefore, aren't a problem for Newton's battery life.

- **IR Port.** If left active, the infrared transceiver can reduce battery life significantly. While we don't think it's really necessary to run to the nearest outlet every time you want to beam something, it's probably a good idea not to set the port to receive beams automatically.

- **Serial Port.** The serial port is another interface that can shorten Newton's runtime. But, because you'll have to be near a telephone wall jack or network or serial connector to make use of this port, it should be a simple matter to plug your Newton into a wall socket during communications sessions. The Apple modem has its own AA batteries which are good for many hours of happy communicating.

How Long For What

Table 11.1 shows expected battery life for Alkaline and NiCad power packs under different operating conditions. These are only estimates, your results may vary.

Table 11.1 Power usage comparison for NiCad and Alkaline powerpacks.

	NiCad Runtime	*Alkaline Runtime*
100% Idle	6 to 10 hours	12 to 16 hours
50% Idle/ 50% Active (normal use)	4 to 8 hours	8 to 12 hours
100% Active	2 to 4 hours	4 to 8 hours
Normal Use with storage card	3.5 to 8 hours	7 to 12 hours
Normal Use with serial on	3 to 5 hours	5 to 10 hours
Normal Use with IR on auto	2 to 4 hours	4 to 8 hours
Normal Use with serial on & with storage card	2.5 to 4 hours	4.5 to 8 hours
Normal Use with IR on auto & with storage card	1.5 to 3 hours	3.5 to 6 hours
Normal Use with Modem card on	.5 to 1 hour	1 to 2 hours

Note: If some of these runtimes seem short, they might be. We tried to err on the conservative side.

Safety First!

We should say that Apple was a little short on battery life data when we compiled our time estimates for this book (and the ones they did give us were demonstratively inaccurate). And, the few weeks we had real, live (not prototype) Newtons really wasn't enough time to run a full suite of tests on battery life. So, the figures we present here are "best guesses" which is another way of saying "guesses." Use these as guidelines but don't be surprised if your results vary, ours certainly did. And, most important, just because we say a Newton with a dead power pack and a fresh coin cell will protect data in internal RAM for up to 12 weeks doesn't mean you should try it out for yourself. The coin cell is for emergencies, don't trust it to protect your data in anything but dire circumstances!

CHAPTER
12

NEWTON ON TOUR

In a manner of speaking, Newton is always on the road. It's so small and light that you'll probably carry it with you wherever you go, whether it's from city to city or room to room.

However, just because Newton is on the go as much as you are doesn't mean that all the places you might travel to will be a suitable habitat for your PDA. Some places are downright Newton-hostile and will make using your MessagePad or Expert Pad while traveling difficult.

Newton is a communications device. This is fine, as long as you can find a place to "jack-in" (plug your modem into a phone socket). However, many hotels, not to mention most foreign countries, will have phone systems that will be difficult, if not impossible, to connect to.

And then there are the hazards of the road. From would-be PDA-snatchers to airport metal detectors, there are many things out in the wild world of the 20th Century that can harm your Newton. The best advice is, as the song says (sort of), "Keep your eyes on the road and your hands on your Newton."

This chapter will give you a quick introduction to some of the issues of using Newton here, there and everywhere. It'll also supply you with some rules of the road that'll help keep you and your Newton together and working.

The Newton Checklist

Be prepared, the scoutmaster says. Good advice that any Newton-toting Road Warrior would do well to heed.

Here is a list of some of the items you'll want to have with you and some things you'll want to check on before you embark on a trip. You won't need these things at the office or puttering around the house. But once you get in that plane, train or automobile, you'll be happy to have a few Newton goodies along for the ride.

Call Ahead. Make sure where you'll be staying has some place where you can hook up a modem. You may have to talk to the facilities manager to get this question answered at some hotels. Also, ask whether there is an RJ-11 (the standard in the U.S., Japan, and Canada) phone jack in the room.

Other establishments, especially those that operate in a big city, may have guest rooms set up for the business traveler with a fax machine, work desk and strategically-located phone jacks and power outlets. If you can, stay in one of these rooms.

Check Out the Airline. If you're flying, make sure to check when making your reservations whether the airline allows the use of electronic devices on its planes. A couple of airlines have a portable computer ban on certain flights, and the attendants consider Newton covered by the ban. This electronics-paranoid policy resulted from the proliferation of battery-powered devices on flights. There is fear in some quarters that the electromagnetic fields (EMF) generated by these devices could interfere with the plane's delicate control and navigation systems. Most airlines will ask you to restrain yourself only during the first and last 15 minutes of the flight, a reasonable policy.

Keep your ears open for news of more stringent restrictions; the idea of an all-out ban is gaining momentum with airline companies that live in fear of the unknown or who might want to rent time on such devices in the future. Greed or fear, whatever the motivation, the digital nomad could be made to suffer the ignorance of others.

Contraband. If you're leaving the country, make sure to check with your travel agent to see what the policy is on bringing devices like your Newton to your destination. There are certain countries where carrying a Newton with you could violate U.S. trade bans. It's because the U.S. government believes the RISC processor technology in your Newton could represent a national security risk (hard to believe, but true).

Also, some countries might restrict the import of devices like Newton. They are probably attempting to protect some local computer company from foreign competition. After all, they don't know that you'd never consider selling your precious PDA!

Check the policy and avoid any unpleasantness at the border.

Branch Offices. If you'll be visiting another office of your company or a client's office and you know you'll want to print or communicate while there, call ahead. Make sure they've got a phone jack you can plug into and, if they have no Newton-compatible printer, be sure to bring the Print Pack along.

Bagging It. If you'll be bringing your personal computer along, make sure you have a bag that can accommodate both PC and Newton plus any other goodies you'll need. Don't put your Newton in checked luggage, the treatment of baggage at airports and train stations is, by now, world famous. You don't want a gorilla throwing your Newton around!

If Newton is the only device you're carrying along, you'll still want some kind of bag or briefcase that can hold you papers, cables, extra batteries and PDA. Remember, most airlines have a two carry-on bag limit. Make sure to stay below it.

Extra Power. Bring at least one extra NiCad pack. In fact, you might want to bring two if one of the packs is getting old. Also, carry along your Alkaline battery holder, just in case. Two NiCads and an empty battery holder probably weigh all of a half pound. We think it's worth it for the added security.

Power Supply and Recharger. You always want your Newton's power supply within reach. If it's going to be a long trip and you expect to use your Newton a lot, bring the NiCad recharger along as well. These two items shouldn't add more than a couple of ounces to your load.

Plug Converters. If you're going overseas, don't forget the plug converters that adapt your Newton's power supply to fit the local outlet (see Figure 12.1). You get all the plug converters you'll ever need in the travel kits available at most consumer electronics stores. Just beware! Some kits include a 1,000-watt voltage converter (it'll probably be in a box about the size of a cigarette pack). Avoid this type of device at all costs. It could fry your Newton's gizzards tout sweet.

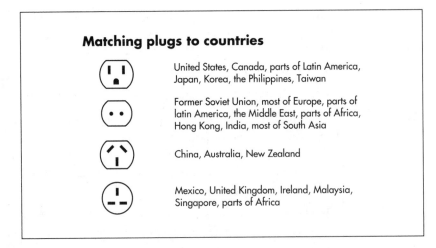

Figure 12.1 Plugs of the world.

A Small Screwdriver. Bring one of these along for everything from freeing a dead battery to removing a stuck phone plug. More than a couple of hotels we've stayed at tried to keep their patrons from unplugging the phone by breaking off the release tab on the plug. You can easily circumvent this measure by inserting the flat (slotted) end of the screwdriver under the plug to release the catch.

A Lint-free Cloth. A cloth can be used for a variety of tasks from keeping your Newton clean to catching spills before they do their worst.

A Current Backup. If you've got a storage card, try to make room for a backup of your Newton's internal RAM. This way, if something happens to corrupt Newton's memory, you can do a factory reset and then restore the internal RAM from the card.

If you have Newton Connection and are carrying your portable computer, you can keep a backup copy of your Newton data on the hard drive. Don't forget the serial cable or you won't be able to hook PC to PDA.

Access Numbers. Make sure you've got the local NewtonMail access number for where you're going. Call Apple for a list. If you're traveling overseas, contact Apple to see if there is a local connection available for Newton. If not, be prepared to call NewtonMail long distance.

Phone Cable. Bring a long (at least 6 feet) RJ-11 to RJ-11 phone cable. A long cable will let you reach the phone jack, wherever it might be hidden.

Phone Converters. If you're traveling to a foreign country, you can try and purchase a phone plug converter for your destination. In some places, most notably Europe, phone jack standards change from country to country (in Germany they can change from town to town!) Another option is to wait until you get there and ask the concierge at your hotel or a friend to help you locate a local phone store. You're much more likely to find the adapter you need in the country where you need it. Remember, ask for the American-to-local adapter.

A Spare Pen. Newton pens disappear with amazing reliability. So, don't get stuck without a stylus.

Optional Stuff

PhoneNet Connectors. Bring your own.

Portable Printer. Another way to ensure you have a way to print when you get where you're going is to bring along a battery-operated printer.

Such printers exist for both Macs and PCs and some can print out very high quality images. The Portable StyleWriter will work, as will a PC printer, as long as you have the Print Pack along. Don't forget to bring the printer's power supply, as well.

Actually, a three-pound printer for your one-pound PDA is probably overkill. But if you need to, there's no better way to be sure you have a way to print than to carry a printer.

Current Conditioners. In some destinations both in the U.S. and abroad, the flow of power is as unpredictable as East Coast weather. If you're worried about a sudden surge in current slam-dunking your Newton, bring along a power conditioner, available at most larger computer stores.

However, if you don't want to drag one of these power bricks along with you, you can avoid trouble with fluctuating power by running your Newton off the power pack and using a NiCad recharger to charge your batteries. If you don't plug Newton in it can never get damaged by spotty power.

The New Wilderness

It can be wild out there. Your average air terminal or hotel room is about as friendly to your Newton as a band of plains Indians are to white Buffalo hunters. Following some of the suggestions in the Newton Checklist can certainly help you be prepared. But there are other tricks you can use to hide in the underbrush while the Indians pass you by.

At The Terminal

An air terminal is one of the most hostile environments you can expose your Newton to. The hazards here are many: airports are one of the most popular hunting grounds for thieves who prey on expensive gadgets like your PDA. And then there's always the Airport Security Gauntlet.

When you head toward your departure gate, you'll likely encounter one of those friendly folks at the X-ray machine who are there to protect your safety. Airport security guards tend to be a surly bunch. They serve a critical purpose, we just wish they could serve a little more graciously.

You have two choices once you arrive at the checkpoint: X-ray your Newton or ask for a manual check. If your Newton is inside some carry-on luggage, just send it through the X-ray machine. Because your Newton contains no magnetic media like a hard disk drive, there is little chance of it being harmed by X-rays. However, you're Newton's internal SRAM or any SRAM cards you might have are very sensitive to EMF. So, be sure to position the bag right up against the rubber curtain at the mouth of the machine. This will keep it away from the motors that power the conveyor belt, which generate very strong EMF.

If you Newton is in your pocket, take it out and ask for a manual inspection. The guard will take your PDA to the other side of the checkpoint. Whatever you do, don't carry your Newton through the metal detector threshold, it produces an electromagnetic field in its search for hidden weapons. This field is of much higher intensity than the one your Newton might contact on the conveyor belt and will almost certainly cause harm. There is a very good chance that the metal detector will corrupt the data in Newton's internal RAM plus any SRAM cards. Only Flash RAM cards seem immune to this effect. Once you've cleared security, turn on your Newton to demonstrate that it isn't some kind of nefarious device. How little they know!

On a recent trip to Toronto, Andy accidentally took his Newton with him through the threshold (he forgot it was in his jacket pocket). Not only did it set off the detector's alarm, it also trashed his Newton's internal RAM. He had to restore his PDA from a backup on his PowerBook.

Once you're past the Security Gauntlet, if you have time, why not steal a little current while you wait? To locate an available outlet, just look on the floor in the waiting areas for those round metal plates. They usually hide outlets meant for maintenance staff use. You can also find outlets near vending machines and, sometimes, on pillars or along the baseboards in the waiting area. If you can't find one, don't sweat it. A half hour on an outlet isn't going to add more than a few minutes of power to your NiCads. But, should you ever need an outlet while hanging around the terminal, it's good to know where to look.

Another thing to watch for in an airport is one of the newer pay phones that come equipped with an RJ-11 jack, like the AT&T Public Phone 2000. If you're lucky enough to spot one of these phones (they're usually equipped with a credit card reader as well), feel free to pull out your modem and make a quick connection to NewtonMail. If you've just arrived and are anxious to send those faxes you prepared on the flight, one of these phones should do the trick.

Assist... Newton Larceny

The second biggest threat to your Newton while traveling are the thieves who specialize in hijacking computers and PDAs from their unsuspecting owners. The expense and relatively small size of the Newton makes it an especially attractive target.

The best way to protect your Newton is to follow this simple rule: always keep your PDA in sight. If it's in a bag, keep the bag slung over your shoulder or snugly clamped between your legs while sitting or standing on line. Whatever you do, don't ever put your Newton down and not pick it up when you stand up. Remembering where you left it a few minutes later is unlikely to help, unless you are very, very lucky.

Just remember, thieves like things to be easy or they wouldn't be thieves. Make it hard for them to get your Newton and they'll go after someone else.

As to whether you can insure your Newton against theft and other disasters, we contacted one of the leading insurance agencies for portable computers. They told us that they don't currently have a policy to cover the loss of a PDA-type device. But, with the coming wave of expensive little devices like Newton, they said they were looking at establishing such a policy. Stay tuned.

Once You Arrive

So, you're off the plane or train and just pulled up to your hotel. Once you're checked-in and safely in your room you have two important jobs: locate the power outlet and the phone jack.

Just follow the nearest lamp cord to locate power and the phone cord to locate the phone jack. You'd be amazed what a scavenger hunt finding these outlets can be in some hotels. Worse comes to worse, you can almost always find power in the bathroom.

The phone jack could be a lot more difficult. Many hotels use phone cables that can't be removed from the wall. They do this to keep the phones from growing legs and walking away. If they do have removable plugs then the plug they use may be some special design that your Newton's plug won't fit into. Then, there's always the chance the phone plugs will be the right type but the phone system won't be. Many larger hotels use digital phone systems that won't work with the analog modem used by most computing devices, including your Newton.

Luckily, some more enlightened hostelries include phone jacks on the phone itself. Check over the phone thoroughly, the jack might be hidden underneath. If that yields no success, then check the wall jack. If it's a solid cable with no sign of yielding an outlet, you're out of luck unless you want to hot-wire the phone system. It is possible to do this with the right equipment, but we believe most Newton users probably won't want to be bothered. To learn more about hot-wiring, get a copy of our first book, *Power-Book: The Digital Nomad's Guide* (we won't mind, really!)

Another, less drastic option is to call the front desk and complain. Perhaps another room is properly equipped or maybe the hotel facilities include a business center. You can always guilt them into letting you into the back office where we're sure you'll find the jack you need. Explain in the most pitiful tone you can manage that it'll only take a minute and will be a big help.

If you're going to be at this location for more than a day or two and your hotel doesn't have the proper phone facilities, we'd recommend transferring to one that does. (See? Calling ahead could have saved you all this trouble.)

Jacked In

If the place where you're staying has the appropriate jack, plug your phone cable in to the phone or the wall and get ready to connect. Next, check the instructions on the phone for how to dial out of the hotel. Almost all hotels will require you enter some kind of prefix, an 8 or a 9 followed by a pause (a comma), which you must enter in your Newton's dialing slip. Also, don't forget to enter the local NewtonMail access number, if you have it.

Next, attempt to connect. If everything works, fine. If you have a problem, make sure you're using the right phone prefixes. You can even manually dial the number to confirm that the connection works. Once you get that loud modem squeal, hang up.

If you didn't hear your modem dial the number, it may be that the local dial tone doesn't register with Newton's modem. This could be especially true overseas. If that's the case, go to the Modem preferences and uncheck the "Require dial tone" box. Then, try the connection again.

In some places, parts of the phone system may still be on the old rotary phone standard. This is true in certain parts of Paris, for example. To address this problem, go to Modem preferences and tap the "Pulse Dialing" radio button so it highlights.

That's it! If none of these efforts pay off, you're probably on a digital system and no amount of tweaking will help.

CHAPTER
13

CARING FOR NEWTON

When danger reared its ugly head, brave Sir Robin turned tail and fled... oh, excuse us, we're just pondering the virtue of discretion.

Danger, trouble of all sorts, is most likely to rear its ugly head when you're least prepared. Well, that's what this appropriately numbered chapter is all about. Being prepared.

The trick to avoiding trouble with your most important information tool is two fold: Take steps to avoid trouble and, when that doesn't work, know what to do to get Newton up and running, again. Newton is so mechanically simple that most of the troubles you're likely to encounter will be software-related. And, thankfully, you're only a Reset away from a solution when it comes to software. Well, almost always.

Newton is an extremely low maintenance device. There's very little you need to do to keep it in perfect physical condition. Basically, treat it as you would a digital watch. Keep it dry, keep it clean, don't throw it against the wall. Oh yes, and don't sit on your Newton. Those Apple ads with Newtons fitting snugly in people's back pockets set a bad example. (Confidentially, those jeans had to be altered to accommodate a Newton.)

Newton Dos and Don'ts

Do Remember This Number. 1-800-SOS-APPL (767-2775, for the alphabetically impaired). Say it again, 1-800-SOS-APPL, Apple's toll-free service line. If you have trouble, and you can't find the solution in this chapter (or you don't have *Newton's Law* with you), call the fine folks at Apple's support center in Austin, Texas, from 8:00 AM to 5:00 PM Pacific Time, Monday through Friday. They'll be more than happy to lend a hand, and if they can't fix your problem, they'll arrange for you to return the Newton for servicing. They're there to help, which is a guarantee that you'll always encounter trouble on the weekends and after business hours.

If you do encounter a critical failure during off-hours, try this number: 1-800-538-9696. The attendant will guide you to your nearest authorized Apple dealer. There aren't too many of those left who actually know how to fix an Apple product, but those that do surely will do all they can for you. Unfortunately, this number and the SOS line are only good in the U.S. For our international readers, check the back of your Handbook for instructions on getting help in your part of the world.

Expert Pad users should commit to memory this number: 1-800-732-8221. It'll get you to Sharp's technical support line. Also, don't forget to register your Newton with Apple or Sharp.

Do Backup. Bad luck steers clear of those who are prepared to deal with it, so, BE, BO (backup early, backup often). Don't let the reliability of your Newton lull you into a false sense of security. All hell will break loose the moment your Newton Connection, or storage card, archives become dated. Check out Chapter Eight—*Ready, Set, Load!* for complete instructions on backing up your data with Connection.

Do Use a MessagePad Case. Covers and cases designed specifically for Newton provide extra protection in all the right places, like stiffeners over the screen. Expert Pad users, who always have a cover on their Newton, don't need to worry about this so much.

Do Keep Something in The Slot. Your PCMCIA slot's only protection is an inserted card or protector. Make sure you're always using a protector when you're not using a card.

Don't Press Hard. Write with a light touch. It'll improve recognition and keep you from permanently fusing the screen's electrostatic layers together. It will also extend the life of your screen, which can wear unevenly.

Don't Be Hot or Cold. Avoid using or leaving Newton in environments with temperatures above 104 degrees Fahrenheit or below freezing. Don't leave it on the dashboard of your car or out on the ice rink, for example.

Don't Get Wet or Dirty. Dust, dirt, grit, and water are your Newton's worst enemies. Although it can sometimes be hard to avoid these elements, because the planet is composed mostly of water and earth, don't take your Newton into situations where the likelihood of contamination is high. So, no long walks on the beach with Newton in hand.

Don't Use The Wrong Pen. Use only pens with rounded, smooth tips that don't, and never have, contained ink of any kind. The empty ball point pen is a no-no.

Don't Leave Your Ports Uncovered. We know those little plastic stoppers can be annoying, but they do serve a purpose: keeping filth out of your ports.

Don't Force Cards or Connectors. If a card or cable doesn't seat itself with a firm push, don't push harder. You'll only damage your Newton's PCMCIA or serial port connectors. Remove it and try again.

Don't Touch the Power. If a cable is damaged, don't use it, replace it. The same is true of batteries. Don't use cracked or leaky cells or power packs. Of course, what applies to Newton applies to applies to power packs. Don't get them dirty, wet, or leave them in the sun.

Don't Turn It Loose. Avoid putting your Newton in a briefcase or bag where it's likely to bang around loose.

Don't Use The Threshold. The metal detectors in airports and many court houses can wreak havoc on your Newton's internal RAM. Have your PDA manually inspected or run it through X-Ray.

Care and Feeding

If Newton's are reliable, they're even easier to care for.

First, invest in a case. We prefer the basic case that Apple sells because it'll give you access to all your ports without having to open it. It's also the cheapest MessagePad-specific case you can buy. Unfortunately, the case won't work with the Expert Pad as it won't hold a PDA without the bracket and lock-down hole on the back.

To keep your Newton clean you need four tools: two lint-free, soft cloths, some Q-tips and isopropyl (rubbing) alcohol. Make one cloth the wet rag and the other the dry rag.

First, always make sure your Newton is off and unplugged before you start cleaning it. Next, take a soft, clean towel and lay it over a flat work area, this gives you a safe place to lay Newton face-down. Always clean Newton sitting down, there's less chance you might drop it.

Use the dry rag to clean dust and other contaminants off the screen. It may be necessary to apply a little pressure to get some smudges off. Be careful not to press hard, you might damage the electronics in the screen. Screen cleaners made especially for computer displays should work as well. But, if you have the option, just use rubbing alcohol. The active ingredient in both are the same.

Sometimes, you'll encounter smudges that won't come off with a dry cloth. In these cases, take your "wet" cloth, dab just a little rubbing alcohol on it and apply it to the smudge. This should remove any fingerprints or other hard-to-remove contaminants. Don't let the screen get wet, especially if enough moisture might accumulate near the seam where the screen meets the plastic shell. Fluids aren't good for your Newton's delicate insides, they can cause short circuits.

Use a little more alcohol on the wet rag to clean the plastic case. Use a Q-tip with a bit of alcohol to clean the serial port and the IR transceiver's window. Dry the area immediately with the other end of the Q-tip. You can use the same procedure to clean the power pack terminals inside your Newton, although these will almost never require cleaning.

Do not clean the power port or PCMCIA slot. Never.

Assist...No Sticking or Sticky Stuff!

Above all, never, ever, under any circumstances stick anything in the PCMCIA slot. Not to clean it, not to remove something that got jammed in there. If you're having problems with the slot, bring your Newton to an authorized service center where they have the tools and expertise to open the Newton's case. Never attempt to open the Newton yourself (you can't without special tools, anyway). Some of the components inside Newton are so static sensitive that even the small static charge put off by your body can damage them, under the right conditions.

You should also run to your nearest service center if your Newton gets wet with something other than water; a dousing with Coca Cola raises issues so complex that Douglas Adams could not explain the consequences in a trilogy of books. If your Newton gets water on it, leave it alone, off and unplugged for two days to dry out, preferably sitting on a cloth or towel. The water will eventually evaporate and *maybe* your Newton will function again. But, if you get something like Coke on your PDA, take it immediately to the nearest service center. Solvents are required to remove the noxious stuff in products like Coke from delicate circuitry.

Dangerous Liaisons

This is the part for those of you for whom trouble has reared its ugly head.

The first kind of trouble we call "bugaboos," annoying, small problems that appear and disappear without apparent cause or reason. If you own a Newton, you'll encounter a bugaboo. No way around it. They don't damage data and they can always be fixed, at worst, by doing a Reset. If that doesn't fix the problem, who ya gonna call? 1-800-SOS-APPL or 1-800-732-8221 (for Sharp).

The other kind of trouble, which you're much less likely to run up against, are system failures. These are unrecoverable errors that require a factory reset or treatment at a service center, to correct. System failures are almost always caused by a fault in the hardware, unlike bugaboos which are usually software-generated.

Bugaboos

Newton attracts gremlins like any other new technology, but unlike most products, the Newton's bouts with bugaboos have been assiduously chronicled in the general press. Most of the early problems can be attributed to the fact that the first Newtons came out two months too early. Since then, Apple has concocted a handful of system updates that take care of most of the problems.

The worst bugaboos are the ones that lock up your Newton. Luckily, these problems are rare since Apple came out with System Update 1.04, but they can still occur. To fix these do a reset, pressing the recessed RESET button hidden behind the battery compartment cover. After a moment, your Newton should ping! And all will be well again. If your Newton seems to have locked up, give it a few minutes to correct itself before you hit the panic button (up to five, if necessary). It could just be locked in thought rather than locked up.

Here's what to do when bugaboos occur:

- Close and reopen the offending application, if possible.

- If that doesn't work, turn your Newton over, open the battery bay cover and hit reset.

- If that doesn't work (highly unlikely, by the way), don't fool around anymore. Just call 1-800-SOS-APPL or 1-800-732-8221.

The Garbage Man Cometh. The most consistently recurring bugaboo that Newton exhibited as we went to press is a problem with digital garbage. Garbage is data that collects in the thin layer of RAM, called system memory, set aside for storing and processing ink. When Newton recognizes ink, it sometimes leaves small traces of the ink data behind in system memory. Over time this stuff collects until the recognizer doesn't have enough memory left to do its job. It's like a digital garbage strike, it doesn't smell bad, but your Newton's performance stinks. When it runs out of memory, your Newton just plain stops; you don't lose data, but you do have to perform a reset.

Apple struggled with the garbage collection problem for the first two months of Newton's life. System Update 1.03, hurried to market to clean up the garbage once and for all, was recalled within hours of its release when Apple discovered it actually complicated the garbage problem. Not only did errant recognizer data cause Newton to run out of memory, but so did several other processes. The first batch of Expert Pads all went out with 1.03, and what a rewarding experience that was for Sharp customers!

As of this writing, System Update 1.04 seems to have reduced the frequency of system freezes. The reset dialog still shows when system memory fills up, too frequently. But now other processes won't call the message.

Stir the soup. Errors in the data soups used by Newton can cause applications to take too long to sift through newly introduced data. If a soup error pops up on the screen, just close the error dialog and the application, then open it again. The problem should go away.

La Turista. In the Newton ROM Version 1.04 era, a lot of folks are plagued by extraneous ink collecting in the forms used by certain applications. For example, the appointment bar in Dates extends itself above or below the time rows on the calendar page. Scrolling only breaks the "real" bar from the false one, leaving a black scar on the top of the screen next to the calendar's month view. Again, closing and opening the application cleans up the screen.

Third-party applications will add to the list of Newton annoyances, because they'll introduce bugs of their own that might interfere with other processes in the highly integrated Newton operating environment. Although, we must admit, few of the applications we tested have caused any problems outside their domain.

Assist... NEWS FLASH: System Update 1.05

Just as we were putting the final proofs of this book to bed, word leaked out of Apple that the company would by November 1993 release a new System Update: 1.05. Thanks to the wonders of electronic publishing, and the kind indulgence of the folks down at Modern Design who did the page layout work on this book (thanks, Carol and Greg!), we just managed to sneak this Assist sidebar in at the last minute. As a result, you may see us refer to System Update 1.04 as the latest version in other parts of the book. Ignore it. This sidebar contains the latest data on system updates.

Few specifics were available on update 1.05. However, two things were known: First, the update will put to rest many of the problems that cause system memory to fill up with digital garbage, which is what usually induces the "memory out" dialog to display. The other is that installing this update will steal 32 Kbytes of Newton's internal RAM which is normally set aside for data storage. As a result, if you're running 1.05, your internal RAM space will be cut to 160 Kbytes.

At about the same time 1.05 becomes available, Apple will start shipping Newtons with a new version of the ROM chip. The ROM is version 1.11 and will give those Newtons equipped with the chip the same bug fixes and enhancements available from update 1.05. Unfortunately, the new ROM will still cost users 32 Kbytes of memory. This is because the system update required to run 1.11 also overflows the banks of the memory space originally allocated to ROM patches.

As a result, it really doesn't matter if your Newton is running 1.05 or 1.11.

By the way, if you're wondering what those version numbers mean, here's how it breaks down. The first digit represents the version of the Newton operating system. (We know, Newton doesn't use an operating system. Humor us, okay?). The second number is the version of the ROM chip installed in the unit.   *(continued)*

> *Assist... NEWS FLASH: System Update 1.05*
>
> The third number is the system update. System updates are specific to each version of the ROM. So, if your Newton says it's running 1.05, that means it's running Newton OS version 1, ROM chip 0 (the first production chip) and update 5. If it says it's running 1.11, then you've got OS 1, ROM chip 1 and update 1, which is the functional equivalent of update 5 for ROM chip 0.
>
> Did all that make sense? At this rate, Apple will need to come out with a PDA specially designed to keep track of all the Newton OS, ROM and update versions. How about calling it the UpdatePad?

Interpreting Error Messages

Most of Newton's error messages are self explanatory and will include instructions for how to deal with the problem. Alright, some errors, like the system memory low message, are less than crystal clear. But, hey, at least it's in English.

Newton will occasionally display an error code instead of a message. These are almost always generated by bugs in software and most can be dismissed. However, if you do get a coded error message, it's a good idea to write the code down and what you were doing at the time it displayed. Then, if the error returns repeatedly, you'll know what to tell technical support.

Here are some of the error codes you might encounter and what they indicate:

Table13.1 Error codes and their meaning.

Error Code	*What it means*
-48002	The store format (usually a PCMCIA card) is too old for Newton to get data off of it. You'll probably need to reformat the card.
-48003	The store format is too new for Newton. Probably formatted by a Newton with a newer version of the ROM. You can reformat it to get the card working.

(continued)

(continued)

Error Code	What it means
-48004	Store is corrupted. This is nasty. It means the card is damaged and data on it can't be used. Try reformatting the card to restore it to a usable condition. If that doesn't work, ask for a refund. Don't take "No" for an answer until the warranty on the card is expired.
-48005	A single object is corrupted. You may need to reenter it, if it's a data object. Look for missing data where you're working to figure out what Newton is referring to. If you don't see anything, or the lack of a key piece of data, you can ignore the message.
-48009 thru -48021	These are soup and store errors that only a programmer should see. If you see one, its probably being generated by buggy software. Call Apple or the developer of the suspect application.
-48022	Another nasty one. It means Newton encountered something it doesn't know how to deal with. If you see this error more than once, try removing installed software. If that doesn't work, call Apple
-48023 thru -48025	A query or index error. If it repeats, call Apple.
-48200 thru -48215	These are object error codes. The only time you see one is if the software you're using is buggy. Contact the developer or Apple.
-48400 thru -48418	Something got into Newton somewhere it didn't expect. This is another of those programming errors you should never see.
-48800 thru -48814	These are all interpreter errors and should never be seen by a user. If you do see one, call Apple.

To display a list of recent errors, tap the overview button while an error dialog box is displayed. About the only thing that you'll learn from the error list is what time and date the error occurred. You'll have to tap each item to see the real error name or code. If it isn't the one you're looking for, tap the overview button again to get back to the list (see Figure 13.1). Now, tap the Get Info button in the top left corner of the error message to see when Newton thinks it occurred.

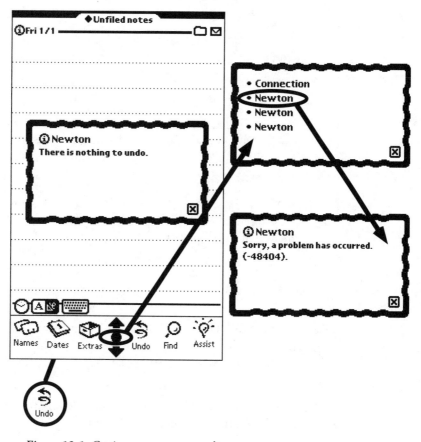

Figure 13.1 Getting an error message list.

Easter Egg... One Small Step For Newton

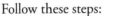

There's another error-related Easter Egg hidden in Newton's ROM. But getting there is kind of tricky!

Follow these steps:

1. Perform a system reset by pressing the RESET button under the battery cover.

2. After Newton restarts and the Notepad opens, tap the Undo icon in the permanent menu. This will produce the "Nothing to Undo" error message.

3. Tap the Overview button before closing the error dialog box.

4. You'll see a dialog box that contains a list. The only two items in the list will both be called "• Newton." Tap the first item in the list. This will show the "Welcome to Newton" error message.

5. Now, tap the Get Info button next to the word "Newton." The date displayed will be 7/20/69, and the time 2:35 AM, the moment that the Eagle landed on the Moon.

Troubleshooting

Like we said above, when danger does rear its ugly head, and it will, it'll be while you're far away from help. This is the Unwritten Newton's Law: Trouble will be inversely proportional to your proximity to the nearest Apple service center.

The following is a list of the most commonly reported Newton problems and their solutions, according to Apple.

Problem: The clock seems to be running fast.
Solution: Hit the reset button.
Cause: This is due to the ASIC that controls Newton's clock being in an indeterminate state. The Newton probably wasn't reset when you first turned on your new PDA.

Problem: Clock loses time.
Cause: The Newton clock is saved approximately every five minutes and upon power down and power up. When a user hits reset during this five-minute stretch, the time used to reset the clock is the last saved (which is probably a few minutes behind the real time). If the Newton has been shut off for a while and reset is hit while the PDA's still asleep, that can really mess up the clock!
Solution: Be sure to turn your Newton on or off and on before using the reset button.

Problem: Recognition stops working.
Solution: Be sure your using a Newton equipped with System Update 1.04.
Cause: See Bugaboos above.
Additional Notes: Having too many items in the To Do list can also fill up system memory. To help keep memory clear, be sure to Delete older and completed items.

Problem: The parallel printer driver that comes with Newton Print Pack won't load.
Solution: Be sure to plug in the Print Pack first and then turn on your Newton.
Cause: When you turn your Newton on, it automatically checks the serial port for the Print Pack and downloads the driver. If you plug in the cable after you turn on the Newton, it doesn't know the cable is there.

Problem: To Do list slows down.
Solution: Delete or move older items to a memory card or back them up with Newton Connection.

Problem: The screen pulses as you write.
Solution: Adjust the contrast up one point and this should no longer occur.

Problem: Scrubbing doesn't work.
Solution: Be sure to write lines that extend slightly over the item being scrubbed. Also, try selecting the item first and then scrubbing it, being sure to begin the scrub outside of the selection.
Additional Notes: When trying to scrub individual characters, be sure to scrub up and down in the same exact spot at least five times to be sure that Newton does not confuse your scrub with the letter "M" or "W."

Problem: You write in all printed capital letters and Newton does not recognize your handwriting.
Solution: Be sure to have handwriting style set to "printed only." The mixed recognizer doesn't deal well with all capitals.

Problem: Newton recognizes many words as one word.
Solutions: Be sure to separate your words Try setting the Handwriting Style preference for closer word spacing. Also, pause briefly at the end of each word.

Problem: Cannot scrub To Do items.
Solution: First scrub the text of the To Do item and then scrub the To Do marker. It is easier to get scrubbing to work if you do it from right to left.

Problem: The snap in the back of the MessagePad no longer holds the Newton in its case.
Solution: Call Apple and ask for a replacement snap.
Cause: If the MessagePad is not placed in the case properly, sometimes the connector can bend one of the pieces of the snap inside the Message-Pad.

Problem: You get the "out of memory" error message and hitting reset doesn't fix it.
Cause: You really are out of memory.
Solution: Delete some items or buy a storage card.

Problem: You get the "cannot complete this task" error message.
Solution: Hit reset and try what you were doing again.
Cause: What you're working on probably exceeded available system memory.

Problem: You get the "Newton still needs the card" error message.
Cause: Could be an application that won't relinquish access to data on the card, or it could be you pulled the card before Newton was done saving something.
Solution: Reinsert the card and wait a few minutes before removing it again. Also, try closing the application you are working in.

Problem: You forgot your Newton or NewtonMail password.
Solution: A cold boot will clear internal RAM and release your Newton from the protection afforded by the password. If your forget your NewtonMail password, call Apple and ask for a new password. When

you receive the password, open the Mail Preferences, tap the Set E-mail Password button and enter the new word. Newton will ask you to confirm the new password.

Problem: You get a message saying you can't store data on your PCMCIA card because it's protected.
Cause: The memory-protect switch on the top of the card is engaged.
Solution: Follow the instructions that came with the card to turn off protection.

Problem: Newton doesn't turn on.
Solution: Check your power sources. If you're in doubt about the state of your battery, plug the Newton into an outlet. If it still doesn't turn on, try hitting the reset button. If that doesn't work, call Apple or Sharp.

The Newton Universe

The Third Axiom: There are more things on heaven and earth than can fit in a mail-order catalog.

Getting the Goods on Newton

So, you've got some scratch set aside for some Newton goodies and can't wait to spend it. Well, you've come to the right place. This section is all about what you can buy to expand your Newton's mind, what tricks you can teach it with third-party add-ons and how you can go about contacting the purveyors of PDA paraphernalia.

The section is divided into three parts: Hot Hardware, Cool Software, and Fast Services. The chapter titles are self-explanatory. If you want to track down a nifty game, just flip to Cool Software. If you've hit the ceiling of Newton's RAM and want to invest in a PCMCIA card, turn to Hot Hardware. And, if you want to get access to an information service that'll help your personal communications assistant earn its handle, Fast Services is where you want a look.

So, before we dive in, some quick advice and a few disclaimers. First, except where noted, we make no guarantee of the applicability or appropriateness of any product for any task. Many of the products you see listed here didn't quite exist when we went to press but should be available by the time you read this. This is a Caveat Emptor world. It was good advice in Rome, it's still good advice today.

Second, where ever possible, we've attempted to confirm all phone numbers and addresses. However, people change, companies move. So, if you dial a number to find out how to get that expense reporter you read about here, and CostaNostra pizza answers the phone, chock it up to the shark-infested waters in which little computer companies must paddle to stay afloat.

Lastly, before you buy from the friendly sales representative who answers the phone, remember, almost any product you can buy direct from a company you can buy mail order or through your local computer superstore—probably for a lot less money. Call these numbers to find out more about the product and to find the local authorized reseller. Most companies are just as happy if you buy that modem from Three G's Computing as they will be if you buy it direct from them. Either way, they make money.

CHAPTER
14

HOT HARDWARE

Newton is a product that holds almost none of the precious margins on which computer dealers and companies built their fortunes. The first thing these people want to do after you buy a Newton is sell you More Stuff.

What Apple's Hawking

Newton Messaging Card
A PCMCIA card with a pager grafted on that makes it look like a cross between a Star Trek communicator and Indian Paint Fungus, the woody protrusions that grow on trees in the Western U. S. It operates on a single AAA battery for up to four weeks. Cool tool for the person who needs to stay in textual contact with the office day and night.

Fax Modem
The Larry Mondello of modems, this PSI Integration-manufactured black box is half the size of Newton and rattles when you shake it. It provides 9,600/2,400 bps fax/data support. See the chart on page 112 for details about protocols supported.

Print Pack
A serial-to-parallel port converter with built-in drivers that let you print to more than 500 supported printers and many more that emulate those printers. Designed by GDT Softworks Inc.

Power Adapter
A universal power supply for the MessagePad and Apple Modem that provides 7 V at .5 amp output on power sources ranging from 100 to 240 V. Four configurations are available to accommodate various types of power outlets:

- In-Line Adapter for the U. S., Canada and Japan
- Right Angle Adapter for international use
- Right Angle Adapter for Australia
- Right Angle Adapter for Great Britain

Apple's power supply comes with a different Newton plug than the Sharp Expert Pad power supply. Don't mix and match. (Actually, the Sharp power supply works in both companies' models.) Since Apple provides a power supply in its packaging, you'll need to buy one only to replace a lost unit or to power both the Apple Modem and MessagePad off AC power. Unfortunately, Expert Pad buyers aren't so lucky. They must purchase a power supply separately.

Battery Booster Pack
The ultimate in geek chic, the Booster Pack is a belt pack that contains eight AA alkaline batteries for up to two weeks of continuous use. It connects to the MessagePad or Expert Pad through the AC port.

Battery Pack Recharger
This compact recharger will put a full day's power into a partially-charged NiCad battery pack in under four hours. You get one rechargeable NiCad pack when you buy the recharger.

Rechargeable Battery Pack
Four NiCad batteries in a sealed, rechargeable pack that fits into the MessagePad or Expert Pad. They provide about four hours of continuous use, depending upon Newton's workload. You can recharge the NiCad pack in the Apple Recharger or by leaving your Newton plugged in overnight.

1 MB Storage Card
A Static RAM card, the 1 MB Apple PCMCIA card includes a battery that should preserve your data for up to five years. After that, the battery must be changed. We heard of several SRAM cards that failed in the first month, but these problems should be remedied with a new order of batteries Apple made recently. The card holds up to 1,250 Name file business cards, 1,000 notes of up to 50 characters, 2,500 calendar appointments of 20 characters, or 400 screens worth of untranslated handwriting or drawings.

2 MB Flash Storage Card
Flash RAM will hold your data for the rest of your life, unless you are very, very young. It requires no batteries, using Newton's power to write data in memory, which cannot be altered while the card is out of the Newton—strong electromagnetic fields can damage these cards, however. The 2 MB card can hold up to 2,500 Name file business cards, 2,000 notes of up to 50 characters, 5,000 calendar appointments of up to 20 characters, or as many as 800 screens worth of untranslated handwriting or drawings.

Sharp's "Multiple Useful Options"

Apple's not the only company that wants to sell, sell, sell peripherals. Sharp gets the show on the road early, charging you for the opportunity to run Newton on AC power. The company has never provided power supply with its Wizard organizers, and they don't let you have one with the Expert Pad, either.

Sharp peripherals, with the exception of the power supply, are identical to the Apple versions:

- Sharp Fax Modem
- PC Printer Cable (Print Pack)
- 1 MB SRAM Storage Card
- 2 MB Flash RAM Storage Card
- Rechargeable Battery Pack (Sharp doesn't currently offer a recharger)
- AC Adapter power supply

Sharp also offers a RS-232 to RS-422 Level Converter for connecting your Newton to a Sharp Wizard. If you already have a cable that links your Mac and a Wizard, it will work with Newton.

Third-Party Memory Cards

Eureka! You've struck cheap memory! Memory cards are the gold standard of the information age. As people move more and more of their personal data onto silicon, the types of cards available to you will proliferate, too. But not all cards are compatible.

Apple uses two kinds of memory chips in its own PCMCIA cards, generic static RAM (SRAM) and Intel Corp.-made Flash RAM. If another manufacturer uses the same chips in a card, it should be compatible with Newton devices.

SRAM
In general, most SRAM cards on the market for the Hewlett-Packard 95LX, 100LX and Omnibook plus the Zeos PocketPC and Sharp Wizard will work with the MessagePad and Expert Pad. Not all cards, however, conform to the PCMCIA 2.0 standard, and these will not get along with the Newton PCMCIA slot—you'll see an error message when it is inserted in the MessagePad.

Flash RAM
Flash RAM cards are a trickier matter. Only Intel Flash memory (the 8-Mbit 28F008SA chips) is compatible with the Newton.

A lot of folks are snapping up SunDisk solid state Flash memory, which tends to sell for less than Intel memory. Tough luck, the SunDisk cards don't work in Newton. Nor will Newton get along with Flash RAM made by Advanced Micro Devices (AMD).

Here, then, is a list of the companies that make Newton-compatible memory cards. Memory prices are very volatile (get it? Memory, volatile, volatile memory? Never mind.) A single glue factory burning to the ground drove the price of one type of memory up by 75 percent in just three months recently, so you'll need to call for the latest prices.

Table14.1 The Third-Party Card Directory

Manufacturer	*Card*
Epson America Inc. 20770 Madrona Ave. Torrance, Calif. 90509 Telephone: 310.782.0770 800.922.8911	1-MByte SRAM card 2-MByte SRAM card

Manufacturer	*Card*
Fujikura Ltd. Tokyo, Japan Telephone: 081.336.1244	2-MByte SRAM card

Manufacturer	*Card*
Hewlett-Packard Co. 3000 Hanover St. Palo Alto, Calif. 94304 Telephone: 415.694.2000 800.752.0900	512-KByte SRAM card

Manufacturer	*Card*
Intel Corporation 2200 Mission College Blvd. P.O. Box 58119 Santa Clara, Calif. 95052 Telephone: 408.765.8080 800.628-8686	2-MByte Flash RAM cards* 4-MByte Flash RAM cards* 10-MByte Flash RAM cards* 20-MByte Flash RAM cards*

(continued)

(continued)

Manufacturer	*Card*

Lifetime Memory Products
305 17th Street
Huntington Beach, CA 92648
Telephone: 714.969.2421
Fax: 714.960.0638

2-MByte SRAM card
4-MByte Flash RAM card

Toll-free international fax numbers:
Australia: 0114.800.126-122
France: 05.90.2188
Germany: 0130.81.4315
Italy: 1678.74213
Japan: 0031.11.4035
Netherlands: 06.022.0531
Norway: 050.12699
Sweden: 020.793.806
United Kingdom: 0800.89.4414

Manufacturer	*Card*

Maxell Corp. of America   1-MByte SRAM card
22-08 Route 208
Fair Lawn, N.J. 07410.
Telephone: 201.794.5900 (ask for information on memory cards)
            800.533.2836
Fax: 201.796.8790 (be sure to put ATTN: Memory Cards)

Manufacturer	*Card*

Mitsubishi Electronics America Inc.   2-MByte SRAM card
Information Systems Division
5665 Plaza Drive
P.O. Box 6007
Cypress, Calif. 90630-0007.
Telephone: 714.220.2500
            800.843.2515
Fax: 714.236.6272   *(continued)*

(continued)

Manufacturer	*Card*
New Media Corporation 15375 Barranca Parkway Building B-101 Irvine, Calif. 92718 Telephone: 714.453.0100 Fax: 714.453.0114	256-KByte SRAM card 512-KByte SRAM card 1-MByte SRAM card 2-MByte SRAM card

Manufacturer	*Card*
Panasonic Co. 2 Panasonic Way Secaucus, N.J. 07094 Telephone: 800.222.0584	256-KByte SRAM card

Manufacturer	*Card*
Sharp Electronics Corp. Sharp Plaza Mahwah, N. J. 07430 Telephone: 201.529.8200 800.237.4277	512-KByte SRAM card

Manufacturer	*Card*
Simple Technologies Inc. 1801 East Edinger Ave. Suite 255 Santa Ana 92705 Telephone: 714.558.1120 800.367.7330 Fax: 714.558.0997	1-MByte SRAM card 2-MByte SRAM card

(continued)

(continued)

Manufacturer	Card
Tote-A-Lap 550 Pilgrim Drive Suite F Foster City, Calif. 94404 Telephone: 415.578.1901 800.952.7867 Fax: 415.578.1914	512-KByte SRAM card 1-MByte SRAM card 2-MByte SRAM card

Manufacturer	Card
Zeos International 530 Fifth Avenue, NW St. Paul, Minn. 55112 Telephone: 612.633.4591 800.423.5891	2-MByte SRAM card

* Available from various vendors, including Apple.

Third-party Modems

Apple has the idea that you should buy a brand new modem specifically for your Newton. Never mind that you have two or three modems lying around the house, even one or two that are smaller than the klunky fax/data modem offered by the purveyors of Newton.

Before Newton will begin a communications session, it sends a series of Hayes AT commands to the modem (Hayes AT is a standard that modem manufactures beat around but never really implement all the way). These commands set up a dialog between the Newton and the modem, and Newton expects certain answers to its commands. The first command it sends resets the modem to the factory settings, obliterating any efforts on your part to make the modem send the replies Newton expects. Then, when the modem's memory has been wiped clean of any special settings, Newton sends a command that returns a list of capabilities in the modem chip set. The wrong answer shuts down the communications session.

Basically, Newton goes to great lengths to make sure you're using the Apple modem. When we asked a friend at Apple about this, pointing out that it was a kind of low thing for a company to do—obsoleting people's current modem—he laughed. It wasn't an evil laugh, but it was a laugh.

Apple doesn't have plans to make third-party modems compatible, it's up to the modem makers to build a Newton-compatible driver for their hardware. Some modems will work with Newton; they must be built with the same Rockwell 224ATF chip set used in Apple's Newton modem and support the right set of Hayes AT commands.

Here are the ones that work, based on our testing and the experience of Newton users on CompuServe and the Internet. We're not suggesting that you go out and buy one of these modems to connect Newton to the world. Rather, you don't need to buy the Apple modem if you have one of these. If you don't have one of these modems, our counsel is to wait a few months, using a borrowed modem in the meantime. Third-parties and Apple will be coming out with new modems. Keep an eye out for a collaboration between Apple and Megahertz Corp. to bring out a low-power PCMCIA modem for Newton.

PSI Integration COMstation One
9,600/2,400 bps fax/data modem with support for V.32 protocols.

PSI Integration COMstation Two
14.4 Kbps data modem with support for V.32, V.42., V.42bis, and MNP 5 protocols.

PSI Integration COMstation Five
14.4 Kbps fax/data modem with support for V.42, V.42bis, and MNP 5 protocols.

PSI Integration
851 East Hamilton Avenue
Suite 200
Campbell, Calif. 95008
Telephone: 408.559.8544
          800.622.1722

Megahertz PCMCIA Notebook Data/Fax Modem with XJACK
14.4 Kbps data/fax modem with support for V.42, V.42bis and MNP 5 protocols. This is the only modem-on-a-card that works reliably with Newton. The XJACK is an RJ-11 jack that fits in the card, and pops out when pressed to allow you to connect to a phone line. Compact and sturdy.

Megahertz Corp.
4505 South Wasatch Blvd.
Salt Lake City, Utah 84124
Telephone: 801.272.6000
          800.527.8677

Supra FAXModem V.32bis
14.4 Kbps fax/data modem with support for V.42, V.42bis and MNP 5
protocols. Always one of best deals in modems; low-cost and very reliable.

Supra Corporation
7101 Supra Drive SW
Albany, Ore. 97321
Telephone: 800.727.8772
          503.967.2400
Fax: 503.967.2401

Zoom FaxModem V.32bis
14.4 Kbps fax/data modem with support for V.17 fax, V.42, V.42bis and
MNP 5 protocols.

Zoom Telephonics Inc.
207 South Street
Boston, Mass. 02111
Telephone: 800.666.6191
          617.423.1072
Fax: 617.423.9231

Cellular Adapters

Cellular phones and computers need a little help from their friends if they
are going to come together to reach out and touch someone (we dare anyone to slip more references to popular music and telecommunications into
a single sentence). A cellular adapter fits between the modem and a cellular
telephone, it emulates characteristics of a regular phone line for the modem
and of a cellular dial-pad for the phone.

Axcell Cellular Phone Interfaces I & II
Applied Engineering Inc.
3210 Beltline Road
Dallas, Texas 75234

Telephone: 214.241.6060
            800.554.6227
Fax: 214.484.1365

The **Axcell I**: Works with AT&T Portable Phone Models 3710, 3730 & 3760 OKI Portable Phone Models 900, 910 & 1150

The **Axcell II**: Works with NEC Portable P200, P300, P201, P301, P400 & P600

Motorola S1688E RJ-11 Adapter

Motorola S1936 RJ-11 Adapter

Motorola S3026 RJ-11 Adapter

Motorola S3027 RJ-11 Adapter

Motorola Inc.
Wireless Enterprise Systems Group
1201 E. Wiley Road
Suite 103
Schaumburg, Ill. 60173
Telephone: 800.331.6456
            708.479.5000 (ask to be transferred to customer service)
Fax: 708.576.0710

The **S1688E**: Works with older Motorola phones that use a Type One transceiver (big, heavy honkers; usually carphones).

The **S1936**: Works with Motorola "bag" phones that use a Type Two or Three transceiver. Bag phones have a separate handset and usually come in a case of some sort, thus its name.

The **S3026**: Works with Motorola portable phones, the brick-like ones that look like walkie-talkies.

The **S3027**: Works with Motorola "flip" phones, the ones that look like Star Trek communicators, like the T•A•C Lite.

CHAPTER
15

COOL SOFTWARE

The Newton architecture provides the raw materials for many different kinds of software. Third-party applications will be weaving the many individual features in Newton together to create new functions that provide more information management muscle.

A calendar can be extended to remind when to change the oil in the car, what day your mother-in-law was born and how often you need to practice your Nine Iron approach shot. The Names file is only the first step toward tying together all the information you collect about a person; a third-party application can let you add notes, invoices, and links to other people so that your contact manager can become the locus of business life. The Assistant can be made to automate many functions in the Notepad, so that a column of numbers can be added, subtracted, or subjected to statistical analysis without first being imported into a calculator application; likewise notes can include new verbs that command Newton and let the Assistant lend you an ever greater hand in managing your day-to-day interactions with the world.

All these features will be available in applications software by the end of 1993. During 1994, the capabilities of Newton will explode into new categories of software we don't know today:

Knowledge Assistants. A class of software that interacts with network-based services to gather information that you'll use at work or leisure. When you need to know about something, your knowledge assistant can find out!

Learning Software. Applications will blend the contents of a book with the intelligence of the Assistant to provide you with customized information. For example, you might be able to buy a guide to world literature that leads you through the great novels of the 19th Century, allowing you to systematically explore the threads of thought you find most interesting.

Electronic Servants. A combination of assistance and network-based shopping services will let you describe what you want to eat during the week. The menus will be analyzed for their ingredients, which will be ordered from a local grocer, who will deliver the fresh foods each day, or once a week, depending upon your preferences (and budget).

The incredibly quick development times enabled by NewtonScript will mean a flood of software for you, the Information Surfer. For now, there are approximately 100 applications for Newton, all created in a matter of a few months and most coming from very small companies. Some are commercial, others are offered for free or for a small fee on online services like CompuServe, America Online, AppleLink and the Internet. Here's the line-up as of October 1993 (we've also included a few applications that have been revealed inadvertently):

Commercial Applications

Personal Organizers and Business Productivity

Ascend

Franklin Quest makes Ascend software, a time-management application designed for use in conjunction with its paper-based Day Planner. Ascend is currently available for Windows PCs and Macintosh. It provides an address book, To Do list, calendar and goals-setting interface. The company revealed that it is working on a Newton version of the application that will be released in early 1994.

> Franklin Quest Co.
> 2550 S. Decker Lake Blvd.
> Salt Lake City, UT 84119
> Telephone: 801.975.9992
>   800.877.1814
> Fax: 801.975.9995

ContactPad

One of the big shortcomings of the MessagePad and Expert Pad is the lack of connections between applications. For example, if you make an appointment with someone, you can't access their phone number from the Dates application, you have to open the Names file or use the Assist to open a dialer slip. Compared to the EO Personal Communicator, which ships with linking features built-in (through a bundled third-party application), the Newton actually seems to fragment your view of data.

Pastel Development Corp. will remediate Newton's deficiencies with ContactPad, an application that examines your data for relationships and lets you browse the connections it finds. Notes, appointments, To Do items, and business cards will be connected. A paper clip icon will appear on items that are linked to other information—just tap the paper clip to get an overview of related information.

ContactPad will also include standard forms that extend the amount of information that can be contained in a person's profile in the Names application. For example, it will include fields that let the user describe the price range and loan qualifications for a prospect.

You can also design your own forms, purchase orders and questionnaires which can be linked to individuals or appointments. So, a psychologist might sit down with a new client and collect their name, address, phone numbers, and clinical information. Later, that data could be linked to notes taken after a session of psychoanalysis.

Pastel Development Corp.
113 Spring Street
New York, NY 10012
Telephone: 212.941.7500
Fax: 212.431.3079

Day-Timer Meeting Assistant

Outlining meeting agendas and following up on tasks before and after a meeting is the forte of the Day-Timer Meeting Assistant from Slate Corporation.

Meeting Assistant leverages the abilities of the Notepad and Dates, providing the ability to create a plan for an upcoming meeting in a custom form. You can attach To Do items to meetings, which remind you about preparations and follow-up items. Meetings created in Meeting Assistant are entered in your calendar automatically. The program also provides the ability to create an overview of all meetings and the attached notes.

Available on floppy disk (Newton Connection software required) or PCMCIA card.

Slate Corp.
15035 North 73rd Street
Scottsdale, AZ 85260
Telephone: 602.443.7322
Fax: 602.443.7325

Day-Timer Expense Assistant

Expense reports are the bane of every business person, eating up valuable time which must be devoted to categorizing expenses, creating reports and tracking when the checks finally come in.

The Expense Assistant streamlines the process with a pre-configured expense template that pops open when you tap the application in the Extras drawer. When a new item is entered, you are given category options, which you tap to add the expense to a specific row in a final report. Expense Assistant maintains a running total for each category or the entire report.

Report templates are built in to the application, so you can print out a professional-looking expense sheet from Newton. Expense Assistant can also export report data to a PC for integration into a corporate accounting system or a spreadsheet.

Slate Corp.
15035 North 73rd Street
Scottsdale, AZ 85260
Telephone: 602.443.7322
Fax: 602.443.7325

Dyno Notepad

Newton's Notepad is disinclined toward outlining; you have to look at everything in a note at all times. When laying out the agenda for a meeting, for instance, you want to be able to view the section names and add notes which you can hide until you need them. That way, you can view the main agenda in a single screen, rather than scrolling through all the notes you've made to find out what's coming after the quarterly report from the Banana Packaging Division.

Dyno Notepad, from Portfolio software, provides the ability to outline a longer document, prioritize items, and create a list of topics and "nest" them in collapsible notes beneath a heading. Tap the bullet and notes associated with the topic appear on the screen. Dyno Notepad provides formatting rulers that aren't available in the standard Notepad application. Say you want to indent a particular passage—just select it and tap the ruler to set a new margin for that text.

You'll also be able to set up project outlines, with due dates, priorities and tracking of completed tasks. Dyno Notepad will ship with several different forms for use when planning projects, outlining a document or agenda, and creating memos.

The program is also compatible with Dyno Notepad for Macintosh and Windows; you'll be able to import and export documents with all formatting intact. Supported file formats include Claris Corp.'s MacWrite, Microsoft Corp.'s Word, Rich Text Format and plain text (without formatting).

Portfolio will be one of the first companies to provide alternative print formatting options, allowing you to create documents that can be printed for use in a Franklin Day Planner, Day Runner, and Day-Timer paper planners. It'll either be part of Dyno Notepad or a separate product (the decision hadn't been made yet when we went to press).

Portfolio Software Inc.
10062 Miller Avenue
Suite 201
Cupertino, CA 95014
Telephone: 408.252.0420
           800.729.3966
Fax: 408.252.0440

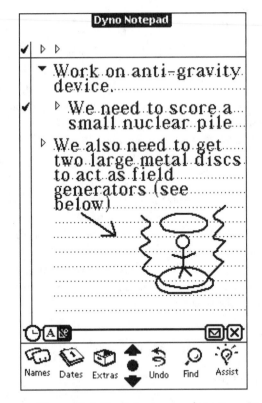

Figure 15.1 Outlining an agenda in Dyno Notepad.

Expense It!

Another expense report application for the Newton, Expense It! provides export connections to Shana Corp.'s InFormed, Claris' FileMaker Pro, Microsoft's Excel and State of the Art Inc.'s MacP&L, P&L for Windows and Momentum Accounting Systems (M•A•S 90/G) for Mac and Windows.

Besides a standard entry form for travel, food, and entertainment expenses, the application lets you edit and print Internal Revenue Service–approved report formats (it's still up to you to make the expenses legal). The form uses Newton assistance to convert your written notes, like "lunch with Andy on Friday," into a meal expense slip with your companion's full name and the date in proper format.

State of the Art Inc.
56 Technology
Irvine, CA 92718
Telephone: 714.753.1222

Personal Time & Billing

Tracking your professional time has always been a paper-to-computer accounting system proposition. Now, with the advent of Newton, you can record the time you spend with a client in your Newton Dates calendar and Great Plains Software's Personal Time & Billing will calculate how much to charge and generate a bill that can be printed or faxed from the MessagePad.

Personal Time & Billing links into your Names database and calendar to follow when you contact each person. It installs in the Extras drawer, and you can open the application to set up client accounts and billing categories (since we don't often charge the same rate for different services, you can create keywords that, when you enter them in a calendar item, tell Personal Time & Billing what rate you are charging for that particular contact). The application also lets you indicate when you didn't charge someone, so that the extra effort you put in is reflected on the bill.

Time billing can also be tracked on a project basis. Open the application to define a project and the people who are working on it. So, when you schedule a meeting with Bob, the account manager at the agency handling the art for a new ad campaign you are designing for the Iguana BBQ chain, the meeting appears on the bill going to Iguana at the end of the month.

Great Plains will also support importing data collected on a Newton into its Dynamics for Macintosh accounting software. That's a powerful addition to the Newton's capabilities, since you can integrate your personal data into the company-wide information network.

Great Plains Software
1701 Southwest 38th Street
Fargo, ND 58103
Telephone: 701.281.0550
Fax: 701.282.4826

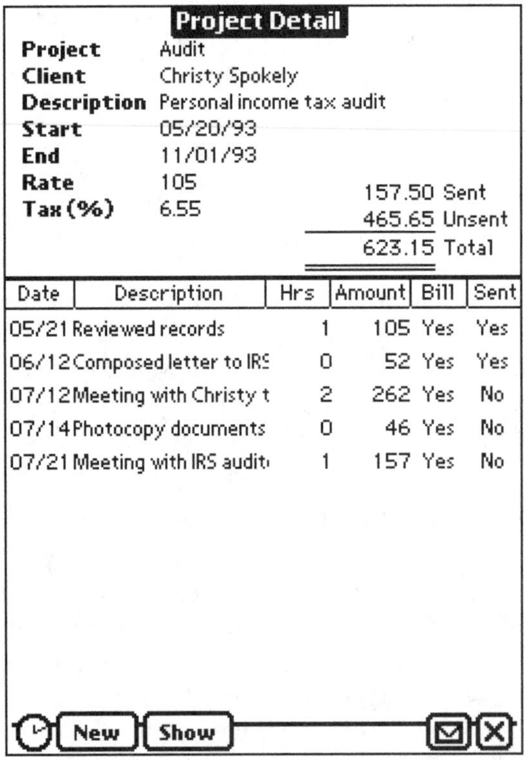

Project Detail

Project	Audit
Client	Christy Spokely
Description	Personal income tax audit
Start	05/20/93
End	11/01/93
Rate	105
Tax (%)	6.55

157.50 Sent
465.65 Unsent
623.15 Total

Date	Description	Hrs	Amount	Bill	Sent
05/21	Reviewed records	1	105	Yes	Yes
06/12	Composed letter to IRS	0	52	Yes	Yes
07/12	Meeting with Christy t	2	262	Yes	No
07/14	Photocopy documents	0	46	Yes	No
07/21	Meeting with IRS audit	1	157	Yes	No

New   Show

Figure 15.2 Up-to-the-minute billing from Great Plains.

PresenterPad

This is one of the coolest and most practical applications for Newton we've seen. How many times have you had to give a talk, but after scratching out your notes and running through it a few times, the talk becomes rushed and disorganized because you are trying to keep your place while living in your allotted time.

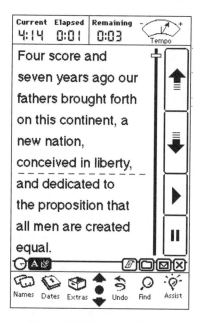

Figure 15.3 PresenterPad puts speaking skills in your hand.

PresenterPad is an outliner and speech-making application that provides:

Portable TelePrompTer. Your text can be downloaded into Presenter-Pad, or you can compose an outline using the pen. Once in the application, on-screen buttons which can be pressed with a fingertip let you control how quickly the text scrolls up the screen, allowing you to set a comfortable pace. The buttons can be aligned along the left or right side of the screen, so right-hander or Southpaw can control the TelePrompTer.

Outliner. Whether you are using a complete script or an outline, the tools for composing your script are built into the application. Likewise, you can download a manuscript from a Mac or Windows PC, then edit it on the Newton.

Time Gauge. A meter at the top of the PresenterPad screen tells you how much time has elapsed, your remaining time, and, if you are using slides, how much time to spend before moving to the next slide. If you feel like you need to speed up, just press the scroll button.

Slide Notes and Manager. PresenterPad lets you control slides on a PC via an infrared link. Your script can be keyed to progress as you move from one slide to the next.

You can be the coolest presenter with a MessagePad in your hand and PresenterPad helping you pace a focused talk. Just remember to give your talk in a lighted room or, at least, stand under a lamp. The MessagePad's reflective screen will not be legible in the dark.

Avalon Engineering Inc.
45 Newbury Street
Boston, MA 02116
Telephone: 617.247.7668
Fax:　　　617.247.7698

Spreadsheets and Calculators

GoFigure

A good calculator does more than just work out a logarithm or calculus problems. A really great calculator is of practical use, too.

GoFigure is both powerful and useful, because it's not afraid to abandon the keyboard interface to provide fields for entering figures that you want to convert. Besides mathematical and engineering functions, it also lets you figure out the due date of a baby, the dimensions of a room in square feet or meters, the complexities of how many calories you burn by running a mile, and conversion of picas to inches and back again, among other things. These are the modules available in the first version:

- Architectural
- Babies
- Dates
- Diet/Exercise
- Film Editing
- Financial
- Grade Point Average
- Typesetting
- Integer/Hex/Binary
- Kitchen Conversions
- Mathematics
- Computer Memory
- Sales Tax/Tips
- Statistics
- Times

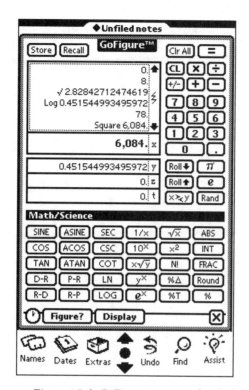

Figure 15.4 GoFigure is a versatile calculator.

Displays can also be changed to accommodate your preferences, so you can use an accounting format or search for answers in hexadecimal.

Available on floppy disk or a PCMCIA card.

Dubl-Click Software Inc.
22521 Styles Street
Woodland Hills, CA 91367
Telephone: 818.888.2068
Fax: 818.888.5405

Lucid 3-D
This spreadsheet, which is already available on the Sharp Wizard and Casio B.O.S.S., will be shipping for Newton in 1994.

Details were scarce at press time, but the approach that the company has taken with its other products is to nest views of the data in a worksheet. For example, each cell in a spreadsheet can reflect the total in another spreadsheet. When you change the data in the nested spreadsheet, the new total bobs to the top level and changes the totals in the main spreadsheet. You can also open up to nine different windows at one time, some focused on different spreadsheets, others providing different views of a single worksheet.

Whether Lucid takes exactly this approach in its Newton spreadsheet, well, no one returned our calls.

Lucid Corp.
101 West Renner Road
#450
Richardson, TX 75082
Telephone: 800.967.5550
214.994.8100
Fax: 214.994.8103

MobileCalc

Transporting the expansive interface of the desktop computer spreadsheet into the narrow margins of the MessagePad is a tremendously difficult undertaking, and one that's critical to making business use of the Newton a viable proposition. After all, the spreadsheet is one of the founding pillars of the desktop computing revolution—if it hadn't been for the ability to work a financial calculation, few companies would have invested in computers for the ordinary office worker.

MobileSoft Corp.'s MobileCalc reduces the interface, but not the power of the spreadsheet. It provides the ability to perform 70 financial, statistical, scientific, and math calculations on your data, as well as a soft keyboard-based method for building complex formulas. It recalculates totals as you change individual cells.

What you do lose with MobileCalc is the capacity of desktop spreadsheets, which sometimes run into the hundreds of thousands of cells. A MobileCalc worksheet can hold 50 rows and 26 columns of cells. All those cells won't fit on the screen at one time, so the application provides a navigational utility that lets you jump from one region of a worksheet to another. The application does accommodate your handwriting in the small cells by allowing you to write in full-size script that is translated and entered into the cell over which you wrote. The controls in MobileCalc let you toggle between number and text recognition in a worksheet.

Available on floppy disk or PCMCIA card.

MobileSoft Corp.
307 Orchard City Drive
Suite 207
Campbell, CA 95008
Telephone: 408.376.0497
Fax: 408.376.0163

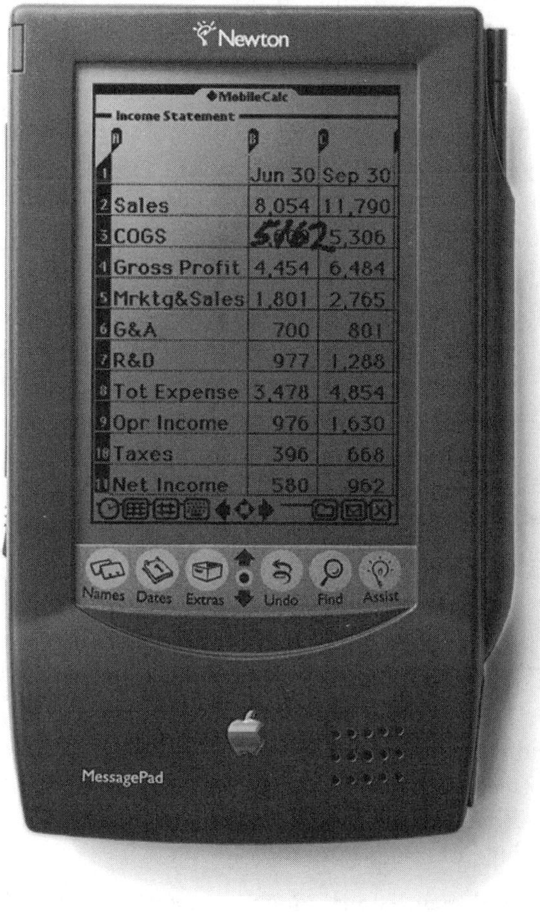

Figure 15.5 MobileCalc—a power spreadsheet in the palm of your hand.

MobileCalc Assistant

It's one thing to open a spreadsheet to work out a business problem, but quite another to get a quick answer to the kinds of mathematical and statistical questions that come up during a meeting.

MobileCalc Assistant ties the functions in the MobileCalc spreadsheet to the Notepad and Newton Assistant. It allows you to write a column of numbers in a note and, by tapping the Assist button, perform a statistical, financial, scientific, engineering, and mathematical analysis. The application adds a battery of new verbs that you can write in the Notepad to control the operation of the Assist feature. For example, you could write a series of numbers on the screen and the word "stdev" to find the standard deviation of the numbers. Highlight the series, tap Assist and, after the entry has been interpreted, a dialog will open that displays the answer as provided by MobileCalc.

Or, in a more practical moment, you could write the total of a dinner check followed by a "15%" to have MobileCalc Assistant work out the tip.

Available on floppy disk or PCMCIA card.

MobileSoft Corp.
307 Orchard City Drive
Suite 207
Campbell, CA 95008
Telephone: 408.376.0497
Fax: 408.376.0163

Money Magazine Financial Assistant

Forms can be as powerful as a calculator or spreadsheet, if they're backed by the right kind of mathematical capabilities. Apple's Starcore software publishing division has taken the kinds of forms that pepper Money Magazine and placed them in an interface designed by PenMagic of North Vancouver, British Columbia, which makes a very fine spreadsheet for the EO Personal Communicator.

Investing and financial planning are the big themes in this application. There are 50 forms dealing with everything from college planning to the net present value of an investment. For example, you can calculate the amount you need to place into savings each year until your children go to college by entering your current savings, the average interest you earn on investments, the cost of education today and the inflation rate. The Financial Assistant examines all the variables and tells you the amount you need to put away.

Available on a PCMCIA card.

Apple Computer Inc.
Telephone: 408.996.1010
Catalog: 800.795.1000

Money Magazine Business Forms

Apple also offers another PenMagic-developed application for business people who need help tracking expenses, planning or decision-making.

Money Magazine Business Forms includes 12 templates for project planning, expense reporting, price lists, invoice and order forms, and budgeting. For the person who likes to believe that more business is done on golf courses than the board room, there's a handicap calculator. You also get a loan calculator.

Apple will let you customize the look of forms, as well as selectively download forms into your Newton from a Mac or PC.

Available on floppy disk only.

Apple Computer Inc.
Telephone: 408.996.1010
Catalog: 800.795.1000

Drawing

DrawPad

Newton's drawing tools are only a little better than using a stick to scratch in the dirt. Saltire Software's DrawPad will let you sketch using various line styles, fill patterns and automatic graphing features.

DrawPad will convert rough drawings into business graphics. For example, you can create a pie chart and change the size of the slices by writing new percentages on the screen. It's strength is the ability to be very precise. DrawPad will generate lines and shapes according to your specifications— if you need a line one inch long, it will be exactly one inch long.

The Newton's screen is the great limitation any graphics application must battle. It's not up to the kind of detail we think most people are used to with desktop computers. For a Newton user who wants better graphics, the only alternative is DrawPad.

We particularly like DrawPad as a source of graphics for notes and letters you create in other applications. There's no better way to put a logo in your letters or a chart on a fax.

Available on floppy disk.

Saltire Software
P.O. Box 1565
Beaverton, OR 97075
Telephone: 503.622.4055
Fax: 503.622.4537

Business Information

GeoAssist: Dun & Bradstreet Business Database
Strategic Mapping has developed a technology for Newton that lets you
drill down through a map of the U. S. to discover the street address, ZIP
Code, and phone numbers of as many as ten million American businesses.

The company will ship custom data sets for individual industries, drawn
from Dun & Bradstreet's directories of American business. Rather than a
single, huge database that Newton would never be able to handle, you'll be
able to get a real estate version that lists local realtors or a banking version
that provides access to the names, phone numbers and financial performance for mortgage brokers. Imagine how powerful a tool like this would
be for a salesperson or an analyst who needs the past year's financial performance for a particular company or industry.

Both the Find and Assist functions in Newton will be enabled in Strategic Mapping's software, allowing you to get a graphical read-out on the
executives and location of Bob's Bank just by writing "Bob's Bank" into the
Find slip.

Strategic Mapping Inc.
3135 Kifer Road
Santa Clara, CA 95051
Telephone: 408.970.9600
Fax: 408.970.9999

Fodor's '94 Travel Manager
A complete graphical guide to restaurants, airports, hotels and good living
in Atlanta, Boston, Chicago, Dallas, Los Angeles, New York, San Francisco, and Washington, D. C. Up to 500 locations are listed for each city.

Fodor's, an Apple Starcore product, provides a guidebook that shapes itself to your latest adventure. For example, you can ask about a particular

type of ethnic food, then choose a restaurant from the list the application provides, after which Fodor's draws you a map to dinner. The information spans the obvious, like where to find the best accommodations, to the obscure but ultimately most important facts, like where to get a good haircut or how to find the museum with the Picasso show.

The Fodor's '94 Travel Manager was co-developed by GeoSystems, an R.R. Donnelly & Sons Co., and Fodor's Travel Publications, a division of Random House. The three companies will ship other collaborative or individually produced titles in the future.

Available on a PCMCIA card.
Apple Computer Inc.
Telephone: 408.996.1010
Catalog: 800.795.1000

Fortune 500: Guide to American Business
Another Apple title, the Fortune 500 guide is a treasure trove of financial and historical information about the largest companies in the world.

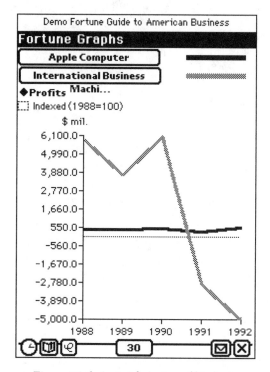

Figure 15.6 An insider's view of big business.

The data includes figures for number of employee, sales per employee, the names of the executive staff, five-year histories of earnings, sales, profitability, and a profile of the corporation. Newton can search for data based on the name of the company, its stock ticker abbreviation, location, and sales figures. You can also view data in graphs or compare the performance of one company with another.

You'll want to update this application annually in order to keep up with the changes, but there are few programs that give you so much information for a flat fee. This could be an investor's best friend.

Apple Computer Inc.
Telephone: 408.996.1010
Catalog: 800.795.1000

GeoAssist: Online Telephone Book Directory
Strategic Mapping will also offer Newton users access to an online directory that contains all the business listings from telephone books around the U. S.

The service will be available in late 1993 for a "nominal" connection fee.

Strategic Mapping Inc.
3135 Kifer Road
Santa Clara, CA 95051
Telephone: 408.970.9600
Fax: 408.970.9999

Portable MLS
Real estate data is some of the most volatile information in the world. Deed information, property values and descriptions of property will be available via a dial-up service that matches the variables entered by the user. For an example, turn to Chapter Nine—*Information Sculptor*.

The cool thing about this type of application is that Newton doesn't need to be connected to the service to use the information. It can be loaded into memory and taken into the field. At the end of the day, you purge the data you don't need and start anew in the morning.

Integration Systems Inc.
625B Purissima Street
Half Moon Bay, CA 94019
Telephone: 415.726.2620
            800.645.4511
Fax: 415.726.9295

Communications

PocketCall

Everyone in the online world considers Ex Machina's PocketCall the most important piece of software for Newton in the first year. The hue and cry for an interface to online information was great, and PocketCall delivers some impressive features. For the rest of the mortals who've never seen electronic mail or a conferencing system, NewtonMail may be a satisfactory introduction to the online universe. But if you get the bug, you'll want to try out PocketCall.

In the course of three demonstrations we saw, the PocketCall software evolved into a thoroughly easy-to-use method for scripting online sessions on the CompuServe Information Service, GEnie, the Official Airlines Guide (OAG), MCI Mail, AT&T Easylink, and cc:Mail Remote. At one point, we also saw a scripting interface to America Online, though it's not clear whether Ex Machina will be able to ship this, since AOL retains proprietary rights to the code that enables its interface.

While logged on to a service, you can browse messages in real-time or you can save them to memory. The application also offers a straight-forward terminal emulation program, which will let you log on to most bulletin board services, Internet providers and some office e-mail systems. A library of commands lets you tap out instructions instead of writing them by hand while the online billing clock tick away.

We especially liked the graphical scripting for major online systems. For example, the CompuServe interface allows you to pick out the forums you want to visit, what messages have been uploaded to the system and which ones you want to download. PocketCall can also be set to wake Newton for an online session while you are away at dinner or sleeping. You'll need a RAM storage card if you want to hold a large number of messages downloaded by PocketCall.

PocketCall's versatility is based on PocketPacks, special modules of code that you must install to enable connections to a particular service. So, the application is a two-part purchase: PocketCall for the basic functions, and the PocketPack for the service of your choice. Once in your Newton, however, a PocketPack for MCI Mail will let you exchange electronic mail with people on the MCI network, directly from your In Box or Out Box.

In 1994, corporate developers and power users will be able to buy Script-Pack, an add-on that lets you create your own online connections for Newton.

Ex Machina Inc.
45 East 89th Street
#39-A
New York, NY 10128-1232
Telephone: 718.965.0309
                800.238.4738
Fax: 718.832.5465

QuickAccess

CE Software Inc. will provide Newton a direct connection to many e-mail systems, including its QuickMail, QuickMail gateways to Apple's Power-Talk messaging services and Novell Inc.'s NetWare networks (via an MHS gateway—ask your network administrator whether you need this).

The software will let you dial in to your local area network to send and receive mail.

CE Software Inc.
1801 Industrial Circle
P.O. Box 65580
West Des Moines, IA 50265
Telephone: 515.221.1801
Fax: 515.221.1806

VoiceAccess

As if your life wasn't complicated enough, you have to deal with voice mail. Mac users who have CTM Development's VoiceAccess voice mail software, which was introduced in 1993, can now control their mailbox from Newton.

VoiceAccess for Newton is free with the Mac application. It lets you dial in to hear messages, record new messages, tell the Mac where to forward messages, and when to shut down, such as after your regular business hours. Messages can also be forwarded to paging software which will dial MobileComm to deliver text to your Newton Messaging Card.

You'll need Newton Connection to download this application.

CTM Development SA
Geneva, Switzerland
Telephone: 011.4122.734.47.47
Fax: 011.4122.734.47.65

Newton Utilities

Elegance

Getting around the Newton interface takes too many taps. But with Elegance in place, most of the main settings are available from a row of tiny icons.

Elegance provides a floating palette, a small bar with buttons on it, that you can place anywhere on the screen. The buttons provide direct access to:

Font list. You can access all Newton fonts, including the third, hidden font, Espy, which Elegance lets you use in the Notepad and other applications. (Future versions of Elegance will come with additional fonts to choose from.)

Font Size. Choose font sizes from 9 points to 48 points, four more choices than are available in the standard Newton Styles settings.

Font Styles. While Newton normally lets you use only plain, bold, and underline styles, Elegance offers: Plain, bold, italic, underline, outline, shadow, condensed, extended, superscript, and subscript. You can also mix font styles, something else Newton can't do unaided.

Pen Sizes. When it comes to pen thickness, Elegance offers the same four choices Newton does, only easier to get to.

Sleep Time. You can open the sleep settings to change the idle time before Newton dozes off. This button also lets you put Newton to sleep immediately or do a reset of your PDA.

Special Menu. This menu contains commands that change the case of selected text, that opens the calculator application and lets you choose the type of keyboard you want to use. You can also get at both In Box and Out Box directly from here as well as perform the system memory garbage-collection routine, without resetting your Newton.

Additional features are expected before Elegance ships, perhaps including a utility for beaming applications that are not copy protected. This is one of those must-have utilities for every Newton user. Once we installed our beta copy of Elegance, we found life much easier in Newton's sometimes tangled web of an interface.

Tanis Development
14 Chambers Street
Fifth Floor
New York, NY 10007
Telephone: 212.385.4444

Pocket Science

KwikPrefs lets you shift the settings in your Newton to meet your changing needs. The problem with traveling frequently between two area codes, or just going home from work, is that the settings for dialing and the credit cards you use may change.

The application lets you set up Kwikkis, icons that represent different groups of settings which reside in the Extras drawer. When you get home and no longer need Newton to dial a "9" to get an outside line, just tap the Home Kwikki to shift the settings to your home telephone line.

KwikPrefs lets you create Kwikkis that include combinations of these settings:

- Country
- Area code
- Prefix
- Long distance service access code
- Calling card number
- Local NewtonMail access number
- Newton volume
- Sleep

Pocket Science also plans to release as a separate product custom templates for fax and printing.

Pocket Science
1157 Littleoak Drive
San Jose, CA 95129
Telephone: 408.446.9372

Personal Software

ClarisGames for Newton

Apple's Claris subsidiary will deliver a game pack in late 1993 that includes Hangman, Enigma, Pegs, and Puzzle, among others. They weren't talking, but then again, would you talk about doing another Hangman game?

Claris Corp.
5201 Patrick Henry Drive
Box 58168
Santa Clara, CA 95052-8168
Telephone: 408.987.7000

Dell Crossword Puzzles and Other Word Games

Loads of brain-teasing fun for the pen-wielding Newtonian. The Dell games package from Apple includes crosswords, cryptograms and word searching challenges. Fun-filled is the marketing word of the day here.

Available on floppy or PCMCIA card.

Apple Computer Inc.
Telephone: 408.996.1010
Catalog: 800.795.1000

Family Safety Advisor

Serengeti Software, the company that developed this application for Apple's Starcore Division, calls the Family Safety Advisor "process" software, instead of a data manipulation application.

It's a set of forms for planning and staying prepared for the kinds of disasters that can beset various regions of the U. S., or the rest of the world, for that matter. When you first turn it on, the user is led through an assessment of their risk of fire, earthquake, hurricane, tornado, flood, and hazardous material contamination (we live in such happy times, don't we?). Then the user provides information to the application: How many people in the house; what kind of insurance they have; contact information for use in emergencies; medical information; and so on.

The Assistant then stores that information—but just think what a relief it would be to have a fax pre-addressed to your mother (or the nearest Kinko's to your mother) after your city's been shaken by a major tremor.

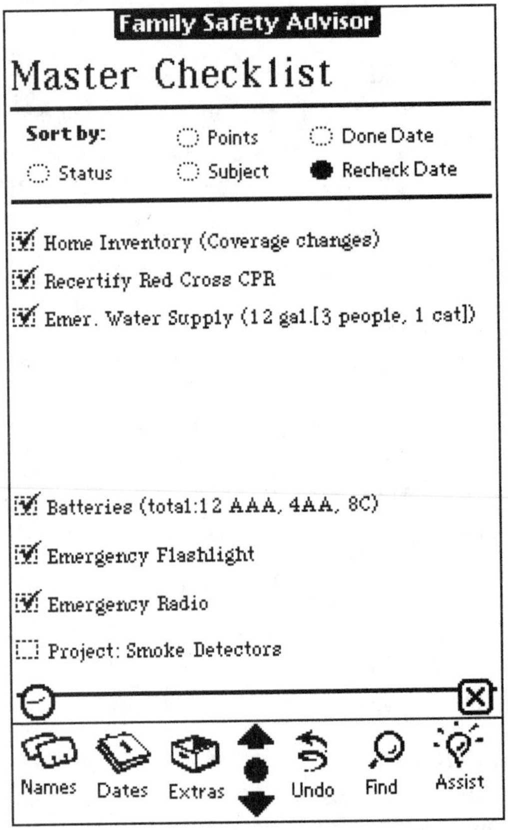

Figure 15.7 Family Safety Advisor won't let you get caught unawares.

Family Safety Advisor also takes you through your house to build an inventory. Then it assesses the risks unique to your home, and helps you prepare for the worst. It will periodically remind you to open the inventory for an update, and to do things like change the water supply or those ten cans of Spam you've socked away.

Available on PCMCIA cards. The name may change before it ships, but it will be distributed by Starcore.

Apple Computer Inc.
Telephone: 408.996.1010
Catalog: 800.795.1000

Fingertip for Golf

Golfers are going to love this application. Fingertip for Golf is an intelligent, digital coach that tracks your game as you play and analyzes the results to suggest what clubs with which you should practice, how to better predict which club you'll need the next time you're stuck with a bad lie, and much more. It also includes bets module that tracks 40 different kinds of wagers.

The really neat thing about the application is how it helps you examine your playing style for opportunities to improve. A practice module, which you'll use on the driving range, reviews your game and makes suggestions about how and what to practice.

Fingertip for Golf tracks your game in a graphical environment, based on a map of the course you're playing. Major courses will be available from Fingertip Technologies, and the company hopes regional and local courses will set up a map that you can download to your Newton before a round. If all else fails and your local course hasn't been mapped, Fingertip for Golf has a course drawing module that helps you create a map of each hole. It checks distances and makes sure your map matches the standard for par scores on a hole, so you don't end up with a 570 yard par three hole.

Available on PCMCIA cards.

Fingertip Technologies Inc.
620 Newport Center Drive
Suite 650
Newport Beach, CA 92660
Telephone: 714.759.9399
Fax: 714.759.0927

Fingertip for Personal Training

In the weight room or on the road, this application uses the same principles to analyze your workout regimen. It calculates your risk factors according to age and past injuries, and helps you pace your progress.

Available on PCMCIA cards.

Fingertip Technologies Inc.
620 Newport Center Drive
Suite 650
Newport Beach, CA 92660

Telephone: 714.759.9399
Fax: 714.759.0927

Fingertip for Sports Analysis

Rotisserie league baseball managers and ardent fans will find their grail in this collaboration between Fingertip and STATS, the company that maintains the statistics used in most major newspapers.

The application lets you analyze the performance of real or imaginary teams using the day-to-day statistics from the Major Leagues. It will provide dial-up access to the STATS database, which you can query each day to get the most up-to-date look at the players and teams.

Fingertip for Sports Analysis takes the statistics several steps beyond the daily papers. You'll be able to compare players and the decisions of coaches with your own arm-chair calls.

Due for the 1994 baseball season.

Available on PCMCIA cards.

Fingertip Technologies Inc.
620 Newport Center Drive
Suite 650
Newport Beach, CA 92660
Telephone: 714.759.9399
Fax: 714.759.0927

Lt. Colombo's Mystery Capers

A role-playing game in which you, the bumbling television detective, try to identify the killer. Nope, it's not Col. Mustard in the Parlor with the candlestick. Fifty different mysteries are included to help you while away a long plane flight.

Available on PCMCIA cards.

Apple Computer Inc.
Telephone: 408.996.1010
Catalog: 800.795.1000

Quicken for Newton

The leading checking account and personal financial management software will be available for Newton in 1994. It will provide online checking, credit card debt management, and portfolio management capabilities.

Intuit Inc.
155 Linfield Avenue
P.O. Box 3014
Menlo Park, CA 94026-3014
Telephone: 415.322.0573

Silicon Casino

Casady & Greene's Silicon Casino puts the pageantry and glitz of Vegas on the dull gray screen of your Newton. It's fun to try your luck and, if you're preparing for a trip to the Neon Gulch of the Southwest, even polish your skills.

The games supported in the first version are:

Blackjack. No splitting a hand and the dealer wins a draw, but you can double down.

Baccarat. Does anybody (besides James Bond) really understand this game? Maybe you will after playing in the Silicon Casino for digital chips. This way it doesn't cost you to learn.

Craps. The range of bets is rather limited.

Slots. There are three machines, $1, $5, and $10. The odds are a little better than Vegas on the $1 machine, but they take it out of your hide on the bigger-money boxes.

Where's the roulette wheel you ask? Maybe the next version.

Available on floppy disks.
Casady & Greene Inc.
22734 Portola Drive
Salinas, CA 93908-1119
Telephone: 408.484.9228
Fax: 408.484.9218

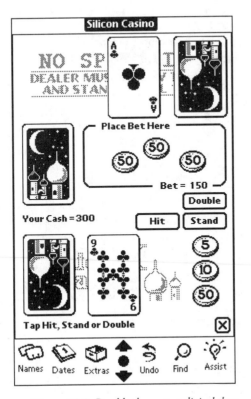

Figure 15.8 Double down as a digital dare.

Professional

CSL Profiles In Hand

Teachers can use this application to collect very detailed notes about their students, enabling a different kind of grading that identifies the key strengths and weaknesses each child needs to work on. For an example, turn to Chapter Nine—*Information Sculptor*.

Requires Chancery Software's CSL Profiles for Macintosh, which collects the teacher's notes into a comprehensive report which they can edit at the semester's end.

Chancery Software Ltd.
Vancouver, British Columbia, Canada
Telephone: 604-294-1233
                800-999-9931
Fax: 604-294-2225

Hippocrates Electronic Medical Assistant

President Clinton doesn't know it, but he was talking about applications like this when he spoke to Congress about reducing paperwork. Hippocrates lets hospitals organize their records, distribute patient charts and doctors' schedules via a network to Newtons. During the day, as they visit patients, doctors can make notes on clinical records, prescribe medicines and order tests. All the information is uploaded to the main computer system at the end of the day.

Prescriptions can be faxed to a pharmacy, saving time for the patient and cutting out more steps in the process. Hospitals can also create their own forms that add Newton intelligence to their networks. For example, Newton could collect data and take care of sorting and routing information that normally is handled by people.

This is a corporate solution, but a very good example of the kinds of capabilities you'll be seeing in many offices, as they embrace mobile computing technologies.

HealthCare Communications Inc.
300 South 68th Street
Suite 100
Lincoln, NE 68510-2466
Telephone: 402.489.0391
          800.888.4344, ext. 130

ProMED

Another variant on the hospital software, the KPMG solution can be integrated into a wide variety of corporate information systems.

KPMG Peat Marwick
Enabling Technologies Services
101 Lindenwood Drive
Suite 400
Malvern, PA 19355
Telephone: 215.889.7800

ComputerBooks Medical Software

Doctors exist on information. They collect symptoms from patients, compare it to clinical experience in formulating a diagnosis, and then consult their own memory or a reference book to make decisions about treatment. ComputerBooks puts four medical reference texts on Newton. They can be searched using the Find and Assist functions.

The company will ship the following in 1993:

Pharmaceuticals. Based on the Food and Drug Administration's drug reference, Physicians' GenR$_x$.

Drug Interactions. Checks the interactions of up to 20 drugs in a single query.

Patient Management. A patient record interface that will be linked via a network to hospital management systems, sometime in 1994.

Physician's Reference I. This module consists of medical analysis forms for 27 tests used in making diagnoses and deciding on a treatment.

Available on PCMCIA cards.

ComputerBooks
P.O. Box 9167
Newport Beach, CA 92658
Telephone: 800.848.2023

Macintosh and PC Applications that Talk With Newton

Newton Connection
Both Apple and Sharp will offer the Connection software, for as long as their collaboration shall last.

Glue
For a complete description, turn to Chapter Nine—*Information Sculptor*. This is a developer's tool, one of the only ones we'll mention, because it could be a very powerful link between the two kinds of data people use most: Personal information and corporate databases.

Oracle Corp.
500 Oracle Parkway
Redwood Shores, CA 94065
Telephone: 415.506.7000
Fax: 415.506.7200

Meeting Maker XP
This group calendaring application works with Newton Connection 2.0 to let you import your calendar into the Newton Dates application. A new Export command in the File menu of Meeting Maker creates an export file which must be loaded into Newton from Connection. It won't be possible to export meetings from Newton to Meeting Maker in the first version.

The company is working to eliminate the Connection step from the process, and hopes to provide full client status for Newton in 1994. This would allow Newton not only to receive calendar items, but to send them to the Meeting Maker server directly.

ON Technology Corp.
One Cambridge Center
Cambridge, MA 02142
Telephone: 617.374.1400
Fax: 617.374.1433

Notify!

Ex Machina's on the other side of the fence, too, sending text messages over paging systems that your Messaging Card can receive. Available in Mac and Windows versions. Make sure you have MobileComm's dial-up numbers to enter when configuring your system. Call MobileComm at 800.685.5555 for information.

Ex Machina will also be delivering Newton frames over the airwaves sometime in 1994, if all goes well.

Ex Machina Inc.
45 East 89th Street
#39-A
New York, NY 10128-1232
Telephone: 718.965.0309
              800.238.4738
Fax: 718.832.5465

PagerPro

A Mac-only pager messaging application that we've found very reliable. It can pass messages from other applications, as well as from a simple message-composition program.

For more information, turn to Chapter Nine.

Caravelle Networks Corp.
301 Moodie Drive
Suite 306
Napean, Ontario, Canada
K2H 9C4
Telephone: 613.596.2802
Fax: 613.596.9659

WinBeep

A Windows-only paging application that can pass messages to Newton from a single PC or an entire network. For more information, turn to Chapter Nine.

Fourth Wave Technologies Inc.
560 Kirts Blvd.
Suite 105
Troy, MI 48084
Telephone: 313.362.2288
Fax:　　　313.362.2295

Shareware/Freeware Top 10

As we went to press, more than thirty shareware and freeware applications were posted on the CompuServe, America Online, and other online services. Many more will be out by the end of 1993. So, rather than waste space on a comprehensive and ultimately outdated list, here are our picks for the best Newton Shareware/Free applications.

You can grab these applications on most of the major services. If there's a dollar figure next to an application, it is shareware—should you continue to use it, send that figure to the developer. Otherwise, all the applications here are free.

Listed in no particular order, since this isn't really a competition.

Tipster $5

Every Newton programmer seems to have tackled the tip calculator as their first application. Of all the ones we saw, this is the best, since it has a slider that lets you scale up the gratuity according to how much you liked the service. You get to set the tip range, and Tipster calculates the total bill with tip.

Author:
Elbert Chen
MaConsulting
1146 N. Central Ave.
Suite 342
Glendale, CA 91202
Telephone: 818.547.3500

Place Settings

This application lets you add the name of your city to the Time Zones map. For instructions, turn to Chapter Seven—*Life's Little Extras.* It's always better to be able to call home Home, rather than Cincinnati.

Author:
David Dunham
Pensée Corp.
Internet: ddunham@radiomail.net

Shopping List

A nicely thought out shopping list manager that breaks out the items into different departments, so you don't have to search through the entire list all the time. Practical and demonstrative of the little bonuses you get in Newton.

Author:
Tom Unkefer
Nomadic Systems
19948 Laurel Ave.
Rocky River, OH 44116
AppleLink: TOMUNKEFER
CompuServe: 763771,470

Newton Book of Days

A demonstration of electronic book technology by Pensée Corp. that lists loads of days you can take off for one reason or another.

Author:
David Dunham and Scott Schwarts
Pensée Corp.
Internet: ddunham@radiomail.net

HotButtons $5

A floating palette of buttons that you can link to applications in the Extras drawer. The first time you click on the buttons, a menu of applications open. Tap one to place its name on the button.

Author:
Cesar Maiorino
17 Kendall Street
Lawrence, MA 01841
Internet: Cesar_Maiorino@bcsmac.bcs.org

AutoDict $10

We've got mixed feelings about this application, but it does serve a purpose. How many times have you written a name in the Notepad and, even though they are in your Names file, the Newton doesn't recognize the name? AutoDict can scan the Names file for first and last names not listed in your personal word list. It runs the search only when you tell it to.

Now, doing so could really slow recognition. But the time you save by avoiding tapping open a keyboard when you want to search for a person's telephone number could balance it out. It's up to you.

Author:
Mac EDV Informations-Systeme
Ziegelofengasse 41/12
A-1052 Wien
Austria
Send credit card information to:
AppleLink: FALK
CompuServe: 100010,501
Fax: 43.1.545.5155.9

Scientific Calculator

Howard Oakley's Scientific Calculator, with engineering and hexadecimal displays, is a great alternative to the vanilla Newton Calculator—for you Mac People, it's a Calculator+ for the Newton Age.

Author:
Howard Oakley
CompuServe: 70734,120

Newton Moon

A calendar that displays the phases of the moon. A nice touch, and a sure way to check if people are going to be weird that day (take it from a former bartender—full moons really do strange things to some people).

Author:
Ken McLeod
AppleLink: THE.CLOUD

800 Numbers

Another electronic book from Pensée Corp., this one lists the toll-free numbers for airlines, car rental agencies, hotels, motels, mailing services and national flower services. Good information to have on a trip or on your spouse's birthday.

Author:
Scott Schwarts and David Dunham
Pensée Corp.
Internet: ddunham@radiomail.net

Newton Names and Note Downloader

It's not Newton software per se, but Danny Goodman's Newton Names and Note Downloader (NNND) is the poor man's way to get names and text files into a MessagePad or Expert Pad. NNND is a HyperCard stack that emulates the Sharp Wizard, allowing you to connect a Newton and a Mac with a serial cable. Launch the Sharp application in the Extras drawer and download contacts into the Name file or text files in the Notepad.

Author:
Danny Goodman
CompuServe: 75775,1731

CHAPTER
16

FAST SERVICES

Networks are changing the way we understand the world, allowing each of us to project our minds into new places and gather new ideas. Here are some of the networks on which electronic mail, conferencing and file archives are available. Many of these do not support Newton as of the printing of this book, but you can bet that one way or another, Newton will let you access these networks before the end of 1994.

Apple Online Services

Apple Computer Inc.
P.O. Box 10600
Herndon, VA 22070-0600
Telephone: 408.974.3309
Fax: 703.318.6701
Needed for Newton to Access: NewtonMail

Third-party Network Providers

AT&T EasyLink Services
400 Interpace Parkway
Parsippany, NJ 07054
Telephone: 201.331.4000
Fax: 201.316.6994
Needed for Newton to Access: Ex Machina's PocketCall.

America Online Inc.
8619 Westwood Center Drive
Vienna, VA 22182
Telephone: 703.448.8700
Fax: 703.883.1509
Needed for Newton to Access: Will support Newton with client software, also due from Ex Machina in 1994.

Commercial Internet Exchange
(A Coalition of Internet access providers)
3110 Fairview Park Drive
Suite 590
Falls Church, VA 22042
Telephone: 303.482.2150
Fax: 303.482.2284

Needed for Newton to Access: No options currently available, though you'll be able to use a terminal emulator to access most Internet providers. Third-party software will be out in 1994.

CompuServe Inc.
5000 Arlington Centre Blvd.
P.O. Box 20212
Columbus, OH 43220
Telephone: 614.457.8600
Fax: 614.457.0348
Needed for Newton to Access: Ex Machina's PocketCall.

GE Information Services
401 N. Washington St.
Rockville, MD 20850
Telephone: 301.340.4454
Fax: 301.340.5306
Needed for Newton to Access: No options currently available, though a terminal emulator will do fine.

MCI International Inc.
2 International Drive
Rye Brook, NY 10573
Telephone: 914.934.6480
Fax: 914.934.6863
Needed for Newton to Access: Ex Machina's PocketCall.

Sprint Inc.
12490 Sunrise Valley Drive
Reston, VA 22096
Telephone: 800.736.1130
Needed for Newton to Access: No options currently available, though a terminal emulator will do fine.

Wireless Network Providers

MobileComm
11800 East County Line Road
Suite 300
Ridgeland, MS 39157
Telephone: 601.969.5134

800.685.5555
Fax: 601.977.8245
Needed for Newton to Access: Newton Messaging Card

ARDIS
300 Knightsbridge Parkway
Lincolnshire, IL 60069
Telephone: 708.913.1215
800.662.5328
Fax: 708.913.4700
Needed for Newton to Access: Products due in 1994

EMBARC Communications Services
(Electronic Mail Broadcasting to a Roaming Computer)
1500 NW 22nd Avenue
Boynton Beach, FL 33426
Telephone: 800.362.2724
Needed for Newton to Access: Products due in 1994

RAM Mobile Data
10 Woodbridge Center Drive
Woodbridge, NJ 07095
Telephone: 908.602.5500
800.662.4839
Fax: 908.602.1262
Needed for Newton to Access: Products due in 1994

AFTERWORD

THE NEXT NEWTON

By Apple's own declarations, the Newton must be deemed a failure if the MessagePad and Expert Pad are the only ones we ever see.

The whole point of the Newton strategy is to get the technology proliferated across as many devices as possible. In years to come there should be Newton VCRs, Newton automobile navigation systems, Newton phones, and even Newton-enabled classrooms. If this doesn't happen, then Newton must be considered a seed that never took root. All those who stood in line to be the first in their neighborhood to own an authentic personal digital assistant will be left wondering how they ever made such a mistake.

Luckily, the immediate future looks bright. Despite the shellacking the first Newtons took in the media, people have bought them aplenty. As a result, Apple has pushed forward with its next Newton design which should reach the store shelves in the first half of 1994. Of course, the MessagePad was supposed to ship about that time in 1993 but didn't make it out until some months later. So, if it's July and no new Newton is in sight, don't lose heart. A technical or scheduling glitch has probably held up the works.

Apple is thoroughly committed to Newton. The company knows that this may be its best bet to make it through another decade. Executives in Cupertino certainly won't let this Newton stand alone as the sole expression of such promising technology.

That brings us to the nature of the next Newton. First, we are obligated to say that Apple has supplied us with no information about their next PDA. Everything we present here is speculation based on reports from reliable sources.

Newton Senior

If you were at the 1993 Macworld Expo in Boston and attended the Newton Showcase you may have spied a prototype which we believe is the basis for the next Newton. Apple has many prototypes and design concepts for possible Newtons, so we could be mistaken. But we don't think so.

The unit was sleek and thin, weighing in at under three pounds (at least, that's how heavy it felt). Although the case was made of clear plastic to show its inner workings, we're sure Apple won't stray from basic black when this unit ships. It had four prominent features: a screen about four inches by six inches; a metal pen sitting in a caddie over the top of screen and secured by a tether; a large battery that slid in on the top of the unit;

and a contoured black window on the upper right corner of the case. It also had an RJ-11 jack on its left side, perfect for connecting to a telephone jack.

Based on information from our sources, this is what we believe the features of that design were:

Case: 8 by 10 by 1 inch

Weight: About 3 pounds

Screen: 640 by 480 pixels, 256 shades of gray and possibly backlit.

PCMCIA Slots: Two

ROM Upgrade Slot: One

IR: One diffuse IR transmitter capable of full-duplex communications with all and any Newtons in the same room. In effect, an infrared network. Great for group annotation of Notepad documents.

Modem: 14.4 send and receive fax/data modem built-in.

Battery: NiCad

There may be more than one version of this big daddy Newton. Expect it come with new built-in applications and be available for well under $2,000. We expect to see an even larger version of this brute of a Newton by the fall of '94 which may support searchable ink (see Chapter Four—*The Written Word* for more on ink technology).

Like we said, we could be wrong. These Newtons may never make it out the door. Certainly, we'd rather see Apple come out with a Newton-powered cellular phone first. But, come to think of it, that's what Motorola is going to do with its first Newton design, which we should see by summer '94.

Other than that, all we have to say is thanks, and we hope you enjoyed the book!

INDEX

Now available

DEFYING GRAVITY

The Making of Newton

($29.95, 196 pages, Beyond Words Publishing, ISBN: 0-941831-94-9), is an in-depth, dramatic account of the story of Newton's creation. It is a techno-logical adventure story; a fascinating case study of the process by which an idea is born and then translated into a product on which careers and fortunes can be made or lost. It is a new kind of business book, one that captures through powerful photo-journalism and a fast-paced text, the human drama and risk involved in the invention of new technol-ogy for a new marketplace.

Toll free ordering
1-(800) 284-9673